SELECTED ESSAYS AND REVIEWS

Selected Essays and Reviews

HAYDEN CARRUTH

COPPER CANYON PRESS

Publication of this book is supported by a grant from the National Endowment for the Arts and a grant from the Lannan Foundation. Additional support to Copper Canyon Press has been provided by the Andrew W. Mellon Foundation, the Lila Wallace–Reader's Digest Fund, and the Washington State Arts Commission. Copper Canyon Press is in residence with Centrum at Fort Worden State Park.

Library of Congress Cataloging-in-Publication Data
Carruth, Hayden, 1921–
Selected essays and reviews / by Hayden Carruth.
      p. cm.
1. American poetry – History and criticism. 2. English literature –
History and criticism. 3. Poetics. 4. Poetry. I. Carruth,
Hayden, 1921– . II. Title.
ISBN 1-55659-107-1
PS305.C35 1995
811'.009 – DC20   95-4425

9 8 7 6 5 4 3 2
FIRST EDITION

COPPER CANYON PRESS
P.O. BOX 271, PORT TOWNSEND, WASHINGTON 98368

Contents

Preface

What have been omitted from this selection are by and large the short reviews of separate books published over the years in newspapers and magazines. I regret this. At least some of these reviews examined works of importance, and a few contain ideas not expounded elsewhere. But the bounds of such a book as this simply must be compressed. I console myself with the thought that those reviews achieved their primary purpose – to introduce new books to the reading public – when they were first published, and that the books in question, if they were truly important, have been written about by others in succeeding years.

Beyond this all essays on music have been left out because they are contained in the book *Sitting In*, which is in print. And all expressly autobiographical writings have been excluded as well because a collection of them is projected for publication in a year or two.

My essays and reviews have been written over a period of nearly fifty years, and many people have been helpful – editors, publishers, librarians, friends, members of my family. I cannot name them all. But I wish to give special thanks to two friends who have been crucial to the publication of this book, James Laughlin and Sam Hamill. In addition Joe-Anne McLaughlin-Carruth has done much of the hard work of selection, and I am immensely grateful, as always, to her.

H.C.
APRIL 13, 1995

SELECTED ESSAYS AND REVIEWS

Dr. Williams's PATERSON

A review of *Paterson* (Book Three). 1950.

THIS THIRD BOOK in Dr. Williams's projected long poem (the fourth and final book is promised "by 1951") is at first reading the most difficult of the three we now have, and at the eighth reading some details of structure and aspects of meaning remain unclear. Nevertheless we can begin to perceive what will be the shape, scope, and texture of the finished work; this book helps to expand and clarify a number of themes, heretofore obscure, in the first two books. When the three are read in sequence they reveal, through interlacing symbols and thematic references, a close and compact development. More than ever it becomes apparent that Dr. Williams has in mind a whole, inseverable poem, not a discrete tetralogy, as many of those who reviewed the first two books were led to assume.

The meaning of the poem so far can best be elucidated through a compressed examination of its symbols. Paterson, then, is a city and also a man, a giant who lies asleep, whose dreams are the people of the city, whose history is roughly coterminous with and equal to the history of America. He is diseased with slums and factories and the spiritlessness of industrial society; his character – usually as observer – walks about, sometimes as a plain citizen, sometimes as a hero, often as "Dr. Paterson," the poet himself. Beside Paterson lies a mountain, which is a woman, upon whose body grow trees and flowers, with the city park at her head. The city-man and mountain-woman are the two basic facts of the poem; they are activated by the four elements. A river, broken by a falls, flows between them and has, beyond its obvious sexual meaning, the further significances of flowing time and of language, usually the fundamental or premental language of nature. Earth is the speaker that knows this language, the "chatterer." Fire is the creative act, in love or art. Wind is, if my reading is correct, inspiration, the integrator, the carrier of sounds and smells. Though generally benign, these forces may be malevolent too, for fire, flood, cyclone, and earthquake all occur in this poem.

Another duality, which is enforced on these basic symbols, is that of marriage-divorce. As divorce is a principal symptom of social disorder, so it is also of historical disorder: the man has been divorced from his beginnings, his sources, as the city is in one sense divorced from the mountain by the river of time and language. Dr. Williams also uses the word *blockage:* man has been blocked from an understanding of his real self in nature by the modern institutions of church, university, commerce, and so forth. Dr. Williams seems to be saying that the only way to escape these blocks is to ignore them, to sidestep them and experience marriage directly. Thus, in the river, it is the falls which is important, the present act and present moment which unite the man and the woman, the city and the mountain, in a "plunge" that "roars" now with the language which lies hidden in the past above and the future below.

This third book has been described by Dr. Williams as a search for a language. Yet much of it is spent in inveighing against what we ordinarily call language. The abstractions of scholarship are the poet's primary anathema, but he extends his disgust to include all human speech. "No ideas but in things," he says repeatedly – the objectivist doctrine carried to its extreme. Abstract "meaning" is the enemy, "an offense to love, the mind's worm eating out the core." The dead authors in the library are "men in hell, their reign over the living ended," their thoughts trapped in inflexible, dead rhetoric. Even the poet's own work is suspect; at one point he admonishes himself: "Give up the poem. Give up the shilly-shally of art."

This seems to put the poet in a difficult situation, since there honestly isn't much reason to be writing a poem (much less to publish it) if one must write in a corrupted language. Dr. Williams's conclusions on this head are not as clear as one might wish, but he appears to be saying that the poet can resolve his predicament through a doctrine of invention. The good language is the language of the river, articulated by and in the falls. The poet cannot hope to imitate the falls, but he can learn from it. By forgetting the past, by writing spontaneously, even carelessly, by grounding all speech firmly in natural objects, the poet can *create* a language in nature that is essentially an act, not a meaning – an act of love and union. By working constantly at a peak of inventiveness, he can elevate this language to a level of independence which is its own justification.

Paterson, when it is finished, will make a great hunting ground for the explicators. There are virtually hundreds of symbols – Dr. Williams would protest my continued application of this word to the *things* of his poem, which he calls, elsewhere, objects; but although one happily and admiringly grants the objectiveness of his objects, their purity and wholeness in his poems, the pristine quality of their existence as identities other than we, one still must insist on the profound meanings and feelings that attach to them, and this is all I wish to suggest by my choice of terms – there are hundreds of symbols and allusions to be tracked down, related, explained, and if he sticks to his text this will annoy Dr. Williams considerably. Essays will be written, for instance, on the many uncomplimentary allusions, often disguised, to T. S. Eliot and his works. There will likewise be essays on the other writers mentioned in the poem (Pound, Stevens, a few younger poets), on the various flowers (extremely important through all Dr. Williams's works), on the dog. Yet I would like to recommend one prior question to the critics before they begin.

Perhaps I can put it best this way. Twenty-five years ago Eliot felt that he should explain some of the sources and meanings of *The Waste Land* in accompanying notes; for Dr. Williams this is unnecessary. We are better readers now. Furthermore Dr. Williams's symbols are made from objects we all know in our own experience, rather than from cultural references, and the meanings given to them are drawn from a common fund of ideas and feelings. But I think we should call on Dr. Williams for another kind of note – a definite note on prosody. He himself sees the trouble, and at one point says to the reader, rather sharply: "Use a metronome if your ear is deficient, one made in Hungary if you prefer." But I think he misses the mark. Any reader with an ear for poetry will respond easily to Dr. Williams's astonishingly pure feeling for the rhythms of the American language. It is not meter or cadence that bothers me, but the line. These lines are not run over, in the Elizabethan sense; they are not rove over, in the Hopkinsian sense; nor are they carefully turned over, as in the poetry of H.D., where breath and sense as well as cadence determine the line-length; they are hung over, like a Dali watch. They break in the most extraordinary places – at least often they do – with no textual, metrical, or syntactical tension to help us feel the movement, or even the presence, of the line-units. If this is done for typographical effect, as sometimes appears, it is ineffectual, for it interferes with our reading. If it is done to indicate a certain way of reading the poem, then we should be told what it is.

Dr. Williams has explained in the past that he uses this device of the short, oddly broken line to obtain the effect of speed in a lyric poem. But *Paterson*, by rough estimate, will be five thousand lines long when it is finished. In such a large dose the effect is, instead, limpidity, constantly bolstered by interjections and typographical novelties; sustained verbal power is seldom achieved.

Perhaps I am a dull reader; if so, these matters can be explained, and in fairness to me they ought to be explained, if not by Dr. Williams then by some prosodist sympathetic to his method. The question of *Paterson's* value as poetry should put the critics face to face with questions they have been dodging for years. What kinds of lines and sentences does one put next to each other to create a long freeform poem? Is it an arguable prosodic hypothesis that the metrical beat, to the exclusion of the line, is the basic unit of poetry? How is aural structure to be sustained in a long poem in which line-values are suppressed?

🙶 . . . .

Stevens as Essayist

A review of *The Necessary Angel.* 1952.

AMONG READERS OF POETRY one sometimes hears: "Ah, yes, Wallace Stevens – a very fine poet no doubt, but how can you account for a man who persists in writing about such silly subjects?" On the one hand, this. On the other, the injustices the man has suffered from those who do take him seriously, critics who have written admirably about Keats or Hart Crane but who have nothing but twaddle to say about Stevens. In this predicament, between the devilishly uninformed and the deep blue connoisseurs, it has been up to Mr. Stevens to save himself, and this he has done by collecting in one volume seven of his important essays in prose.

Stevens is a poet who believes in the supremacy of poetry. Unlike many of his colleagues, who turn to traditional dogmas or outside disciplines for their support, he refuses the opinion that art is a game, a propaganda, or a ceremony.

For him poetry is a means toward truth and he says it unabashedly. It is our best means, for its implement is our greatest faculty, the imagination, superior to the philosopher's reason or the scientist's empiricism. And poetry, if it succeeds, possesses also the power to bestow upon its participants an automatic byproduct – ennoblement.

Thus Stevens gets down to fundamentals immediately, to the level of the artist, his own studio. And his main point is that the poet's imagination is useless unless he or she brings it to bear squarely upon reality. For him reality is the vastly differentiated, often discouraging presence of this actual world, untinctured by intimations of any further intelligence. It is a reality of almost unlimited beauty for those who can deal with it imaginatively and in its own terms. The poet who can order and make comprehensible an aspect of this reality, through the imaginative conjunction of resemblances, participates in the discovery of a truth. He ennobles himself and his readers, and to him belong the moral and intellectual rewards of nobility. Reality is for the poet, as for all people, the "necessary angel," whose protection saves him among word-workers from becoming only another radio announcer howling across the wind.

As a poet Stevens's duty has been to write poetry, to explore reality. He has written many poems, many admirable poems, some truly great poems. But as a poet who feels the insecurity of the poet's position in the modern commercial, pragmatic, positivist world, Stevens has given himself the secondary duty to write about poetry. He has made a definition of poetry; he has studied the way poetry works. He has given us several theories of the processes of imagination, theories about metaphor, analogy, and resemblance, theories about epistemology and human personality. He has been especially concerned with the way poets look at reality, the way each person sees a tree differently, for these various views comprise what we can apprehend of existence, and they are our *raison d'être* as sensible beings.

But what do we usually hear about Stevens? Among his admirers he is a high romantic, a direct descendant of impressionism, a mage of the poetic ritual. Among his critics he is a funambulist, a hedonist, a decadent. Both parties have been too much impressed by the externalities of his style, his eccentric rhetoric and his occasionally rococo vocabulary. They have failed to see the kind of precision he has obtained through these means. They have seized upon and exaggerated those poems which present an exotic view of the world, poems of Florida and Tehuantepec, and they have neglected the poems which extol the august beauty of mundane things.

The fact is that the ideas Stevens expresses in these essays, and that he has always expressed in his poems, bear a much closer affinity to Wordsworth, to Sidney, or to certain poets of the pagan world than they do to the decadents of the late nineteenth century. Insofar as our world is decadent in comparison with some other, I suppose Stevens is too, though I should prefer to use some such word as *refined* or *elaborate*. The nobility that Stevens has sought is obviously not Homer's, it is modern, intellectual, and subtle; it is heroic only in its spiritual or esthetic staunchness. Perhaps it is not nobility at all, but a kind of very good intelligence or very intelligent goodness that we in our moral sedentariness can still aspire to. But whatever it is, it is not foolishness or frippery. It is earnest, though not deadly earnest, and its products – Stevens's poems – are serious works, constructed to a measure which allows no extraneous or supercilious ornament. It is inconceivable that a poet whose concept of poetry is the one enunciated in these essays could be vulnerable to affectation or preciosity, though he has his disguises. Stevens has created a theory of the value of poetry which is as austere as any ever conceived, and his poems are hard grapplings with reality, out in the open, away from the cul-de-sacs of spiritual remoteness that have trapped so many of the rest.

The development of Stevens's thought has been, if one hesitates to say logical, at least consistent and in a line with its own objectives. Most of his ideas are not original – his affinity to Wordsworth has already been pointed out by J.V. Cunningham – but they have been rigorously tested by the poetic conditions of modernity. Nor has Stevens tried to write criticism. His essays are more nearly an operating program for poets, for one poet particularly, Stevens himself. Hence they are an important adjunct to, or defense of, his poetry; and in this sense at least, though I think also in others, they are indispensable.

I do not want to turn from these essays without noticing their extraordinary qualities as literature. Like his poems, Stevens's prose contains many prodigious remarks: "The centuries have a way of being male"; "The supreme example of analogy in English is *Pilgrim's Progress*"; "When we look back at the period of French classicism..., we have no difficulty in seeing it as a whole." These will scare the scholars half out of their wits. So much the better; a little area must be reserved. But we know that Stevens likes to shock us, and we laugh and look for the most outrageous and exotic surmises, until all at once they are no longer outrageous and exotic but the astute and respectable thoughts of a man who lives in West Hartford, Connecticut. These are rich essays, simply constructed but richly and elegantly written. They contain many examples, an anthology-full of quotations from the most various and delightful authors, all much to Stevens's purpose, but all exciting to come across for their own sake. All told *The Necessary Angel* is as pleasant, instructive, and inspiring a book as I have read in a long, long time.

. . . .

Write Little; Do It Well

A review of *Collected Poems*, by Yvor Winters. 1953.

No POINT in being sententious or plausible or coy in circumstances like these: you say what has to be said.

Yvor Winters's *Collected Poems* contains at least a half-dozen lyrics that are, though unassuming, the equal of anything written in the United States since the death of Emily Dickinson. I hasten to say this the more quickly because I feel people all over the country are awaiting this book with grim pleasure and will rejoice now in the opportunity to berate its author without much reference to the quality of his work. We have our deplorable literary "racket"; once it was called the "game"; we are perhaps even pleased with it; its hazards pique our small mettle while our innocence believes that in the end History will effect conclusive judgments, raising all good poets to their proper rank in spite of our present contentions and maneuvers. Well, History just may not. Winters has braved the racket, he has defied it. In the literary "world," though certainly not in the real one, he has taken a critical position of defiant isolation, from which he has launched his attacks. He has appeared often angry, unfriendly, bitter. He has attacked not only individual poets but the whole poetic evolution in which most of us, until lately, had thought we were flourishing, the "revolution of the word," the expiring *symboliste* heritage. Perhaps we should not be surprised that many dislike and fear him, or that they may try to retaliate upon him in reviewing, or not reviewing, his *Collected Poems*.

Yet I am sure it would be a monstrous shame if Winters's poems were ignored or rejected now. They are too good for that, and we have too much to learn from them.

Like Ezra Pound, Winters has insisted first on the indispensability of good writing, the ordinary, basic craft of language without which sensibility is helpless; but he has been more methodical than Pound in telling us what good writing is and even how we may hope to achieve it. No talk of the word, the embracing, affective, supercharged word! No talk either of associations, ambiguities, levels, multiple referents, and the like. (Though these things, he would say, all exist.) But instead, composition: fine metric, right rhyme, structural integrity, the good art of syntax. And like Pound also – the similarities between the two are less obvious but more instructive than the dissimilarities – Winters began from scratch, a rebel against the Georgian allegiance, and he was a student of comparative literature, as it is called, rather than the follower of a single poetic mode. But Winters refused Pound's easy and predatory scholarship; he turned not to folkish Provence or unfathomable China, but to the hard poetry of the English Renaissance, to

> *Gascoigne, Ben Jonson, Greville, Raleigh, Donne,*
> *Poets who wrote great poems, one by one.*

And his poems bespeak these men, no doubt of it. His little lyrics have the resilience of Gascoigne, the elegance of Raleigh at his best, plus the urbanity of Jonson, the tough sinew of that urbanity:

> *The sirens, rising, woke me; and the night*
> *Lay cold and windless; and the moon was bright,*
> *Moonlight from sky to earth, untaught, unclaimed,*
> *An icy nightmare of the brute unnamed.*

And from the whole spirit of that time, Gascoigne to Herbert and Marvell, Winters has taken a marvelous sense of the stanza:

> *High noon returns the mind*
> *Upon its local fact:*
> *Dry grass and sand; we find*

No vision to distract.
Low in the summer heat,
Naming old graves, are stones
Pushed here and there, the seat
Of nothing, and the bones
Beneath are similar:
Relics of lonely men,
Brutal and aimless, then
As now, irregular.

Anyone who cannot hear, and relish, this intricately simple interplay of sentence, line, rhyming quatrain, and stanza – it is the first stanza of the main part of the poem called "To the Holy Spirit from a Deserted Graveyard in the Salinas Valley" – probably has no business reading poetry anyway.

Yet listen to these phrases: "And moves down coldly solvent ways"; "Bright soul on hands and knees"; "The spring has darkened with activity"; "I see the trees flame thin, in watery lines"; "drenched in arrears"; "meaning by a moment made"; "a scheme of air."

What I am trying to show with these examples, though the space is too short, is the pervading quality of Winters's poetry. It is perfectly unmannered, in spite of some of the intentional archaisms. A second-rate poem by Winters could be mistaken for a second-rate poem by someone else, which would be difficult in the case of Eliot or Stevens or Cummings. Yet without a manner, Winters has a style, an habituation to his own apprehension of language. A poet's style, in this sense, is hard to define; it is the paratype of his or her personality. Certainly Winters has taken much of his feeling for language from his reading of Renaissance poetry or French poetry of the last century; but equally much, if not more, is totally modern. Here is part of his advice "To a Young Poet":

Write little; do it well.
Your knowledge will be such,
At last, as to dispel
What moves you overmuch.

What is "such ... as to" but today's prose, the language of a technological civilization, lapsing into poetry, with more than a touch of post-romantic irony in the syntactical arrangement and the rhyme with "overmuch"? There are many like instances. There are also a good number of "o'ers" and "ere's," and there is a "clime," to which I object rather strenuously, not simply because these are archaic or "poetic" words, but because they are so closely associated with cultural attitudes distinct from the poet's own that their intrusion militates against the basic seriousness of his work. I would say the same thing about Pound's early poems, in which similar archaisms were used, often to great poetic advantage; but the charge is more damaging against Winters than it is against Pound precisely because Winters's poems are more serious, i.e. less in the nature of literary artifices, than were Pound's imitations of Browning and Arnaut Daniel.

Winters took a long time to achieve his mature style, and he has left enough of his early poetry in this small book to show the evolution clearly. The first poems are *imagiste* exercises, sometimes compressed into mere one-line notations. Then comes a group of poems in imitation of early William Carlos Williams, though never with Williams's clarity and lightness; some of these are very bad, though no worse than most of the poems written by other young and rebellious poets after World War I:

> *Belief is blind! Bees scream!*
> *Gongs! Thronged with light!*

A number of translations follow, from the thirteenth-century Galician, from French and Spanish poetry of the sixteenth century, from Baudelaire, Verlaine, and Rimbaud. These are impressive often but still not fully integrated, not *inwrought* (in a Hopkinsian sense); they give the appearance of being ill at ease with themselves. Then nearly halfway through the book the mature style begins to emerge in a series of sonnets. These are often crabbed and obscure; unnecessarily so, I think, and with some I am still searching for the way in. But the best of them, "Apollo and Daphne," is a first-rate sonnet on a set classical theme. One thinks of Yeats's Leda sonnet. It is large in conception and more sinuous – Winters would say, with disdain, "affective" – in language; but Winters's sonnet has great force and clarity, and it shows, in the lines

> *And all her heart broke stiff in leafy flame*
> *That neither rose nor fell, but stood aghast,*

how he can merge without imprecision, thus making the poem almost leap into focus, such contrary sounds as broke-stiff-stood-aghast and all-leafy-flame-fell. Nearly all the best poems follow after this, the last third of the volume.

Like any poet with a seasoned style Winters can deal with a great variety of topics. Many of his poems come from mythology and scholarship, and are academic in the best sense – intentionally devoted to recorded values. Others are taken from the poet's experiences as a father, a young student, a Civil Defense official, a breeder of show dogs (airedales, he would insist), a teacher. Three poems rise from Winters's spirited work in behalf of David Lamson, who was tried for murder in California, and very questionably convicted. There are poems "On the Despoilers of Learning in an American University," "To a Portrait of Melville," "On the Death of Senator Thomas J. Walsh," and "In Praise of California Wines." If these sound like the titles of set pieces, the inference is not mistaken; but the themes are set by the poet himself, out of his own objectified desire and experience, as, one imagines, Saint Anselm set for himself the theme of the Ontological Proof; the poems, though generalized, have that same force of personal authenticity. And in them all, several motifs predominate. One is the mystery of Christian experience. I take it Winters is neither believer nor agnostic, as these terms are used. Basically he is a rationalist, as we know from his criticism, but beyond that, like other rationalists, he has a profound realization of the mystery itself, and of its two centers beyond the edge and in the nucleus of human thought. In his earlier poems he speaks in terms of anxiety and insanity, "the blank pain of Doom," "the hazards of insane inheritance." But in his most recent work, especially in "To the Holy Spirit," Winters has achieved a reconciliation with mystery and ignorance, almost a faith in them, and his pain and anxiety he dismisses "into irrelevance." With this resolution has proceeded, as well, a resolution of language: in the earlier poems are the "slow cry," the "slow flame," "the instant blurred"; in the later, only words that are sure and self-contained. Fear of the mind's limitations, a kind of insanity, spurred language too, beyond its capacity, until the fear was overcome.

About three years ago in *Poetry* Winters wrote: "In a period of critical muddle-headedness such as our own, I have had to divert a good deal of my energy into prose, if only to keep my own ideas in order." Maybe so; one can see how a person might feel this way. But in looking back one can see the priggery of such a remark as well. And Winters goes further. He says: "Write little; do it well." Write well, by all means, but why little? This is a kind of solemnity that won't hold up. Yet it is a part of Winters's whole attitude toward poetry. Leaving aside questions of personality, is it justifiable? This book of Winters's collected poems is either too big or too small: too big, according to Winters's own rigorous concepts, since it still contains, after all the paring down, poems that are inevitably less good than others, which therefore could have been deleted; too small, from my standpoint, since it confines the poet's obvious great gifts and his lively, generous sense of the contemporary within bounds that are uncomfortably narrow. There is about this book – not individual poems but the whole collection as a structure of editorial and critical judgment – a reticence so self-conscious that it becomes arrogant, and this is unhealthy.

Some of the best poems in the book are: "The Slow Pacific Swell," "On a View of Pasadena from the Hills," "Orpheus," "The California Oaks," "Sir Gawaine and the Green Knight," "Time and the Garden," "A Summer Commentary," "To the Holy Spirit."

Finally let me dispel any intimation I may have given that Winters is finished. Nowadays the custom is, if you are a successful poet, to bring out your collected poems when you are about fifty and have six or seven volumes behind you. The fact is, these poems are not collected, but selected, and like Winters, you always have to say, rather ungraciously, "This volume contains everything I wish to keep." This is like the boy who picks up his marbles and goes home. Obviously it is a fine thing to have this selection of Winters's poems in one book, but the air of finality about it is unfortunate. Winters's best poems, I believe, are his most recent, and I feel certain he will not stop writing now.*

---

* He did stop, however. As far as I know he never produced another poem of real force after "To the Holy Spirit." A pity. Yet for that poem alone I feel justified in reprinting this review, which otherwise does not please me now (1994), not at all. I haven't tried to conceal its ineptness and callowness, but I have cut and revised it more than most of the others.   [*cont'd...*]

🙋 ·

Without the Inventions of Sorrow

A review of *The Collected Poems of Wallace Stevens*. 1955.

OPULENCE – it is the quality most of us would ascribe to the poetry of
Wallace Stevens before all others; profusion, exotic luxuriance. We
have a permanent impression of poems which teem with rich, strange,
somehow forbidden delights. Just to read again the titles of his poems
is to awaken this sense of the extraordinary abundance: "Tea at the
Palaz of Hoon," "The Bird with the Coppery, Keen Claws," "Sea Sur-
face Full of Clouds," "The Man with the Blue Guitar," "Mrs. Alfred
Uruguay," "The Owl in the Sarcophagus," "Angel Surrounded by
Paysans," "The Irish Cliffs of Moher" – and hundreds more, of course.
They surround us, as it were, like an incomparable gallery.

Nor is the idea of a gallery out of place in speaking of this collected
edition of Mr. Stevens's poems. I was continually impressed, as I saun-
tered among the hundreds of poems, by the way in which they present
to us the whole movement of this century in art; no exhibition of paint-
ings could be more expressive of the modernist's aims and methods.

Winters *was* an academic poet, and whether in the best sense, as I suggested, or in the
worst makes little difference now. The pendulum of taste has swung so far away from aca-
demicism in *all* its senses that I doubt ten young people in America know Winters as
either poet or critic. Yet a dozen or more of his poems will be in the anthologies forever.

As for his criticism I return to it occasionally, as I return to Pound's, for simple pleasure
in its language. Wrongheaded and cantankerous both men could be, God knows. But their
clarity of judgment and vigor of expression in particular instances are as refreshing as
spring water in the desert. You could make up a marvelous anthology of literary aphorisms
from the prose of either of them. How people could write in those days! Not at all like
today's poets who, if they condescend to criticism at all, do so as if they think some
godawful disgrace attaches to the ordinary English declarative sentence. Winters was
wrong, of course, in his basic attitude. He was at least wrong in historical terms. What has
been, has been: the whole post-romantic efflorescence, our heritage. It had its glories and I
see no point in denying them – as Winters continually did. If reason is at variance, then
reason must be adjusted. Winters could not do this, and I remember the remark of a friend
in graduate school to the effect that he couldn't make head nor tail of Winters's criticism
until he saw that the whole endeavor was motivated by fear of personal insanity. That is the
truth, I think. But it is also true that a great deal of what Winters wrote against the course of
Anglo-American thought and feeling in the nineteenth and twentieth centuries remains a
necessary proviso, something we must take into account and incorporate within our ap-
preciation of the very processes he was attacking – as the smidgen of regret in any love af-
fair deepens and enriches the experience.

Of course the poet's very graphic way with imagery reminds one natu-
rally of painting; the bright Mediterranean colors and the arranged in-
teriors, as in the opening lines of "Sunday Morning," recall to me most
clearly Matisse, though there are many other connections and associa-
tions. The chief point, however, is that in these poems the many
influences on the art of our time can be seen plainly: French, pastoral,
metaphysical, Homeric, and so on; and the many aims: to originate, to
shock, to re-examine, to analyze, and above all to deal uncompromis-
ingly with the realities of the contemporary world.

In point of time Stevens's career as a writer has been coextensive
with the development of modern art, at least in this country, and the
career itself, as recorded in these poems, reveals the stages through
which we have come to believe the masters must always pass. The
chronology is not definite, but the main lines are clear. There are the
early masterpieces of conventional technique – "Sunday Morning"
and a few shorter poems in regular blank verse. There are the poems in
which this technique begins to shift under an experimental impetus; of
many examples, "The Comedian as the Letter C." There are the sheer
experiments, often fragmentary and uncharacteristic, and there are the
excesses – poems in which a manner that has pleased the poet for a
time is pushed too far, into conscious or unconscious self-caricature.
There are the variants on a constant theme – many of them apparently
impromptu – of the middle period, when the poet was working toward
a strong and individual style with which he could master any material
no matter how complex or "unpoetic." And there are the later poems
which sometimes revert to an old simplicity, though with the reso-
nance gained from the years. The progression has been accompanied –
quickened, pervaded, impelled – by a relentless amendment and
elaboration of the poet's theme – his insistence on the centrality of hu-
man imagination in the scheme of things – and the lavishness of his in-
vention has never diminished.

But why do we always come back to our impression of opulence?
One thinks immediately of the abounding images from the natural
world:

> *The rocks of the cliffs are the heads of dogs*
> *That turn into fishes and leap*
> *Into the sea....*

It is true that the rivers went nosing like swine,
Tugging at banks, until they seemed
Bland belly-sounds in somnolent troughs....

On an old shore, the vulgar ocean rolls
Noiselessly, noiselessly, resembling a thin bird
That thinks of settling, yet never settles, on a nest....

The cricket in the telephone is still.
A geranium withers on the window-sill.

But do they really abound? It has been much more difficult than I ex-
pected it would be to find these four detachable examples, and even
they are not truly representative. The fact is, most of the poems are
single metaphors, short, whole, compact, even spare; the images are
used frugally and pointedly; they are integral and functional, never
merely decorative. Even the long poems are generally composed of
short sections, separated and numbered, which each conform to this
pattern of lyric rigor, and the few long poems which do comprise sus-
tained passages of narrative or exposition are surprisingly unadorned –
not counting "The Comedian as the Letter C," which we can now re-
gard as an early experiment. In other words, the poems themselves,
when we examine them without preconceptions, contain neither
denser nor more ornate imagery than we should expect to find in 534
pages of poetry by anyone else, and in many cases the comparison,
especially if it were with the work of his contemporaries, would show
Stevens's poems to be the simpler in design, structure, and figuration.
    Perhaps then it is a question of the poet's subject, his *materia*.
Many of the poems, true enough, and especially the earlier ones, do
convey an exotic scene, a Caribbean radiance of sun-drenched seas
and forests. "Hibiscus on the Sleeping Shores," "The Idea of Order at
Key West," "O Florida, Venereal Soil" – these and many others, most
of them from *Harmonium,* the poet's first book, are clearly visions of
splendor. But the first poem in the second book is called "Farewell to
Florida," and thereafter Stevens's characteristic scene is not tropical
but northern, and he gives us as many celebrations of drab and wintry
occasions as of summer. Again I was surprised to find how few poems
are in fact devoted to outright flourishes of earthly glitter.

The poems from *Harmonium* are doubtless the best known. They have been republished many times in anthologies and repeatedly discussed by the critics. They have become a regular part of university courses in modern literature. And many of them are brilliant; it isn't surprising that they are used as displays. But they are not as good as the later poems, and emphatically they do not reveal the qualities of Stevens's whole accomplishment. The advantage of this collected edition is the prominence it gives to the main body of poems.

I think we conclude finally that in the texts themselves the language is the only constant ratification of our sense of the poet's opulent invention. There is nothing new in the idea of Stevens as a master of language. But to explore the pages of this collection is to be astonished, literally, by the range and intensity of his rhetorical genius. It is not virtuosity, for the virtuoso's performance is theoretically attainable by anyone who works hard enough, whereas Stevens excels at what only he can do. It is a perfection, a pressing extension within the formulations of his own strict style and prosody, of the aptitude for naming, which lies at the base of any writer's talent. Someday perhaps an industrious scholar will count the number of different words Stevens has used; certainly it would be interesting to see that magnitude measured. Stevens delights in odd words, archaic words, foreign words that he can wrest to an English meaning. In this respect he is like Whitman, but to my ear better than Whitman, for I am never embarrassed by Stevens's importations: he dominates and controls the foreign words with an uncallow, unprovincial authority Whitman never achieved. More exactly, Stevens is Elizabethan in his attitude toward language, highhanded in the extreme. When all else fails he derives words anew, gambling with recognizable roots and associations:

> *The grackles sing avant the spring*
> *Most spiss – oh! Yes, most spissantly.*

Such delight in language is infectious, and we are convinced, as we should be, when Stevens says to us:

> *Natives of poverty, children of malheur,*
> *The gaiety of language is our seigneur.*

Stevens is the delighted craftsman whose delight is, in part, the access of gratification which comes upon the exercise of mastery. His pleasure is endless because it is part of his work, past and present; it is transmissible because we too, in reading his poems, share that mastery.

True poetry is instinct with this delight – and with much more, of course. With meaning which transcends its verbal properties. With a passion which makes whole the verbal elements. As it happens, Stevens's delight in language is concomitant to his entire vision, his argument. If there is space in this short tribute for only a glance at one or two technical aspects of his poetry, I think we can be sure that for many readers in years to come the meaning and the passion of Stevens's poetry will be its dominant rewards. Certainly as readers and critics become more familiar with the whole body of work, we shall see more and more clearly how *humane* has been the impulse behind this delight that is interpretive of our actual world. Make no mistake, these poems have been written as solace for intellectual and moral hardship, not simply as verbal indulgences. Even now, in this book of beautiful, impeccable, famous poems, we have something so intimately a part of our time and scene that we are almost persuaded to say, appropriatively: "This is what we have been able to do; by these poems we are willing to be known."

To Fashion the Transitory

1956.

THE PROBLEM OF TIME in Edwin Muir's poetry dominates all others, and I suppose this allies him to the so-called metaphysical tradition in modern literature. But it is a loose and problematical alliance. If the metaphysical tradition is characterized in part by certain habits of significant ambiguity in thought and substance, or by a certain mental posture of irony which infiltrated the liturgical sensibility of medieval writers and which has endured as a creative mode in the erotic and political imaginations of Renaissance times and our own, then by contrast Muir's poetry is straightforward, singleminded, and virtually Wordsworthian in manner and tone. Muir is a fabulist, a poet of dreams and visions; he relies for his effects upon a high degree of poetic realism. By poetic realism I mean not a naturalistic technique but a deeper realism that makes matter-of-fact use of the poetic conventions for what they are – the easiest, clearest, and most economical means of coming to terms with the substance of one's feelings and imaginings. Muir lived for a number of years in central Europe and devoted a good deal of time to translating modern German literature, especially the novels and stories of Kafka, and it is not surprising that he should have learned something from the writer who, more than any other, has demonstrated the use of a conventional medium for the realistic embodiment of fantastic substance. But at the same time it is important to recognize that the essential ingredients of Muir's poetic manner, as well as the main elements of his thought and feeling, took form before he began translating Kafka, and that few other poets have equaled the skill with which he has used the conventions of English prosody – his verse-making, song-making genius. Some of Muir's poems are among the best that have come from Great Britain during the first half of this century.

Time, for Muir, appears under its ancient aspect of the thief, a doubly invidious figure because it steals away in "deadly days" and "melting hours" the objects and values that it alone has been able to create. Eternity, especially in the earlier poems, is simply time's extent, with the awful blanknesses of prehistory and posthistory at either end:

> So, back or forward, still we strike
> > Through time and touch its dreaded goal.
> Eternity's the fatal flaw
> > Through which run out world, life, and soul.

But at least one other kind of eternity, the eternity of mind, in which human beings escape from the flow of time into the permanence of conceptual or symbolic actions, appears in many poems, and in the later poems a third kind of eternity, akin to that of traditional Christian belief, offers something like a resolution to the time problem. The progression from an amorphous materialism through the eternity of the mind to something "more than half Platonic" is evident in the poems.

Because men and women are able to exist both in and out of time, they possess, against time's depredations, an existential advantage that is unique (discounting angels): the abilities to remember and to dream. By these means they create their own time. In the eternity of mind, dreams and memories – together with fables, their universalized counterpart – furnish the very substance of meaning; life is fabulous, and in the individual experiences of it the great events are enacted again and again, so that its meaning is perpetually reinforced. The individual's dreams and profoundest memories are prefigured in humanity's fables. Muir would admit, I think, that these concepts are more than faintly Jungian. But this does not imply a direct connection; the ideas were "in the air" thirty years ago, and in any case it is clear that Muir worked them out in terms useful for him solely in his poems. Perhaps this concern for meaningful archetypal figurations aligns Muir after all with the metaphysical and post-symbolist tradition considered in its functional aspect, but with this difference: Muir disdains the search for objectifications among the intellectual conventions of the age and instead confines himself to the task of constructing a modern typology from the pristine sources of experience – myth and dream. This is perfectly evident in the poems. Each of them is an assault against time, a failing assault, of course, as all such assaults must be, written out of the eternity of mind to recreate and reinterpret the perpetual fable of man's dreams and memories. This is hard substance, and the poems have about them, beyond their verbal utilitarianism, a kind of obduracy of spirit that we associate with the Scotch-Presbyterian sensibility. How many of the poems derive from actual dreams we cannot tell; yet certainly many of them, especially such Kafka-like poems as "The Escape" and "The Interrogation," have the quality of dreams – terror and absurdity reduced to the commonplace occurrences of the mind. Images of anxiety recur throughout the poems, and though one does not wish to speak in clinical terms about them, several poems are superb reenactments of anxiety itself:

> But when you reach the Bridge of Dread
> Your flesh will huddle into its nest
> For refuge and your naked head
> Creep in the casement of your breast,
>
> And your great bulk grow thin and small
> And cower within its cage of bone,

While dazed you watch your footsteps crawl
Toadlike across the leagues of stone.

That exactness of subjective detail, cast in the ordinariness of conventional verse, is what tells us that Muir himself has crossed such a bridge more than once. And even more prominent in the poems than anxiety is its aftermath, melancholy, the irreducible sadness of the person who cannot complete the gesture of acceptance and resignation:

I do not want it so,
But since things so are made,
Sorrow, sorrow,
Be you my second trade.

The central fable to which Muir returns again and again is, of course, that of fallen humanity, for the Fall is the universal fable of our entrance into time, into history, the moment when we begin to dream and remember. "What shape had I before the Fall?" he asks. What "dragon brood" roamed the earth then? His dim memories of a splendidly heraldic age haunt his poems, and he speaks of "the journey back," back beyond our ancestries to the fabulous origins. Little by little the primal place grows clearer, and the journey itself, back through the eternity of the mind, lightens new corners of dreamed and fabulous experience. The patterns of value consolidate. Of the search for Eden, Muir writes:

If I should reach that place, how could I come
To where I am but by that deafening road,
Life-wide, world-wide, by which all come to all,
The strong with the weak, the swift with the stationary,
For mountain and man, hunter and quarry there
In tarrying do not tarry, nor hastening hasten,
But all with no division strongly come
For ever to their steady mark, the moment,
And the tumultuous world slips softly home
To its perpetual end and flawless bourne.

And in dreams and memories the "deafening road" is traveled cease-lessly, the road that opens out from Eden and carries us to our only compensations – the transitory values of our mutual arts and the per-manent values of our shared and inherited experience. Our experience is legendary, embodied in dreams and fables that are known to all of us. And in its largest aspects it transcends our arts:

> *Old gods and goddesses who have lived so long*
> *Through time and never found eternity,*
> *Fettered by wasting wood and hollowing hill,*
>
> *You should have fled our ever-dying song,*
> *The mound, the well, and the green trysting tree,*
> *They are forgotten, yet you linger still.*

In his *Autobiography* Muir says that he did not begin to write poetry until he was thirty-five. One somewhat regrets the loss of the youthful work, but his mature poetry makes up for it, so beautifully written. In many ways Muir brought to his poetry the ideal verbal equipment, for like a number of other modern writers whose work is important to us Muir came from a linguistic backwater of the British Isles, in his case Orkney; his native speech, a dynamic, still logopoeic dialect, has been a noticeable factor in his poems, as have the remnants of Nordic myth that survived among the island folk during his childhood. On the other hand Muir has not allied himself with the nationalistic poets of Scot-land; perhaps as an Orkney man he was too much out of the main-stream of even Scottish provincial life to identify himself with it. In-stead he has chosen the hard lot of literacy in the cosmopolitan world – wisely, I think – and has devoted himself to the available audience and the usable resources of the mind. The result is a poetry of the modern sensibility at its broadest self-consciousness, a poetry which, in its use of dreams and memories and in its strong idiom, objectifies an endur-ing, undermost reality, beneath appearances of time or place. Like the surrealists, Muir deals with our perpetually incipient apprehensions of what is; but unlike them he is concerned with the broadly human in-gredients, not with the individual ego. Elsewhere I have called him a subrealist. The term is somewhat misleading, but perhaps it conveys the distinction I have in mind.

Muir's preference is for what John Crowe Ransom has called the common line, the folk measure of ballad and hymn. Some of his poems on legendary or heraldic themes are in fact ballads transmuted or refined, and thus belong to an old tradition of British literature. They are lyrical ballads of a new order. But Muir has often used the pentameter too, and one of his commonest stylistic devices is the play of long, intricate syntactical units against the simple regularity of standard English meter. The opening sentence of "The Labyrinth," for instance, extends for thirty-five lines without effort, surely an enviable feat. Some of his shorter lyrics consist of a single sentence. These qualities are a part of Muir's poetic realism, a style that does not shun inversions or other "unnatural" or "literary" constructions provided they derive from the force of reality in thought, feeling, and dream, and this real substance is what one comes back to repeatedly in writing about his work. The closest he himself has come to a discussion of technique is his poem "All We":

> *All we who make*
> *Things transitory and good*
> *Cannot but take*
> *When walking in a wood*
> *Pleasure in everything*
> *And the maker's solicitude,*
> *Knowing the delicacy*
> *Of bringing shape to birth.*
> *To fashion the transitory*
> *We gave and took the ring*
> *And pledged ourselves to earth.*

And yet one is not aware of the "delicacy"; it lies in the poetic act, in the discriminations and perceptions, not in the poem. The object, the poem itself, is instead shaped of earth, not perdurable, in fact transitory, but nevertheless ingrained with the maker's love and the most lasting elements of human nature and experience; and such poems as "The Annunciation," "The Journey Back," "Variations on a Time Theme," "The Island," and "The Horses" will last for a good many seasons in the eternity of the mind.

ల . . . .

The Closest Permissible Approximation

A review of *Waterlily Fire: Poems 1935–1962*, by Muriel Rukeyser. 1963.

THESE are the opening stanzas of an early poem by Miss Rukeyser:

> *The drowning young man lifted his face from the river*
> *to me, exhausted from calling for help and weeping;*
> *"My love!" I said; but he kissed me once for ever*
> *and returned to his privacy and secret keeping.*
>
> *His close face dripped with the attractive water,*
> *I stared in his eyes and saw there penalty,*
> *for the city moved in its struggle, loud about us,*
> *and the salt air blew down; but he would face the sea.*

And one of her recent poems begins:

> *Great Alexander sailing was from his true course turned*
> *By a young wind from a cloud in Asia moving*
> *Like a most recognizable most silvery woman;*
> *Tall Alexander to the island came.*
> *The small breeze blew behind his turning head.*
> *He walked from the foam of ripples into this scene.*

Force, directness, affection for the separate word and the various parts of speech (especially participles), knowledge of cadence and syntax as components of meaning rather than vicissitudes of fabrication – we can have no doubt at all of the poetic genius behind these lines. Painters speak of the "painterly" qualities of a certain work, meaning the way in which the medium itself becomes important to the esthetic and moral experience, the paint on the canvas an embodiment of thought and feeling (as opposed to the schools which regard the medium as ideally a transparency). There is an analogous quality in Miss Rukeyser's poems. We are always aware of their language, of the way she has worked it into shapes and movements that are basically idiosyncratic.

Often this is extremely effective. Sometimes, on the other hand, it leads to the kind of excess we call mannerism, as in the long passages where she writes without verbs:

> *Eyes on the road at night, sides of a road like rhyme;*
> *the floor of the illumined shadow sea*
> *and shallows with their assembling flash and show*
> *of sight, root, holdfast, eyes of the brittle stars.*
> *And your eyes in the shadowy red room,*
> *scent of the forest entering, various time*
> *calling and the light of wood along the ceiling*
> *and over us birds calling and their circuit eyes.*
> *And in our bodies the eyes of the dead and the living*
> *giving us gifts at hand, the glitter of all their eyes.*

One can see how this might happen; a search for immediacy, a hunger for language genuinely experienced – it was what impelled the imagists. But Miss Rukeyser's characteristic poem is rather long, complex, full of allusion and other intellectual and cultural machinery. I miss the motion-making words that would lend quickness. Instead the effect resembles an impasto, colors heaped on one another until the surface is thick and lightless.*

But Miss Rukeyser's best poems are very good indeed. Aside from their virtues of language they possess many virtues of substance. I admire especially the breadth of her response. Personal anxiety and desire are powerfully represented in her work, but so are the exterior aspects of experience, and not just in lyrical or ironic meditations on nature. Her world is essentially urban, her poems occur in a context that is implicitly – and often explicitly – technological and political. She seems to know a good deal about architecture and machinery and what happens at political caucuses, the whole texture of actuality right now, and she is very successful in giving us a sense of the combined attraction and repulsion all of us feel in such an environment. It is refreshing. But more than that it is evidence of artistic responsibility,

---

* NOTE IN 1994. Clearly the participial way of writing has become extremely popular since Rukeyser, and in the hands of fine poets, e.g., Adrienne Rich, Len Roberts, and many others, it produces fine results. I forgot my own first principle: there is no such thing as inadmissible poetry and what works, works.

which in itself is meaningful, adding to the emotive power of a work's objective particulars.

Analogous to this is another aspect of her work that is somewhat more difficult to speak about. I mean her vigorous, brave, and I think nearly absolute honesty, this being – honesty – the nearest permissible approximation, in most of our lives, to an absolute of faith. Let us agree on what seems obvious to me: that a large part of lyric poetry is a kind of prayer. Where does this leave the poet who cannot acknowledge a supernatural existent? You may go backward and forward through the anthologies of modern poetry and find this problem on almost every page. Ninety per cent of the poets are too lazy to deal with it, using such terms as "Lord" and "my God" with the implied reservation that they are fictions. Or they impute a fake divinity to great men, mountains, dead rodents, and such. But suppose you are absolutely honest; suppose, in the straits of reason and experience, you must deny the supernatural but assert the ultranatural, those extreme susceptivities of consciousness which govern our spiritual and moral lives; and suppose you even raise ultranatural experience to a superpersonal level, the racial or the pan-human; do you then agree to call it by the name of God, do you stand up in church and say the Credo with your fingers crossed (as was lately recommended by that noted British humanist, Basil Willey)? Miss Rukeyser does not. This is the quality of her honesty. She recognizes that there is a point at which symbolism as a poetic technique turns into a substantial instrument of mendacity. I don't say she is an objectivist; far from it. She is no doctrinairian of any kind. And I don't say she has solved the problem. Consider it solely as a tactic of vocabulary: what terms shall the poet invent which can assume the richness and versatility of terms refined in centuries of religious usage? Remember that even the most determined anti-Christians from de Sade to Sartre have argued in basically Christian terms, because there are no other. It would be mere obstinacy to ask Miss Rukeyser, or any single poet, to do a job which requires a sustained community of genius. Yet I know no other body of work in which the problem has been met more squarely than in hers; nor, generally speaking, any poetry which has brought more imagination and lyrical firmness to the task. Make no mistake, these poems are deeply felt – prayers, I should say, desperate prayers for the things the poet needs but cannot command in the political-technological nightmare of the modern state: peace and justice. For this reason her poems are intrinsically, connately a part of our ethical crisis, which begins to show at least some sign of turning into a genuine social crisis, and as such they ought to win the prior respect and endorsement of us all, especially since the substantial honesty of the poems is inseparable from their superiority as works of art.

Poets Without Prophecy

1963.

BEGINNING WITH WHOM? – not Eliot – with Arnold perhaps? – well, beginning rather a long time ago the meaning of the words *poem* and *poet* shifted finally from a matter of substance to a matter of technique. Today we can find vestiges of that older way of speaking. In the backwoods where I live people still say, when you tell them a lie, "Oh, that's poetry," and I suppose somewhere people may still exclaim, "How poetic!" upon seeing a sunset. We do not say these things. We consider them offensive. For us a poem is a work of art, a composition of verbal materials, a thing, and the poet is the maker who makes it.

I don't want to suggest that we are wrong; certainly I don't want to excuse the sentimentality and unctuousness which were the end products of the old view. But I would like to point out that these end products were a long time in coming – centuries, in fact – and that there distinctly was something grand and ennobling in the idea that a poet was to be known not by his art but by his vision; something more than grand and ennobling, something essential. And we have lost it.

I don't know what to call it precisely. It's hard to move back into that area of old custom without falling prey to the soft, foolish terms it spawned so readily toward its close. But let's extend to one another the charity of understanding and agree on an acknowledged orotundity: "the larger vision of humanity." Once the poet was our spokesman, and not our oracle, our advocate and not our secret agent, or at least he or she was as much the one as the other; and if the poet did not speak for us, all of us, fully and warmly, if the poems lacked the larger vision of humanity, we said he or she was deficient in one of the qualities which, virtually by definition, make a poet.

This attitude survived among the older poets of our time, though their own theories about poetry tended to suppress it; the larger vision of humanity was still a part of their poetic instinct. The *Cantos, The Waste Land,* and *Paterson* are alive with it; Frost's poems reveal an unmistakably general feeling; so do the poems of Cummings, Aiken, Ransom; Stevens veiled his concern under his marvelous verbal textures and his epistemological preoccupations, but it was there, especially in the later poems where a sense of brooding pity underlies almost every word. Even Marianne Moore, whose writing has never appealed to me, conveys a kind of coy consciousness of sodality in her least timid poems. The point is that all these poets came into the world at a time when the poet's direct responsibility to the human species at large still hadn't quite been laughed out of existence. They themselves were the ones who set off the final burst of laughter when, in order to discredit the impressionistic views of the previous age, they directed their attention away from the representative role of the poet and toward the poet as experimentalist, hierophant, artifex, oneirocritic, or what have you.

It should be clear that my topic is poetry and politics, though I have chosen to work my way into it by means of concepts which show political feeling as what it really is – concern for others – rather than as mere partisanship.

Next came the thirties, the time when poetry was avowedly political, the time of Archibald MacLeish, Muriel Rukeyser, Alfred Hayes, and the British socialists, the time equally of the Southern Agrarians. I myself find this poetry refreshing to read today, especially the radical poetry; its motives and objectives were so forceful that often a kind of vividness was the result, against which our own verse, striving for greater richness, seems only muddy. I wonder if we aren't ready for a revival of interest in proletarian writing, similar to the Jazz Age revival which occurred a few years back. Serious attention is being given again to John Steinbeck, thanks to his Nobel Prize, and this is to the good. Others also deserve reconsideration. I nominate Malcolm Cowley and Kenneth Fearing and Langston Hughes. Nowadays they are scarcely thought of as poets, yet they each wrote first-rate poems.

At the same time one cannot avoid seeing that the larger vision of humanity became more specialized in the poetry of the thirties, narrowed and reduced, and that this constriction grew even tighter in our poetry of the war. We had some fine war poems, things like Eberhart's "Fury of Aerial Bombardment" and Jarrell's "Death of a Ball Turret Gunner"; they have become standard anthology pieces. Yet if we compare them with the poems of the First World War we see a great difference. In the poems of Wilfred Owen, for instance, or even in such a highly wrought work as David Jones's *In Parenthesis,* the larger vision is instinct in every word and very profoundly expressed in some; but Jarrell's gunner, whose remains are washed out of his turret with a hose, is a far more specialized figure. He does not live in our minds as a fully realizable exponent of our own suffering. The figures created by Bill Mauldin and Ernie Pyle, though shallow, come closer to this and closer to the Tommies of Owen's poetry. This isn't Jarrell's fault. He is a fine poet, and the reason for his narrowed sensibility (which I don't think he desired at all) lies in the cultural evolution of the century. There had been an attrition of poetic consciousness. Far too complicated a matter to be easily explained; yet I think we can all see the difference between Owen and Jarrell, and I think most of us can concede that it is connected with the increasing refinement of the poet as a self-appointed agent of sensibility in an insensible and ever more hostile society.

Since then this erosion of the larger view has reached a point at which poetry has become almost totally apolitical. The supreme political fact of our lives is the atomic bomb. Am I wrong? It is enormous; it occupies the whole world. It is not only what it is but also the concentrated symbol of all hatred and injustice in every social and economic sphere. Speaking for myself, I have lived in fear of it for fifteen years, fear that it will go off, one way or another, and kill me and my family and my community, or render our lives so intolerable that we won't wish to go on. Maybe I am more timorous than most people; I believe actually some Americans never think about the bomb. But poets? That would be incredible. No matter how hard they try they cannot escape being included among society's more percipient members. Yet if one were to judge by their output one would have to believe that poets are the least concerned people in the world, not only on their own account but on everyone's.

Poetry, under the editorship of Henry Rago, is as representative of the various groups among American poets as any single magazine could probably be. I have just gone through all the issues for 1961, the only recent year for which I could find a complete set on my shelves. The year produced 335 poems by 139 poets, and although I skimmed through them rapidly, it has still taken me several hours to make up a count; I didn't go so quickly that my figures are likely to be off by more than a little. In the whole year I found two explicit references to the bomb, one a passing seriocomic remark, and ten poems on the general theme of suffering in war, two of which were translations from foreign poets of an earlier time. There were a great many poems on sex in its various aspects, religion, growing old, being young, thought and feeling, the uses of knowledge, themes unintelligible to me, and painting, music, and poetry.

That's it, of course – Poetry. The only topic poets will admit. Time after time they say so. Robert Creeley, one of the best alive, asserts his allegiance to "the poem supreme, addressed to / emptiness...." At the other end of the country, Howard Nemerov, a good academic poet, speaks of himself as:

> *Dreaming preposterous mergers and divisions*
> *Of vowels like water, consonants like rock*
> *(While everyone kept discussing values*
> *And the need for values), for words that would*
> *Enter the silence and be there as a light.*

Could anything be plainer? And I believe you could find statements of this precise credo – belief in the poem as an isolated act of absolutely and solely intrinsic goodness – in ninety percent of the books published by American poets in the past ten or fifteen years. There are a couple in my own.

Not spokesmen then. But hermits, lone wolves, acolytes – building poems in the wilderness for their own salvation.

The poets will retort in two ways. First they will say that art has always been lonely work, that the artist must use his or her own experience, and that ultimately he or she must put together a personal vision of reality – or, as some would say, discover it – within the self. This is self-evident; but it does not require the poet to withdraw so far from the general experience of the time that he or she becomes merely a specialist pursuing specialized ends. In fact it ought to mean just the opposite: that the poet, within the self, identifies and augments the general experience in such a way that it will excite a renewed susceptibility in everyone else.

Second, the poets will say that their isolated poems are acts of an implied political significance. They will say that in evil times the individual person exerts a force for good by carrying on his or her private endeavor with exemplary diligence and honesty. They will say that by refining their own purity as artists and by rejecting the false values of the world they are expressing a political attitude of considerable importance and firmness, and are doing so in terms more durable than could be used in direct statements about immediate political objectives. In the past I have said this myself, and I do not think it is sophistry. But it comes close to it. Politics is practicality, and a political act is by nature an act committed in the context of immediate objectives. And isn't the "context of immediate objectives" simply a jargonistic equivalent of the "larger vision of humanity"? This context still exists, I grant you, in the very remote background of today's estranged poetry. But when the correlation between the output of *Poetry* magazine and the leading headlines of, for example, the *New York Times* is as disparate as my little tabulation for 1961 indicates, then the context has receded so far that it no longer furnishes a useful field of reference to most of the people who read the poetry.

This is the point. The larger vision has been turned over to the newspapers, to the so-called industry of so-called mass communication. I imagine there's not a single reporter covering the discussions at Geneva for whom the larger vision isn't so fully, consistently present that drinking and weeping are the only ways to get to sleep at night. But poetry is not their job; and if they are good reporters they know this and steer clear of it.

The Beats are the exception to what I have been saying. At least so they seem at first, though I wonder if they aren't simply the other side of the coin. I mean the hard core of poets who still flourish their Beat credentials. Among them we find explicitly political poems in great numbers, poems designed to incite impeachments, riots, revolutions, etc. To my mind they fail. The best of these poets is perhaps Gregory Corso, an exceedingly talented poet who has written two dozen really good poems, enough to make anyone envious. But all these good poems are nonpolitical, most are apolitical, and the best are not particularly Beat. His most popular poem is a diatribe called "The Bomb," but for me it seems only a long composition made up partly of rant and shapeless anger and partly of attempts to exorcise the bomb in the name of some numinous human essence; it turns politics into a sort of gang war supervised by the old ladies from the settlement house. In short it contains no poetry, no imagined transmutation of experience, no single realized image to which our thought and feeling can cling. In this respect – that is, the reintroduction of poetry to politics – it seems to me that the Beats, whom we all hoped (some of us secretly) would succeed, have failed almost completely, and what success they have had has been on the wrong level.

Poets are never liberals or conservatives, they are always radicals or reactionaries; and today public life rejects these indecorous extremes. True, the far Right has worked up something resembling a movement in recent years, but it remains intellectually disreputable. On the Left, in spite of sporadic efforts in New York and California, those of us who are long-standing anarchists have to agree there isn't much doing. In other words the political attitudes usually endorsed by poets are now amorphous, disintegrated, anachronistic, without programs. Yet this ought to be exactly the political condition in which poets can flourish and in which politically directed poems – and I mean *poems* in the completest sense – can be written without becoming debased by doctrinaire points of view. I cannot speak for reaction; but it is hard for me to believe that any radical poet in the country today lacks a point on which he can stand firm, a point from which, as the spokesman of us all, he can attack known injustices and stupidities. Isn't the bomb, our monstrous, inescapable, political absurdity that stands for all our violence, all our racism, sexism, greed, and evil, the place to begin? And why isn't it happening?

Théophile Gautier, while discussing his fellow writers, said: "To be of one's own time – nothing seems easier and nothing is more difficult. One can go straight through one's age without seeing it, and this is what happened to many eminent minds."

Yes, of our time too. We poets have gone straight through fifteen years without seeing them. One can think of a hundred reasons: the extraordinary burden on us of the poetry of our immediate past, the long evolution of formal preoccupations, the sociology of the culture hero; but none of these, or even all together, can suffice against the bomb, none can explain two poems out of 335. Only blindness can explain that. I think American poetry, to speak of only that element of our civilization, is stupefied by massive neurosis – terror, repression, spasmodic hysteria – and I cannot conceive of a therapy ingenious enough to cure it.

Multiple Disguises

1963

THE WORK of Denis de Rougemont, taken as a whole, seems to me obsessed, conventional, disorderly, and unprofitable. Such was my opinion formerly, and since this new book, *Love Declared: Essays on the Myths of Love*, adds nothing exceptional to what de Rougemont has said before, such my opinion remains. I state it in these somewhat vehement terms because I find I more and more resent authors who believe they may serve the modern world by offering it exercises in analytical simplification. Many of these authors are extremely clever; de Rougemont is of course much more: a finely gifted, beautifully learned person. But to me our culture is so obviously not simple and so obviously never was simple that anyone who suggests he can explain it to me in a book arouses my indignation. By now a great many people have made exactly this suggestion, and my tolerance is about gone. I am perfectly willing to grant my animosity: the work of de Rougemont is an intellectual fraud, and it makes not a whit of difference that it is also a pious fraud.

Is there any other way to describe a piece of cultural analysis which is so driven by enthusiasm for its schematic concepts that it denies not only history but what everyone knows to be true from the experience of daily living?

Love in the Western World, the book in which de Rougemont first attempted a full-scale account of his ideas, was published in France in 1939, and has enjoyed a considerable vogue ever since. I imagine the main points of it are known to most readers, but a summary will be useful. Human experience, according to de Rougemont, is ruled by two types of love: first, *agape* or Christian love, which is a love between equal persons and is typified by marriage undertaken for purposes of procreation; second, *eros* or passion, which is a love between unequal persons, which shuns marriage and thrives on separation, which is ultimately not love of a person at all but love of Love, and which ideally ends in the death of the lovers. The two arise from fundamental religious sources. *Agape* is a development in human terms of the Christian theories of Incarnation and the absolute qualitative separation of God and man; these ideas, in spite of the doctrine of sin, permit holiness on earth and happy love in life. *Eros*, on the other hand, springs from the Oriental and specifically Manichaean belief in a totally divisive conflict between evil and good, in which evil is identified with the world and the body, and good with heaven and the spirit. *Eros* entered the main current of Western civilization, still according to de Rougemont, with the Catharist heresy of the twelfth century (deriving from the Bogomils of Bulgaria and ultimately from the teachings of Mani in the Near East), and its primordial literary expression in the West was in the songs of the troubadours. De Rougement suggests that most Provençal love poetry was disguised devotional poetry of the Catharist or Albigensian church, in which the lady of the poet's song was a stereotyped representation of the Lady, Sancta Maria Sophia, Eternal Wisdom, the Light of Heaven and Bride of God, to whom the poet vowed allegiance, for whom he swore himself (hypocritically or not) to chastity, and with whom he hoped presently to unite himself in death. The whole apparatus of *cortezia,* the laws, the courts, the rituals, the prescripts for *vray amor,* was no more or less than a clandestine and consciously disguised analog of the heretical Catharist rites – so de Rougemont suggests, although he tempers his historical radicalism by saying that he is more interested in the cultural intent of his analysis than in the determinable history of ideas. After the Albigensian Crusade, that nightmare of religious brutality, the Catharist heresy was fragmented and driven underground by the Inquisition (whose atrocities we can all too well imagine in our world of terror today), and its literary counterpart, now beginning to lose its conscious ground in religion, moved to the north and became linked with Celtic literature. The result was the Arthurian cycle, and the epitome of this cycle was the legend of Tristan and Iseult, in which de Rougemont finds all the necessary ingredients of the erotic myth par excellence: the love of Tristan and Iseult is an adulterous relationship of unequals, it thrives on separation (to such an extent that the lovers invent needless obstacles whenever external circumstance fails to provide them), and it ends in the blissful death of the lovers. From this point on, de Rougemont traces the Tristanian myth as it becomes further and further attenuated and dissociated from its religious source, through Faust, Don Juan, the romantic boom, and into our own time, when in an almost wholly profaned but very widespread form it has issued in the cult of the movies, the commercialization of sexual imagery, and especially the breakdown of marriage; its political corollary is the totalitarian passion. This summary greatly truncates de Rougemont's schematism, and in particular his analysis of the Tristan legends, which in itself is a marvelous study in critical exegesis.

The new book, *Love Declared*, adds nothing essential, though it refines and extends some of the concepts. The principal change is the elevation of Don Juan to a mythical status equal and opposed to that of Tristan within the erotic hierarchy. Thus Western culture is now seen to vibrate between serious, sacramental Tristanism and comic, impious Juanism, depending upon its periodic *rapprochements* with the religious sensibility; all this, of course, still being subordinate to the broader antinomy of eros and agape.

A thoroughgoing critique of de Rougemont's theory of love would be valuable except for one consideration: we have had our fill of critique. What we need now is affirmation. And this is my first comment on de Rougement: he writes from the point of view of a committed Catholic, he praises agape and blames the world's ills on eros, and yet almost his entire work is devoted to a critical discussion of eros. He returns to the articles of his disapproval again and again, obsessively and without adding anything new. His hope lies, apparently, in some unrealized synthesis of *eros* and *agape*, but he is exceedingly vague on this point, and his discussion of *agape* consists solely of statements that it derives from the Christian commandments to love God and love thy neighbor and that it is good. Yet the problem of married love is far more important and probably far more difficult than the historical analysis of heresy, as some Catholic philosophers are beginning to recognize. Certainly in the modern world the complex "institution" of marriage can no longer be reduced to the prescriptive formulas of the historical Church.

Second, like any good Catholic de Rougement anathematizes the

Manichaean dualism, and yet his thought is formed in the same mold. It is interesting to note that in the revised edition of *Love in the Western World,* published in 1956, de Rougemont introduced a number of terms from existentialist philosophy as well as the word *existentialism* itself, applying them to his own position. I don't mean to suggest that this was conscious trimming; de Rougemont acknowledged his debt to Kierkegaard, for instance, from the first. Yet there does seem to have been some attempt to shift the philosophical tone of the argument. In spite of it, and in spite of the essay in the new book devoted to a definition of the person, de Rougemont remains as far from the existentialist attitude as anyone could be. His work is built on dualisms – eros/agape, Tristan/Don Juan – and moreover he insists that Tristan and Don Juan are not persons but forces. (Compare the humane Juan of Montherlant or the absurd Juan of Camus with de Rougemont's eternalized sex maniac.) This is what I mean by analytical simplification; its sign is the dualism and its direct provenance is absolutist idealism. This seems to me a far more insidious and pervasive aspect of fundamental Platonism than the ambiguities which may persist in our sexual mores. And the manipulating of ideals in de Rougemont's manner seems to me far less satisfactory (questions of religion aside) for the person who is *rationally* concerned with the predicament of modern civilization than the realism and relativism of writers like Camus, whatever other shortcomings they may have. At this state of intellectual history we have no need to be reminded of the determinative power of myth. What we need are suggestions for ways to escape it.

Third, the question of ordinary experience. In one of his most recent statements of the distinction between *agape* and *eros*, de Rougemont writes, "Eroticism begins where sexual emotion becomes, beyond its procreative goal, an end in itself or an instrument of the soul," (*Love Declared,* p. 35). This sounds very neat, which is what makes me suspect it. *Agape* equals Christian marriage which equals sex for the purpose of procreation; *eros* equals adultery which equals sex for its own sake. But at this point, though I suppose it is indiscreet to say so, I begin to wonder if de Rougemont, who has set himself up as the leading philosophical authority on love, has had any experience of it himself. Is anyone who has ever gone to bed in order to make love unaware that the primary motive for doing so is immediate, sensory pleasure? – susceptible to almost endless refinement no doubt, and thank God for that, but sensory and thus immediate nevertheless. In other words marriage, so far as it is definable at all, is a combination of *eros* and *agape*, or better yet a tension between them, immensely rich and changeable, and any writer who denatures the complexity of this fusion is doing marriage a disservice, not a service.

Fourth, de Rougemont says that the decline of poetry and the rise of the novel, that is, the shift from lyricism to narrative and drama, begins with the transference of the erotic literary center from Provence to the north and with the loss of eroticism's sacral meaning. In other words *Tristan* is the first novel and de Rougemont's work, as he says, is in one sense an investigation of the novel as the preeminent Western literary discipline. But what are we to say about a critic of the novel who doesn't mention, for instance, Dostoyevsky? Is it possible that the crucial importance of Dostoyevsky and the line of moral sensibility descending from him cannot be explained in the terms de Rougemont has invented?

Fifth, the historical pivots of de Rougemont's theory are the twelfth century and modern times. The twelfth century was "precisely," as he insists, the time when the erotic myth entered Western civilization; sometimes he pins it down even more narrowly than that. But is this likely, considering what we know about love? Is it possible, considering what we know about Augustine, Scotus Erigena, the schools of Chartres and Arras, to keep solely on the philosophical side? Were human beings all continent, up till A.D. 1130? Does the work of Reinach, Cornford, Schroeder, Dupouy, Stoll, Hoernes, etc., etc., mean nothing? Fertility and procreation have been powerful ideas, of course, and we have had many explanations of their role in ancient and medieval religions; but there is plenty of evidence also that our species has nearly always made a place for the sexual urge as such, for pure eroticism, in religion, life, and art. Indeed if this is not the meaning of Paul's "better to marry than to burn," then it has no meaning. De Rougemont asserts further that the twelfth and twentieth centuries are notable for the breakdown of marriage which occurred in each era, under the influence of ascendant eroticism. But here he is venturing into the area which he otherwise excludes from his philosophico-literary analysis, namely, social history. If he mentions the breakdown of marriage at all, then he is obliged to investigate the social factors – for example, the collapse of feudalism, collapse of capitalism – which probably are more important than the cultural factors. At least he ought to acknowledge that, without history, his literary or even mythological criticism of human behavior is in the realm of fantasy. No poet, but only a critic, would arrogate so much responsibility to his own discipline. For that matter, why didn't the modern breakdown of marriage occur during the great upsurgence of erotic romanticism from Kant to Wagner, rather than a hundred years later when almost the entire Western cultural leadership was in revulsion against it? I don't say these matters cannot be explained; I only say they are wonderfully, magnificently complex. I repeat: any simplification is a degradation.

De Rougemont's accomplishments are praiseworthy, of course. He has given us, for example, a modern definition of the soul which seems practicable from almost any point of view, and though this is implicit among other writers, I know no one else offhand who has done it explicitly. It is useful work, as is much of his mythological exegesis and some of his comparative analysis of oriental and Western religions. But all these accomplishments are ancillary to his main objective. Let us proclaim the end of the age of critique. It has lasted long enough. A cultural philosopher who adopts the methods of critique is living off the work of the past and hence is circumscribing the range of his achievement even before he begins. The change won't be easy. It will require a mental insurrection. It will require a displacement of knowledge – at any rate secondary, derivative knowledge – by invention. But if obsolescence is the mother of revolution and necessity the mother of invention, I'd say the only thing lacking now is an obstetrician.

🖋 . . . .

Pursy Windham Lucigen
1964.

PERCY WYNDHAM LEWIS was born in 1882, and like the rest of us began by sponging off his mother, the difference being, however, that he refused to be weaned and kept it up until he was nigh on to thirty; whereupon the poor lady, who was none too well nourished herself, died. Percy's hysteria, when no one, and more especially his "mother country," would offer a surrogatory tit continued the rest of his life, or nearly; and a more pitiable, childish, and ultimately tedious spectacle is unlikely to be found among English men of letters, or among the latter-day Parnassians generally.

Unflattering as it is and even, if you like, "dirty," this is all the reader of *The Letters of Wyndham Lewis,* edited by W. K. Rose, can conclude. Or almost all. The book itself, handsome and substantial, has been edited with scholarly care and also with a certain warmth and imagination; but beyond that, since the selection Professor Rose has made from the extant correspondence comprises, he says, only about a fourth, we must, being ignorant of the rest, reserve final judgment of his editorial skill. Nevertheless he appears to have done a good job. More important, we are told that the selection is representative, we notice that the book is dressed up with baby pictures, footnotes, copious prefaces, etc., and we conclude that the project is attended with scholarly earnestness and an air of quasi-finality. Hence I see no reason why we should withhold our judgment of its subject, Lewis himself. Like all collections of letters, this is a book about a man. In this case the man was also a painter, a novelist, and a critic; but it was not the painter, novelist, or critic who wrote these letters, it was the man. Those who offer us the letters are, by so doing, inviting us to judge the man alone. Nor is this judgment trivial: first, because the man happened to be a figure of some importance in his time; second, because the man indubitably did create the paintings, novels, and works of criticism.

Percy was born on board his father's yacht, which had been tied up for the occasion at Amherst, Nova Scotia. His father was a wealthy young Canadian, his mother a good-looking young Englishwoman. Not long afterward, however, they separated, and the mother took Percy to live in England, where she sent him in due course to various public (private) schools. She had a hard time. Percy's father was frequently in default of child support, and we are left with the impression that he was squandering his substance in the fleshpots of the Maritimes; though for that matter as far as I know no one has troubled to investigate his side of the story. At any event Mrs. Lewis maintained herself and her son through her own ingenuity and hard labor in various shoestring enterprises, chiefly shopkeeping. Percy was at the same time washing out of the schools to which he had been entrusted, and at age sixteen, when he stood twenty-sixth in his class of twenty-six at Rugby, he gave it up as a bad job. Later he attended the Slade School of Art, where his talents for drawing were recognized and encouraged. In 1902 he went abroad, and until 1910 lived in Paris, Madrid, Munich, and the Netherlands, attended occasional lectures, made paintings and drawings, dressed in a black cape, and generally pursued *la vie bohême,* as it was still properly called in those antediluvian days. The only letters offered us from this period are those to his mother. They are filled with cheerful condolences for her hardships, both physical and financial, and with reports on his expenditures for lodging, food, and models. During most of this time he apparently sent his dirty laundry home to London to be washed, and his letters often contain requests for books and other articles to be enclosed in the returning packages. Most of the letters also contain requests for money. In 1907, when he was twenty-five, he wrote: "Chère Maman, Well, so long as you give me enough to keep me in food, etc., and pay for the stove, etc., it's all I can expect...." Etc., etc., etc. At the same time one ought not to deprecate the affectionate tone of these letters; it seems clear that mother and son were held in a close if desperately unequal relationship by a deep mutual need.

Lewis had always mingled writing with his art studies, but we cannot tell how serious he was in his first attempts, of which we have no specimens. They were poems, apparently, and were destroyed by Lewis, or perhaps suppressed by his executors after his death. In 1909, however, he sold a story to Ford Madox Hueffer's important *English Review,* a success which led him, in 1910, to return to England and establish himself in London. Quickly he became engaged in the ferment of the new esthetics, along with Pound, Hulme, and the rest; the story is well known. The part played by Lewis is somewhat difficult to assess. Certainly he was not the leader; but he brought from France a genuine Fauvist and Cubist enthusiasm, and no doubt his knowledge of the plastic arts contributed something valuable to the program. Beyond this his personality must have been congenial to the others. The word *biting* as applied to intelligence has lost its meaning through overuse, but it can be momentarily restored by saying, emphatically, that this was the quality that distinguished Lewis from Pound, acerb as the latter could be and often was. In later years Lewis disputed with Pound for the credit of having originated vorticism. The truth seems to be that although Pound invented the term and contributed several characteristic pronouncements to their joint magazine, *Blast,* it was

Lewis who did most of the work and furnished most of the ardor. And without doubt he was the one responsible for exporting the new sensibility from the literary to the artistic centers of London; he was busy during these years with exhibitions, workshops, art publications. Concurrently he kept up his other writing. He was extraordinarily productive, in short, as he continued to be for the rest of his life. In 1914 he began serious work on his first novel, *Tarr*.

The war was, for Lewis as for everyone, a waste of time, yet he took to it with aplomb. After casting about unsuccessfully for an easy commission, he enlisted as a common soldier, trained in an artillery battalion, and won a second-lieutenancy in the regular way. At the front, though he grumbled eloquently over military snafus, he was a fearless and even enthusiastic soldier. Those who have read Mitchell Goodman's classic novel *The End of It*, will have an illuminating cross-reference for the following sentences from a letter to Pound dated September 1917: "Ainsi, I was F.O.O. (forward ob officer) of the Group three days ago, and on that occasion had the extreme gratification of seeing, in the midst of our barrage, a large Boche fly into the air as it seemed a few feet beneath me. From the ridge where I was observing things I looked down into the German front line as you might into Church Street."

Tarr was published in 1918. It was the beginning of a maniacal spate of activity which produced, in the next twenty years, more than twenty books, a great many paintings and drawings, and a steady outpouring of pamphlets, little magazines, manifestoes, reviews, and other ephemera. The letters during this period tell us nothing about Lewis himself; he is a disembodied epistoler. We know, for instance, that he was married in the late twenties, but the letters contain no mention of it, and at this moment, having just read his lifetime's correspondence, I can't think of his wife's name. I find it hard to imagine anyone else's letters that would leave me similarly uninformed. We do not know where he lived or in what circumstances. We know nothing of his tastes in clothing, food, landscape, climate, architecture, music, or manners. During much of this period he wrote his letters from a deposit box in the Pall Mall. In short Lewis's desire for secrecy became a mania, the private half of the mania which, in public, expressed itself in delusions of persecution. The letters we have in this volume are chiefly of three sorts.

A small number are affable but impersonal communications to friends who were so staunch they refused to quarrel with him, for example, the painter Augustus John and the poet Roy Campbell. A larger number are requests for money. And the largest number of all are simply a flood of disputation: insults, vituperations, cavils, a sea of self-fomented troubles. His enemies were publishers, rival authors, critics, agents, gallery and museum directors, bureaucrats, the entire cultural community; his Enemy was Anglo-Saxon civilization from top to bottom. Well, many of us might agree, but not, decidedly not, in Lewis's terms. He belonged, or wished to belong, to an "elusive but excellent community," the "party of genius," "outside any milieu or time"; but it was too "elusive," it didn't exist, and this nonexistence, thrust continually into his face, exasperated him to the point of unabated bad temper. But more than bad: evil.

Why? What was it all about? In one of his more temperate remarks Lewis spoke, late in his life when he was reviewing a new sculpture by Henry Moore, of "how important it is to know how to circumvent the natural platitude of the dimensions of life." There it is; he had been saying it for thirty years, and he continued till his death. Whatever other faults he had, he was neither dishonest nor obscure, and his style, though complex and overheated, hit with ringing clarity upon the crucial words. When he said "circumvent" he meant precisely that; and when he said "platitude" it was like a snarl. Life was unbearable, reality was unbearable, nature and the body were totally corrupt; their adherents, the naturalists of every camp, were not only corrupt but conspiratorial; only art and the mind could preserve the "aristocracy of intellect" from the nihilism which had resulted, paradoxically, from an emotionally charged misreading of Nietzsche. And thus Lewis joined the antirealists, the modernists, those who would invent Being from the misapprehended dynamisms of esthetics. He became for England what Gottfried Benn was for Germany – the parallel is astonishingly exact – and if his course was the opposite from that of Céline's in France, they both had begun at the same point and their effects were similar: Céline destroyed the body through exercises of nauseated lust, Lewis destroyed it through the annihilating decrees of his revulsed and frigid mind. These and their allies created the New Parnassus, which their disciples have turned into the New Philistia. Lewis's

novels are peopled by Ideas, beings of Style, creatures as sexless as
himself, for only these could exist in the unreality of the devalued and
denatured universe; and if as a painter he acquired among the élite a
certain reputation as a portraitist, it was because he bestowed upon his
sitters a firm, machine-like flesh, which sometimes seemed desirable in
the thirties. He was England's Léger, but totally without Léger's
humor and compassion. Politically Lewis's course was predictable and
remarkably similar to that of his continental comrades: outspoken, un-
qualified support of Franco and Hitler.

When the second war came Lewis left England and went to North
America, boarding ship the day before England declared war on Ger-
many. No matter how Professor Rose minimizes this escape, the infer-
ence is unavoidable: Lewis left his country because he feared for his
safety after his years of Nazi vociferation (even though he had publicly
changed his mind about Hitler the year before). But once in North
America, where he suffered from the climate, the people, and the re-
strictions of the war, he gradually slipped into a new self-delusion,
namely, that he had left England solely for financial reasons and now
wished nothing better than to return. If only he could raise the fare for
the clipper flight to Lisbon and thence to London.... Of course he
could not.

Frankly I was so nauseated by these wartime letters that I skipped
over to the final section of the book: Lewis at home again, the grand
old man ensconced finally in the admiration of younger writers, critics,
and publishers. The metamorphosis at last occurs. The tone of his at-
tacks softens, though the attacks continue until the end, and he now
spends a good deal of time writing in kindly condescension to his dis-
ciples and well-wishers. He resumes friendships with Eliot and Pound
on a much more equable basis than formerly, and he keeps up a steady
though ineffectual campaign to secure Pound's release from St. Eliza-
beth's. He dispenses generous and chiefly sound advice to younger
writers. He becomes, in short, Le Vieux, the only role he could con-
ceivably play with any degree of charm. It was during this period that
those who are now his advocates, including Professor Rose, first met
him and corresponded with him. What accounted for the change?
One can't be sure. I doubt that the tragedy, a very real tragedy, of his
blindness was enough to bring it about, or even his eventual knowl-
edge that the loss of vision was caused by an inoperable growth inside

his head that was methodically killing him. Lewis had been quite criti-
cally ill in the thirties (though the nature of his illness, like everything
else about his personal life, is darkly hidden) without any moderating
result, and his suffering during the war had merely changed him from a
blaster into a whiner. More likely his mellowing was simply an effect of
the new sympathy he detected in the reactionary intellectual milieu of
postwar England, coupled with the natural decline of energy in his ad-
vancing years. The old battles were over, after all, and if he had aban-
doned his outposts, so had his adversaries. Stephen Spender, who
only yesterday had been the young radical, was one of the first to offer
his services as a reader when news of Lewis's blindness became
known.

This book of letters gives us a man who grew from adolescence to
senility in one movement. Emotional maturity and that part of intellec-
tual maturity which rests upon emotional factors were denied him. He
belonged, without a doubt, to the Party of Genius; we look back on
that Party only with regret, first that its brilliance was so perverse, sec-
ond that we lack its means in pursuing our so much more serious ends.
What estimate the years to come will place on Lewis's works I do not
know, of course. I shall be surprised and sorry if his writing comes to
be valued as art, that is, as something necessary to the life of humanity
in a condition of civilization. But I won't be surprised if a few of his
many works, especially *Childermass* and *The Revenge for Love*, retain a
reputation as glittering examples of what can be done within a conven-
tion of sterility. In either case I refrain from judgment. I don't say a man
may not create his own reality from considerations of style. So may a
man raise himself by his own bootstraps, speaking in terms of the inner
synthesis. But for the onlookers it remains merely a feat of levitation,
a curiosity, a sideshow which exists simply by virtue of its a priori
irresponsibility, and in the present instance the performer happens
also to be a remarkably ugly man. I am content to pass on to the next
attraction.

✌ ·

Upon Which to Rejoice

1965

MRS. TROLLOPE'S OPINION of American religion was low – uniformly, doggedly low. And nowhere did she speak more to the point than in her footnote describing the effect of American religion upon American writers: "The mind of a man devoted to letters undergoes a process which renders the endurance of the crude ignorant ranting of the great majority among the various sects of American preachers intolerable; and accordingly they have taken refuge in the cold comfortless stillness of Unitarianism." Mrs. Trollope's pen was not always up to her ambition, as here in the first part of her sentence, but in "the cold comfortless stillness of Unitarianism" she surpassed herself. I came across it in my copy of her *Domestic Manners,* the fifth edition published in 1839.

The first edition had appeared in 1832; and in the fall of the following year a young graduate of Harvard Divinity School, William Greenleaf Eliot, emigrated from New England to St. Louis, where he founded – or rather helped to found – three institutions: the St. Louis branch of the Eliot family; the city's first Unitarian church, which became one of the strongest in the West; and Washington University, where Hegelianism, in the teaching of W. T. Harris and his colleagues, rose to its clearest and most orthodox American expression a few decades later. (Harris, who was a distinguished philosopher and educator in his time, founded and edited the *Journal of Speculative Philosophy,* was appointed United States Commissioner of Education, was associated at various times with Peirce, Royce, Bronson Alcott, and William James, and was largely instrumental in adapting German idealism to the service of American free education, free westward expansion, and free enterprise generally.) When William Greenleaf Eliot's grandson was born in 1888, he came into an intellectual environment that combined Eliotean gentility, Unitarian cold stillness, and Hegelian cosmic rationalism into a mood of petrified expectancy. He did not like it. Yet exactly one hundred years after Mrs. Trollope's remark, T. S. Eliot was writing of the "still point of the turning world," and doing so

moreover in Mrs. Trollope's own England. Mrs. Trollope would have
objected to the current notion that the poet went there to discover his
"still point." She would have said he brought it with him.

Professor Howarth has written at length about this early environ-
ment in his study of the influences exerted upon Eliot by relatives,
friends, and others. Since Howarth does not actually know, any more
than the rest of us, what was happening inside Eliot's head at the vari-
ous stages of the poet's work, his book, from a scholarly point of view,
must be classed as an entertainment; but it is interesting and in part
suggestive. Howarth's conjectural slickness, as a matter of fact, can set
off whole chains of it in the reader's mind. For instance, Karl Jaspers
and Gabriel Marcel were both born in the same decade as Eliot. What
would have happened if Eliot had gone to Europe, to Germany, for his
education, instead of to Harvard? Like his two contemporaries, he had
a penchant for spiritual philosophy and an attachment to concrete
experience. Taken together, these suggest, at that time and with that
background, a young man extremely likely to have been impressed by
the new currents stirring in European philosophy, namely, the exis-
tential.

Practically speaking, the opportunity did not exist. Eliot was an
American, and an American at that time was still a provincial, and a
provincial was still an idealist in the academic sense. At Harvard, Eliot
wrote his doctoral thesis on the idealism of F. H. Bradley, performing
adroitly in a worn-out mode. Now that it has been published for the
first time, fifty years after it was written, we can see both Eliot's supe-
rior philosophical gifts and the dead end to which he applied them.
Certainly he would have become a poet in any case; but his recogni-
tion of this dead end must have corroborated his natural tendency. For
the young American idealist of 1915, the way of philosophy, tempo-
rarily or not, was closed; but the way of poetry was open.

The poems are what we have, a new collected edition that is hand-
somer than the familiar green volume of 1935, to which it adds the
Quartets and a section of short poems written since 1940. Reading it is
a great pleasure, and a slow one, not only because the poems demand
one's close attention but because so many issues have consolidated
around the poems that from line to line, sometimes from word to word,
one must make new judgments. I shall omit my own particular obser-
vations, which are probably those of many readers in recent times. His

writing is often stiff; his political and cultural attitudes are antedilu-
vian. What it comes to is this: ninety percent of the critical profusion
surrounding Eliot's poems is wrong; the commentators must begin
again. A number of the most celebrated poems are his worst (for he
was quite capable of bad writing, e.g. in "Gerontion"), and some pas-
sages upon which the sensibility of our era is thought to rest simply do
not mean what most people think they mean. Eliot's gravest defect, I
think, has been his apparent lifelong temptation as a poet to write for
an effect; in each phase of his work there are brilliant, hollow-sounding
lines, places where we miss the genuineness of Yeats (crazy as he was),
for instance, the sense of complete emotional commitment. Yet for me
the power of the writing is still there, mounting steadily until almost
the last word, and I find myself remembering the defects for reasons
which do me, I believe, no great credit. Eliot's chief virtue has been his
willingness to experiment; this is not what most people think now that
Eliot has become so firmly a figurehead of the Establishment, but it is
perfectly plain on the pages of the book. Every major poem is not only
a technical advance over previous work, it is a technical departure – a
movement into something completely new. I am not sure that this can
be said of any other important poet in English. And Eliot is important;
he always will be, make no mistake about this. His departures give us
our clearest examples of responsibility in the arts. These, and not his
opinions, justify his leadership. Beyond that, he has enlarged our po-
etic diction enormously and made it consonant with the whole range
of contemporary experience, which is the first and perhaps the only
universal criterion of importance that we can infer from the history of
poetry.

The point raised by Mrs. Trollope is a confusing one. I who have
never been in England find myself on her side, at least in this instance:
I do not care for coldness and I take small comfort from stillness. Yet
these are what another American has transplanted to England, and en-
forced there chiefly through his poems, although partly through his es-
says and other literary activities. Eliot's coldness is the aspect of his
work that repels me: his idea of authority based on literalness; and I
see no way to pretend that it is not as much a part of the poems as of
the essays. His stillness, considered abstractly, is for me fantasized
post-Nietzschean nihilism. Yet like thousand upon thousands of oth-
ers who share my feelings, I find these elements in his poems, though

not in his essays, harmonious and esthetically moving; and this I think is the ultimate criterion not merely of importance but of greatness.

🖎 ·

Ezra Pound and the Great Style

1966.

To READ the criticism of Ezra Pound's poetry is to subject oneself to a bewildering experience. Most of it, certainly the best of it, has been written by people who are, or were, Pound's disciples; people who have gone to him as to a sage, seeking to immerse themselves in the influence of his compendious mind. And yet these people, in the books they have written about Pound, are the very ones who cast us most rudely into bewilderment.

Almost in one voice they announce, as if they had made an immense discovery, that Pound's great work, the *Cantos*, is a failure, that his economic and social opinions are pigheaded, that his scholarship is not only full of error (all scholarship is full of error) but actually stolen and faked. But then why do these people bother to write about his poetry? Why do the rest of us go on reading it all our lives long? Why, decade after decade, have we continued to be interested in this man, who has been such a peevish critic of our civilization and whom most Americans believe to have committed treason, at least technically, against our country – though this has never been proven juridically? Bigger traitors and acuter critics vanish into oblivion overnight, but Pound has held the American imagination for fifty years, and scarcely a month goes by without some new revelation of his celebrity in our popular press.

The answer is simple yet seldom, and almost never simply, stated. In great works of art we recognize a great and splendid light; perhaps not *in* the works but *behind* them, a luminosity beyond the realm of art, which only artifacts of the first magnitude permit us, still darkly, to descry. It is a radiance we find in the ceiling frescos of the Sistine Chapel, in passages from Dante and Shakespeare, in some of the music of J.S. Bach; or occasionally in stranger places, like the final part of *Gulliver's Travels* or certain episodes in *Huckleberry Finn*. Always we stumble when we try to define this light. Even the words we apply to our own state of consciousness when we are seeing it remain inexact: wonder, exaltation, the gentle shock of sublimity. Yet we know what it is; and of all the poets in our time who have written in English none has revealed it more clearly and consistently than Ezra Pound.

Because we are unable to define the light, we often speak of it in terms of style, the concrete appearance of works in which the light is present; and because style too, in its fully realized entirety, is indefinable, we often choose to speak of inferior examples, which give themselves more readily to analysis. Here are four lines from Pound's translation of an ode from the *Shih-ching,* which is the Chinese anthology of ancient poems and songs.

> *Wen, like a field of grain beneath the sun*
> *when all the white wheat moves in unison,*
> *coherent, splendid in severity,*
> *Sought out the norm and scope of Heaven's Decree.*

These are a long way, a very long way, from Pound's best. They show him at work in a conventional mode that impedes the characteristic movement of his verse, yet they are still quite good, especially the first couplet. And how daring. How closely Pound courts prosodic absurdity. For here he has used a device that tempts all poets from time to time, usually with comic results, and he has brought it off: the "perfect" rhyme. Not only that, he has used two perfect rhymes, since *Wen* and *when* are almost indistinguishable, at least to those who cannot speak Chinese. Pound has bracketed his couplet in two monumental chords, like two strokes of the tonic in a fugue, between which the separate elements are allowed their intricate play. And notice the intricacy: the narrowing or funneling parallelism in "field beneath white wheat," the syncopation of "all the white," the sudden retardation of "moves." Indeed one could write at length about the prosody of these two lines alone.

But are they true? Only great learning and patience could say with any pretense of authority, and even then the answer would be only that – a pretense. Thousands of factors, and I'm not exaggerating, impinge on this single judgment, or for that matter on almost any literary judgment. But as nearly as I can tell these lines are true: true to the original

poem, the coherence, splendor, and severity that Pound names in his
third line; true to the legend of King Wen; and true above all to
Pound's vision of the light. The real question is: what is Pound's
vision?

All told it is extremely complicated, as we should expect from so
complicated a man. But in essence, like the visions of all great men, it is
a vision of goodness, the good that exists somewhere in the universe,
the excellence at the heart of experience, which is obscured from us
most of the time by the imprecision, not to say chaos, of our human ar-
rangements. Pound himself rarely speaks of the good, but more often
of equity, order, an honest wage, the importance of ceremonial obser-
vances, and the like. In fact his vision is close to the idealization of
human nature that was found on the nineteenth-century American
frontier, where Pound was born; it is a pastoral vision, and today it
seems almost quaint – or would if Pound hadn't shaped it in his mag-
nificent style.

Ancient Chinese civilization and particularly the Confucian tradi-
tion have been important to Pound for several reasons, but chiefly
because he found in them the ideal of a just secular order. On this
account he has been accused, by those who miss the point, of mere
secularism, which is preposterous. What Pound is interested in is not
secularism but wholeness and union: of spirit and form, mind and
body, man and nature. He connects the Confucian ideal with many
scriptural and mythological counterparts in Asia and the Near East,
and with a long line of religious feeling in Europe. If these Western
connections begin in the temple at Eleusis rather than in the temple at
Jerusalem, this is not because Pound denies biblical wisdom – that of
Abraham or that of Jesus – for he has expressly confirmed it, but rather
because he believes this wisdom to have been distorted and vitiated by
the political, economic, and military policies of the Church and the
Christian rulers. This may or may not have been the case, but it is at
least an arguable view, and certainly one held by many historians more
exacting than Pound.

Thus Pound's affinities in European civilization have been with
Eleusis, the Roman mystery cults, the ritual marriage to the corn god-
dess, with Gnosticism, the Cabalic tradition, the Albigenses, which in
turn connect him with his second consuming passion, the marvelous
and heretical literature of the troubadours, or rather the entire devel-

opment from the Provençal poetry of courtly love, with its close though possibly unconscious paraphrase of Catharist liturgy, to the crowning works of Cavalcanti and Dante. In these areas Pound has made important contributions to criticism and scholarship.

One cannot say the same for some other enthusiasms into which his quest has led him, the chief of them being, of course, his long excursion into economics. For two decades or more his vision of light appeared to have dwindled to his own personal, not to say eccentric, interpretation of Social Credit, the perfectly respectable hypothesis propounded by C.H. Douglas. Many people, owing in part to Pound's dilations on the subject, and probably also in part to those of certain Créditiste members of the Canadian parliament, will be surprised to learn of the respectability of Douglas's theories; but whether or not one accepts them they are at least serious and well intentioned, and they have been elaborated with a considerable degree of technical competence. Undeniably Pound's enthusiasm for economic solutions has borne results that have been sometimes ludicrous, as in his blunders concerning American history and monetary theory, and sometimes extremely sad, as in his blind appreciation of Mussolini. The effect on his poetry is unmistakable; it appears in the fourth line I have quoted from the Chinese translation, where the words *norm* and *scope*, which Pound used to give precise technical meaning to Confucian economic hypotheses, fail to work poetically. On a much larger scale the *Cantos* give us whole pages of political rant that serve no poetic purpose whatever, and this has induced some critics, among them Noel Stock, whose *Poet in Exile* is perhaps the best and toughest general analysis of Pound's writing that we've had so far, to explain the "failure" of the *Cantos* by saying that at some point Pound abandoned poetry and the objectives of poetry, and turned instead to an attempt to rewrite history and impose his own political ideas. But even if this criticism weren't based on a too-narrow definition of poetry, the charge would be untrue, and for two reasons.

First, even though much of Pound's political writing and nearly all his political activity have been wrongheaded and wasteful, they derived without question from his vision of the good: that has been his obsession. It would be hard to imagine a social critic more disinterested than Pound. Hotheaded, impulsive, irascible, yes; but you may search as you will through his poems, essays, prose fragments, and personal correspondence (as far as it is available) and you will not find a scrap of a personal motive – no private ambition, not even a general desire for power, since he has continually thrown away the power he actually had. Indeed, after saturating oneself in the enormous variety of Pound's writing, one begins to realize that although at first one had thought the image of Pound himself stood out clear, in the end it is only a series of masks, almost caricatures: the man himself is evanescent. And because his vision of the good is a unitary vision, in which poetry, agriculture, and economics are expressions of the same generative force in the human spirit, no separation of fundamental human activities is possible. The only separation is the light from the darkness. Pound is our most farsighted poet; he sees poetry in a treasury report, provided the report is true and signifies a just distribution of the products of human labor.

Secondly, to say, as Stock does, that Pound could ever become a nonpoet is simply absurd. It couldn't be, any more than a peach could become a watermelon. I don't mean that he was born a poet, or was endowed by the gods with poetry; no Platonic inference is required. He began with great verbal talent, obviously; but he was formed as a poet in his youth, between the ages of fifteen and thirty, when he studied poetry as I think no one ever did before, unless it was Dante. It is said that once he wrote a sonnet a day for a year, and then destroyed them all. He studied nine languages, seeking the poetry in each of them; he wrote and rewrote his own work every day, insisting on the necessity for labor and thought and continual experiment. I cannot believe that any genius so sculptured in a poetic attitude – to use one of his own favorite similes – could ever change. And in fact it didn't; in spite of the history and politics, his poetry is there on the page, right up to the last cantos and the most recent translations.

A great deal of nonsense has been written about the *Cantos*. Much of it comes from a misapprehension for which Pound himself is partly responsible. When he began the *Cantos* he announced that he was at work on an epic, and later hinted at parallels with the *Divine Comedy;* from time to time he indicated that his work was going according to plan, that it had a comprehensive formal structure. Well, his forty years' labor did not turn out quite that way. Whether or not this is regrettable is a meaningless question, since we cannot imagine what the *Cantos* might have been under some other dispensation. But we can see readily enough what they are, once we put aside our preconceptions. They are the second half of Pound's collected poems, the first half being the volume called *Personae*, which contains the poems he wrote before he began the *Cantos*. If the *Cantos* have more unity than the collected poems of other poets, this is what we should expect, for they embrace persistent themes and they do proceed, though waywardly, from a hell to a purgatory to, in the last cantos, a kind of paradise; but at the same time they remain, as we should also expect, miscellaneous: good and bad, lively and dull, important and unimportant, like anyone's collected work. We need a *Selected Cantos,* just as we have selected editions of the works of other famous poets, eliminating their less interesting productions. As a matter of fact Pound himself has made such a selection, which will be published in due course if all goes well, and no doubt other editors will eventually make other selections. Whether any of these, including Pound's, will be good or bad remains to be seen; but in principle nothing prevents them from being at least useful, or possibly much more. Meanwhile we have the *Cantos*, numbered 1 to 109, plus a few later fragments that have appeared in magazines. They are an epic, yes; but only in the sense that any poet's lifework is epical.

Can they be finished? A friend of mine who is also a good friend of Pound's was visiting him once not long ago when Pound suddenly opened a drawer, took out a sheet of paper, and thrust it into my friend's hands. "There, that's the ending" – to be tacked on wherever the main text ultimately stops. Then the paper was snatched back, and my friend's memory of it remains naturally somewhat vague. But I shall be surprised if, when the ending is finally given to all of us, it turns out to be the precise, climactic statement that Pound's admirers expect, and I even hope it will not be: I cannot believe that any brief passage could sustain Pound's entire vision of light. In one sense the *Cantos* were finished some years ago, perhaps at the end of the Pisan section, when the main areas of feeling and substance had been distinguished and exploited, or in cantos 90 and 91 with their recapitulation of the main themes and their beautiful vision of a culturally united world. Pound himself has suggested that the paradisal elements in the last cantos may be unavoidably weak or insecure: "It is difficult to write a paradiso when all the superficial indications are that you ought to write an apocalypse." In another sense, of course, the *Cantos* will never

be finished. And their unfinishability is, like that of a few other mo-
mentous works – Kafka's *The Castle*, Mahler's Tenth Symphony – an
intrinsic part of their meaning.

It is a question of style then; but this too has been muddled. There
are styles and there is Style. Styles are objectified artistic embodiments
of personality, elaborations of manner – style is the man, as somebody,
I think Rémy de Gourmont, has said. Among Pound's famous contem-
poraries we have many such styles, transmitting to us their authors'
various selfhoods, to which we respond variously. I can read Wallace
Stevens and William Carlos Williams with pleasure, T. S. Eliot with a
certain reluctant sympathy, and Marianne Moore in utter coldness; but
I can recognize all these poets easily, and I believe my responses to
them have less to do with the merits of their writing than with the
equations of temperament existing between them and myself. Even
Yeats, who wrote poems that affect me with a kind of crippling delight,
remains a stylist only in this smaller, personal sense. Pound alone in
our time has created Style – the huge, concrete, multiform artifice that
transmits to us the impersonal light beyond art, and from which the
artist himself drops away. Pound's best poetry attracts every literate
sensibility without reference to temperament or sympathy; it tran-
scends taste. The *Iliad* was written by a man who is a myth, *Hamlet* by
a man so uncertain that people spend lifetimes arguing over who and
what he was. So with Pound: he is evanescent, and his work – *Perso-
nae*, the *Cantos*, the translations – stands as fully self-sustaining. If
parts of it are boring, is that the unforgivable sin some critics have
averred? Of course not. We forgive, gladly, Homer his catalogues and
his endlessly repeated epithets, Shakespeare his *Henry VIII* and *Merry
Wives*.

Pound well understands the difference between himself and his con-
temporaries (though his relationship to Williams is more complex
than the others). For him it was the difference between symbolism and
realism, and he chose the latter. Where Yeats and Eliot had looked for
an "objective correlative," an image upon which to impress their par-
tial and individualized feelings, Pound insisted that the observed detail
must stand by itself, an image in the concreteness of its own meaning,
its identity. Hence his poetry is detailed, and set out in beautifully ex-
act language, for exactness is the key to his sense of beauty.

Pound once said, speaking less than half in jest, that if he had the means he would build a temple to Demeter in Fleet Street. That is primary: the goddess sought through so many incarnations: Isis, Cythera ("crystalline"), Dione, Sophia, Eleanor, and all the others. The good: meaning proportion, plenty, the spirit of earth at work in man's heart. "Nothing matters but the quality of the affection" – so he has written. Homer began it and Pound – what shall we say, has he ended it? This only, I think, is the question to which critics and poets must address themselves now. What meaning has Homer or Ezra Pound in an age of inverting values? What role is left for the goddess of fertility when fertility itself has become a nuisance? How shall our children live in a world from which first the spirit, then history, and finally nature have fled, leaving only the mindless mechanics of process and chance? Will any place exist for a humane art in a society from which the last trace of reverence – any reverence – has been rubbed out? As a matter of fact I think a place will exist, will be made; but it won't be easy. Revolutions of sensibility have occurred before in the world, overturning whole libraries of masterpieces, though none so swift as ours.

To create beauty from sterility, value from meaninglessness, this is the work to be done, and less the philosopher's than the artist's (if ultimately a distinction may be made between them). One way to begin is by investigating Style. But although our studies of how Style works, how it recurs and is transformed, inevitably become abstruse and absorbing, they must not be permitted to obscure the fact that it does work – the reality of Style in our lives. The great Style, the suprapersonal Vision of Light, whether in "Lycidas" or Canto 45. In this respect Ezra Pound's poetry is certain to be more and more important to us as time goes on.

✍ ·

Materials from Life

1967.

OUR EFFORT to conceptualize love must have begun nearly as soon as people found out that lying together is warmer than lying apart – I am not facetious – and in the millennia since then it has generated thousands upon thousands of works, theoretical and imaginative, which most people agree are among the finest products of the human mind and heart. In the face of this it is difficult to decide that a new book, just received and just read, makes a significant addition to what has gone before. It is doubly difficult when the work in question lacks the flair for expression and the versatility of feeling which the topic has inspired in the great minds of the past – Plato, the Psalmist, Ovid, Plotinus, Augustine, Bernard: this is a formidable company. Too formidable; and although our minds inevitably do draw comparisons, surely their doing so betrays the unamiable side of our character. The fact is that Irving Singer, in his book called *The Nature of Love,* says what no one has said before, or at all events what no one has said explicitly and systematically. And if his writing is neither as graceful nor as assured as one might wish, nor always perfectly lucid, it is still good enough; it has wit and verve; it is far better than what we normally find in professional philosophy. Above all Singer writes with no ostentation of technical virtuosity, and his book will be understandable to any reader who has even a passing acquaintance with philosophical aims and methods. Certainly it is an important book, and certainly a very good book. It has the kind of goodness we associate with originality and modesty and a genuine desire to serve.

Of course one may be mistaken. Perhaps somewhere a book exists that duplicates Singer's. The theoretical literature of love is immense, even the recent parts of it, and I have read no more than a little; I imagine no one has read it all. Theologians of every persuasion, including the pagan, have been especially productive in our time. Such books as Martin Buber's *I and Thou,* Etienne Gilson's study of Héloise and Abelard, Simone Weil's *Waiting for God,* the essays and sermons of Paul Tillich, and even, in its implications of new human discoveries of love, Teilhard de Chardin's *The Phenomenon of Man* – these and many others are popular and doubtless have helped great numbers of people, although all such works, I think, including the last named, suffer from a necessary ultimate regressiveness in Christian thought. The secularists have been less prolific, if you do not count the quacks and semiquacks – the sexologists – who have enjoyed such a field day with their manuals. Secular philosophers have been impeded and embarrassed by the great burden of Freudian and other naturalistic apparatus which was handed to them years ago. Albert Camus, for instance, had an *attitude* toward love, which may be worked out in more or less detail from suggestions contained in *The Fall*, but I doubt that he had a *concept* of love. Most philosophers simply evade the issue. Jean-Paul Sartre, more serious and more rigorous, has given us his "theory of existential psychoanalysis"; but it is an awkward, difficult, technically moralistic theory; and although few of us would care to reject his notion of the importance of choice as validating our theoretical human "authenticity," at the same time the famous "freedom" that goes with it remains elusive and obscure in the experience of our lives, particularly in the experience of falling in love.

Singer performs a more useful service. Where Sartre began his discussion of being with a consideration of consciousness in alienation, Singer begins with consciousness in love, and what he has produced is a phenomenology of love, having all the credibility and simplicity that Sartre's work lacks. (The sheer tenebrosity and poundage of Sartre's book on Jean Genêt seems especially needless in the light of what Singer has done.) I do not mean of course that Singer has outperformed Sartre; his aim is both narrower and shorter. But within the limits of a discussion of human affective experience Singer, from a general philosophical orientation similar to Sartre's (so the reader deduces, although Singer himself does not say it), has moved in a direction both more fruitful and more easily verifiable than Sartre's.

The heart of Singer's conceptualization lies in his first twenty-five pages. He begins with the accepted notion that "love is a way of valuing something," either a thing or a person, although we agree generally to confine the discussion to love of persons. Singer then analyzes love-as-valuation into two functions. The first he calls appraisal, which in turn he divides into two types. "Objective" appraisal is the discovery in the beloved of values which are commonly and publicly agreed upon. It is objective, of course, only in the sense that it is publicly verifiable, since a change of taste may easily overturn it: the objective value of Gina Lollobrigida is appraised differently, at least in some respects, from the objective value of Jean Harlow. The second type of appraisal is what Singer calls individual appraisal, this being the private valuation made by the particular lover who finds in his particular beloved values corresponding to his needs: she is blonde and he dislikes brunettes, she is rich and he disapproves of poverty, and so on. (I apologize for sexing the lover and the beloved; it is a flaw built into our system of pronouns, and it plagues every discussion of love. But naturally the affective mechanisms work both ways, equally.) Both objective and individual appraisal are merely the *discovery* of values which already exist in the beloved, and by themselves they do not, according to Singer, suffice for a description of love, even though the values in question may go far beyond mere sexual attractiveness. What is needed is the addition of the other half of love-as-valuation, which he calls bestowal. Bestowal occurs when the lover assigns or ascribes to the beloved, values which she does not necessarily possess in objectivity, but which in a sense she comes to possess as a consequence of her lover's act. For them the bestowed values are real. Thus loving consists of three forms of valuation, of which two are incidental while the third – bestowal – is essential. The beloved may be good looking, which is a commonly held value discovered through objective appraisal; she may speak Chinese, which is a value only in respect to her lover's particular needs and is discoverable only through individual appraisal; and she may suffer from a hideous speech defect, which her lover turns into a charming mannerism by bestowing upon it a value it does not possess in "reality." Through their acts of mutual bestowal, in other words, the lovers transcend considerations of mere desire, convenience, and need, which may be requisite to their love but which can never constitute it. Bestowal is the necessary and defining element of love.

Many important consequences issue from this conception of bestowal, it seems to me, but I shall keep my discussion to three.

First, bestowal is always, essentially, and crucially gratuitous. It may occur with rhyme – it often does – but never with reason. It is the free invention of value, emanating solely from the lover's affection and directed solely toward the beloved. It has no end or object beyond the beloved, not even the gratification of the lover's needs, since these require an appraised value; it proceeds directly and solely to the beloved as a *person*, a *someone*. This is important. It is one means by which Singer attacks the Freudian deterministic concept of love as subliminal narcissism. Singer gives love a content beyond necessity. His argument is analogous to Sartre's, of course, since both of them are concerned to restore autonomous selfhood to the human animal, but it seems to me that the idea of gratuitous bestowal is a sharper, simpler counterfoil to nineteenth-century naturalistic determinism than Sartre's ideas of choice and a mankind "condemned to be free."

Second, because bestowal is always, essentially, and crucially gratuitous, it is always and essentially creative. From feeling, the lover creates value, which is then bestowed on the beloved, thus creating in the beloved an augmented being; or rather, more strictly, an augmentation of being. At the same time the lover's act is self-creative, an augmentation of the lover's own being, because it enlarges his or her capacity for response: clearly it would be impossible to create a *value* to which the lover did not respond. Being as such, then, is the consequence, if not strictly the product, of love, and what could be more creative? (Singer's concept of bestowal is thus closer in some respects to Jaspers than to French sources.) The meanings of all this for secular philosophy are fairly obvious, and some are obviously dangerous, but for the moment I shall simply say that one important meaning is the freedom of love. Not so much a freedom of choice, as Sartre would have it, for the "selection" of the beloved is always hidden, even if it is not ultimately adventitious; but a freedom of invention, of creativity. It is the freedom of making rather than the freedom of affirming, of initiative rather than response. Thus the lover's freedom is a continuing enrichment, not a source of anguish, and surely this interpretation is closer to our real experience of love than Sartre's. It is very evidently closer to our experience of love as manifested in our erotic poetry.

Third, because bestowal is always, essentially, and crucially creative it is always and essentially imaginative. That is to say, love is functionally esthetic. Here is where one chief danger lurks. For human imagination operates inevitably in terms of ideals, call them what one will – forms, models, gestalts, universals, noumena. Any artist knows from his or her working practice that it is impossible to create a representation of anything without the intrusion of prior knowledge; we cannot so much as "see" anything as it actually is – certainly not our beloved. Hence idealization is an inevitable part of love. But we know too that the processes of idealization tend to place the image of the beloved under this or that sign, to lead away from a consideration of the beloved as a person and toward a consideration of the beloved as a meaning; ultimately they may end in aims and objects totally separate from the beloved. The trick is to show that this need not be the case, that idealization need not inevitably or necessarily lead away from the person, but on the contrary may lead back to the person and may, so to speak, reinforce the person; and to my mind this is a point which Singer has failed to make with sufficient force. On the other hand this volume is only the first of several he intends to devote to his theory of love, and I am sure he will have much more to say about idealization later on.

The 350 pages which follow this introductory section of Singer's book are devoted to a critique of the principal theories of love from the beginning of the Greco-Hebraic tradition to the end of the Middle Ages. Although he obviously has an enormous knowledge of the literature and does not hesitate to bring in obscure texts when he needs them, Singer concentrates on Plato, Aristotle, the Old Testament writers, Lucretius, Ovid, Paul, Plotinus, Augustine, and the medieval writers from Bernard of Clairvaux to Thomas Aquinas, ending with the radical revisionism and reversionism of Martin Luther. Much of this material will be familiar to Singer's readers; any philosopher who decides to proceed in terms of systematic criticism, historically arranged, runs the risk of boring his audience. Singer's reading of the texts in question is acute and clear, but not strikingly original. What comes through most prominently from his discussion is an impression of sweetness in the intellectual tone; not so much in the writing as in the sympathy of mind he brings to great writers in the religious tradition. Clearly, although he works from a standpoint outside that tradition, Singer finds much that is attractive in the Christian philosophers, as in the saints and mystics. And who can doubt that their great effort of love, prolonged in intellectual jeopardy over so many barbarous centu ries – right if it was right, or wrong if it was wrong – did in fact save the world?

Singer makes two exceptions to his rough chronological arrangement. The first stems from an embarrassment in his materials. Since all his texts come from the period of Western religious flowering, Singer lacks naturalistic texts to use for foils. The incipient naturalism in parts of Aristotle is not useful for his purpose, and Lucretius is too elementary, while Ovid is a special case. Hence Singer displaces Freud, who on other counts as well is his bête noire, from a comfortable niche in our own era, and takes him back to the Middle Ages to act there as the foremost theoretician of naturalistic love. This is no injustice to Freud, it may even be a kind of honor, yet sometimes the juxtaposition of Freud and Saint Thomas or Martin Luther seems a trifle odd. Perhaps in the circumstances it isn't surprising that the Viennese doctor always comes off second-best.

But the ultimate point of the critical parts of Singer's theory is that both traditions, religious and naturalistic, not only fail to explain love, as we understand it now, but impede it, misdirect it, and even destroy it, at least conceptually. In both cases this happens through the misuse of the processes of idealization, for both philosophies, through their idealizations, direct love away from the person and toward an ideal object existing outside the competence of human valuative faculties, on one hand toward God and on the other toward Nature; and thus they both deny to human love the function of bestowal which, as Singer has argued, is the indispensable constitutive element. Reduced to this brevity, the argument is full of holes, of course. God is conceived in many ways; so is Nature; the entire evolution of the human loving relationship to both is marvelously intricate. Yet Singer's argument, detailed but not difficult, holds up throughout, I think. It is sound intellectually and experientially, and it points always back toward ourselves. It is the first step toward the accomplishment of the task we must perform for ourselves, an absurd but imperative task: to find a way for modern human beings to love one another without external sanctions. This is the essence of Singer's book.

But in addition Singer's critique performs another valuable service, the rigorous redefinition of the chief terms in Christian theories of love, *agape* and *eros*, as well as the reintroduction of two important subordinate terms, *philia* and *nomos*. All these have been seriously muddled by religious popularizers for centuries. (A case in point is a new book by Ralph Harper, who, however, is no popularizer, his *Human Love: Existential and Mystical,* to which we turn with good will and a certain sympathy for the author's intention; but we find in it the same woolly use of terms, particularly the reduction of *eros* to a virtually meaningless animal impulse, and the same glib religious and idealistic concepts that have already estranged us from most of the speculative literature of modern love.) Singer has done well to bring semantic precision back to the discussion. He has done it by tracking his terms to their philosophical sources in ancient texts, then by analyzing their evolution. I don't say this is a unique distinction, but such rigor is unusual, and we are grateful to find it in a book of this kind.

Singer's second departure from his chronology is the omission of the entire episode of courtly love in the twelfth century. This, he says, together with its effluence in the romantic tradition generally, will be the subject of another volume; or possibly two – he does not state his plan exactly. The "heresy" of *vray amor* and its subsequent influence upon European civilization down to our own time has been for years the special province of Denis de Rougemont, and has been muddled by him, both conceptually and historically, almost beyond belief; so that for this reason alone I should think many people must look forward with agreeable expectation to Singer's next book. But I, for my part, look forward even more to the final volume of his projected series, the one that he will devote to modern love; for then, it seems to me, he must come at last to an end of critique, and must shift his aim to an affirmative philosophy of love – especially, I hope, to the consideration of the role of idealization in human love and in life generally.

For isn't the real significance of Singer's work the fact that it is open, at least implicitly, to immense possibilities? By now I am sure many readers of this commentary wonder why I began it by calling Singer's book new and original. What is original about the idea of gratuitous and creative bestowal – except perhaps the term itself? Isn't it a common part of our attitude to life now? It is; and when I began to read Singer's book I said to myself, "But of course, this is what I have thought for years." Love for its own sake or for *our* sake, creative human love as a condition of unsanctioned being, is part of our overwhelmingly secularized culture; we find it everywhere – in our movies, poetry, fiction, in the hortatory materials that are thrust at us constantly from every moral stronghold, including the religious – to which it ought to be anathema. Love, despite the state of the world, is our existence, and creativity is its touchstone. This is how our loves now work if they work at all; this is the idea we try to impress on our frolicsome children when we tell them what is really meant by making love, not war. But all good philosophy takes its materials from the life in which it is born. Singer has crystalized our attitude toward love. And in doing so he has searched out its elements systematically and has made them into a good instrument for criticism. He has a long way still to go. I, no more than another reader, have access to his plans, and all I can say to him is that I hope he won't be deterred by the professional objections his colleagues are sure to raise to his work, objections I would not raise myself even were I competent to do so. I confess I have a kind of vision: the final overturning of the Cartesian apple cart. We have known for a long, long time that the *Cogito* is a false hope, with all its supervening burden of self-divisive consciousness. We have seen it as a vitiating element in all Western culture, including much of our own existentialist thought. We know perfectly well, from our whole experience of intellectual, social, sexual, and military history in our time, that if we have any virtue in meaninglessness and absurdity, it is our capacity, not to think, not to feel, not "to see ourselves," but to love; and hence to imagine, because love, not necessity, is the mother of invention – to imagine, meaning to bring together, to synthesize, to act undividedly in the existential wholeness of the human spirit. Yet for two thousand years no important new philosophy has begun with love as the explicit starting point, and I can't help asking myself, naively or not: Wouldn't it be wonderful if it happened now?

🖎 . . . .

Delmore, 1913–1966

1967.

POETS THINK a good deal about words and the qualities of words, naturally enough since in the broadest sense words are their livings (though ultimately it comes to more than that). I have been thinking lately about the word *ruth*. A discredited word, marked "poeticism" in the dictionary. It turns up commonly in poetry written on the most amateur level, where it rhymes invariably with *truth*, but you seldom see it anywhere else. In my own case it is well known to me yet doubly discredited, because it rhymes with – indeed is part of – my own name, as I discovered when I was a schoolboy and whiled away the tedium by fiddling with the meanings of *hay, den, car,* and *ruth*. But with one exception I can think of no serious writer of the twentieth century who has used the word. You might expect it would be a very useful word, rooted firmly in the Anglo-Saxon origin of our language, an active word, meaning mercy, compassion, Aristotelian pity, yet more vigorous than any of these. Ruth suggests not merely a passive state of sympathy, but the compassionate attitude as something outgoing and efficacious. Perhaps this is because when we think of ruth we think also of the story of Ruth in the Old Testament: "Whither thou goest, I will go," though as nearly as I can tell by consulting the etymological dictionary there is no linguistic connection between the English word and the Hebrew feminine name.

Is it significant that in our society today we use the word only in its negative form: *ruthless*? Delmore Schwartz would have thought so.

He is the exception I spoke of. He used the word *ruth* again and again, trying, with the kind of poetic courage that comes close to folly, to find the combination of prosodic and thematic factors that would allow a rehabilitation of the word. It went with another favorite word of his, equally unfashionable, the word *hope*. How well this rehabilitation succeeded in individual poems is a matter of taste. To my mind some of the poems are masterpieces. But in his whole work and his whole life, Delmore failed. He had to fail. His vision of a world of ruth and hope was shattered again and again, and no poet shows us more clearly the ruthlessness of our own society. Incidentally I make no apology for calling him Delmore, because it is impossible to call him Schwartz; he was always just "Delmore" to everyone, friends and strangers alike.

The truth is that our society today, in spite of all our recent cultural pretensions, is as hard on poets as it ever was. Granted, many poets are fed and housed better than they were thirty years ago, and their work is published more promptly and sometimes more effectively, but only provided that they teach, recite, perform, expound, exhibit – in short, that they tickle the institutional vanity of the age. Those who cannot or will not do this suffer in one degree or another the tyranny of a social machine more highly institutionalized, more ruth-less, than ever. Delmore suffered it in the greatest degree. It destroyed his life.

Then there is a complementary truth, which is even more depressing. Simply this: that the smaller society within the larger – the society of poets which ought to be the reverse of the larger society, which ought to be the society of almost pastoral grace and creativity that Delmore envisioned – is instead racked by its own desperate tyranny, the tyranny of competition, envy, vanity, professional avarice. This is what destroyed Delmore's work. Not all of it of course, for his best poems and stories and essays make a little group of splendid pieces. But Delmore never produced the body of fine work he could have produced and would have produced, as we cannot avoid recognizing, in other circumstances.

Delmore's terrifying, lonely, evil death in the summer of 1966, when he fell gasping with a heart attack at 3:00 A.M. in a hotel corridor – and the wrong corridor at that, significantly enough, because the room he was looking for, his own last home, a tawdry, littered cubicle – was two floors above: this rotten death nevertheless brought, in a wry, unhappy way, a sense of release to his old friends. For the first time in years they could speak publicly of their affection and admiration for him without fear of immediate recrimination. Not one of them, as far as I know, had escaped the wild accusations that Delmore issued during the years of his deepening psychopathological crisis. Some of his paranoid delusions were so outrageous and complicated that everyone laughs at them, even people who have the best reason to understand the depths of anguish from which they sprang. Delmore's aggressions had the fantastic quality of an invention by Rube Goldberg. And of course his old friends were silenced by them. They had no choice but to withdraw in the face of such unappeasable hostility, though they continued to help him, silently and indirectly, when they could.

Now during recent months we have seen a number of tributes written by Delmore's old friends. Invariably they recall him as a young poet, someone fun to be with, a bright talker, hard-minded and humorous, tireless, looking for a good time, full of the élan of being a poet in the company of poets. In the eyes of these people he seems an attractive, lively, gifted, romantic figure.

I never knew him well, though I saw him off and on over the years. He was somewhat older than I. When he was poetry editor of *Partisan Review* he published some of my first poems, and we had an amiable correspondence. In his dealings with younger writers he was always helpful and interested, I think. He had many teaching jobs, including some real plums at posh universities, and although often he was unable to last out the term of his contract, his students felt warmly about him and frequently went to look him up later in New York. Toward the end these young people, students and others who found him in the bars around town, were apparently the only ones who were close to him.

In the early fifties I took a job in a publication office on Fifth Avenue overlooking the park, where Delmore worked too on a part-time basis. He came in one day a week to write one-paragraph reviews and blurbs and do other little chores. He did not like the office, and although I worked there every day for a year I never felt comfortable in it either, and often on "Delmore's day" he and I would take off in midafternoon and go to one of those bars on Madison Avenue where the woodwork is darkly polished and the mirrors are shadowy. These places would be empty at that time of day; the bartenders would be busy setting up for the cocktail crowd; Delmore and I would lean on the bar with our big, expensive highballs that neither of us could afford, and talk about... almost anything, I suppose. Poetry and baseball, since we shared these interests, and then I recall one time when I tried for an hour to explain to him my devotion to jazz and to the musical qualities of jazz. It didn't work. Like most poets – I have always been especially annoyed by the poems on jazz that William Carlos Williams wrote – Delmore continued to think of jazz in essentially nonmusical, sociological terms. But what I remember most of all is his appearance. He still looked rather boyish, like that old photograph in the Oscar Williams anthologies, but his features were somehow softened, hazy, blurred, and his voice was so quiet that I had to bend my head to listen. I had the impression of great sadness and sweetness. It was as if he was lost and knew he was lost, and had almost – not quite – given up caring about it. The exhilarated spirit his older friends remember was never apparent to me, but rather a quietness and a desire to cling to little things, little actions and objects, as if from a simple attachment to littleness for its own sake. He looked and spoke like a defeated shipping-house clerk. I could imagine him on the point of adopting some far-out hobby, like growing dwarf trees, to occupy his declining years.

Impressions of lost afternoons! And who knows how many of those expensive highballs set off fuses that detonated in catastrophe ten or twelve hours later?

Anyway Delmore was lost – it wasn't just my imagining. Not long afterward the roof fell progressively in, the nightmare of his final decade began. When he died he was fifty-two years old.

What we have left is his work. He began very early – his first published writing appeared in *Partisan Review* when he was twenty-two years old – and he won almost instantaneous success. His poems and stories had a romantic warmth that seemed more than appealing after the "proletarian verse" of the deep Depression, and at the same time they were vigorous and fresh, products of a strong personal vision; they offered a sense of direction at a time when the defeat of human aspirations in Spain and the buildup for a new world war were creating anxiety and twitchy sensibilities everywhere. Here was a proper romantic. Delmore acknowledged his model – Shakespeare – and it seemed almost unheard of. He wrote sonnets – how strange! – and gave them high-powered first lines in the proper sonneteering tradition. It was a part of his almost foolish poetic courage. Yet it worked; the sonnets were good, and they still are – some of them probably among the best of their kind in American literature.

There was a charming simplicity about Delmore's early work, though never simplemindedness. He was of course a product of his time. He claimed somewhere that he began studying existentialism in 1935, three years before Sartre published his first book, in which case Delmore was one of the most precocious philosophers in America; but he was exaggerating, he often did. The point is that he was aware, with his quick, intense mind, of the main currents of the intellectual world of which he himself had so rapidly become a part. He was aware, too aware for his own good, of anxiety and nihilism, of obsessive guilt and responsibility, for these themes formed much of the substance of his work for years to come. He was not only aware of these elements of the era's awareness, he fought against them – in his own way. Always he clung somehow to his concepts of ruth and hope. He turned them and twisted them, he did everything he could to rescue them from the absurdist denials of Sartre, Camus, and their American followers. Hope was reasonable, damn it! – so he insisted. It was the only value that could bring mankind through the incredible horror of the war and the whole stupidity of modern life.

In almost no time at all Delmore found his work in great demand and found himself in a position of considerable power in the literary world. He was an editor of *Partisan Review*, which without doubt was the best connection a young writer could have in those years. The pages of other reviews opened to him as if like flowers; teaching offers came to him; he was lionized and studied. He entered what must have been a period of insanely intense activity. New poems, stories, and essays appeared frequently. Plans were announced by his publisher for a long autobiographical poem and for a translation of Baudelaire's *Fleurs du mal*. But then came the probably inevitable collapse. For whatever reasons – and although I am sure they were complex, still the simple pressure of sudden success must have had a lot to do with it – Delmore began producing work so bad that one can hardly believe it was written by the same person. The long poem was abandoned before it was finished, though parts of it were published, and the translation, when it came out, was so poor and so riddled with error that it had to be withdrawn from circulation. Consider how great a blow that must have been. And the decline that set in then continued for a long time, for years. A new collection of poems in 1950, *Vaudeville for a Princess*, contained so much poor work that Delmore himself was able to include only three poems from it in his selected poems of 1959.

The old models had disappeared, the ones that had guided his first work, Shakespeare, Keats, Kafka, Baudelaire. Instead Delmore's poetry began to look more and more like a pastiche of his contemporaries and rivals. Auden, Thomas, Roethke, Lowell – for a while Delmore's writing was like a roll call. He seemed to be trying to beat everyone at his own game. It was hopeless, ruthless, as Delmore himself must have begun to realize. Then at last he found his own voice again, a drier voice that formerly, running in longer cadences and in a rhetoric of bitterness that burst out of itself continually toward joy. These were his last poems. Above all they spoke of endurance:

> *Poetry is better than hope,*
> *For Poetry is the patience of hope, and all hope's vivid pictures...*

It was not a reconciliation, we cannot imagine that in Delmore's case; but at least we can trust that his last work gave him moments, perhaps hours and days, of rest in his turmoil.

Delmore's stories, perhaps because he took them less seriously than his poems, were always good. He was a marvelous storyteller. His prose was real prose, not a poet's typical posturing, but straight and clear and strong and flexible, and he could manage a complicated story line without stress. He never wrote a bad story, as far as I know, and he wrote some that are superb; the only trouble is that there are so few of them altogether. He could have been one of the great masters of the short story. Then finally we have his criticism. He wrote a lot of it, mostly magazine reviews but also some longer essays, all intelligent, lucid work. Like all criticism much of his is ephemeral, but some has permanent value. I remember especially a long review of Faulkner's *A Fable*. Perhaps it took a poet to do justice to that so often unjustly criticized masterpiece.

The personal factors in Delmore's illness are largely unknown to us, and will remain so until somebody – I hope a very intelligent some-body – writes his biography. But the public factors in his failure are not. To be a young Jew and a young poet in America in the thirties and forties was a brutal experience. We know this because so many others were hurt by it. Delmore was simply one of the most gifted. He wrote splendid stories and poems, but how much more good work he might have done! – if only he had been given the chance to escape from the pressures of racial tension and competitiveness, a chance to create a consistent, integrated body of writing. I wish that somehow he had gone away when he was about twenty-five, had gone out West perhaps, to live on the desert or in the mountains. He wouldn't have liked it, he was too much a city boy. But if he had been forced to stay until he learned to like it, until he learned to recognize the strength he pos-sessed within himself....

Well, maybe it would have been no better for him. We can do noth-ing to help now at any rate. We can only take steps to secure and distin-guish his work. I hope some publisher will soon bring out an intelli-gently edited selection of Delmore's best poems, stories, essays, and reviews. There are enough to make one good-sized and extremely fine volume, and it is a book we cannot afford to do without.

🖎 ·

A Meaning of Robert Lowell

1967.

A BOOK REVIEWER looking at Robert Lowell's new book, *Near the Ocean*, for the first time would find good reasons to be annoyed with it and to say so forcibly. The book itself, for one. It is a pretentious vol-ume; printed on expensive paper, bound in heavy cloth and stamped in three colors, decorated with twenty-one drawings by Sidney Nolan, designed lavishly and wastefully in an outsize format, jacketed in var-nished sixty-pound stock: in short, a very self-conscious-looking collector's item or piece of coffee-table swank, which might easily pro-voke a reviewer into a little investigation. He could learn without difficulty, for instance, that publication of the book had been post-poned several times, and that the price had been announced progres-

sively at $4.95, $5.50, and $6.00. Why? Our reviewer would soon dis-
cover that the longest piece in the book, a translation of Juvenal's
Tenth Satire, had appeared in a magazine version, in *Encounter*, only a
few weeks before the book came out, and he would see significant
differences between the two texts. He would surmise that last-minute
revisions had been made in the poem – hence, very likely, the delays in
publication of the book – and he would wonder if other equally im-
petuous revisions had been made in other poems, especially the per-
sonal ones whose texts are spattered with ellipses. He would wonder
also if the resetting of so much type had required the increases in price.
He would read the note at the front of the book, in which Lowell,
speaking of Nolan's drawings, says, "May my lines throw some light on
his" – apparently meaning that the poet hopes a certain reciprocity of
example will ensue between texts and illustrations. But what a curious
way to say it, what a slip of the two-edged pen. As for the drawings
themselves, would indeed, our reviewer might exclaim, that the poems
could illuminate them, they need it! Next he might look at the table of
contents, where he would count the titles, seven poems and six transla-
tions, and wonder if readers should be asked to pony up six dollars*
for so small an offering of untried work. Finally our reviewer would
turn to the texts themselves, where he would find, first, an ill-assorted
group of translations from classical and Renaissance poems, not
Lowell's best, and second, among the original pieces – the slight heart
of this slight book – one conventional tribute to Theodore Roethke
and six personal poems: strange poems, not poorly written in the usual
sense, on the contrary fairly glittering with the acuity and verbal pa-
nache we expect from Lowell, and yet so awkward nevertheless, so
fragmentary, devious, elliptical, and even stilted that they seem – well,
to make the best of it, bewildering.

How could our reviewer fail to give the book an angry notice?
Highfalutin ostentation: nobody likes it. All the less do we like it in
contrast to Lowell's other books, which, in their quiet formats and
with their modest crosshatch illustrations by Francis Parker on the
title pages, make an attractive and more reasonable appearance. *Near
the Ocean* looks unmistakably like a "big production" that was sup-
posed – if not by Lowell, by someone – to catapult the poet into the

---

* Equivalent to $26.27 in January 1994.

cushiest seat in stardom, as if he weren't sitting there already. But by its own overreaching, it has failed.

Our reviewer, if he had an inquiring mind, would not be satisfied simply to castigate the book's appearance, however. He would wish to find out why Lowell wrote these strange new poems, and what purpose their new style is intended to serve. In short he would change himself, if he were able, from a reviewer into a literary critic. He would study all Lowell's work, he would divide, classify, elucidate, analyze, and compare, and he would give us a schematic judgment which might or might not be useful to us, and which might or might not have something to do with the poems.

Incidentally, if he were a proper scholar, he would begin his essay with a review of previous critical opinions, which in the case of Lowell's poetry comprise a truly splendid range: from servile adulation (in the New York clique) to contumelious rejection (among the West Coast paradisiacs). Obviously this hodgepodge offers a great opportunity to a critic who fancies his own rhetorical prowess.

For my part I am no critic. More's the pity perhaps, because I do find, like our hypothetical reviewer, that I am unwilling to rest on the simple distaste aroused in me by Lowell's new work, a distaste which is uncertain at that, inconsistent and unformed. I would like to know more. In consequence I must attack the poems in the only way I can, namely, as a fellow poet, someone who has worked the same side of the street for roughly the same period, and who presumably knows something about the difficulties of the job. This is what I propose to do, that is, to look at the poems less as finished works than as objects coming into being. Indeed, for reasons I shall elaborate, I think this is the only way one can look at Lowell's work of the past fifteen years.

The risks in my method are great, of course. One is that I shall stray from my literary topic into what is normally considered personal or biographical. To those who may charge me with this, I give two answers. First, I shall not stray far because I do not know Lowell personally, having met him only twice, for a few minutes each time and at an interval of more than a decade. My knowledge of the man comes from what I have heard during twenty years on the edge of the literary world. Secondly, in dealing with poetry as personal as Lowell's, or as personal as most poetry written nowadays in America, the risk of infringing upon the poet's privacy is properly speaking no risk at all. An invitation has been extended to us: why shouldn't we accept it?

The place to begin, then, is with a biographical datum. Robert Lowell is, and for some years has been, the most envied poet in the country. The consequences of this are many, but for the moment I wish simply to enforce the fact. I envy Lowell. Everywhere I go among literary people I meet only others who envy Lowell. The reasons for it are obvious enough: his great advantages. First, the advantage of his birth in a distinguished family. One does not wish to insist on this, but at the same time it is not negligible. No doubt being born with a ready-made cultural and social status is sometimes a hindrance, but it is a help too, and in our hearts most of us would be glad to put up with the one if we could thereby attain the other. Secondly, the advantage of talent and intelligence. I am not speaking of the particular concrete expressions of these properties, but of the properties themselves. From the first Lowell's poetry has had an inner force bespeaking his great native gifts. It has put him in the class of wonder boys, along with poets like the early Auden and Dylan Thomas who, however idiotic they may sometimes look in other respects, were simply unable to write a trite or flaccid line. Most of us must cultivate poorer gardens. If we console ourselves with the idea that the best crop sometimes comes from meager soil, nevertheless we yearn often enough, in our adverse labor, for the facility of mere brilliance. Thirdly, the advantage of success. Let anyway say what he or she will, Lowell is our leading poet. It is a fact. He has power, influence, and an enormous reputation. His books, for example, are kept in print and they sell steadily – what a joy that must be! We all, I know, are reasonable creatures, and we recognize that success is more often a nuisance than a blessing. But are we so inhuman that we deny our envy of those who have it? I hope not.

Of course envy is a tricky thing. It takes many directions. At bottom it accounts, I believe, for ninety percent of the critical response to Lowell's work, the wide range of opinions, and it accounts too for the concentration of responses at the extremes of the scale: adulators at one end, detractors at the other. As for the adulators...but why not call them by their right name, the flatterers? In their multitude we dismiss them; and we need add only that although their opinion in the long run may turn out to be right, and Lowell's poetry may be seen to

be precisely as great as they say it is, if this happens it will be not be-
cause of, but in spite of, what they themselves are saying and doing
now. The detractors, whose motives may be equally disreputable, are
nevertheless forced by the nature of their position to take a more dis-
criminative view, and hence their expressions of opinion may be actu-
ally helpful to us in making discriminations of our own. At least I shall
go on that presumption.

Myself, after discounting as well as I can my own factor of envy, I
find that my uncritical, working man's response to Lowell's achieve-
ment changes from time to time but generally hovers between the two
extremes. In each stage of his poetic evolution Lowell has written a few
poems that seem to me extremely fine, and he has also written poems
that seem to me mannered, pointless, incomplete, and obscure. In-
deed, try as I may – and I have tried again and again over the years –
some of his poems, particularly his earliest and then again his latest,
remain incomprehensible to me, as dark and profuse as a pot of
Bostonian whistleberries. Moreover I cannot escape the feeling that
some of this obscurity has been purposely, even crassly, laid on.* For
me, this is the single largest detracting element in his work.

One point, however, I wish to make perfectly clear. Lowell's posi-
tion of leadership seems to me not only to have been earned but to be
altogether suitable. I say this on two counts. As a man, Lowell has
given us more than enough evidence of his firmness and integrity – one
thinks of his conscientious objection during the war and all that it en-
tailed, his refusal to attend White House sociables, and many other
such actions – to substantiate his moral fitness for the role. As a poet,
he gives us this same integrity in art. When I read his poetry, however
negative my response may be to its effect, I know I am in the presence
of an artist *in extremis*, operating, I should say struggling, at the limits
of sensibility and technique. This is a quality which we consider pecu-
liarly American, a kind of hardrock Yankee pertinacity, and to me it is
peculiarly attractive. Who was it that said he would fight it out on this
line if it took all summer? An American military man, I believe. When I
read Lowell's lines, I feel that he has fought it out upon them for years.
This is tough and homely and American. It is admirable. It is what
leads me to place Lowell alongside William Carlos Williams, rather

---

* Lowell has admitted as much. See his *Paris Review* interview.

than in the company of other older poets to whom he bears a closer superficial resemblance. It is also what leads me, in the perennial confrontation of artists with the world, to rest content under his leadership. If my standing behind him will add to the strength of his position, he may be sure I am there.

So much for preliminary considerations. The phases of Lowell's poetic evolution are so well known that I need indicate them only briefly. We may dismiss his first book, *Land of Unlikeness*, which was published in a limited edition that few people have seen; Lowell himself effectively dismissed it when he republished its main poems, considerably revised, in *Lord Weary's Castle*, the book that established him with one shot as a leader of his generation. Written in the first flush of enthusiasm after his conversion to Catholicism, the poems were highly charged devotional lyrics mixed with autobiographical elements, presented in an elaborate formal dress: close rhymes, exact meters, a heavy reliance on couplets, and an equally heavy reliance on the rhetoric of allusion. It was a virtuoso performance. At its best, in perhaps a fourth of the poems, it showed a young poet writing with genuine spontaneity in the strict forms of the English metaphysical convention, while bringing to them his own distinct voice and idiosyncratic manner. In short Lowell had done what everyone had been saying could not be done: he had invented a new style. In his next book, *The Mills of the Kavanaughs*, he stuck with it, but most readers considered the book a falling-off, especially the long title poem. What this poem, a dramatic narrative in monologue, showed was that the ability to sustain narrative tension across the librations of discrete pentameter couplets is lost to us: the suspension bridge has replaced the viaduct.

Lowell waited eight years to publish his next book. Then, in 1959, he presented us with a change of appearance so radical that it seemed a reversal. The formal manner was gone; no pentameters, no rhymes, no ornate rhetoric. The book, called *Life Studies*, which more than recouped his reputation, gave us instead poems in open, loose measures, without rhyme, in a diction that seemed easy and almost insouciant. The heart of the book was a group of autobiographical poems so intensely candid that critics immediately called them "confessional," an unfortunate choice of terms. It implied that Lowell was engaged in public breast-beating, a kind of refreshing new psycho-exotic pastime, or in a shallow exercise of "self-expression," long ago discredited; whereas in fact his aim was far more serious than that.

The following two collections of poems, *For the Union Dead* in 1964 and *Near the Ocean* this year, have continued to explore themes of autobiographical candor, but have gradually reverted toward formalism. Not the baroque formalism of *Lord Weary's Castle*, however. Now the meters, though basically iambic, are cast in rough lines of trimeter and tetrameter, punctuated with purposefully inexact rhymes. The diction is more extreme, more peculiar and concise, than in *Life Studies*, and the syntax has become progressively more taut, split up into smaller and smaller units. This has gone so far in the latest poems that one can scarcely find a complete sentence from stanza to stanza, but only phrases, expletives, stabs of meaning. The effect, although entirely different from the high style of *Lord Weary's Castle*, nevertheless brings us back to an obscurity and artifice that seem to denote another reversal; the simplicity of *Life Studies* has been jettisoned.

In effect Lowell made, in *Life Studies*, a considerable leap into a new area of poetic experience, which he has been exploring since then through increasingly elaborate means. Why he did this, what was in his mind, are questions readers must try to answer if they would understand the actual meaning of Lowell's experiment.

I have said nothing about the translations, perhaps because they are a source of embarrassment to me. Over the years Lowell has made a good many, including a couple of long ones and a whole book of short ones, from many languages, called *Imitations*. When this book was published in 1961, I reviewed it enthusiastically. The density and tonicity of the best translations took hold of me and persuaded me that Lowell had reached far toward the intrinsic qualities of the original poems, especially in his Baudelaires. Since then my friends who know Baudelaire better than I have informed me with cogency that this is not true, and that I had no business reviewing such a book in the first place. Of course they are right on both counts. Aside from the intended alterations of sequence and literal meaning, which Lowell acknowledges, there is, for instance, the way in which Baudelaire's characteristic elegance, deriving from the fluent, almost sinuous buildup of stanzas and longer passages, is fragmented and rigidified in Lowell's choppy phrasings. And there is the way, too, in which

Baudelaire's tainted post-romantic sense of beauty is both reduced and roughened in its passage through Lowell's anguish-ridden, New Englander's sensibility; the flowers of evil become merely evil flowers – a considerable difference when you stop to think about it. Lowell's detractors seize on these points, and others, as ammunition for their campaign, which is made easier by the evident inferiority, when judged against any standard, of some of the other translations. The Villons are quite bad, the Rimbauds and Pasternaks barely passable. But I continue to feel that the best of the Baudelaires, Rilkes, and Montales are excellent Lowells indeed, and this is all he had claimed for them. He does not call them translations, but imitations. Perhaps he should have gone further and specified that what he was imitating was not the poetry of Baudelaire or the rest, but the poetry of Lowell; perhaps he should have chosen another title, for example, *Appropriations* or *Assimilations*. No matter; the point is that Lowell has made a perfectly legitimate effort to consolidate his own poetic view of reality by levying upon congenial authentications from other languages and cultures. The best of his translations go together with the best of *Life Studies* and *For the Union Dead* to make up the nucleus of his mature work, the organic unity of which must be apprehended by those who wish to form reliable judgments.

Even at the most superficial level of technique, the prosodic level, Lowell's evolution, both his successes and his failures, offers a fascinating study to people who are interested in the disciplines of poetry. This is usually the case when important poets change styles. Consider Lowell's commonest prosodic device, the suspended or Hopkinsian upbeat produced by ending a line on the first syllable of a new unit of syntax, a phrase or a sentence. He made it work well, not to say famously, in his early poems, but when he abandoned strict pentameters he had more trouble with it. How do you employ this very useful concept of extreme or total metrical enjambment when your line-structure has been purposely deregularized? It is the old story: you can't have your cake and eat it too. Simple as it appears, this is a crucial problem, perhaps *the* crucial problem, of contemporary unmetered poetry, which different poets have met in many different ways. Some have adopted the practice of reading their poems with abrupt pauses at the end of each line, but this is an oral strategem that seems to have little connection with the actual dynamics of the poem. Denise Levertov has gone further by rationalizing the line length and rhythm in terms of "organic form," a concept which appears, however, to be incompletely worked out at this stage. Like her, Lowell has preferred to work on the page, that is, within the poem's prosodic structure, but with indifferent success in many instances. Conceivably such a simple matter as this, which is nevertheless extremely important in terms of Lowell's natural style, lies behind his recent return to more exact, or more exacting, meters.

But that is a topic for another discussion. What I am interested in here is something prior to poetry. Before a person can create a poem he or she must create a poet. Considered from the limited perspective of artistry, this is the primal creative act.

Imagine Lowell seated at his work table on some ordinary morning in 1950. *Lord Weary's Castle* has been out for four years; already its triumph is a burden. The poems in *The Mills of the Kavanaughs*, now at the press, have been finished for a year or more, and are beginning to slip into the past, to seem stale, remote, and incidental – like the verses of one's friends. Now I have no idea what Lowell would be doing in such circumstances, probably brooding and daydreaming like the rest of us, but for the moment let me ascribe to him a simple, orderly, god-like self-mastery that neither he nor I nor Charles de Gaulle can claim in actuality. In 1950, given that marvelous perspicacity, he would have had to ask himself two questions. In essence, what is my theme? In general, what is my defect?

One does not ask these questions once and then go on to something else; one asks them over and over, as one asks all unanswerable questions. A serious poet moves progressively toward his essential theme, though he can never reach it, by means of exclusions, peeling away, from poem to poem, the inessential, working down to bedrock; and he examines every word he writes for clues to his defect. In the case of Lowell we cannot doubt that he works in such a state of constant tension and self-interrogation. Yet it seems clear to me, even so, that at some point around 1950 he must have asked these questions with special intentness. Nothing else can account for the change of poetic stance so strikingly evident in *Life Studies*.

What had Lowell set out to do in his first poems? He had set out explicitly, I think, though ingenuously, to build on the Donne-to-

Hopkins tradition of devotional poetry in English, to write poems of faith. The evidence in the poems themselves is unmistakable. Consequently he had produced a rather large number of set pieces in a high style, such as the poems on Jonathan Edwards and other historical figures or events, affirming a public devotional aspiration. This is what all young poets do, isn't it, one way or another? They begin, or at least they try to begin, where the mature poets they admire left off. They do this in the compulsion of their literary zeal, in spite of the evident unfeasibility of it, owing to the irremediable disparity of experience. At the same time Lowell interspersed among his devotional pieces various autobiographical elements, usually disguised and highly wrought, set out in the same taut, allusive, difficult style as the rest, but genuine autobiography nevertheless. I think it must have become evident to him by 1950 that in spite of the very great but purely literary success of the devotional set pieces, these autobiographical poems were the more alive, the more interesting, and ultimately the more comprehensible.

Poems like "Mr. Edwards and the Spider" and "After the Surprising Conversions" are good specimens of their kind, but like all their kind they are sententious. That is to say, a large part of their meaning is a stable and predictable element of the general cultural situation, with which the poems are, so to speak, invested. (And under "meaning" I intend the entire affective and cognitive experience of the poem.) But the autobiographical poems or partly autobiographical poems, like "Mary Winslow" and "At the Indian Killer's Grave," work themselves out in their own terms, within their own language; and in spite of the high gloss of artifice which remains upon them, they speak with urgency.

All this is even more evident today, fifteen years later. The most prominent motifs of the poems in *Lord Weary's Castle* are the Christ, the Crucifix, and the Virgin; they are repeated on almost every page. Yet they remain inert. They are not personal realizations, they are not symbols, they are merely tokens (which perhaps, in the tradition Lowell had chosen, is all they can be). The personal motifs on the other hand – personal guilt, personal death, personal violence and desire – are what carry the poet along, and they are connected, not with devotional aspirations, but with his experienced life. He returns to them again and again in poems about himself, his mother and the Winslow family, and his father, Commander Lowell. In *Life Studies* he

simply relinquished one set of motifs, the former, and took up the
other. The resulting augmentation of his poetic stature – his personal
stature as creator within the domain of his poetic materials – was enor-
mous.

As I say, Lowell cannot discover the precise specifications of his
theme, which is lucky for him. If he were to do so, he would be clapped
into silence instantly. Nor can we do it for him, which is equally lucky.
All we can do is brood, as he does, over his lines and the shadows be-
hind them, tracking down the motifs to see where they lead. In my own
recent brooding I turn especially to two lines from the poem called
"Night Sweat" in *For the Union Dead:*

> *always inside me is the child who died,*
> *always inside me is his will to die…*

Simple enough; explicit enough. They are one expression of the radi-
cal guilt that seems to lie at the base of Lowell's poetic nature. It is a
guilt which took form like any other, leaving aside psychoanalytical
factors: first from elements of generalized cultural guilt, in Lowell's
case the New Englander's shame over the native Americans and the
Salem women, which has exercised an obviously powerful influence
on his imagination; then from guilt that all men feel, with deep neces-
sity, for the deaths of their own fathers; and finally from the horren-
dous events of contemporary history. But what is the punishment for
the crimes that produce this pervading guilt? It is personal death. We
all know this, from the first moment of our mortal recognition. Yet
against this Lowell casts again and again his instinctive belief in the re-
mission of sin, or rather his knowledge, his feeling, of his own undi-
minished innocence. Then what can our death be? What is our guilt?
There is only one answer, outside absurdity. Our death is our sin, for
which we pay in advance through our guilt. Our death is a crime
against every good principle in the universe: nature, God, the human
heart. And we, the innocent, are the responsible ones – this is the idea
Lowell cannot forego. We bear this crime like a seed within us. Our
bodies are going to commit it, do what we will. Our bodies are prepar-
ing our death at every moment. They are going to carry out this mur-
der inexorably, while we stand by, helpless and aghast.

This is the ultimate Yankee metonymy, you might say. Puritan death

as punishment for sin contracts, under the paradox of benign tran-
scendentalism, to death as sin. Naturally it is a theological monstrosity.
It is impossible. Yet in the human and poetic sphere, it is a validity of
staggering force. And it lies at the heart of the American sensibility, a
far more cogent explanation of our attitudes, including our racism and
violence, than, for example, Leslie Fiedler's mythologized sexualism.

Well, all this is highly conjectural. There are scores of other, doubt-
less better, ways to approach Lowell's theme, I'm sure. Yet I feel this
progressive identification of sin, guilt, and death can be traced fairly
directly from such poems as "At the Indian Killer's Grave" to "Night
Sweat" and beyond. The two lines I have quoted strike close to it.
They are literal. When Lowell says "inside" I think he means inside:
he is carrying this sin-death around in him like a monstrous pregnancy.
I would almost bet that if he suffers the common nightmare of artists,
the dream of male parturition, it is a dead thing that comes out (at
which point, if he hasn't awakened, his dream may be suffused with
bliss).

Meanwhile Lowell has his defect, for which he should give thanks.
It permits him to relax into the mercy of technical self-criticism. Not
that it is easy to deal with; quite the contrary. Like all fundamental de-
fects, it is a function of his personality, and hence wears many faces. I
call it the defect of pervasive extraneity; but it could have other names.
One aspect of it is quite clear, however, in *Lord Weary's Castle*, the
laid-on metaphysical obscurity. This was the fashion of poetry at the
time, and Lowell accommodated himself to it easily and naturally, and
without the least poetic infidelity. We must bear in mind in considering
fashion that a fashion during the period of its ascendancy is not a fash-
ion; it is merely what is right. In composing the poems of *Lord Weary's
Castle*, Lowell had no sense, I'm certain, of doing anything but what
was necessary. He had no sense of *doing* anything at all, except writing
poetry as it is written. Nevertheless the obscurity, like the ornate style
and the use of inert figures from a general cultural conspectus, was
clearly extraneous to his main themes and objectives, as he could see
five or six years later, and he gave it up; this was his defect and he
chopped off its head. But it sprang up elsewhere, hydra-like. Other as-
pects of it were more difficult to see. For instance, in the title poem of
The Mills of the Kavanaughs, he had shown his inability to sustain the
long units of poetry, and at the same time his great talent for the short

units: the line, couplet, phrase, and isolated image. These are his *forte*.
Lowell can rap out a single sharp line with extraordinary facility. The
trouble is that these brilliant strokes may contribute nothing to the
whole fabric and intention of a poem; they may be merely extraneous –
pervasively extraneous because in spite of their irrelevance they do sit
within the total structure and they cannot be eradicated once the poem
has acquired a certain degree of distinctness.

In a poem called "The Scream" from *For the Union Dead*, Lowell
writes of the time when his mother gave up her mourning:

> *One day she changed to purple,*
> *and left her mourning. At the fitting,*
> *the dressmaker crawled on the floor,*
> *eating pins, like Nebuchadnezzar*
> *on his knees eating grass.*

We have all observed this, of course, a woman crawling on the floor,
her mouth full of pins, to adjust another woman's hem – at least all of
us have observed it who are over a certain age – and we are struck, con-
sequently, by the originality of Lowell's simile. It seems to me abso-
lutely genuine; I have never encountered it before. Hence the pins and
grass collapse together spontaneously in our mind like a perfect super-
imposition of images. I am charmed. Only when I stop to think do I
realize that Nebuchadnezzar and what he stands for have only the re-
motest connection with this passage, and that the dressmaker herself is
a figure of no importance in the poem. As an image, this is a brilliant
extraneity: the defect at work.

And what shall we say about the appearance of the new book, its
crass and confused ostentation? This is gross extraneity and nothing
else.

In short, Lowell's defect is a temptation to mere appearance, to
effects, trappings – to the extraneous. And it arises, I believe, from a
discrete imagination, that is, an imagination which works best in dis-
junctive snatches. I suppose some people would call it an analytic,
rather than a synthetic, imagination. His problem as a poet during the
past fifteen or twenty years has been to continue digging toward his es-
sential theme, while at the same time turning, if it is possible, his defect
into an advantage.

So far I have been writing about Lowell as if he were an isolated case, but the reverse is the truth. He is a poet of his time. The shift of focus in his poetry has been one part, a very small part, of a general shift in artistic values and intentions during the past quarter-century.

When was the last time in our Western civilization that a writer at his work table could look at a piece of writing and with complete confidence call it finished, self-enclosed and self-sustaining, autonomous – a work of art in the original sense? I'd say in poetry it must have been at the time of Pope, and in fiction, since the novel lags behind, perhaps as late as Flaubert or Turgenev; but actually no one could draw the lines so precisely. The change from one notion of art to another was very gradual. All we can say with certainty is that sometime during the nineteenth century – that changeful time! – the old idea of the enclosed work of art was dislocated in the minds of serious artists: Heine, Rimbaud, Strindberg. Such writers began to see that art is always unfinished; and from this arose the concept of its a priori unfinishability, that is, its limitlessness. For a time – quite a time – the two concepts ran side by side; many artists tried by various means to combine them. In the forepart of our century, for instance, we got the idea of the circularity of artistic structure, from which derived the work of art that was both limitless and enclosed: *The Waste Land* and *Finnegans Wake*. These were grandiose conceptions. They made art into something it had not been before, a world in itself.* They were helped along by the general collapse of values in the post-Nietzschean cultures of Europe. Some artists, despairing of their own painful nihilism, even tried to substitute for the reality of the world the anti-reality of art – or of style, the word, whatever – believing that only by this means could they create a bearable plane upon which to enact human existence and build a consistent scheme of values. I am thinking of such men as Gottfried Benn, Céline, and Wyndham Lewis, or in a different way of Breton and the surrealists. Of course Hitler's war

---

* An extreme statement; in one sense art had always been a world apart. The "immortality" of the poem was a desperately held notion of the Renaissance, and was transmitted through succeeding generations of poets – poets of every school – down to recent times. But in another sense the enclosed *and* limitless masterpieces of 1910–1940 did introduce something new. The possibility of an art that was not only distinct from "objective reality" but contradistinct, a plane of being divorced from and better than the corrupt world of non-art; and this engendered a philosophical departure far more serious than, for instance, the shallow Yellow-Book estheticism from which it partly sprang.

smashed all that, proving the ugliness and irresponsibility of it. Reality was reality after all. We came out of the war badly shaken, clinging to the idea of existential engagement. Henceforth, contrite as we were, we would be responsible and free, creative within the real world. Yet what could this mean in a reality over which we had no control, a reality in which we, the conscious element, possessed nothing but the lunatic knowledge of our own alienation, what could we create? We decided – and to my mind the inevitability of it is beautiful – that what we could create was life. Human life.

It was not a retreat into anti-reality. In looking back we saw that, after Nietzsche, we had been living in a crisis of intellectual evolution, a terrible blockage and confusion; we had been absorbing what Jaspers calls "the preparing power of chaos." Now we were ready to go forward. Now, in freedom and responsibility, we began to see the meaning of what we had known all along, that a life is more than a bundle of determined experiential data. (For the biggest horror of our crisis had been the complex but empty enticements of Freudian positivism.) A life is what we make it. In its authenticity it is our own interpretation and reorganization of experience, structured metaphorically. It is the result of successive imaginative acts – it is a work of art! By conversion, a work of art is a life, *provided it be true to the experiential core.* Thus in a century artists had moved from an Arnoldian criticism of life to an existential creation of life, and both the gains and the losses were immense.

The biggest loss was a large part of what we thought we had known about art. For now we saw in exactly what way art is limitless. It is limitless because it is free and responsible: it is a life. Its only end is the adventitious cutting off that comes when a heart bursts, or a sun. Still, the individual "piece" of art must be objective in some sense; it lies on the page, on the canvas. Practically speaking, what is a limitless object? It is a fragment, a random fragment without intrinsic form, shading off in all directions into whatever lies beyond. And this is what our art has become in the past two decades: random, fragmentary, and open-ended.

Hence in literature any particular "work" is linear rather than circular in structure, extensible rather than terminal in intent, and at any given point inclusive rather than associative in substance; at least these are its tendencies. And it is autobiographical, that goes without saying.

It is an act of self-creation by an artist within the tumult of experience.

This means that many of our ideas about art must be re-examined and possibly thrown out. I have in mind not our ideas of technique, derived from the separate arts, but our esthetic generalizations, derived from all the arts. Such notions as harmony, dynamism, control, proportion, even style in its broadest sense. How do these criteria apply to a work that is not a work at all, conventionally considered, but a fragment? I do not say they do not apply; I say the applications must be radically redetermined.

As readers, where does this leave us? In a mere subjective muddle? Sometimes it seems so. For that matter why should we read another person's poems at all? Our life is what concerns us, not his or hers. Is this poet a better observer than we, a better imaginer, a better creator? Can this poet's self-creation of his or her life assist us in ours, assuming a rough equivalence of human needs and capacities? Perhaps; but these too are subjective criteria. What then?

All I can say is that the most progressive criticism we have now *is* subjective, resolutely so and in just these ways. It asks what a poem can *do* for us. The reason we have so little of it is that we are unused to such methods, we are fearful – justly – of the sentimentalism and shallow moralism such methods might reintroduce into our frameworks of sensibility, and we do not know upon what principles to organize our new subjective criteria. Our critics are still years behind our artists, still afraid of the personal, ideal, practical, and contingent. For strangely enough, these four properties are just what we preserve in fragments but often destroy in wholes. Working philosophers know this. In a grave correspondence to human limits, an apothegm is better philosophy than an organon.

Still, I see some evidence here and there that the critics are beginning to stir themselves.

What Lowell thinks of all this he hasn't said. He has written almost no criticism, and apparently does not intend to write any. I salute him! But at all events we know that he has been working for twenty years in the heart of the movement I have described, among eastern writers and artists. He has been associated with painters who gave their work the unfortunate names of abstract expressionism and action painting, and with theatrical people who have used such concepts as the happening and nonacting acting; these being half-understood designations for the artist's life-constructing function. This has been Lowell's milieu. Of course he has shared it with many other writers; what I have been discussing in terms of Lowell's work is a shift or tightening of artistic intention which cuts across every line. And one thing more is certain. Whatever the rationale, or whether or not there is any rationale, we cannot read Lowell's autobiographical writing, from *Life Studies* to *Near the Ocean*, without seeing that we are in touch with a writer who is in fact making his life as he goes along, and with a degree of seriousness and determination and self-awareness that surpasses the artistic confidence of any previous generation. He has resolved to accept reality, all reality, and to take its fragments indiscriminately as they come, forging from them this indissoluble locus of metaphorical connections that is known as Robert Lowell. No wonder he is enthusiastic.

Hence we see that in his translations, and for that matter in all his work, Lowell's methods are distinct from those of Ezra Pound. This is a distinction we must be careful to draw, I think, because Pound's methods have become so much second nature to us all that they blur our recognition of the principal fact about the two poets, namely, that the historical gulf separating them is enormous. Thus when Pound wrenches and distorts Propertius in the translations from the Elegies, or when he capsulates writing from many sources in the *Cantos*, he does so in the interest of a general program of cultural aggrandizement conducted from a base of personal security. There is no uncertainty of values in the *Cantos*; in this respect the poem is as old-fashioned as *Candide* or Boethius. Nor is there any uncertainty of poetic personality. The writer – *ego, scriptor,* as he signs himself in a couple of places – is a steady and reliable, if sometimes rudimentary, presence. Pound's work in effect is an Arnoldian criticism of life on a very grand scale, which is only possible because the critic looks out from the secure bastion of his own personality founded on a stable scheme of values. Lowell on the other hand is a poetic ego without fixtures: in a sense neither being nor becoming, but a sequence of fragments, like the individual frames of a movie film, propelled and unified by its own creative drive. This does not mean that Lowell's work lacks values; his poems are as strenuously moral as anyone's. But his objective is not critical, nor even broadly cultural; it is personal; and the moral elements of his poetry are used, not as precepts, but as the hypotheses of an experimental venture in self-validation. In his autobiographical work, both translations and original poems, Lowell employs many of Pound's devices, perhaps most of them, but his ends are his own – and this makes all the difference. It means a radically different creative outlook, issuing in new poetic justifications and criteria.*

And so I return to my starting place; for I am sure everyone knows that the hypothetical reviewer with whom I began is really myself, and that all this speculation springs from the moment when my review copy of *Near the Ocean* arrived in the mail. I have already said that I do not like the sequence of autobiographical poems which forms the heart of this new book. Let me add to this three further points.

1. Why has Lowell moved progressively away from the simplicity of *Life Studies* toward a new formalism? Is it only a reversionary impulse? Is it an attempt to give greater objectivity to the random, fragmentary materials of his autobiography by reintroducing elements of fixative convention? Is it from a desire to make fuller use of his talent, that is, to turn his defect to advantage by emphasizing prosody and syntax as means both for suggesting the discreteness of experience and for unifying it within the poem's linear flow? No doubt all these reasons, and others, are at work. But the result is a too-great concentration of effort upon the verbal surface – to my mind very unfortunate. We now have poems which are compositions of brilliant minutiae, like mosaics in which the separate tiles are so bright and glittering that we cannot see the design. A mosaic is fine, it is the model par excellence for poetry in our time, but if we are to see the pattern the separate pieces must be clear and naturally arranged; and in the best mosaics the colors are subdued rather than gaudy.

2. In point of substance I ask, still in a firmly subjective mode, what are the most useful parts of autobiography? To my mind the most interesting of Lowell's poems are those from his present or recent past, concerning his wife, divorce, children, illness, imprisonment, and so on, but these are few and small compared to the great number about his youth and childhood, ancestors, his visits to the family graveyard. I

---

* In 1994 it strikes me that what I described in this paragraph, and in the entire essay, is the transition from modernism to post-modernism as we use those terms today. Most people now do not think of Lowell as a post-modernist; stylistically speaking, perhaps he isn't. But wherever one draws the line, the seeds of rejected modernism are in Lowell's work and his influence on younger writers in this respect was profound.

detect a faint odor of degenerate Freudian sentimentalism. Have we not had enough of this, and more? We are interested in the man, the present, unfinished, lively being. If the term *confessional* is to be applied to Lowell's work, although I have said why I think it is inadequate, then I suggest he has not confessed enough. In particular one topic is lacking, or nearly lacking, for such poems as "Beyond the Alps" hardly scratch the surface: I mean Lowell's conversion to the Church of Rome and his subsequent – should I say recusancy? I scarcely know. He was in and then he was out, and the real drama remains for us a mystery. Surely this touches the man. And surely it touches many issues of our time: justice, probity, the individual and the mass, the role of love in society, even peace and war. In effect I advocate a stiffening up of autobiographical substance, a colder and more realistic view. Let the rigor now reserved for verbal superficies be applied to the exact new content of experience.

3. But judgment fails. In this art it has not found its place. If I were to suggest one ultratechnical criterion still available to a poet in Lowell's circumstances, I would say: relevance. Be random, yes, fragmentary and open-ended – these are the conditions of life – but scrutinize every component of your act of creation for its relevance. The advantage of random observation is not only in what comes but in what is let go. Avoid the extraneous like the plague. Lowell does not always manage it, and his defect is not the advantage it might be. His style, though more deeply in-wrought than before, is still too much like a shell, a carapace, an extraneity. We see again and again that the most difficult work of imagination is not when it soars in fantasy but when it plods in fact. And what a force of imagination has gone into these poems! A man's being, fought for, fragment by fragment, there on the page: this we can recognize. And we know that in such poetry the risk of failure is no longer a risk but a certainty. It must be taken, eaten. The very poem which seems most awkward to us may be the one that will wrench us away finally from the esthetic fixatives of the conventions of irresponsibility, and release us into responsible creation. If we read Lowell's new poems in the light of the problems he is facing, we will know that although we must, since we are human, judge them, our judgment is not something superior or separate, it is a part of his struggle, as his struggle is a part of ours. In this knowledge we may discover what we have been groping toward for centuries: not humility,

which as artists we do not need, nor magnanimity, which I hope we already have, but the competence of human freedom.

𝒦 ·

A Turn in the Rhyme

1968.

IN THE MID-1950s when Karl Shapiro began publishing what he called, ironically, his "bourgeois poems," accompanied by essays that rudely attacked T. S. Eliot and other members of the Establishment, many thought this a puzzling outcome. Wasn't Shapiro too a member of the Establishment? An extremely popular, attractive poet, learned, witty, well-spoken, correct, a virtuoso of poetic form? A Pulitzer Prize-winner, a consultant on poetry to the Library of Congress, etc.? Quite true; hence his revulsion from his own work seemed sheerest apostasy. Many critics accused him of trying to retrieve a slipping reputation by capitalizing on the new Beat phenomenon.

But his accusers were wrong, as they could have told if they had taken time to study all Shapiro's work. They would have learned, first, that no poet has ever been more honest or intelligent about his own writing, and second, that the inner necessity of revolt had been evident in his poetry long before the Beat movement came to notice.

All this is perfectly clear in the new *Selected Poems*, which is a splendidly edited model of what any selected edition should be. Shapiro has chosen generously from his past work, and equally from each phase of it; he has declined to revise old poems. Consequently this book, unlike most such books, is a genuinely useful epitome of his whole work.

Shapiro's earliest poems, written in the 1930s, won immediate popularity. Formalistic, rhymed and metered, witty, ironic, dressed in the smart Marxist-Freudian diction of the time, they were, in short, Audenesque, like most poems by young Americans of that period. Today the style seems terribly dated. Here is the opening of the poem called "Hospital":

> *Inside or out, the key is pain. It holds*
> *The florist to your pink medicinal rose,*

The nickname to the corpse. One wipes it from
Blue German blades or drops it down the drain;
The novelist with a red tube up his nose
Gingerly pets it. Nurse can turn it off.

With our recent experience of camp, how easily we could make fun of this. It is an absurd style at worst, falsely tough and falsely objective, from the same period that gave us James M. Cain and "Terry and the Pirates." Yet at his best Shapiro wrote with immense tact, an instinct that stopped him short of absurdity, so that poems like "Hospital," "Auto Wreck," "Skiers," and many others may be read without disdain as set pieces from that era, which suddenly come alive – stark, lucid, and humane. Even the wretched novelist with his nose-tube becomes a convincing figure of human pathos.

But the style was a dead end, obviously. We note that all Shapiro's good early poems are from his first book, dated 1942. His second, in 1944, was a falling off, though it won the Pulitzer Prize; already he had begun repeating himself. The next year, in *Essay on Rime*, a remarkable book-length poem on the problems of contemporary poetry, he expressed doubt concerning his own poetic practice, and thereafter he began softening his diction, lightening his rhymes and meters. But although he wrote fine poems, including the sequences called "Adam and Eve," "Recapitulations," and "Poems of a Jew," these remained basically conventional and clearly not the answer to his doubts.

So the revolt came. It was impelled by many factors, no doubt social and broadly cultural as well as narrowly literary; and it was a complete revolt, since the "bourgeois poems" bore almost no verbal resemblance to previous work. Blocky, free, prose-like, iconoclastic, touched with apocalyptic insight, they seemed, coming from Shapiro, actually shocking. Today their shock is gone; we can see that shock was a very minor part of their original intention, if it was a part at all. They were simply what Shapiro had to do at that point. They remain fresh, shrewd poems which we read today with approval and pleasure.

ALL TROPIC PLACES SMELL OF MOLD

All tropic places smell of mold. A letter from Karachi smells of
mold. A book I had in New Guinea twenty years ago smells

*of mold. Cities in India smell of mold and dung. After a
while you begin to like it. The curry dishes in the fine
Bombay restaurant add the dung flavor. In the villages
dung patties plastered to the walls, the leavings of the cows
the only cooking fuel. The smell rubs into the blood.*

*Paris in the winter smells of wood smoke and fruit. Near the Gare
St. Lazare in the freezing dusk the crowds pour slowly down
the streets in every direction. A police van the size of a
Pullman car goes at a walking pace. The gendarme keeps
jumping down from the rear like a streetcar conductor in
the old days. He is examining identity cards of pedestrians,
especially the females. A girl comes swinging along, her
pocketbook in rhythm with her behind. She is bareheaded
and wears a raincoat. The gendarme examines her identity
card. She is motioned into the paddy wagon.*

*Salzburg, the castle smells of snow and peat. Baltimore, old oaken
bucket. Portsmouth, Virginia, roses and diesel oil. Dublin,
coal dust, saccharine whiskey, bitter bodies. Damp gusts of
Siena doorways. Warehouses of Papeete, acrid smell of
copra, frangipani, salt water and mold. Smell of rotting
water in Hollandia.*

*Unbreathable jungles, parks subtle and cool. Backstage the ballet
dancers wipe their sweat; "the entire stage stinks like a
stable." Sewer gas of beauty parlors. Electric smells of hair
in rut. Talcum powder, earliest recollection. Rome, the
armpit of the universe.*

There is more to this than meets the eye – or the nose. As I say, it is
fresh and it is shrewd too, sardonic, intelligent. But it is not moving, as
Shapiro seems to recognize, because recently he has begun working
toward renewed concentration, sometimes in rhyme and meter, more
often in free forms of greater density than the "bourgeois poems." The
last poem in his book, "Aubade," a free poem which deals allusively
with many motifs from the medieval erotic tradition, is one of his best.

Perhaps *Selected Poems* contains a few masterpieces. Frankly I hope so. I hope some of these poems turn out to be genuinely durable. They are such ingratiating poems to begin with, so lively and readable, so original in every respect, that one can't help wishing them well. At the same time the book offers a fascinating record of poetic honesty, courage, and willingness to change, a record that young poets should read carefully and study. Yet for all this one hopes also that the book is only a prelude to the real fruit of Shapiro's revolt, which surely is still to come. In human terms it seems unfair that a man in his fifties, after thirty years' work, must gird himself for his greatest effort. As Shapiro's friends we cannot ask it. As readers, however, we are insatiable and relentless, and we ask everything, scarcely pausing – though let us in fact pause here – to say, Good Luck!

Melancholy Monument

A review of *The Complete Poems,* by Randall Jarrell. 1969.

RANDALL JARRELL was a romanticist of the generation which came to adulthood during the miserable 1930s. That is to say, he found himself as a young man in a society whose most active intellectual centers were dominated by the thought and style of T. S. Eliot and, behind him, Irving Babbitt. Jarrell reacted as did most of his young fellow poets: he launched into a search for a way out of the social and cultural order which seemed to him, and which was, superannuated. More than this, he launched – in spite of his southern politesse, for he was born in Nashville and graduated from Vanderbilt, the home of the Agrarians, Fugitives, and of southern élitism in general – with a radical eagerness as intense as that of any of his northern contemporaries. Among romanticists he was an especially pure example. He was what Jacques Barzun has called an *intrinsic* romanticist: a poet existing outside the primary epoch of romanticism who still exhibits the romanticist's primary characteristics.

What these characteristics are is open to question. But leaving aside the secondary characteristics, such as the romanticist's commitments to freedom, individualism, irrationalism, and so on, certainly one of his primary characteristics is his hang-up between man's power and man's misery, between the vision of glory and the experience of degradation. "Man is born free, and everywhere he is in chains." In his youth this is precisely the paradox that Jarrell saw in the world around him: at the top a culture oriented toward tradition and devoted to the methodical delectation of esthetic virtue, at the bottom a society sick in every member and vitiated by pain and injustice. As the 1930s advanced – Harlan County, Abyssinia, Detroit, Spain – the realities were unmistakable. But so were Jarrell's longings. For years the commonest locution in his poems was the phrase "and yet...," uttered sometimes wistfully, sometimes mordantly, sometimes in hollow despair.

To surmount this impasse between innocence and experience (using Blake's terms) the romanticist seeks a faith, or at least a synthesis, that will define and accommodate both sides of the paradox. Historically speaking, few have managed it, especially among poets. Probably the commonest way out has been through radical social action, based on Hegelian concepts of history. For poets a surer but much more difficult course has been the ascent from romantic agony to genuine tragic vision, which in turn destroys its own romantic base by imposing upon it the classical order of the tragic world – the world of fate and of Promethean pathos and steadfastness. The great example, of course, is Goethe. In our time we have the smaller but very instructive case of Theodore Roethke. He began with a verbal and mental style different from Jarrell's, yet with much the same poetic materials, the same view of nature and human reality; but he converted them into an at least sporadically consistent tragic vision. Roethke continued to write with more and more depth of feeling until he died, while Jarrell, almost exactly contemporary, dwindled away into fragments and exercises.

Not that Jarrell didn't try. Social action was effectively denied him, since his connection with the amorphous, self-doubting radicalism of the *Partisan Review* was doomed from the start to futility. Conventional religious faith was also apparently inaccessible to him. But he tried other means of escape, especially by pursuing romantic revulsion from experience to its logical ends in dream and fantasy. Time and again, especially in the poems of his middle years, he constructed elaborate dream visions, significantly Germanic – not to say Gothic – in style, from within which he looked out at the objective world and denounced it. But the stress of actuality always supervened. Jarrell was sane, excruciatingly sane, and he could never secure his dream beyond the limits of a few separate, though quite splendid, poems.

Similarly he tried, but only half-heartedly, to commit himself to the mystique of creative impunity, the cult of *l'homme d'esprit*, the anti-world of style and imagination; he tried to give himself, not to the meretricious élites of Gottfried Benn or Wyndham Lewis (he was too radical for that) but to the commonalty of alienated poets, descendants of Baudelaire who preserve themselves from social, moral, and metaphysical blight through the integrity of their autonomous creative endeavor. In a few passages he sounds surprisingly like Vachel Lindsay preaching the "gospel of beauty." But it is noteworthy that Jarrell's most consistent statement of this purist philosophy occurs in neither his poetry nor his criticism but in a story for children, *The Bat Poet*, which in spite of the skill and good taste evident in its telling remains basically a propagandistic fable intended to affirm the superiority, or at least the specialness, of the poet in the community of animals. Jarrell himself didn't believe it, or only half believed it. He could not forego the exquisite anguish of the romanticist's dual attachment to vision and reality, innocence and experience. In the end he was left in the wilderness of romantic nihilism with no base but sensibility.

The results are evident. In his criticism Jarrell gave us vibrant readings of individual poets, Frost, Williams, and others, but no theoretical statement of basic value. In the last twenty years of his poetry, although the dream poems and a few others are interesting, he fell more and more into fragmentary utterance, false starts, scraps and notes, and especially into set pieces – "story poems" and "character poems," updated Robert Frost – that lacked the verve of his youthful work. Then too there was the endless translating and retranslating of the German poets, especially Rilke. What Jarrell needed, I think, in order to write successfully was an occasion which gave him not only the enclosed reality of a particular episode but a chance to remove it to a certain distance from the complexity of the ordinary world; and the only sustained occasion of this kind which occurred in his life was World War II. Jarrell's war poems are his best in every sense. They are the most alive poetically, the most consistent thematically.

All this is what I have thought for some years, and in reading *The Complete Poems* I find it confirmed. The book would be a compendium at best. Here is Randall Jarrell complete and completed, the same who so enlivened our literary and social consciousnesses only a short time ago; at least the time must seem short to readers of my generation. Now he is gone, stuffed in a great fat tome, to be looked at and put away in the corner of a low shelf. Well, the poems deserve far better. Some of them are great.

The book contains all Jarrell's poems from his previous books, plus three additional sections: one for new work written between his last book and his death, a second for poems published in magazines but not previously collected, the third for earlier unpublished poems. It is, we are made to understand, complete. But this is the only book of its kind that I know in which we find no hint of the person upon whose authority we are to accept either its completeness or its other attributes, which seems odd. It has no editor as far as anyone can tell from reading the book or its dust jacket or the ancillary press releases from the publisher.

It gives us, however, a considerable bulk of poetry, in which the war poems are a distinct, superior unit. They are not many, perhaps thirty or forty altogether. But even if they were fewer they would be a remarkable achievement. How anyone can write while soldiering is difficult to understand; as someone who went through the war unable to write a word, I can only marvel. But Jarrell had been writing for nearly ten years before America entered the war. His early poems are sometimes mannered or imitative and often artificially opaque; but from the first, as nearly as one can tell, he wrote with ease. When the war came he already possessed a developed poetic vocabulary and a mastery of forms. Under the shock of war his mannerisms fell away and his basic skills came into concerted action. He began to write with stark, compressed lucidity.

Nowadays we commonly hear critics declare that World War II produced no memorable poetry. Even a critic as acute as George Steiner has said that the poetry of 1940–1945 is without "the control of remembrance achieved by Robert Graves or Sassoon" in 1914–1918 (see Steiner's *The Death of Tragedy*). To this I can only reply that if I know what "control of remembrance" means, in my experience the poems of Jarrell have it, and they have it preeminently. I am certain that other readers of my age, those who were there, find in these poems of soldiers and civilians, the dead, wounded, and displaced, the same truth that I do. And it is not merely the truth of Friday night at the vfw; old dogfaces may use their memory to corroborate the materials of Jarrell's poems, though few will do so, but the *truth* is *in* these poems – it is an esthetic presence.

Warfare gave Jarrell the antagonist he needed; not fate, not history, not the state, not metaphysical anxiety, but all these rolled into one – The War – that brute momentous force sweeping a bewildered generation into pathos, horror, and death. Today our young dissenters and resisters sometimes ask us why we didn't resist as they do, why we were willing to go along with the militarists. Unsuccessfully we try to explain that there were a number of reasons, but that in any event willingness had nothing to do with it. But we don't need to try any longer, it is all there in Jarrell's poems. The irresistibility of the war, the historical inexorability of it, the suffering of all its victims, Americans, Germans, Japanese – Jarrell wrote it down with equal understanding, equal sympathy. And he wrote it then, there, at that time and in those places, with power, spontaneity, and perfect conviction. Against what I have said already about his poetry, I must in basic honesty conclude with an amendment: in his war poems Randall Jarrell did rise, as if in spite of himself, to his moment of tragic vision, with its lucidity and starkness, in the "ordinary" occasions of life as a soldier.

Spenser and His Modern Critics

A review of *The Poetry of The Faerie Queene*, by Paul J. Alpers; *Spenser's Allegory of Justice in Book Five of The Fairie Queene*, by T. K. Dunseath; and *Reading Spenser: An Introduction to The Faerie Queene*, by Roger Sale. 1969.

WE WHO WERE brought up to literature by the great poets and critics of the years before mid-century are inclined to regard *The Fairie Queene* with disdain – the longest poem in English! that allegorical bore! interminable rhymes! ghastly pseudo-diction! – and hence to suspect its readers of callowness, pedantry, or worse. "The eccentric few," Eliot called them, while Leavis dismissed Spenser's poetry as "too simple a fact to need examining afresh." William Empson, that maverick, has been almost alone among recent British critics in his attention to the poem, which after all is the acknowledged British epic.

And though I may be wrong – I probably am but it doesn't matter, because my impression rather than my error is what signifies here – I cannot remember a single essay by a prominent American critic, Blackmur, Ransom, Tate, Burke, or anyone, which deals with Edmund Spenser.* Thus our disdain has a certain sanction, which we in turn magnify by projecting it backward. We have come now to look upon all Spenserians throughout literature as a breed apart, a secondary manifestation, inferior to the Shakespeareans, the Sons of Ben, or the admirers of Donne and Herbert. Not that we aren't aware of Shelley's enthusiasm, just as we may recall Milton's remarks in *Areopagitica* or Dryden's qualified approval in his essays; but these we easily wave aside. Consequently we are surprised to learn that Spenser, from a time well before his death until the present moment, has been the object of a vast critical attention, perhaps vaster, more varied, and more intelligent than that paid any other poet in English; and we are positively shocked to find that the poem itself, *The Faerie Queene*, is not only readable but downright enjoyable – the whole 35,000 lines of it.

What kind of poem is it? Certainly not the kind that many of us have been led to expect. First, it is not an ordinary allegory, not a piece of Aesopian fablery. Secondly, it is not dry-as-dust sermonizing, a versified *Pilgrim's Progress*. Thirdly, it is not an exercise in an antique mode, for although in some aspects it may be "the last poem of the Middle Ages," in most its spontaneity and contemporaneity are what strike the reader with greatest force.† Fourthly, it is not a prettified and excursive chunk of Renaissance pastoralism, a versified *Arcadia*. Fifthly, although it is imbued with Christian and even churchly concern, it is not pietistic, not in the least, but is secular in its outlook, a poem of great psychological realism. In short Fairy Land is not the dream country that we may have been led to believe from our generalized knowledge of late-Renaissance pastoralism, as in *A Midsummer*

---

* Of course I do not mean to slight C.S. Lewis in England or Rosamund Tuve in America (or anyone whom I have overlooked). But although Lewis has written at length and enthusiastically about Spenser, the purely literary cogency of what he says is impaired by the undisguised religious base of his judgment, or at least it is for me, while in the case of Tuve, her prominence has come only lately – mostly, alas, since her death.

† The still very common notion that Spenser's writing is overloaded with intentional archaisms was disproven some time ago. See B.R. McElderry's article, "Archaisms and Innovation in Spenser's Poetic Diction," PMLA 47 (1923), pp. 144–70.

Night's Dream. It is our land, hard, multiform, unsatisfactory, greatly and poignantly beautiful. It is where we are right now.

And so on and so on: it is easy to say what the poem is not, much harder to say what it is; which explains the long critical labor that has attended it. From the beginning people of sensibility have tried to define the poem and their own responses to it: Thomas Rymer, William Temple, Sir Kenelm Digby, and many others of the time; thence into the eighteenth century, John Hughes, John Upton, Thomas Warton, Richard Hurd; and the nineteenth and early twentieth, through all the changes and ranges of romantic impressionism and philological academicism. Much of this work is brilliant. I do not see how anyone who looks into even a little of it (which is as much as I have done) can fail to be struck by the human splendor of this love that only intelligence can display: so much warmth of heart engendered by great words on a printed page. I recommend, for instance, Thomas Warton's *Observations on the Fairy Queen of Spenser* (1752). Granted, parts of it seem laughable, especially where Warton seeks to account for Spenser's appeal in terms which will not embarrass his neoclassical devotion to the *Ars Poetica;* but elsewhere I was astonished to see Warton's depth of insight and the acuity of his readings; I believe that with respect to his methods at least, and very likely with respect to much of his substance, his work could be published today without apology. Then there is the Variorum edition of Spenser's works (Johns Hopkins, 1932). What its reputation among scholars may be I don't know, although they certainly rely on it. But for the general reader who wishes to have everything needed to take pleasure from *The Faerie Queene*, including imaginatively selected excerpts from all Spenserian criticism up to 1932, the Variorum is a blessing and a perfection.

My own experience of *The Faerie Queene* has been recent and intense. I had read only bits of it years ago, never the whole thing. Now I plunged in, and it was a marvelous adventure. One by one, very quickly, my preconceptions fell away. I found myself going on – and on and on and on – with all a voyager's satisfactions of sensible novelty. Not that I wasn't confused. *The Faerie Queene* must be one of the most mixed-up poems in the world. Characters disappear in mid-story and never return, totally unrelated episodes are juxtaposed, the plot (if you can call it a plot) is so loosely organized that no reader could remember all its parts; yet the movement of the verse sweeps everything before it, so that one reads in perfect contentment, overwhelmed by difficulties one is scarcely aware of. Many commentators speak of this, of being "entranced" or "carried away" by the poetry. But though I know what they mean I dislike their choice of terms, which seems to indicate that the reader is towed along by the poem in a state of shock. Nothing could be further from the case; one reads this poem actively, almost aggressively, hungrily. And in spite of the bulk there is no surfeit. One reads as one breathes, and neither poem nor atmosphere ever seems too much.

For my part the greatest difficulty was with the rhymes. Four thousand Spenserian stanzas! Most modern poets would quail at the thought of forty. And of course the well-known paucity of rhyme-sounds in English is at the root of the trouble. Sometimes I thought that if another stanza rolled into view with hight/pight/wight/night or sayd/ayd/apayd/upbrayd for its terminations, I'd heave the book in the fire. But this was usually when I had been reading for several hours and my strength was failing anyway; and as I read further I became less and less disturbed by the repeated rhymes, more and more appreciative not only of the need for such a stanza but of its suitability, elegance, and power; for only that stanza, with its intricate rhyme scheme and its total stop at the end, could impose order and limit on a poetic style which otherwise must be the most fluid ever conceived in English:

> High ouer hilles and ouer dales he fled,
>   As if the wind him on his winges had borne.
>   Ne banck nor bush could stay him, when he sped
>   His nimble feet, as treading still on thorne:
>   Griefe, and despight, and gealosie, and scorne
>   Did all the way him follow hard behind,
>   And he himselfe himselfe loath'd so forlorne,
>   So shamefully forlorne of womankind;
> That as a Snake, still lurked in his wounded mind.

> Still fled he forward, looking backward still,
>   Ne stayd his flight, nor fearefull agony,
>   Till that he came vnto a rockie hill,
>   Ouer the sea, suspended dreadfully,
>   That liuing creature it would terrify,

To looke adowne, or vpward to the hight:
From thence he threw himselfe dispiteously,
All desperate of his fore-damned spright,
That seem'd no helpe for him was left in liuing sight.

But through long anguish, and selfe-murdring thought
He was so wasted and forpined quight,
That all his substance was consum'd to nought,
And nothing left, but like an aery Spright,
That on the rockes he fell so flit and light,
That he thereby receiu'd no hurt at all,
But chaunced on a craggy cliff to light;
Whence he with crooked clawes so long did crall,
That at the last he found a caue with entrance small.

$$(3.10.55-57)$$

This is Malbecco's last flight, after the final loss of his beloved, faithless Hellenore, and shows him being transformed, in an action far more complex and subjective than anything in Ovid's *Metamorphoses*, into the eternal personification of *Gealosie*: good Spenserian verse, some of his best, strong, supple, economical, and perfectly clear in spite of the difficulty of the material; but parse it if you can. Spenser's syntax is a curious combination of formalism with informality, at once elaborate and casual, like nothing else in English.* His connectives are often merely that, all those *that's, whom's, wherein's,* and *whenas's* linking together illogical constructions, full of ambiguities.

Nought vnder heauen so strongly doth allure
The sence of man, and all his minde possesse,
As beauties louely baite, that doth procure
Great warriours oft their rigour to represse,
And mighty hands forget their manlinesse;
Drawne with the powre of an heart-robbing eye,
And wrapt in fetters of a golden tresse,
That can with melting pleasaunce mollifye
Their hardned hearts, enur'd to bloud and cruelty. $(5.7.1)$

---

* It approximates to "stream-of-consciousness" writing four centuries later.

Whose is the "heart-robbing eye," beauty's or the warriors'? Yet we hesitate not a moment in the reading, for the ambiguities are open and simple, like the flow of words, and never forced.

Fluidity and simultaneity, these are the qualities of Spenser's verse, giving us, in the four-hundred-year-old poem, a feeling of great presence; and isn't this exactly what our poets today are striving to achieve in their purposely fragmented writing? But because in the centuries since *The Faerie Queene* we have become so habituated to logical or pseudo-logical speech, their efforts seem mostly awkward and destructive – forced indeed. To Spenser it came naturally; and as I followed his verses I became more and more aware that what I was reading was essentially a modern poem.

This seems to be the statement, bizarre as it may appear, toward which the critics are reaching, toward which they have been reaching for two hundred years; though as usual they are chary about it. Of course the ambiguities of the verse and the uncertainties of the allegory have required a long period of groundwork in conventional explication and textual study. I suppose the pinnacle of this work, or one of the pinnacles, was Josephine Waters Bennett's *The Evolution of the Faerie Queene* (Chicago, 1942), a remarkable book. With immense learning Bennett put together all external evidence, historical, biographical, and literary, to reconstruct Spenser's writing methods during his twenty years of intermittent work on *The Faerie Queene*, and although some of her conjectures are doubtless farfetched, her general conclusion seems unimpeachable; namely, that Spenser did not write *seriatim*, as most previous critics had inferred, but instead "planned and wrote in episodes and narrative sequences which he fitted into his larger plans as best he could, replanning the whole, probably more than once, and rearranging and revising his materials as his plans matured." Certainly this is what any working poet today, after looking at the size and scope of the poem, would conclude offhand, though Bennett's argument, derived from wholly nonsubjective sources, is no less fascinating for that. In fact one point which I found offensive in the work of younger critics, who in the past decade have begun to approach *The Faerie Queene* from a new starting place, is their nearly unanimous scorn for Mrs. Bennett and her colleagues of thirty or forty years ago, especially since their attitude is so unnecessary: Bennett's conclusions and theirs are by no means incompatible. Even Paul

Alpers, who of all critics has least cause for a grudging view of his pre-
decessors, having produced a "pinnacle" himself, is not immune from
it. But that's the way the generations succeed one another in poetry as
well as criticism, and no doubt in every other domain. In the old days
you had to kill your father; now it's more likely to be your mother.

The title of Alpers's book, *The Poetry of the Faerie Queene*, is some-
what misleading because Alpers is not concerned primarily with
Spenser's verse, his prosody, diction, etc., but rather with his meaning.
Indirectly, however, the title is justified because Alpers finds the mean-
ing in the poetry. Is this simple-minded? Nevertheless Alpers is oper-
ating at a notch above anything in previous Spenserian criticism. Con-
sider the preconceptions which he must knock down in order to make
his argument; for him the meaning is not in the narrative sequence, not
in the fiction, not in the sermonizing, not in the play of character, not in
the pictorial or iconographic representations, and neither in the moral
nor in the historical allegory; all of which have been cornerstones of
prior Spenserian exegesis. Instead Alpers argues that the meaning is in
the poetry; i.e. in the figures and formulas that Spenser has chosen to
express the values about which his feelings cluster. Alpers writes: "For
Spenser the meanings of locutions and formulas are inherent in them,
and are as independent of a putative speaker as they are independent
of specific dramatic situations within the poem." In short the poem is
not its explicit content but its rhetoric, and its meaning is a psychologi-
cal meaning, a shifting self-elaboration of human attitudes and states of
feeling arising in and from the conflict of values expressed in the
poem's verbal flow. It is in the mind of the reader, or somewhere near
it. It ascends above the poem, so to speak, and floats there like a luster
between the reader and the obscure actions of the narrative. "The
poetry is a mode of understanding, not of experience."

Consider the typical "event" in *The Faerie Queene*. A knight under-
takes a quest, the achievement of which will represent his attainment of
a particular virtue: holiness, temperance, etc. On the way he is beset by
misadventures, usually involving combat with other knights or with
dragons or monsters. Now three points must be made. First, these
"actions" are perfunctorily described and their outcome is never in
doubt; sometimes the descriptions are so vague, so detached from the
narrative fiction, that if we read them literally we have hardly any idea
of what is happening. Secondly, the opposing knights or monsters are

almost always personifications of weaknesses within the hero's own personality, which he must overcome in order to attain his quest. Thirdly, the hero himself is a personification, never a character; at best a generalized human force, part of the fabric of social and metaphysical destiny in which all our emotional values take form. Putting these three observations together, Alpers shows that the meaning of the poem, or the poem itself in the fullest sense, moves above and around these token actions with a fluidity which exactly corresponds to the fluidity of the verse. It is in effect a modern poem, a meditative lyric, whose meaning, or value, is engendered not in its objects or symbols but in its shifting patterns of rhetoric.

Of course Alpers overstates his case, as he must if he is to differentiate clearly between what he is doing and what has been done before. Actually it would be strange indeed if Spenser had constructed his labyrinthine allegory for no purpose but to sustain his word-spinning; surely *some* of the meaning is allegorical. But Alpers has performed a great service in showing how the full meaning escapes the allegory. For by 1580 no allegory, even Spenser's, could any longer support the complex feelings in the minds and hearts of Renaissance civilization, and the pressure of this excess of feeling was precisely what induced the human overreaching that we now call poetry in the full sense of the term, viz. the *creative* use of language. Poetry entails belief; its growth is a function of declining traditional faith, or alternatively, a displacement of faith into new (and human) sources of creative energy. Thus we have *The Faerie Queene*, a modern poem, a very human and existential poem, and above all an accessible poem. And thus we acquire a weapon to use against the whole tribe of critics who would deny our access through their scholarly mystifications, the allegorists, numerologists, iconographers, and others who insist on the poem's obscurity or specialness. Of these the latest is Frank Kermode, who has argued brilliantly that Spenser's conscious aim was to conceal his meaning – that Spenser was in love with Queen Elizabeth or something equally problematical – just as the Provençal poets, according to Denis de Rougemont, made their erotic poetry into concealed analogues of the heretical Albigensian liturgy. But this is brilliance wasted; for whatever may be the case with the troubadours, we know from immediate experience of the poem that Spenser's purpose was the opposite of esoteric. His whole attitude is a plea for easy understanding, a plea whose earnestness cannot be mistaken, and his poem, though assuredly complex, is as open as the skies.

Another recent and helpful book is T. K. Dunseath's *Spenser's Allegory of Justice in Book Five of The Faerie Queene*. Dunseath sets out to rehabilitate the fifth book from the nearly universal deprecations of previous critics, who have found the quality of writing in Book Five, and in the latter parts of the poem generally, a falling off from that of the earlier books, and who have complained of the excessive bloodthirstiness of Artegall and Talus as they pursue their quest for justice. As to the former, I myself was conscious of no decline in Spenser's power as I read into the second half of the poem, although I noticed a change of tone. On the contrary I felt the writing of the last three books to be better and more lively and varied than that of the first three, although in individual passages the judgment would not hold up. Indeed for my taste the opening canto of Book Four contains the most versatile and workmanlike narrative writing of the entire poem. At the same time in Book Five I was shocked, I confess, by the way Artegall and Talus, who is less a "gentle squire," on the pattern of earlier episodes, than Artegall's henchman and enforcer, lop off heads and push people over cliffs and spread decimation in their path, all in the name of justice; and I was shocked also by Spenser's virulent suppression of libertarian political concepts. But I overcame my shock quickly. We must remember that if Spenser was a true Renaissance man, implanted with the idea of the Prince, his only alternative in late sixteenth-century England would have been some form of sectarian and puritanical separatism, which could scarcely have produced *The Faerie Queene*. Dunseath, shrewdly and convincingly, analyzes each of Artegall's adventures to show how the knight purifies himself of various aspects of injustice, until he becomes what his name implies: Artegall, Arthur's Equal – a point previous critics seem not to have appreciated. Thereafter the two, Artegall and Prince Arthur, actually join forces to complete their quest together. This tells us a good deal, not only about Artegall, but about the shadowy figure of Arthur himself, both here and elsewhere in the poem. Spenser has introduced Arthur into each book as the ultimate masculine representative of generalized virtue, or what Spenser calls magnificence (magnanimity); but by the time he came to Book Five he had clearly begun to regard justice, not magnificence or the more chivalric virtues of holiness or chastity, as the great subsuming virtue, and Arthur/Artegall as its great champion. This strongly reinforces the secular and existential meaning of the entire poem and gives us a clearer notion of its structure. For if we must impose a "structure" on the poem that Spenser left unfinished – he had originally contemplated twelve books, or possibly twenty-four – then it seems to me that the first five books make a natural unit. In the fifth book, as Dunseath points out, all the previously unfinished business of the poem is brought to an end: the marriage of Florimell and Marinell, the betrothal of Britomart and Artegall, the conclusion of many secondary love quests, the final unmasking of Duessa, the recovery of Guyon's horse and Florimell's girdle, the humiliation of Braggadochio, the dissolution of False Florimell, etc. Book Five, the Legend of Justice, is the end and apex of the poem's entire opening thrust, in other words, and Book Six, with its new material and its excursion into pastoralism, is like an epilogue. In a surprising number of ways Spenser's Book Six is analogous to Shakespeare's *Tempest*.

One point which Dunseath in his scholarly reserve fails to make is the clear application of Book Five to ourselves. We can read it, and we do, far more sympathetically than other readers of the past century have read it. Spenser, we are told, wrote most of Book Five after he had returned to Ireland from a visit to England in 1590, a visit during which he had been greatly disappointed not only in his personal ambitions but in what he saw at Court. The dreams of the early Elizabethan years, dreams of a great and glorious and virtuous realm which Spenser had taken with him to Ireland long before, had now vanished, replaced by venality and corruption and bitter dissension in the ruling hierarchy. Spenser must have been writing in a frame of mind very similar to ours. We too need only look around to see that in a land without justice no other virtue, public or private, can flourish long; we too are deeply aware of the need for action. I hope we can do without Talus, and perhaps even without Artegall in the hesitant phases of his quest, but can we carry on much longer without an Arthur? Our political corruption and social injustice are overwhelmingly manifest, and many passages of Book Five strike home to us with force.

Dunseath is careful in his choice of terms: Book Five is a culmination, not a dénouement. In this undramatic poetry there can be no climax of involvement. When Dunseath says that Spenser's "is a poetry of awareness, not resolution," we are reminded of Alpers's statement that "the poetry is a mode of understanding, not of experience." This is the dominant theme of the new Spenserian criticism. It is the controlling idea, for instance, in Roger Sale's *Reading Spenser: An Introduction to The Faerie Queene*, which is a small book, satisfactory as far as it goes and in effect a reduction of much material in Alpers's book; but I wonder if, in the case of *The Faerie Queene*, these introductions, guides, and pedagogical manuals serve a purpose. I believe that even for rather inexperienced readers the best course is to plunge directly into the poem. Plunge in and keep going. And the same applies to the criticism: we should forego introductions and begin with one of the "pinnacles," Alpers or Bennett or some other, it makes no difference; quickly one book will lead to the rest. Nor should we ignore the criticism, which is not only fascinating in itself but essential to the poem. Because *The Faerie Queene* is a mode of understanding first of all, and because understanding functions on many levels and from many points of view, no single reader working on his or her own can hope to discern more than a small part of the poem's meaning. At the same time the criticism is necessarily held close to the poem by the nature of the task, since here our understanding is wholly verbal and the poetry is everything; criticism cannot stray far into speculative generalization nor distract us from the poem's splendor. More than two hundred years ago Warton concluded his *Observations* by writing: "Much of the pleasure that Spenser experienced in composing the *Fairy Queen*, must, in some measure, be shared by his commentator; and the critic, on this occasion, may speak in the words, and with the rapture, of the poet." I too can think of no conclusion more fitting than to borrow, with Warton, those words and that rapture.

> *The waies, through which my weary steps I guyde*
>   *In this delightfull land of Faery,*
>   *Are so exceeding spacious and wyde,*
>   *And sprinckled with such sweet variety*
>   *Of all that pleasaunt is to eare or eye,*
>   *That I, nigh ravisht with rare thoughts delight,*
>   *My tedious travell doe forget thereby;*
>   *And, when I gin to feele decay of might,*
> *It strength to me supplies, and chears my dulled spright.*

                                                              (6.1.1)

🐦 . . . .

The Writer's Situation

A contribution to a symposium published in *New American Review*, April 1970, edited by Theodore Solotaroff.

1. WHY DO YOU continue to write? What purpose does your work serve? Do you feel yourself part of a rear-guard action in the service of a declining tradition? Has your sense of vocation altered significantly in recent years?

2. Do you believe that art and politics should be kept apart? Has this belief changed or grown more complicated during the past decade? What influence has the politicization of life during this period had on your work?

3. What are the main creative opportunities and problems that attract and beset you in your work? Which movements, tendencies, writers, if any, do you find yourself identifying with or supporting? Which ones do you oppose?

4. Has writing entered a "postmodern" era, in which the relevance of the great modern writers (Joyce, Eliot, Mann, Faulkner, et al.) has declined? If so, what seem to be the literary principles of the postmodern age? If not, what principles of modernism are still dominant and valuable?

5. Has there been a general collapse of literary standards in recent years? Are you conscious of a conflict between your past standards and your present ones?

6. Have literary criticism and journalism kept pace with, and faith with, the best fiction, poetry, and drama produced in the sixties?

Speaking personally – I hope pertinently – your questionnaire is embarrassing.

1. I'm damned if I know why I continue to write. I don't think I'd know in the best of circumstances, but right now I'm particularly embarrassed because a few months ago I quit. Resolved: no more. My poetry was a dead end, themes scrambled and uncertain, sense of a creative locus hopelessly lost: no diction, no instinct for form. I would cease, if not forever at least for a good long time; to let the internal forces recompose themselves. But within days I was at it again, secretly,

little nips like an alcoholic housewife's, but then more and more openly; until now, being pressed for income, I've even begun sending out a few poems to the magazines. I suppose my experience is any poet's. On the rottenest day, when my head aches and my allergies rage, when the sky drips snow likes rags of underwear, the poem occurs. Sometimes whole strings of them, flung on paper, scraps to be sorted and studied afterward. I conclude that part of my mind, the central, most important part, thinks poetically, and can think no other way. Good or bad, the poems must take form as long as the mind is functioning at all.

Sense of vocation? I haven't any, not with respect to poetry. In reviewing and editing, yes. There my sense of vocation, or at least of obligation, is strong; obligation to other writers, to editors and publishers, to the cultural mechanism at large – to keep it going and still unrigidified, so it may serve young poets as they come on and contribute to its essential, usually overlooked ingredient in our civilization. Paradoxically, in bread-and-butter writing I am an idealist, but in creative work a pragmatist. My poetry serves no one but myself; other service is incidental, a byproduct. My poetry is what has brought me, it almost alone, through a life too often shaped by illness, poverty, isolation, and other perplexities. At root I see no distinction between poetry and philosophy; at root I see no distinctions among any of the necessitous activities of human self-consciousness in face with its own fearsome being.

I serve no tradition, even the one I am fond of. And if that is declining, it will ascend again, no doubt with a different aspect. Tradition: a misused word. The thing itself, what the word stands for, does not exist. It is a myth, and like all myths it cannot die. It may go to sleep, like the princess of the thorny rose, and during its slumber extraordinary changes may occur; but as long as human sensibility continues, someone will always come to kiss it awake again.

2. Here also I am embarrassed, because I must seem to brag. I am a radical born and bred, from a long line of the same, and have *always* believed that art and politics cannot be kept apart. I began by thinking this was taken for granted – the elder poets seemed to confirm it – only to discover it was not. More than ten years ago when I wrote a piece for *The Nation* insisting that poetry must incorporate specific social, economic, and political materials, my friends, including some who are

now among the foremost radical poets, were appalled and even fright-
ened, as if I had attacked the roots of art. They demanded that we, as
poets, maintain our "purity," not seeing that purity in their sense
means esthetic death.

Two points need to be made. First, what I was saying then was said
not for politics' sake, but for art's. I doubt that politics needs art, cer-
tainly not for its immediate ends. Propaganda and art have no real
points of contact; and if art sometimes becomes politically effective, as
happens more often than many people think, so much the better. But
art needs politics, just as it needs the other elements of life – sex, meta-
physics, the natural world, and so on. Art without politics is a lie, in
bad faith with itself. But this has an important corollary. Many poets
today are going around saying the need of the times is for this or that
kind of art; we must all become more and more radicalized, we must
fracture tradition, form, even language itself. But this is just the kind of
prescriptive criticism I deplore. Let each poet speak for himself or her-
self, let each say what *his* or *her* poetry needs, not mine. Art may not be
autonomous, as the New Critics tried to make it, but it is autochtho-
nous: it inhabits its own territory. Art needs life, all life; but as servant,
not master, as material, not exemplary form. Many of us are excluded
by personal circumstances from political activism, but our experience
is no less valid poetically than other people's. Art which shapes itself
to the "need of the times" may turn out to be no art at all.

Second, if my personal radicalism has been consistent from the be-
ginning, there has been nevertheless a change in my understanding of
poetic means. Twenty years ago I was greatly puzzled by the question
of how to break into the autonomous poem of the forties and early
fifties with my radical concern. I was impressed by the way Pound's
Cantos fell apart when he introduced specifically political argument.
Not only that – for one could, and I did, say that this was caused by the
antihuman and hence antipoetic quality of what Pound was arguing – I
was also impressed by the way ninety-nine percent of the rest of the
political poetry of the thirties, most of which had been written by poets
whose hearts were in the right place, had similarly fallen apart. My
own early political experiments were mostly dismal, not poems at all
but rants and curses. Now we have had a decade rich in further experi-
ments, by poets of every formal persuasion, and the problem no longer
bothers us. The political content of poetry is seen to be quite at ease in

its esthetic function. We wonder why we were ever puzzled. But we were, and the strides we have taken in this respect are worth noting. Some critic should study them.

As I say, art serves neither the tradition nor itself nor the times; it serves the artist, the needy human creator. And in so doing, I believe, it is faithful to both itself and mankind at large. The tradition evolves willy-nilly; it takes care of itself. And all this is perfectly congruous with what LeRoi Jones (our Shelley) means when he says that poetry is revolution.

3. Recently I had the job of assembling a large anthology of twentieth-century American poetry. To help with the notes I sent a questionnaire to all its living contributors. One question was similar to this of yours, about movements, schools, affinities, etc. But I think without exception the poets replied that they belonged, each one, to no movement whatever and were totally independent of any groups or associations; and this was just as true of those whom we all unhesitatingly identify with particular factions as it was of the genuine mavericks. Apparently poets are people: they don't like being classified.

For years I have been called an "academic" (even though I've lived in the backwoods exclusively, far from the academy), and for years I've resented it.

In truth I think formal distinctions among poets are beginning to recede, even in popular taste, and are being supplanted by questions of faith, essence, or thematic preoccupation. We see that the Black Mountain poets, for example, are much closer to some academic poets than was previously thought. From dissimilar origins and by disparate routes, the poets converge. For myself I know that the problems of poetry which hold my attention are the problems of this epoch of life, and that they preoccupy equally the sensibilities of my friends who share my general attitudes, Denise Levertov, Adrienne Rich, Galway Kinnell, J.V. Cunningham, and then many others not known to me personally. Naturally we write about these problems in different ways, using different characteristic modes and voices, just as we have differently colored eyes, different tastes in food, and different illnesses. But what holds us together and distinguishes us from others who do not share our general attitudes (such as the doctrinaire religious poets, the poets of wit, or the pop poets) is far greater and stronger than what separates us.

I don't mean to downgrade problems of form, which are the driving force. For me, although I am as sure as anyone that conventional English prosody has been played out (except in the hands of a few very strong, idiosyncratic poets), rhyme is still close to the verbal heart of poetry, at least Western poetry, and measure is essential: identifiable and *predictable* measure. I underscore predictable. This, in my judgment, is what measure means: the reader's (listener's) ability to anticipate the *next* beat, as one does in music. To find ways to use these components without stiffness and without lapsing into specious diction is my technical problem. But it is inescapably technical, and I don't think it warrants much discussion outside the workroom.

...Am I being evasive? Now, later, while retyping my reply, I have second thoughts. If the formal problem is technical, and hence fundamentally private, this doesn't make it any less tough; and tougher still is the thematic problem, the sense of breakup and confusion in poetic attitudes. I don't know which causative factors are personal and which are external. Certainly the personal ones are important: my reaching a difficult age (forty-eight) for artists, my awareness of faltering strength and talent, my knowledge that what I had to say in the first half of my life has now been said, if not as well as I wish, then at least in forms which I despair of bettering, and other factors too private to mention. But the external factor is important too, this extraordinary acceleration of sociocultural change through which we are living. Every day my mail brings books and magazines that open new perspectives of form and experience. The creative opportunities, as you call them, are indeed great. The danger is that insecure poets will be paralyzed, not liberated. I can't assess all these considerations. But I do know that they were what made me quit, and that if I have resumed writing sooner than I expected, nevertheless I have lost the sense of continuity, the sense of moving through an integrated personal myth, which I once had and which I think is the most important property any poet can possess. Now ideas for poems come at me like bullets flying from all directions; they are gratifyingly many, but they come from disparate sources and are often contradictory, in both form and substance, leaving me overwhelmed, bewildered, and scared. And I suspect many poets my age feel the same way.

4. A huge topic. I've written about it for years, but in fragments, scattered reviews and essays, always lacking the opportunity (and perhaps the courage) to attack it systematically. In short: yes. Certainly

writing since 1945 is new, certainly the great writers of the earlier period have less relevance for us than they once did.

Say that with Nietzsche came the final and total collapse of traditional systems of value, replaced for a while by an amorphous esthetic optimism, which in turn collapsed with World War I. The writers who began work then began in a void – nihilism, absence of values. (The Lost Generation.) Hence they sought substitutions for reality, some by turning backward (Eliot and his followers), but many by asserting the antireality of art. It sprang from the Yellow-Book estheticism of the nineties, with affinities in Renaissance and romantic notions of the "eternity" of poetry; it was called by many names, the "revolution of the word" (as in Jolas's *transition*), the Jamesian or Flaubertian apotheosis of style, and so on. It had its root in Kantian esthetics, in Coleridge's concept of "imagination," but in essence it was an attempt to create, by sheer power of human invention, a new plane of existence in artistic form upon which the search for value, especially the search for identity, could proceed. Many, like Yeats and Mann, participated only tangentially; others, like Pound, Eliot, and Joyce, were nearer the main thrust, though probably never conscious of its full implications; a few, like Wyndham Lewis, Céline, and Gottfried Benn, were conscious advocates; and it is no mistake that these last three were all friendly to Hitler's regime. Benn was the clearest, with his introduction of the "phenotype," a new human being, a mutant who could function solely in terms of style.

Well, these hopes were disappointed in the second war. Reality, real reality, with its ovens, the *gauleiter's* deportation orders, its disregard for style, its passionate misery, supervened. The structural finesse of *Finnegans Wake*, the imaginative concision of *La jeune parque*, the stylistic autonomy of *Nightwood* or *Les enfants terribles*, were seen to be no antidotes to the world as it is. Contritely, artists turned back toward reality, back toward human rather than artistic responsibility.

Against all this imagine the larger movement which began a century ago, more or less, and which has intensified noticeably in the past two decades. Call it existentialism if you will; the term is not right, but no one has thought of a better. Do not, however, call it a philosophy, though elements of it have been adumbrated by technically trained philosophers. It is, to my mind, a great shift of human sensibility, comparable to medieval theism or Renaissance humanism, and like them it entails a change in our conception of our own human place in reality. If theism was anthropomorphic, if humanism was anthropocentric, then our era is anthropo-eccentric; we exist on the edge of reality. This is no intellectualization, but a profound and popular ethologic retooling. The consequent shift of values is immense. Now we recognize that in meaninglessness we are our own sole value, and that art is our chief instrument in the imaginative creation of this value, the turning of human experience into human meaning, the making of selves.

All terribly oversimplified; more than that, hypothetical. Yet I believe it could be documented by a mind sufficiently encyclopedic. And the result in American poetry of the past fifteen years is clear to me, cutting across every division, from Lowell to Olsen, from Berryman to Ginsberg. The emphasis is on the life, no longer on the self-contained "work of art," and we have, not mere autobiography, not mere "confession," but life coming into being on the page, fragment by fragment. Hence the great literary forms break down, style becomes functional again. Our former obsessive idea of the masterpiece disappears. The random poem, open-ended and fragmentary, becomes the norm: we see it everywhere. And this leads directly to today's concepts of radical and revolutionary anti-poetry, the poem considered solely as an *act* of fragmentation. There is a danger in this, as I have said above. We may lose the poem altogether, and I think it is important at this point to remember that the esthetic function *in se* is still legitimate, still indispensable.

Of course many writers are working yet in the essential prewar modes, especially novelists hung up on the ideas of Robbe-Grillet and Nathalie Sarraute – the persisting modernists. We see writers like John Barth and John Fowles fooling away their talents in endless novelistic puzzles, a pastime which seems to have reached an ultimate reduction – I hope it's ultimate – in *Word Rain* by Madeline Gins. But American poets, I'm glad to say, have been almost entirely free from this kind of formalistic irresponsibility. They are artists, yes; resolutely so; but artists acknowledging a participatory rather than exclusionary function. Not popular artists, not "people's poets" or "proletarian poets," but poets writing both from and for the eternal, suprapoetic, existential crisis – for all of us.

What principles of modernism are still dominant and valuable? I don't know about principles; after what I've said it should be clear that

I think we must understand the "principles" of the great prewar writers in ways that most of those writers themselves did not and could not. But once we have said this, their value remains enormous. Pound, Eliot, Joyce, Mann, and the rest: they were great writers, giants. For one thing they taught us to read. For another they taught us to write. What more can one ask?

Optimism is untrustworthy. Yet I believe we are living in the early phase of an era which may become one of the most extraordinary episodes in human evolution, the justification at last of self-conscious intelligence in its own terms, if only we can find means to contain our own technology and keep from being blown up.

5. No. And no. Quite the contrary. Standards are tough today, and awareness of them is widespread. I see slipshod writing among young poets, but I'd say proportionately less now than I saw twenty years ago when I was editing *Poetry*.

6. I read so little criticism I'm hardly qualified to comment. What I do read is discouraging. Older critics are still trapped in the irrelevant, insoluble impasse of Kantian divisiveness, while the younger are so ill-informed historically that they cannot conceptualize our present state of the arts. To my mind the best American criticism is still Kenneth Burke's; his books are crammed with leads that younger writers ought to be following. As for journalism, that's something else again. I have been a newspaperman, like my father and grandfather before me, and I have a higher regard for the profession than most of my friends have; but I don't believe its problems enter the present discussion.

A Focus, a Crown

A review of *Autobiography*, by Louis Zukofsky. 1970.

RECENTLY, after years of neglect, the poet Louis Zukofsky, whose *Autobiography* is one of this year's most valuable literary events, has come into a certain vogue, especially among younger writers known as the Black Mountain poets and their followers. They find in him a poet new and modern and yet their elder, a poet whom they have discovered, a poet who for a long time has been doing more or less what they themselves wish to do, doing it in their style and manner. They are right, of course, although Zukofsky wasn't quite all that undiscovered before they came along.

He began writing seriously in the 1920s, influenced by two older poets who soon became his friends, Ezra Pound and William Carlos Williams. In 1927 he began his major work, a poetic sequence called simply "A," which is still in progress. During the thirties he became the effective leader of a group of New York poets called the Objectivists; they were known for a time, but were then eclipsed by the massive popularity of Eliot, Yeats, and the American poets dominated by European and symbolist influences. Zukofsky continued at work in virtual darkness. He produced a couple of anthologies, a long and deeply inquiring study of Shakespeare, an extraordinary and controversial translation of the poetry of Catullus, and a steady stream of new poems.

Now we have his *Autobiography*. Though it is in some respects the most fragile of his works, depending for its very existence upon the prior existence of the others, and though it will probably attract fewer readers than the rest of his books, still it seems to me the purest of them all. It is like the topmost jewel in a crown. Without the support of the other jewels it might be merely an emptiness or a glitter; but in its setting it draws together the luster of the whole, making a formal focus and apex, a point of concentration and particular lucidity.

First, however, the book must be described, for it is scarcely a conventional autobiography. It comprises fifteen short poems reprinted from Zukofsky's other books and set to music by the composer Celia Zukofsky, the poet's wife, who has appeared in most of his other works and has collaborated on several of them. This short collection is prefaced with a short note and interspersed with five even shorter paragraphs. These paragraphs set forth a few, very few, public facts of Zukofsky's life, the barest possible summary, written in prose that is undistinguished to the point of multiple clichés and stiff journalistic syntax, such as you might find in any dictionary of biography.

Readers acquainted with the originality of Zukofsky's other prose will not doubt that this effect is intentional, and to them his implication will be clear: the poet's life, beyond these few publicly ascertainable facts, is his own affair, while his real autobiography, meaning the aspects of his mind and feeling which we all deserve and need to share, is his poetry. More than that, his truest autobiography is these poems set to music.

Thus we have a very pure and lucky example of a work whose form embodies its meaning, whose form *is* its meaning. Take the merest externals and put them together: the title (*Autobiography*), the authorship (man and wife), and the main text (poems and music). These data incorporate the themes of all Zukofsky's writing from the beginning. Life is a function of art, that is to say, of the creative imagination making from experience the structures of significant feeling which we call personalities. Its form is fundamentally conjugal – conjugated, joined. And its concrete enduring manifestation is music, toward which all other arts and all significant actions incline as toward their fulfillment. Finally and above all, the force, the motive energy, is love. These are crude statements, explicit and limited. But they are as near as statement can come to the essential meaning, implicit and unlimited, of the *Autobiography*, which itself makes no statements. It exists. It is at one with itself, without abstraction. It is its own fullness and resonance of meaning.

In short it is an emblem. Normally we do not think of emblems in the traditional sense as products of individual genius, but rather as broadly cultural artifacts, things slowly evolved from the common mythopoeic mind. Many such artifacts are still fixed in our consciousness, in spite of our state of cultural erosion. Zukofsky's *Autobiography* is smaller than most of these, as we should expect since it is of one mind's making, but it shares their clarity and resonance within simplicity. It could only have been made by an intense imagination engaged for a long time with its own materials.

Music has always been a large part of Zukofsky's poetry, both linguistically and thematically. One of my favorite passages is this prologue to a longer poem, here called "A Song for the Year's End" (addressed to the poet's wife and son – Paul Zukofsky, who is a concert violinist – and if the substance seems fuzzy in extract, it makes perfect sense in the larger context):

> *Daughter of music*
> *and her sweet son*
> *so that none rule*
> *the dew to his own hurt*

with the year's last sigh
awake
the starry sky and bird.

Once in another connection I wrote that the sounds of this poem could be analyzed if one were sufficiently clever and patient. Presumably, with the techniques of modern phonemics, a chart of them could be made. But it would still be only a chart, however complex, and it would still be only approximate. We know how these sounds work in our mouths; we could, with our astonishing clinical methods, teach a deaf person to say them; but we do not know and may never know how they work in our verbal imaginations, which have been formed from far too many unknown cultural influences ever to be tabulated. We can only declare that these sounds do work.

There are rhymes in the poem obviously, and assonances and consonances, but these are not the music of it. Music is made, not from repetition - boom, boom, boom – but from variance within repetition; in other words from change, from modulation. *Music-rule-dew-hurt-year's-starry-bird:* it is a unique and wonderfully satisfying modulation of sounds. And it is organized by a rhythmic structure, in line-length and accent, which is perfectly complementary and again unique and satisfying. These are a few, but only a few, of this short poem's musical elements.

And I think they are exactly brought out in Celia Zukofsky's setting, for four voices with piano accompaniment. I cannot speak technically about this. I have played the parts on my clarinet and have sung them to myself, which is the best I can do in my circumstances. The music is grave but not solemn, with perhaps a more propulsive feeling than the words alone suggest. Its tonal movement is descending, then ascending, in minor harmonies, and a somewhat syncopated effect comes from the different timings of words in treble and bass. I like it very much. It seems an effective piece of music in itself, and a combining of conscious modern musical experience with strong feeling for the tradition of song, especially the seventeenth-century tradition.

As I have said, Zukofsky's young admirers are perfectly right when they insist that he is a distinctly contemporary poet, their fit comrade-in-arms, not only with respect to verbal practice, since most of his work is more vigorously contemporary in tone than the intentionally archaic passage I have quoted, but especially with respect to his attitudes toward experience, some of which prefigured by two decades the wave of European existentialism that came to us after World War II.

But Zukofsky is vigorously traditional as well. I am certain he would have no truck with the young people's antagonism to learning even if probably he does, like them, decry our educational methods. I do not see, for example, how anyone whose ear is attuned to the evolution of English song from Shakespeare to Campion to Dowland to Milton's *Comus* can fail to recognize the relationship between that and the passage I have quoted or many others I might have quoted, even though Zukofsky rarely uses standard rhyme and meter; and I believe an analogue also exists to elements of the Jewish lyrical tradition.

Zukofsky is deep, implicitly and explicitly, in the literary historical matrix. I hope young poets will see this, and see that it in no way weakens, but on the contrary strengthens, his essential humane relevance. To put it another way, the real history of literature is the history of love.

Perhaps I was wrong to suggest that because this book derives from Zukofsky's others it will have fewer readers. In another sense it is complete in itself, needing only the warmth of blooded, breathy voices for its fulfillment. The express addition of music to these texts may attract readers who would not be drawn to the poetry alone, reversing the process I first had in mind. I hope so. Certainly I recommend these songs to all amateur singers and instrumentalists, especially recorder players. The music is easy, yet different and appealing. And why not recommend them to professionals too? I should be most grateful for a recording by performers who could do these songs full justice.

Whether or not this book is widely used, however, or even if I (heaven forbid) should be the only person who ever uses it, Louis and Celia Zukofsky's *Autobiography* is here – this life made in collaboration and fully achieved, a verifiable human success in our present doleful balance of human failure.

✒ . . . .

Poet of Civility

A review of *Collected Shorter Poems, 1927–1957,* by W.H. Auden. 1970.

THIS NEW *Collected Shorter Poems* supplants Auden's unsatisfactory *Collected Poetry* of 1945 in at least three ways. First, it offers a longer span of Auden's work, thirty years in all. Second, it gives us the poems in chronological arrangement. Third, it presumably contains Auden's final accounting for the years in question, since a number of previously collected poems have been left out and many have been revised. I shall confine my remarks to these three heads.

1. The *Collected Shorter* contains three hundred poems, which comprise Auden's central achievement. His long poems, like *The Sea and the Mirror* and *The Age of Anxiety,* are omitted, and of course one must look elsewhere for the plays, librettos, essays, travel sketches, polemics, and so on. But these other works are – and most were intended to be – ancillary to the short poems, which means that the *Collected Shorter* is the book upon which Auden's reputation will chiefly rest in the long run. Not that it is complete; Auden is still at work and in any case he has cut off the collection at 1957, explaining in the foreword that this was the year when, owing to a shift of his summer residence from Italy to Austria, his work entered a new phase. (Like most of us, he apparently writes his poetry on vacation.) Everywhere in this book, however, Auden's modest, scrupulous view of his own work is evident, so that one suspects his real reason for excluding his work of the past ten years all the poems from *About the House* (1965) and whatever others have appeared in periodicals since then – is his feeling that he is still too close to it to judge it properly.

2. The arrangement of poems in the 1945 *Collected* was frankly miserable; alphabetical in order of first lines, a jumble of early by late, comic by elegiac, didactic by erotic. It gave the reader no impression whatever of Auden's development. The new arrangement, chronological as it should be, is far handier. In a few cases Auden has departed from chronology even here. The sequence called *Horae Canonicae,* for example, his parabolic meditations on the theme of Good Friday writ-

ten in the late forties and early fifties, is displaced to the very end of the book, no doubt as a sign that Auden considers it his best poem, or at any rate the poem whose impact he prefers to leave in the reader's mind. But all told the order is reliably chronological, and it reveals a consistent evolution. The changes of Auden's style that had seemed abrupt when they occurred now look like natural transitions, so that from the entire span we receive a clearer impression than ever of the role Auden has played; doubtless an unconscious role at first, but then, I think, as the years passed, an ever more conscious one. What he attempted was the assimilation of the specific English literary tradition to the modern poetic revolution. Put another way, it was the restoration of orderly flow to the mainstream of English poetry after the interruptive activities of the Pound-Eliot generation, yet without abandoning their insights; and all for the sake, probably, less of the specific literary mainstream itself than of the values carried by it: civil speech, social progressivism, philosophical humanism, enjoyment as a primary component of esthetic theory, intelligence, and the functionally corrective place of art in society. It is not after all the outlanders of English literature with whom we associate Auden, the Blakes and Chattertons; instead his roots are in the public, professional, cosmopolitan tradition from Dryden to Bridges and Masefield. To revitalize the values of this tradition, to modernize them, and enforce them against the pandemonium of social disruption, successive Fascist wars, and British cultural complacency – this was his work. And his knowledge of his own relationship to the English mainstream was not altered by his need to write more and more from a position of dissent. (See the poem called "We Too Had Known Golden Hours.") It was exasperating work, and actually drove him away from England while he was still a young man. Yet has there ever been a less successful expatriation? To this day, after nearly thirty years of living abroad, Auden remains the English man of letters par excellence.

3. From these unpromising, because so miscellaneous, sources, namely, the fragments of English formalist tradition, the liberating impulses of modern prosody, the vocabulary of Marx and Freud and Frazer, the moods of Kafka and Hesse and Proust and Brecht, and with many hints picked up from his own contemporaries (for there are poems in which he is hardly more than an amanuensis for Koestler, de Rougemont, or Graham Greene): from these unpromising sources

Auden put together his early style, full of caustic poeticisms, broad understatements, sudden savageries, unexpected allusions, and with heavy reliance on the rhetoric and conventions of thriller fiction.

> *And the minerals and creatures, so deeply in love with their lives*
> *Their sin of accidie excludes all others,*
> *Challenge the nervous students with a careless beauty,*
> > *Setting a single error*
> > *Against their countless faults.*

> *O in these quadrangles where Wisdom honours herself*
> *Does the original stone merely echo that praise*
> *Shallowly, or utter a bland hymn of comfort,*
> > *The founder's equivocal blessing*
> > *On all who worship Success?*

> *Promising to the sharp sword all the glittering prizes,*
> *The cars, the hotels, the service, the boisterous bed,*
> *Then power to silence outrage with a testament....*

And so on. It was a period style, very alive and novel then, very dated now. Yet the point is that Auden himself was sensitive to its databulity before anyone else and began to modify his style while he was still young, toning down its mock violence, lengthening its syntax, subduing cadence and rhyme, until in his late work he ended with a kind of talky essay-poem that resembles the poems of Marianne Moore, but more sprawling than hers, more personal, more inclusive, more prone to generalization and sentimentality; the poetry, in short, of his "bucolics" (his term) and household poems. Thus, while remaining committed to "literary" values, he moved from a merely eccentric to a genuinely personal style. And of course the Oxonian accent is unmistakable throughout.

In his revisions for this new volume, Auden has reinforced this poetic development retroactively. From the early poems he has cut out many self-conscious poeticisms – the apostrophic *O*'s, for instance – and he has smoothed syntax and structure to give the poems more fluency. His revisions have been both extensive and intensive: a remarkable feat. He is the best reviser I've ever encountered. In the thirty or so poems I have examined in both the 1945 and 1967 editions, only one or two have escaped unchanged, though many revisions are slight, no more than the work of an itchy pencil. But where Auden has gone to work seriously to improve an old poem the results are often spectacular. As a technician he is superb. His revisions give us a lesson in versewriting that ought to be instructive to any young writer of no matter what stylistic predilection. In the poem from which I have quoted, "Oxford," Auden has rewritten almost every line he chose to keep, and he has cut the whole poem from nine stanzas to four. Was such drastic revision worthwhile? The poem was no world-beater to begin with. Yet I think Auden's effort is justified, because he has reduced a pretentious set piece to an incidental but graceful and intelligent little poem, worth keeping in his collected edition. His revision of the famous poem on the death of Yeats is more daring, if only because the poem in its earlier version was so well known; he has taken what seems to me the enormous risk of removing three stanzas. It works. The poem is instantly raised to a new level of somberness and genuineness, even if it sounds peculiar to us at first, and hence is truer to its original intention.

In many poems of the middle period, the 1940s, he has changed locutions toward greater literariness, but a literariness of his own particular kind. In one poem "the orgulous spirit" – a thumping Auden-ism if there ever was one – becomes now "the spirit orgulous," and we see at once that it is even more characteristic. The greatest changes I have found are in the sonnets originally taken from *Journey to a War*. In 1945 they were called "In Time of War." Now they are called "Sonnets from China"; they have been reduced from twenty-seven to twenty-one in number, their sequence has been reordered, all have been revised, some completely rewritten, and one new sonnet has been added. To my mind these are notable improvements. I doubt that anyone coming to Auden for the first time in this new book would be aware of the amount of tinkering that has gone into these sonnets, yet the new sequence is demonstrably better than the old one. I don't mean that the *poetry*, the conceived essence, is improved, but the poems are far more readable, and hence our approach to the poetry, whatever its interior values may be, is easier. Perhaps the fact that Auden's poems *can* be rewritten in this way, years after their first appearance, says something about them. I think it does. This is mainstream poetry, poetry in the specifically literary, public, professional tradition, poetry that calls attention to itself precisely as artifact, as something *written* – and hence as something rewritten or at least rewritable. It is not poetry cast forever into an unchangeable form by the white heat of personal vision.

Incidentally many titles in the new book have been altered. A reader who wishes to look up a particular poem must often rely on the index of first lines, and sometimes even that won't help.

What shall we say about these values of the specific English literary tradition, values of intelligence, decency, literacy, humaneness, civility, responsibility? Even though condescension, complacency, and blindness have often gone along with them, we could use a little more of them in the world of social reality these days, whatever place they may have in the world of poetry. Certainly in 1945, in the exhaustion produced by years of war and brutality and terror, they seemed, cast as they were in the rhetoric of a querulous, nerve-worn intellectuality, exactly right. But now it is a long time since I have heard anyone speak of Auden's poetry with real concern. And he meanwhile has proceeded further and further into literariness, and has propounded again and again his notion of art as a "secondary" reality, a game, a pastime. My impression is that the young generation, reared in the knowledge of the bomb and in a totally changed social environment, doesn't bother to read his poetry at all. Certainly there are anthology pieces in Auden's book, like the poem beginning "Doom is dark and deeper than any sea-dingle" (formerly called "Something Is Bound to Happen" and re-titled "The Wanderer" in the new book), or the song beginning "Lay your sleeping head, my love" (now called "Lullaby"), poems we will always remember. But those stretches and stretches and stretches of genteel, polysyllabic garrulity? The action is going on down in the street now, yet Auden is still back in the parlor, gabbling away. Maybe after the action is over, if it ever is, we can all return indoors and resume where we left off. But does anyone seriously propose that we will be the same men and women then, able to respond as before? I suspect no famous poet ever "aged" so fast. Auden strikes me now as somebody "back there," a contemporary of... well, I dislike saying it but I can't avoid it: this poetry reads like something out of the two-dimensional past where everyone lives at once, Coventry Patmore, Goldsmith, Lucan. The poems are fodder for graduate students. They scarcely exist, except for the few people in the world today who still take pleasure in reading old books.

🖎 ·

Seriousness and the Inner Poem

1971.

THIS AFTERNOON as I walked beside my brook a half mile above my place where the channel enters a broad, heavily wooded gulf I was thinking about the way my sense of poetry has been unsettled and put at odds with itself by the general upheavals of taste in recent years. This was no rarity; any afternoon or any walk these days might find me thinking about the same thing. It is a hard, obsessive topic. There in the gulf, where I clambered along the rocky, rooty bank, my attention was turned half outward, half inward. The brook in that place moves like a zipper down a fold of earth, its channel straight, its current swift, until it hits a barrier of tipped-up Green Mountain bedrock, which shatters the flow. Four or five noisy little waterfalls spill into four or five mean-dering little channels that simper through a low, soggy, ferny sump. Then farther on, the brook regathers itself and continues as before.

Sometimes I think my feelings about poetry have become so con-trary and self-divided that they will never find their way out of the sump and into a regathering again.

I stopped and stood looking back up the gulf to the simplicities there, the undivided brook, the leaning birches and rain-brightened autumn leaves. My antecedents had been simple too. When the war was done with me in 1945, like thousands of others I found myself res-cued by the GI Bill from the work I had been trained to do earlier; I could go to graduate school and put off earning a living. I jumped at the chance, and landed, unsuspecting, in the thick of Modern Poetry, which today is called Academic Poetry. It was a common enough case.

I have my reservations about that term *academic*. God knows most of us were antiacademic in those days, we despised the demands of scholarship, and many of our heroes were the same poets as those ad-mired by the liberated young poets of today: Pound, Williams, H.D. When people call my own early poems academic it infuriates me, because I know that many of them were written in times of crushingly real trouble when academicism in any of its senses was the furthest thing from my mind. If I used the forms and styles that I had seen in the books of popular poets of the day, it was because my substantial need left me no energy for formal experiment, and because my circumstances gave me no opportunity to learn about those of my contemporaries who were beginning to write in other ways.

But the discrimination of merits and flaws in the poetry of mid-century is too big a question, and too tangled in sectarianism, to be attempted now, though ultimately the job must be done. Certainly much of that poetry *was* academic, and getting more academic every day, as we ourselves were aware. It was no great trick to break with such excess when I came to realize what my contemporaries in other sectors were doing. The poems of Denise Levertov moved me deeply when I first saw them in about 1955, so do some poems by Allen Ginsberg, and from them I went on to other poets, Creeley, Duncan, Corman, and so on, and then into the whole efflorescence of the sixties, Merwin, Wakoski, Berry, LeRoi Jones, Philip Levine, and many others, hundreds of others. But what a mixture! Ginsberg's furor next to Creeley's precisionism, Corman beside Jones beside Wakoski beside Berry – a real hodgepodge. And if you add poets from the earlier period whose works are still moving and good, Tate, Ransom, Stevens, Jarrell, Shapiro, Lowell, Bogan, John Peale Bishop – the list is very long – where does that leave poetic taste? Are there no general criteria, covering everything? Am I condemned to eclecticism, that dirty word?

I was brought up against this problem with particular force a couple of days ago when I found a poem by John Crowe Ransom quoted in a place where I had not expected it. I was reading some letters by Jack Spicer, the California poet who died in 1965 and who is acknowledged by all concerned to have been the real leader, virtually the guru, behind the "renaissance" of West Coast poetry a decade or more earlier. Spicer was completely committed to poetic talent and insight, as distinct from technical proficiency, and to the chances and triumphs of poetic language, and from this he moved further and further into occultism, until in his final poems, formally unlike anything called by the name of poetry elsewhere, he claimed to be giving readers only what had been dictated to him by invisible external powers. In short he was not the poet to whom one would look for an appreciation of poetry in the academic or rationalist traditions. Yet there was this poem by Ransom, "Piazza Piece," quoted in Spicer's letters. Not Ransom's best, but a fine poem anyway and worth quoting again.

> – I am a gentleman in a dustcoat trying
> To make you hear. Your ears are soft and small
> And listen to an old man not at all,
> They want the young men's whispering and sighing.
> But see the roses on your trellis dying
> And hear the spectral singing of the moon;
> For I must have my lovely lady soon,
> I am a gentleman in a dustcoat trying.
>
> – I am a lady young in beauty waiting
> Until my truelove comes, and then we kiss.
> But what grey man among the vines is this
> Whose words are dry and faint as in a dream?
> Back from my trellis, Sir, before I scream!
> I am a lady young in beauty waiting.

(Do young readers need to be told that in the American South *piazza* means, or once meant, *veranda*, and that a dustcoat was an overgarment worn while driving in an open vehicle?)

The gist of Spicer's commentary on Ransom is in one sentence: "The way to read this poem (and most of his) is not to let the deceptive skill hypnotize you into not hearing the poem." How simple. The New Critics, perhaps including Ransom himself, would have said simpleminded. Yet for my part I have seen no statement about Ransom's poetry more perceptive than this. We recognize at once how it ties in with the common complaint of young poets today that rhyme and meter distract them from the real content of poetry. For Spicer, as for most older readers, Ransom's skill is not a distraction but a hypnosis; yet the effect may be the same. We lose ourselves in wonder for these rhymes so modestly doing their work in perfection, the way Ransom breaks from the traditional Petrarchan sonnet to bring in that wonderful rhyme of moon/soon, the diction so consistent in its mock-romanticism – or is it mock-mock-romanticism? – this tonally flawless interplay of syntax and meter, the structural finesse that creates such an augmentation of meaning in the repeated lines. And then the originality too: has there ever been another sonnet like this? If so, I am unaware of it. What magnificent writing! We lose ourselves in wonder of it to such an extent that we lose the poem. Because the poem is not the writing, neither the particular prosody nor the sonneteering tradition; it lies within, existing there as a song and a cry, fulfilling its own language exactly. Nor is this anything to do with sentiment. The poem is the entire and practically unlimited spectrum of unanalyzable but recognizable structures of feeling and thought, of thought-full feeling, which arises from the words in their immutable relationships: for example, "But what grey man among the vines is this / Whose words are dry and faint as in a dream?" The poem is neither good nor bad, but true. And if as I believe – probably contrary to Spicer, though his opinion was never made altogether clear as far as I know – Ransom's skill, which may deceive or hypnotize some readers (especially emulative poets), is antithetical to the poem but necessary and supplementary to it, then perhaps we have the glimmerings of a criterion.

So much may be said for "Piazza Piece." How much more then for "Blue Girls," "Bells for John Whiteside's Daughter," and "Winter Remembered"? These were the poems, with others of a like order, by which I had chosen to represent Ransom in a big anthology of American poetry I put together a couple of years ago; and when bound galley proofs were sent out last summer ahead of publication to poets and critics who might help promote the book, I received a letter from an old friend who is also an old and close friend of Ransom. It was a bitter letter, and the bitterest of my friend's reproaches concerned my treatment of Ransom. He complained that I had used only the slighter poems, the elegiac and gently ironic poems, and had left out the tougher, more philosophical, generally later poems, which he thought would show Ransom as the serious and important writer he has really been. Specifically he said I should have chosen, in addition to the poems I did choose, two others called "The Equilibrists" and "Painted Head." He accused me of turning Ransom into "a charming minor poet."

Well, charming minor poet is what we usually call Sir Thomas Wyatt, George Crabbe, John Clare, Padraic Colum, and many others, and personally I wouldn't mind belonging to that company at all, at all. What else is there – except oblivion on one hand and the fluke of great-

ness on the other? But aside from this, and aside from the fact that I do
not especially like the two poems recommended by my friend, and
aside from the further fact that neither I nor any anthologist can turn
Mr. Ransom into anything but what he is, the more critical point re-
mains that my friend has tried to impute seriousness and importance
to a poem by reference to the seriousness and importance of its topic. I
think this cannot be done. A topic may be serious and important in the
affairs of human beings, in philosophy, in science, in politics, and it
may even be serious in other ways in poetry, but when we are talking
about seriousness and importance as indicators of poetic value or es-
thetic efficacy, then the topic is a neutral factor and seriousness is an at-
tribute of the poem, the intrinsic real poem. In art, to say it another
way, the quality of feeling is important, not what is felt.

Are Ransom's later poems truly serious? In their argumentative or
discursive method they give me an impression of great earnestness, but
not of seriousness. They are efforts of thought, after which come efforts
of language, somewhat lagging. I see no poems in them at all. But in the
earlier lyrics about the deaths of little girls and boys or about growing
old or about romantic frustration I see, beneath the layers of irony, very
great seriousness indeed; total seriousness. Here the intrinsic poems,
originating in a spontaneous response to the enigmas of life, swell with
limitless self-augmentation of imaged feeling, thought, and association,
which is another way of saying that they are serious. And this in turn is
another way of saying that they are neither good nor bad, but true. Of
course I have no way of telling what place Ransom may finally occupy
in the scale of poetic reputations, minor or major or somewhere in
between. But I believe it will be determined by these serious early
poems, "slight" though they may be, and not by the earnest later ones.
I hope it will be a high place, because I personally like these poems
very much, and I now think I did not include enough of them in my
anthology.

That which is neither good nor bad then, but true and serious....

I return occasionally to the essays of T. S. Eliot, which seem to me
deeply inset in our literary consciousness, not as touchstones in the
Arnoldian sense but as a sort of gad, taunting us with their wrong intel-
ligence and perverse brilliance to try to correct them, and to try to
measure up. In the preface to *The Sacred Wood* Eliot wrote: "Poetry is
a superior amusement: I do not mean an amusement for superior

people. I call it an amusement, an amusement *pour distraire les honnêtes gens*, not because that is a true definition, but because if you call it anything else you are likely to call it something still more false. If we think of the nature of amusement, then poetry is not amusing; but if we think of anything else that poetry may seem to be, we are led into far greater difficulties." But Eliot was leading himself into difficulties, unnecessarily. He was a famous word-twister; he could invent newspeak by the yard. But is any species of amusement the same as poetry? The answer is flatly no, no matter how you redefine the word; not even if you say that *amusement* means *seriousness*. Yet we can see how Eliot fell into his predicament; the poems of Ransom show us. We are hypnotized by that marvelous skill of writing, or perhaps like Eliot we are honest people distracted by it, and this is amusement, a kind of amusement. If we do not know how to conceive poetry except in its formal properties, we may conclude that this amusement is all of poetry, as many people have, including W. H. Auden, who went so far as to say that poetry is a "game." But then what do we do with our knowledge that in reading we have actually undergone something more? We have been *moved*, we have been *shaken*. There is no question about this, as the slightest self-scrutiny reveals to us. Ransom's poem is terrifying. And what has moved and shaken us is the serious poem within the hypnotic amusement. That is clear, at least to me. What is less clear is the way in which the amusement, as secondary, is an indispensable supportive element of the primary seriousness; yet I am certain it is.

Eliot himself came to a similar view twenty years later when he was writing less as a critic than as a working poet and editor. He spoke of *genuineness* and of how it might be applied as a rule of thumb in the judgment of poetry. He seems to have meant by this his own sense of the congruence or incongruence between a poet's experience and his or her language; if they fitted, if the experience filled out the language and left no emptiness of rhetoric or bombast or ornament, then the poem was genuine. He was, in other words, edging toward seriousness as a criterion. But he was afraid of it, reluctant to go very far in exploring it; and I think this was so because of his fear of the subjective. Like the other critics and poets of his time, in their revulsion from the scientific or naturalistic thought of the late nineteenth century, he felt he needed the buttress of objectivity in his ideas and feelings if he was to stand firm against his enemies. He needed to fight them in their own terms. Though he despised their reliance on concepts of external verification in their material domain, he was still dependent upon external verification in his own spiritual and esthetic domain. In this he was profoundly a part of our philosophical past, so much of which has gone into the "rational proof" of irrational knowledge (see Eliot's doctoral thesis on the philosophy of F. H. Bradley), and of Western, as opposed to Eastern, thought. In this he was a true "academic." And at this point, I think, we discover the real difference between American academic poetry and the poetry that came after it.

The ways to say what happened in American poetry during the sixties are probably countless. I am inclined at the moment to say, for example, that English poetry, meaning all poetry written in any kind of English, has been haunted for almost four hundred years by what Kit Marlowe, who was born in the same year as Shakespeare, would have written if he had not been killed in a barroom fight at the age of twenty-nine. Spicer would probably not have said this; his young followers certainly would not. No matter. I am my peculiar self plus my peculiar training, and what I say is helpful to me because it occurs in my terms; it may be tangentially helpful to others too. The point is that the latent subjective in Western culture, which has broken through to the surface sporadically (as in Marlowe's *Faustus* and *Dido*), has broken through again. Its effect is large, but we cannot yet say how deep or enduring. For the present, however, we are willing to adopt truth and seriousness as the criteria of poetry, even though we have no idea what they are. We are willing to say what was anathema to the academics, that each reader is his own best critic. We are willing not only to say it but to assert it, to make it a principle of action. We agree that our judgments of seriousness lack objective verification, and that in consequence we can have no unanimity, or probably even preponderance, of belief, but we say it doesn't matter; we say we have, in literature past and present, more than enough poems to go around, however multifarious our beliefs may be.

Finally we say that we are justified in our beliefs by our awareness that the test of seriousness is not simply our sense of a certain urgency in the poem, or a certain "tone" or "mood," but our sense of personal movement and change in reading the poem. Our subjective judgment is firmly experiential; that is our verification. For we believe that the function of the poem, which lies within amusement, is to create us, to extend our beings indefinitely in evolving structures of thought and feelings. This is what we have learned in our long and repeated observations: of war, of peace, of mass, of solitude, of learning, of ignorance. The whole meaning of social force and natural force, and very likely of metaphysical force, is the unimportance, not to say vacuity, of life as it actually is; that is, in single conscious units. Force, the manifestation and outward being of social and natural reality, is our destruction; it annihilates us, it depersonalizes us, it changes us from human beings into objects for manipulation, or into figures on a chart. We resist by means of the poem, which is our self-creative act, whether we are, in the narrower sense, "creators" or "spectators." There are other means of resistance too, of course, and we do what we can to halt or impede the demolition of our habitat. But these other means are at best negative and preventive, and hence they lack ultimate seriousness. Art is our only positive creative resistance. Art is our ultimate seriousness.

Art is also our mystery. So be it. The structures of the poem arise by inscrutable means and are unified by infinite and indefinable connectives. We love to speculate about such things. Our speculations fill the pages of our magazines. But speculation is as far as it goes, and in the end we see that this too is a kind of amusement. For if the mystery is ever penetrated and art becomes a matter of objective or a priori understanding, that will be the end of seriousness and the end of humane, as distinct from technological, civilization.

This is the value of art, the real value; not a heritage, not a treasure or a tradition, but an ever-renewable creative efficacy. Of course we must remember that all serious and true works, past or present, are equivalent in this respect and are in this sense treasures. Where would we be without their life-giving powers? Repeatedly our experience is shattered against the force of reality, and our self-awareness goes meandering in disintegration and self-division, until it is regathered and reshaped in a total creative act, which is an organized aspect of being, a whole particular scene, serious and true. And then we continue as before, perhaps stronger but certainly no weaker, until a final shattering.

彡〜 . . . .

Fallacies of Silence

1973.

NOT MUCH literary criticism these days is granted the éclat that came almost as a matter of course to certain brilliant and valuable works a generation ago. Probably not much deserves it. Yet one recent essay is being celebrated in ways that remind us of the earlier time. Its title is "Silence and the Poet," its author is George Steiner, and a few days ago I read it. It is worth attending to.

Steiner's main concern in his published criticism has sprung from his perception of the terrifying interrelationships among literature, language, and contemporary history, particularly as experienced in Europe during the period that ended in 1945. How, Steiner asks repeatedly, could the wardens of the infamous camps have been devoted, as we know some were, to the great expressions of German humanism? How could the *gauleiter* who spent his evenings closeted with the eloquence of Goethe, Heine, or Fontane, use that same language the next day for composing warrants to send children into torture and death? What becomes of the poet in such a world? What becomes of his responsibilities, to his art and to his humanity? What happens to language itself when it is so abused? What remains of the essential value of the word, or of our faith in the meaning of meaning?

These are disturbing questions. All who lived through those years, even in America, have asked them, and have submitted, reluctantly or readily, to the reversions of shame, guilt, and despair entailed in them. But without doubt Steiner, whose personal and family history connect him intimately with the European cataclysm, has asked them with more purpose than most, and with great urgency, so that his responses are sharpened and remarkably well articulated. This is evident in his writings that evoke the German social and cultural milieu in and after the Hitlerian episode, or in essays dealing with the works of particular authors who lived and wrote during that time. But the essay in question is not of this sort; it is more general, conjectural, and polemical, an argument in applied esthetics; written, if one may judge from its tone, in a white heat of concern. Like many such works it is confused and overwritten, replete on the one hand with a sense of humane commitment that produces on the other an imperious rhetoric, as if to clear the way for deeply felt but questionable propositions. As a sign of its author's feeling the essay is forgivable, perhaps commendable, but as a passage in literary theory it needs more study.

The essay is in two parts, undifferentiated and poorly joined. In the first Steiner attempts to show how poetry, taken as the generalized verbal motion of the human imagination, contains within itself three tendencies of transcendence: toward light, toward music, and toward silence. But we see at once how confusion enters. The three are not consonant. As his example of transcendence toward light, Steiner chooses the passage which would occur to all of us, the ending of the *Paradiso*, which is one of the few moments of genuine transcendence in our literature. But Dante makes it perfectly clear that this is precisely what it is, transcendence, elevation from one level of perception to another, not mere transference between two modes of sensuous perception: not, in other words, the transformation of word into landscape, sound into sight or touch, verbalism into plasticity, but a movement from "outer" to "inner" light, away from sensuousness altogether, into the metaphysical. Dante says his eyesight must be purged or made pure (*sincera*) before he can "see" the lofty light that in itself is true (*alta luce che da sé é vera*), which I take to mean that his eyesight is refined of materiality and removed, as such, from his actual eyes. Dante says:

> *Cosí la mente mia, tutta sospesa,*
> *mirava fissa, immobile e attenta,*
> *e sempre di mirar faciesi accesa.*

It is his mind which, "full rapt, was gazing, fixed, still and intent, and ever enkindled with gazing" – his *mind*, not his eyes; his mind in all the cognitive immediacy and autonomy that medieval psychology gave to it; his mind fixed and immobile, that is, beyond sense and without will. And if his speech fails when his mind is struck by the divine light (*la mia mente fu percossa da un fulgore*), the failure does not persist into the time of actual composition, for the language, the singing but simple tension of the last canto, is the verbal triumph of the whole poem.

Transcendence, literal, actual, absolute, is what that canto is about, as all readers recognize, and what the whole *Paradiso* has been leading

up to. But with Steiner's second category, the movement toward mu-
sic, we enter a different dimension and find ourselves in an incongruity.
Here we have not transcendence but transference. By pointing to vari-
ous examples Steiner shows how Western poets have striven in their
language toward pure sound, as if music were a superior kind of ex-
pression, as indeed many poets have believed, including poets of every
age and school; in short, the Orphic theme, a dominant in Western tra-
dition from ancient times to the present. The evidence is abundant
and well known. We agree with Steiner's account of it. But two further
considerations occur to us, which Steiner does not mention. First, the
movement toward music is not a movement from sensuousness to
metaphysicality; properly speaking, therefore, it is not transcendence
at all but mere transference from one mode of sensuous perception to
another, from verbalism to tonality. It concerns two ways of perceiving,
but both on the same level, involving two of our five physical senses,
sight and hearing. Second, the Orphic tradition, so closely attached to
the idea of music, is nevertheless a worded tradition, a literary tradi-
tion, the property of poets, not of musicians. There is, I believe, an
equal but contrary or complementary tradition in music, although few
musicians, naturally enough, have written about it. I mean the striving
toward language, especially in the development of instrumental music
from post-Renaissance times to our own. What is the syntax of Bach,
the rhyming of Mozart, the rhetoric of Beethoven and Bruckner, and
the whole expressionist tendency from Brahms to Debussy and
Mahler to early Stravinsky – to say nothing of the speech-like textures
common to African-American jazz – if it is not a striving toward utter-
ance, toward statement, toward idea; an attempt to combine sounds in
such a way that they will create an ultrasonic meaning based on a pro-
jection of sublimated rationalism? Thus each mode strives toward the
other in an effort to surpass itself. But however far poetry and music
move horizontally toward each other – and certainly we have seen their
limits extended in recent decades – this does not entail a movement
vertically out of their common sensuousness. Neither can move be-
yond its own being-in-this-world. For if the medium is not the message
– and I certainly hope it is not – it is indubitably the substance, the
substantiality, and even Dante had to resort to language that does not
break down in order to tell us of the time when language did break
down.

In his third category, the movement toward silence, which is his most important for the purposes of the essay in question, Steiner cites two examples, Hölderlin's decline from poetry into madness and Rimbaud's escape from poetry into the life of action. True enough, these are species of silence. But leaving aside the probabilities that Hölderlin's silence was not the silence of silence but the silence of bedlam (a distinction to which some of us can attest) and that Rimbaud's flight was motivated merely and negatively by the same intellectual disgust with poetry which at moments overtakes most of us, leaving aside, that is, the fact that these two remarkable poets can be interpreted only in terms of themselves, we must still deal with the *mystique* of silence which has without doubt drawn heavily upon their examples and which has become increasingly prominent in Western literature of the past century. Steiner affirms that this is what he means: the myth, the cult. He indicates the role that silence has played in the thought and feeling of poets as diverse as Shelley and Valéry. But there are kinds of silence. In Steiner's essay they are not distinguished. The silence of wonder, for instance, is not the silence of defeat. And both are very different from the silence we actually discover in poetry, which is not true silence at all. It is silence as an incorporate element in the medium or the technique, silence as a verbal ploy. Thus we see poets relying on the elocutionary pause, suggested typographically, as intrinsic to modern prosody, in ways analogous to the use of silence by composers like John Cage or of empty space in the grouped figures of Henry Moore or the "cage" sculptures of Herbert Ferber. Silence has become a mere extension of style – useful, informing, expressive.

In other words it seems to me that the first part of Steiner's essay is a confusion not only between transcendence and transference or two different kinds of experience, it is a confusion between experience and reflection, between poetic ends and means. All of us, whether we are religious or not, agree that moments of immediate, ultrasensuous experience do occur. We may refer to them pseudo-rationalistically, using such terms as *insight* and *intuition*, or we may identify them subjectively and metaphorically: the divine light, the music of the spheres, the stillness at the heart of eternity – light, music, silence. In all these cases, however, we mean a real transcendence, a movement out of ourselves, an ecstasy (Greek *ekstasis*, "a putting outside of") in which we abandon our ordinary sensory locus. In the case of silence particularly, we mean real silence, a breakdown and cessation of language – language being the paradigm of our intelligent presence in the material world. We mean the silence which signifies direct perception with no interposing sense-mechanics: the mystic's confrontation with God, the naturalist's moment of dissolution in universal force. At the other end of the scale, we know that a poet faced with the degradation of language, its drift toward meaninglessness in the lying utterances of politics and commerce or in the simple erosive monotone of mass culture, may suffer, in his or her dismay, a breakdown or dislocation of poetic language itself, a stoppage, and a consequent paralysis of imagination, resulting in silence – again real silence, the silence of defeat, of nihilism. These are the extremes, absolute silences, beyond sensuousness, God-bestowed or devil-inspired; they are the bounds of poetry. Indeed poetry is bounded by silence on all sides, is almost defined by silence. And doubtless it does strive toward its bounds in its search for ends, namely, for newly perceived and recorded experience. The poet seeks *his* or *her* new experience in *his* or *her* new words, careless of the fact that neither experience nor words can be new. Steiner regards this as a case of the artist's risk taking. It is a Promethean raid on the inarticulate, which by ellipsis becomes a raid on the power of the Word, the all-meaning divine silence. It is a crime which the poet commits in the hope of bringing back new vigor to human speech, but for which he may pay instead the penalty of being struck dumb. This is a highly mythic view, romantic and charged with fatalism. Fortunately we have good reason to think that in its search for means, as opposed to ends, poetry is more reasonable and returns to its own center, the region of greatest articulation. Sensuousness, the substance *ex natura rei* of imagination, cannot surpass itself; to name silence is to break it; and Dante, who babbled at the sight of God, spoke good vulgar Italian afterward when he wrote his poem. Moreover he was careful to discriminate, with beautiful Dantean lucidity, the two occasions into two modes of experience, the mystical and the material, each with its own qualities and needs.

From this Steiner proceeds in the second part of his essay to a consideration of the writer's predicament in contemporary history, especially in totalitarian societies. He describes eloquently the degradation of language in our time. It is something that all responsible writers live with and know: the way whole swaths of our vocabulary are stricken from us by the subversions of the press, the advertising industry, and politics. We live among masses of rotting wordage like rats on the town dump. We must steal our scraps of meaning from the useless mounds of decay, while the area in which we can move freely grows ever smaller. The true language, living language, contracts before our eyes. Confronted with this, Steiner recommends that we write less, saving our few remaining words, so to speak, for the occasions of greatest personal and human value; and in the extremest situation, where language has been completely debased by the lies and atrocities of totalitarianism – for it is clear that no barbarity can be committed that has not first been conceived and ordered in human speech – he says we should not write at all. Silence is best. But I hope I have shown how this projection of his mythic fatalism into the present social predicament of the writer does not follow from his earlier argument. I hope I have shown how his confusion between ends and means, between transcendence and transference, between the metaphysical and sensuous modes, and especially between silence as a product of wonder or defeat and silence as an extension of style, leads to a practical absurdity. About real silence we can say nothing, literally. It has no words. How can it be a social or political mechanism? Stylistic silence, on the other hand, has its uses; but they must be examined in utilitarian terms. We know that one poet who relies on pauses and rests as part of technique may be reduced to stuttering fatuity, while another succeeds in reinforcing basic poetic structures. We know that when we are faced by the official interrogator it is both courageous and reasonable to shut up if we can. But silence as a principle? Silence as an invariable means, a kind of standing on our dignity, a withholding of ourselves from the world to signify our denial of the world's subverters and perverters? No, I can't accept that. Steiner himself has nothing but praise for the Jews of the Warsaw ghetto who continued writing, lucidly and with conscious artistic and human integrity, throughout the prolonged agony of their own destruction (pp. 155–68, *Language and Silence*).

In short, within his three tendencies of "transcendence," which he treats as if they were of one kind, Steiner has confused two modes of human experience, the corporeal and the spiritual (to use antiquated terms); and from his confusion he has attempted to infer rules of prac-

tice for poets in their craft. It can't be done. He ends by assigning to
one kind of silence, poetic silence, values derived from the other kind
of silence, ecstatic silence. It is a contradiction, almost as if he asked
the poet to be wordless in words. And such a muddle is dangerous, I
believe, not only because it destroys our concept of the poetic function
and misconstrues the poet's role in society, but because it introduces
false distinctions into our view of the relationship between art and re-
ality, between the poem and its object, or between the poetic mind and
the human body.

Where does this imputed contraposition of the human and artistic
come from? It is insidious. I have said elsewhere that it is a product of
post-Nietzschean disillusionment, especially as it was worked out in
the literature of style during the first half of our century; it was an at-
tempt to supplant the chaos of devalued existence with the order of
style, the reality of fiction; it was at the heart of the modernist impulse.
But whether or not that historical conjecture is right, let me repeat,
with *all* the great theorists: art and life, art and reality, art and the world
are the *same thing*. The integrity of one is the integrity of the other.
The word and the act sink or swim together.

We are not the only writers who have served in a time of verbal de-
generacy. Indeed it seems to have been the case almost always, poets
deploring the sad state of their language. Were the Elizabethans, to
choose a difficult example, verbally motivated only by enthusiasm for
their new vocabulary, imported from overseas? Or were they equally
concerned to amend the outworn Skeltonic language they had inher-
ited? We can't tell. But certainly by the time of the Augustans, decay of
language through popular or official misuse had become a serious
affair. Swift and Pope spent half their lives decrying the scribblers, the
jobbers, and the time-serving pamphleteers; and the *Dunciad* ends
with a terrifying vision of the world reduced to chaos through verbal
dullness, one of the great infernos of modern literature. And so it con-
tinued through the romantics and post-romantics to our own time. For
sixty years Pound insisted on the corrective function of poetry, both in
language and society – in basic morality.

But has anyone before this ever recommended silence? Seriously, as
a major poetic means? We live encompassed by a verbal civilization
whose structures become visibly useless from day to day, worn out,
broken, befouled. Our public persons, whether disc jockeys or evange-

lists, salesmen or senators, are driven to ever more frantic outbursts in their efforts to revive the meaning of language that they themselves have decimated. Worse – at least in some respects – our poetry itself weakens as its growth becomes more massive, forms overburdened with stereotypes, styles machine-made and plastic; or so it seems to me. But still, does anyone recommend silence? That would be an apocalyptic view. Yet even apocalypse itself is a poetic event, a revelation caught and held in words.

Poetry moves toward its own center, where the fount of language flows most freely. That is its going ahead, its renewal. It returns from the frontiers of experience bearing chaos and revolution, the rawness of events, which it submits to the regulative conceptualizings of our permanent, concrete, basic, human modes; that is, to language. How do you correct the misuse of a word? By using it rightly. How do you combat the schoolteacher who in common ignorance subjects your child to a confounding of *mundane* and *menial*? You distinguish meanings; with the child at least, with the schoolteacher if possible. We need not less but more good writing. This is *not* a defense of the establishment. Traditions come and go. My point is that they come and go *in language*. I am making a plea for courage among writers, and for a recognition that the means of poetry are what they are and what they have always been.

As for those who live oppressed in states of total, totalitarian inhumanity – and we Americans are aware that I may turn out to have been talking about ourselves – I say that all who are artists or who acknowledge art depend on them as on no others. Let silence be their tactic, never their strategy. The least sentence spirited from prison or ghetto or death camp is our treasure; the test of humanity in its extreme moment is its choice of words. Not cries, not groans, though these may have eloquence too when we know the context, but chosen words. Think of George Jackson choosing his; not always rightly, yet in his anguish so often exact and just and true – so very, very often. Indeed I think no man is a writer who does not know himself in prison. And if the torturer has a taste for Schiller, or the mace-sprayer by chance has at one time responded to Melville, this does not change Schiller and Melville. Words once fixed in rightness cannot be altered by mere replication, no matter how barbarous the mind in which it may occur. Only the use of words for new evil, original evil, debases them.

Then write. Write well. Honestly, meaningly, imaginatively, and from the center. The *stylistes* are elsewhere, studying silence. They are no help to us.

A Location of J. V. Cunningham

1972.

SOME POEMS, probably most good poems, need no criticism because they speak for themselves. But seldom does this relieve the critic from his work. Poems, like their authors, occur in time, submerged in historical muddle and encumbered with social and cultural appurtenances which, though bearing scant relationship to the poems themselves, still obscure them from general understanding. Hence the real – and menial – work of criticism is to dispose of this excess. A critic is a sort of sergeant-at-arms: ostensibly there to make a show of authority, but actually to answer silly questions and keep the tourists moving. Rarely is he permitted to use his power by excluding somebody from the congressional chamber; and as for admittance, the senators march past him with scarcely a nod. Perhaps he is obsolete.

At all events I wish to write briefly about the poetry of J.V. Cunningham, which is surrounded by just this kind of confusion. Though clear and independent in itself, needing no criticism, its value has been widely misunderstood, even by astute readers. For a time nothing could be done to clear the muddle because to attempt it would entail a discourtesy – though not a real discourtesy, only a seeming one – to another poet, older, highly valued in himself, and known to be hypersensitive. Now that time has passed, and unfortunately the work can begin.

I'm sure everyone knows what I mean. Cunningham began to write poetry when he was a student of the late Yvor Winters at Stanford in the 1930s. In fact he was one of a number of students who were knit together by the resemblance of their poetic methods and their adherence to Winters's poetic theory; they were known everywhere as "the Winters group." Winters himself introduced most of them to the public in an anthology he edited, *Twelve Poets of the Pacific* (1937). And he particularly praised Cunningham on a number of occasions, including one full-length, independently published essay, *The Poetry of J.V. Cunningham* (1961), which was flattering and probably embarrassing to its subject. Yet in this Winters showed the good judgment that was usually his when he was writing affirmatively, which wasn't often, as opposed to his lack of discrimination when he was angry and bent on disparagement; for we see now that although some of his other students, during the thirties and later, produced interesting, valuable, mostly forgotten poems, Cunningham is the only one who has achieved independent stature as a poet.

Even so, most readers still think of Cunningham as a "Winters poet." They confuse the two men; worse, they compound them. They regard the poetry of both as a common product, in which the poems of one are interchangeable with those of the other. But this is folly. In styles, tones, modes of feeling, and topical preoccupations, the two are not only distinct but far apart. Only a culture as diffuse as that of American poetry in the twentieth century, with its engrossment in schools, influences, and affinities, could compress in readers' minds the difference between two such dissimilar poets.

True, the influence, if it was an influence and not simply a congruence, of Winters upon Cunningham was profound. Cunningham would be the first to acknowledge it. The two agreed, early and firmly, that they occupied common ground, confronting an enemy together, viz. the whole mainstream of modern Western poetry. The list of their shared dislikes includes every catchword of modernist textbooks: "symbolism," "connotative language," "free verse," "associative linkage," etc., etc. In general their views rest upon two principles. First, that poetic form in itself neither possesses nor logically can possess *affective* efficacy, and that in consequence conventional form, with its proven *esthetic* efficacy, is best. Secondly, that the substance of a poem should be organized in terms of rational progressions, and should be connected, plottable, paraphrasable. Not that a poem is a work of logic or a mathematical proposition. But if I interpret Winters correctly, he did believe that because feeling is aroused in a poem only through the intercession of the mind, it may be most dependably aroused by materials that are verbally organized in terms of ordinary mental procedures. Ideas are the coordinates of emotion.

Chiefly the work of defending these positions fell to Winters, who complained from time to time of the loss it meant to his poetry, though we assume that his vehemence and enthusiasm in carrying it forward betray a fundamental enjoyment. No one ever took more delight in controversy. Cunningham by contrast has been far less aggressive. Apart from important essays in medieval and Renaissance scholarship, he has produced little criticism: two or three brief statements on prosody, an interesting examination of Wallace Stevens, a few other pieces. For my part I wish he had not written even this much, for while it is a slight part of all his work, contributing little to the total effect, it is also narrow and doctrinaire. His poetry speaks for itself and is sufficient; his criticism, in speaking for everyone, falls short. I still cannot see, after years of watching the critics, how anyone can confront a shelf of poetry embracing every imaginable mode and maintain the possibility of prescriptive criticism; yet time and again they do it, especially critics who are also poets. Perhaps for certain strongly creative personalities a belief in not only the universal but the exclusive applicability of their own technique is a psychological necessity. Beyond that what can it serve?

From this base of shared theory the two men work separately and differently in their poetry, as we should expect. They were of different ages, backgrounds, interests. Winters's poetry is French, a point which as far as I know has not been adequately understood. His early studies were concentrated on French and Spanish literature, and his early poems, published in the 1920s and later suppressed, were the work of a young man in the first enthusiasm of his contact with French literature of the years before World War I. Winters himself, from the vantage point of his later combative sectarianism, placed the blame for his early work upon Pound and Williams (see his entry in *Twentieth Century Authors*, 1942). But this cannot account for the unmistakable, if indiscriminate, international flavor; a flavor, I judge, of Apollinaire, Larbaud, Forgue, Reverdy, maybe Supervielle, and even more of the pages of *The Little Review, Broom*, and other expatriate magazines of the time. From this beginning Winters worked backward through the French nineteenth century, stopping briefly with the Symbolistes and Mallarmé, lingering with Baudelaire – he wrote many sonnets with a characteristically Baudelairean sinuosity and strength – and ending in a Gautier-like clarity and concision, with a preference for trimeter and dimeter lines. This is a very abbreviated account, but I believe it will stand up to scrutiny. My point is the French peculiarity I detect from beginning to end and in every aspect – prosodic, dictional, and even thematic. I suspect Winters would have been more at home intellectually in France than he was in California, in spite of the cordiality of his feeling for the Pacific milieu. But he never went. Sometimes it seems as if he could never get close to anything he liked.

Cunningham's locus is entirely different. His studies have been in Latin and Renaissance literature, in philosophy and mathematics, and in the late-medieval rhetoricians, Erasmus, More, Scaliger, Ramus. He has written important essays in Elizabethan scholarship, especially on Shakespeare and Jonson, and his own poetry is Jonsonesque. I do not hesitate to pin it down more narrowly; the characteristic Cunningham poem is a direct development from Jonson's *Underwoods*, or rather from the short poems in that collection. He has the same lightness of touch, the same half-smiling sorrow, the same awareness of the ideative content of life – a very different tone from that of a Winters poem, even when the two are using the same meters. Yet there is nothing antiquarian about Cunningham's usage, and this apparently must be emphasized since many readers today feel that no one can imitate the poetry of the past without betraying the present. Cunningham is a scholar, like all poets he is in some sense an imitator, his sensibility is embedded in tradition; yet his approach to writing is totally and individually creative. The evidence of this, the peculiar tension and inalterability of truly self-contained poems, is seen in every line. Once one grants that for certain temperaments archaism of form and diction is not a striving for effect but a natural mode, and once one concedes to the poet his right to an idiosyncratic, not to say anomalous, place in literary society, Cunningham's poems come forward as the products of our age, on an equal footing with those of any poet alive.

[UNTITLED]

Poets survive in fame.
But how can substance trade
The body for a name
Wherewith no soul's arrayed?

No form inspires the day
Now breathless of what was
Save the imputed sway
Of some Pythagoras,

Some man so deftly mad
His metamorphosed shade,
Leaving the flesh it had,
Breathes on the words they made.

THE DOG-DAYS

The morning changes in the sun
As though the hush were insecure,
And love, so perilously begun,
Could never in the noon endure,

The noon of unachieved intent,
Grown hazy with unshadowed light,
Where changing is subservient
To hope no longer, nor delight.

Nothing alive will stir for hours,
Dispassion will leave love unsaid,
While through the windows masked with flowers
A lone wasp staggers from the dead.

Watch now, bereft of coming days,
The wasp in the darkened chamber fly,
Whirring ever in an airy maze,
Lost in the light he entered by.

MONTANA PASTORAL

I am no shepherd of a child's surmises.
I have seen fear where the coiled serpent rises,
Thirst where the grasses burn in early May

And thistle, mustard, and the wild oat stay.
There is dust in this air. I saw in the heat
Grasshoppers busy in the threshing wheat.
So to this hour. Through the warm dusk I drove
To blizzards sifting on the hissing stove,
And found no images of pastoral will,
But fear, thirst, hunger, and this huddled chill.

[UNTITLED EPIGRAPH]

These the assizes: here the charge, denial,
Proof and disproof: the poem is on trial.
Experience is defendant, and the jury
Peers of tradition, and the judge is fury.

ENVOI

Hear me, whom I betrayed
While in this spell I strayed,
Anger, cathartic aid,
Hear and approve my song!

See from this sheltered cove
The symbol of my spell
Calm for adventure move,
Wild in repose of love,
Sea-going on a shell
In a moist dream. How long –
Time to which years are vain –
I on this coastal plain,
Rain and rank weed, raw air,
Served that fey despair,
Far from the lands I knew!

Winds of my country blew
Not with such motion – keen,
Stinging, and I as lean,

Savage, direct, and bitten,
Not pitying and unclean.

Anger, my ode is written.

I said at the beginning that Cunningham's poems need no criticism, which is all the more true because his most difficult poems, his earliest – difficult not in method but in obscurity of reference – have been glossed by the poet himself in a prose work called *The Quest of the Opal* (1950). Yet now I wonder if some readers, especially young readers whose training is so different from what we took for granted a few years ago, may not need help in recognizing the quality of writing in these poems. I mean the quality of versewriting. Notice how, within strict rhyme and meter, the language flows in poetic naturalness, neither forced nor padded; implying by "poetic naturalness," as distinct from the naturalness of speech, a language of tightened and rhetorically varied syntax. No extra words to fill out the meter; no twisted syntax to make a rhyme. (The very spare use of adjectives, in poetry as in prose, is a sign of verbal control.) Some people think that anyone can do this who grubs and revises earnestly enough. But if Pope, Gray, Keats, Tennyson, and Browning couldn't do it, why should we think it easy? In his best poems Cunningham writes with a skill that seems to me not only rare but astonishing. Not that good versewriting is enough to make good poems, but it helps. Sometimes good versewriting seems rarer than good poems.

A further respect, though not the last, in which Winters and Cunningham differ is in their ages. Winters belonged to the generation of Tate, Warren, MacLeish, and the others who began to write just after World War I; Cunningham to the generation whose beginnings were associated with the Depression and World War II. This has meant a difference of poetic aims. Winters's poems are not impersonal, but he in his time could still work in a convention built upon poems of large, general concern, a convention which held in reverence the idea of the masterpiece – an objectively valued poem on a set theme. Ten years later, when Cunningham began, the convention was dying fast. His poems are shorter, more restricted in aim, and far more personal; personal to the point of intimacy. Robert Lowell's autobiographical poems have been called confessional by some critics, an inappropriate term; but granting its rightness for the moment, we see immediately that Cunningham has "confessed" far more than Lowell, especially in his later poems; we see that Cunningham is actually close to those of his own generation against whom he thought he was writing, poets like Lowell, Elizabeth Bishop, Berryman, Roethke, Olson, Delmore Schwartz. He is indelibly a part of that scene, an important part. And perhaps it is worth noting that although he has occasionally used syllabic meters from the beginning, including some fine hendecasyllabics (as fine as Rexroth's), he has turned to them more and more in his recent work, especially in such autobiographical poems as the sequence called *To What Strangers, What Welcome* (1964).

The volume of Cunningham's output is small, but compact and without waste, tough, distinctive, filled with strange flint-like intensity. "The judge," he has written, "is fury," and the poet is "deftly mad." We cannot doubt the authenticity of these works of despair, bitterness, and intransigence. I suppose Cunningham will be linked with Winters in anthologies and textbooks for years to come, but I hope I have indicated the reasons why he deserves to be considered in his own terms. Which poet's work a reader will prefer is entirely a matter of taste. For what it's worth I prefer Cunningham's.

To this I add a word about the epigram. It is a dead form, killed long ago. We can scarcely imagine now its popularity in the sixteenth and seventeenth centuries in Europe. In Germany in 1697 an anthology of *Ueberschriften oder Epigrammata* required six volumes to do its work and contained 200,000 specimens; and though nothing so compendious appeared in English, there were many collections and scarcely a poet failed to try his hand. From More and Scaliger to Lessing and Hazlitt, the critics sought to define and regularize the concept of epigram. Many epigrammatists, like John Owen (1560–1622), a Welsh schoolmaster whose twelve books were bestsellers throughout Europe – though he made little money from them, and Jonson tells of Owen "sweeping his living from the posteriors of little children" – many such poets wrote in Latin, so their works are practically unavailable to most of us. In fact the Latin tradition continued for a long time. Landor's Latin epigrams are said to be both more numerous and better than his English poems. In the 1890s schoolboys at Winchester were required to produce three Latin epigrams a week. No wonder the epigram died.

The epigrams of Martial, acerb, bawdy, with a punch line at the end, were the great influence on English epigrammatists of the Renaissance, though a gentler tradition, deriving from the earliest Greek poets of the *Palatine Anthology*, was evident too. (Many of Herrick's short poems are properly epigrams.) What happened to these traditions is debatable. I suppose they wore out. In the eighteenth century you might think Pope's genius was the soul of epigrammatic feeling, but actually, with his heavy diction and cadence, he contributed to the deterioration of the form, which declined even more in the hands of Gay, Garrick, Goldsmith, Lord Lyttelton, Walpole, and others. Wit was extinguished in verbal emptiness and elegance, though Burns at his best wrote a few passable examples. In the nineteenth century, under the criticism of gentility, the decline turned into a downfall. Henry P. Dodd, who edited an anthology of epigrams, mostly unreadable, in 1876, wrote in his introduction of the "injurious effect" of Martial – "the wit of a point is attractive to men of refined taste," he said, "but if sting be added to it, lower tastes are gratified" – while the unsigned article in the *Encyclopedia Britannica*, eleventh edition, called Martial's influence "as baneful as it is extensive." Gentility condemned, in other words, what the Renaissance had admired and what had produced ninety percent of the epigrams we remember. By the end of the century the epigrammatic spirit survived only in prose (Oscar Wilde), in comic epitaphs, limericks, and other folk verse, and in fake sentimental imitations of Oriental poetry. The *Cambridge History of English Literature* does not mention the English epigram, though it gives a few paragraphs to Owen, in all its fifteen volumes, a shocking omission.

In our century the spirit of the age is contrary to epigram, whose aim is public, rhetorical, and conventional. Only in a context of fixed values can the brief unargued moral conceit make its point. In 1944 the poet D. S. Savage wrote: "[Today] the sincere artist is forced to examine anew every aspect of experience, to approach it originally.... He can no longer rely on any external authority." And we acknowledge how well this exemplifies our predicament. In such circumstances what poet could write epigrams? What poet would wish to? The epigram, which had been for poets of the Renaissance a definite and major genre, was now not only unpracticed but unrecognized. The only scholar in modern America to devote attention to it was, as far as I know, Hoyt Hudson, and he died before he finished his work.

Yet the epigram is not dead, it is very much alive, and the point of

my brief historical summary is that Cunningham has been responsible
for its resuscitation, he almost alone. True, scattered here and there are
other epigrams we remember in modern poetry, by Roethke, Bogan,
Paul Goodman, Jonathan Williams, and others. But only Cunningham
has concentrated on the form as a major category of literary endeavor,
something worth doing for its own sake. As with his other poems, he
has taken his formal impetus straight from the center of the Renais-
sance, from Jonson, from Owen and Martial and the Latin tradition
generally; to which he has brought his contemporary sensibility. As for
"external authority," the poet who will search in the right place will
find it. It is common sense, earth wisdom and street wisdom, the prag-
matic underlore of our, or any, culture. This has always been the ele-
ment in which good epigrams take form, Martial's, Jonson's, or
Cunningham's; only a rococo civilization could pervert the epigram to
social punning and dilettantism. At all events, though the epigram is a
demanding form and Cunningham has produced some poor ones, his
good ones are remarkable. They may be the best in nearly three hun-
dred years of English.

1.

Dark thoughts are my companions. I have wined
With lewdness and with crudeness, and I find
Love is my enemy, dispassionate hate
Is my redemption though it come too late –
Though I come to it with a broken head
In the cat-house of the disheveled dead.

2.

Soft found a way to damn me undefended:
I was forgiven who had not offended.

3.

In whose will is our peace? Thou happiness,
Thou ghostly promise, to thee I confess
Neither in thine nor love's nor in that form
Disquiet hints at have I yet been warm;
And if I rest not till I rest in thee
Cold as thy grace, whose hand shall comfort me?

4.
Lip *was a man who used his head.*
He used it when he went to bed
With his friend's wife and with his friend,
With either sex at either end.

5.
All in due time: love will emerge from hate,
And the due deference of truth from lies.
If not quite all things come to those who wait
They will not need them: in due time one dies.

6.
I married in my youth a wife.
She was my own, my very first.
She gave the best years of her life.
I hope nobody gets the worst.

7.
You ask me how Contempt *who claims to sleep*
With every woman that has ever been
Can still maintain that women are skin deep?
They never let him any deeper in.

8. Night-piece
Three matches in a folder, you and me.
I sit and smoke, and now there's only two,
And one, and none: a small finality
In a continuing world, a thing to do.
And you, fast at your book, whose fingers keep
Its single place as you sift down to sleep.

9.
It was in Vegas. Celibate and able
I left the silver dollars on the table
And tried the show. The black-out, baggy pants,
Of course, and then this answer to romance:
Her ass twitching as if it had the fits,

Her gold crotch grinding, her athletic tits,
One clock, the other counter clockwise twirling.
It was enough to stop a man from girling.

10.
The night is still. The unfailing surf
In passion and subsidence moves
As at a distance. The glass walls,
And redwood, are my utmost being.
And is there there in the last shadow,
There in the final privacies
Of unaccosted grace, – is there,
Gracing the tedium to death,
An intimation? Something much
Like love, like loneliness adrowse
In states more primitive than peace,
In the warm wonder of winter sun.

Robert Frost

1975.

THE LEAST ONE CAN DO when the centennial celebration of Robert Frost's birthday comes around, if one is American and a reader of poetry, is to get down his *Collected Poems* and try them again – another confrontation, as it were, in the apparently endless business of coming to terms with our most difficult and most famous poet. Well, this is it. He was born in 1875, and I have just performed my own new and dutiful confrontation. And I can't say it has advanced me one inch closer to a resolution of my ambivalent feelings about the man and his work.

It is a long business indeed, this coming to terms with Frost. In my case it began in public school forty-odd years ago. Frost was the only living poet to whose work I was introduced then, though I think the name of Sandburg may have been mentioned; Frost was the only one worth considering. In fact I was told expressly that poetry as a serious vocation was dead, had been killed by the idiocies of the radical modern poets, and that the art had become merely a hobby for idle men and women who published their verses in the magazines I found in my own home, the *Saturday Evening Post* and the *Ladies' Home Journal*. What I read in those magazines confirmed what I'd been told. Thus Frost was placed at once into the company of Browning, Longfellow, Byron, and Shakespeare, the standard poetic fare of public school English classes. And what I read in Frost's poems tended also to confirm what I was told because although I lived in a small New England town which at that time still closely resembled the farming communities in the poems, I nevertheless felt that the attitudes of the poet were old-fashioned, safe, comfortable, and approved, the products not of a contemporary imagination but of one that was turned backward. At any rate they had little to do with the reality of my own life.

Partly this was true, my feelings were exactly right, as none of many later and I hope more intelligent readings has disaffirmed; and partly, I suspect, my response was controlled by my teachers, who did not show me any poems from the possibly disturbing or unusual segments of Frost's work. Yet in spite of my dissatisfaction with aspects of substance, I could gratify my teachers without counterfeiting because I liked some of the poems immensely, and I still do. It was a question of being able to identify my own speech with the idiom of the poems, and of being immediately taken by their rhythmic and phonetic patterns, their whole verbal texture. And I still am taken. Is this illegal? If we read Shakespeare for the sound of his language, may we not read any other poet the same way? Yet plenty of fashionable people nowadays will tell you that verbal effect of any kind is not only disjunct from the "real poem" but somehow inimical to it.

What my dissatisfaction with substance was pointing to, though I had no way of knowing it at the time, was the division in Frost's poetry, and apparently in his character, that has been noted since then by many critics. Twenty years after my days in public school Randall Jarrell wrote an essay in which he called attention to the dark side of Frost. He said that the public mask created by Frost, the persona of a shrewd and genial Yankee sage, was a contrivance only, a piece of public relations, and that at heart the poet was a troubled, doubting, anguished man. Jarrell said further that the poet's most popular poems were connected with this public, genial aspect of his self-image, and that like it, they too were at best contrivances, while his really genuine poems were all products of his darker side. Jarrell's essay, which is a model of what a critical essay should be, made a considerable impression because it put into the open and schematized something many readers had felt all along. They may have differed somewhat with Jarrell's selection of the poems he thought were genuine, but they agreed with his general estimate. Consequently for a while it became easy to deal with Frost. All one had to do was set aside the public image of the poet as something false, created by him for meretricious ends, and then set aside with it all the light, folksy, quaint, optimistic poems that seemed to express meretricious and contrived sentiments. One was left with a few deeply moving poems and with a poet who was, *au fond*, both real and private, worthy to be accepted and admired by those of us who were devoted to serious modern poetry.

We all knew the story of how Ezra Pound had helped Frost get his first book published. But we also knew that later in life the two poets had disliked each other about as much as any two people can.

But the question was more complicated than Jarrell thought. Since Frost's death in 1963 his adulators in the press and poetry societies have been continually upset by the disclosures of his biographers, who have shown us a man of monumental vanity. Apparently the mask of geniality hid a raw and wounding temper. Theodore Weiss has an interesting poem called "Yes, But..." (in *The World Before Us*, p. 249), based on the contrasting manners of two poets who visited him in their old age: William Carlos Williams, who was "complaining," "struggling just to be somebody," "always open, always desperate," and who was uncertain and doubtful of himself and "could not read to the end of a verse"; and Frost, who was the older of the two but still "sturdy as an ancient oak," "no doubts shaking him," "intoning his poems well over an hour with tremendous relish." And another friend of mine who knew Frost in his last years has spoken of the annual crisis when the Nobel Prize was given to someone else. I gather Frost went to his grave embittered and indignant because the prize was never his. Well, prizes are nice, most of us like to get them, but most of us know they mean next to nothing too; and the Nobel is no better than any other. For my part I care nothing about the person; I never met Frost and saw him only once, at a reading in Chapel Hill in about 1941. Moreover I am willing to accept, at least here and for the moment, the common notion that vanity is necessary to the artistic personality, that all of us who

write suffer from it and must suffer from it, and that the diffidence of
Williams was only vanity in another form. Still the fact remains that
Frost was a conspicuous case, and the further, more important fact re-
mains that the effect of this is evident in his poems.

What one finds on rereading the *Collected Poems* is a relatively small
number of first-rate pieces and a much larger number of unsuccessful
ones. I don't mean the failures are "bad poems"; a few are, but scores
and scores of them are poems that almost make it – almost but not
quite. Usually they contain fine descriptions, pointed imagery, apt and
characteristic language; but then at some point they turn talky, insis-
tent, too literal, as if Frost were trying to coerce the meaning from his
own poetic materials. And in fact I think this is exactly what he was try-
ing to do. Call it vanity, arrogance, or whatever: Frost came to distrust
his own imagination, and believed he could *make* his poems do and
say what he wanted them to. His best poems, nearly all of them from
his first two or three books, were poems in which meaning and feeling
had come together spontaneously in their own figures and objects.
They were esthetically functional creations in the fullest sense. Frost
saw that this had happened, then spent much of his life trying to make
it happen again, trying to coerce his poems in formulaic and predict-
able ways. He ended not with poems but with editorials.

Here is one of his most popular poems, "Stopping by Woods on a
Snowy Evening":

> *Whose woods these are I think I know.*
> *His house is in the village though;*
> *He will not see me stopping here*
> *To watch his woods fill up with snow.*
>
> *My little horse must think it queer*
> *To stop without a farmhouse near*
> *Between the woods and frozen lake*
> *The darkest evening of the year.*
>
> *He gives his harness bells a shake*
> *To ask if there is some mistake.*
> *The only other sound's the sweep*
> *Of easy wind and downy flake.*

The woods are lovely, dark and deep,
But I have promises to keep,
And miles to go before I sleep,
And miles to go before I sleep.

This is not Frost's best poem. Probably his best are his long ones, too long for quoting in a short essay. But it is a good poem, to my mind quite genuine, and its meanings and feelings, larger than any stated in the poem, do emerge indirectly but unmistakably from the arrangement of images, rhythms, sounds, and syntax; we all know this, and Frost knew it too. The story is told that he wrote the poem at dawn in a state of near exhaustion after working all night on a longer poem that wasn't going well. He wrote it easily and quickly. And it turned out to say more than he knew he was saying, which is just what all of us who write poems recognize and long for. Frost longed for it too. He longed to repeat it. But his longing drove him to attempt the coercion of experience by means of contrivance and conscious control.

On the next page of the *Collected* is another very well- known poem, "For Once, Then, Something":

Others taunt me with having knell at well-curbs
Always wrong to the light, so never seeing
Deeper down in the well than where the water
Gives me back in a shining surface picture
Me myself in the summer heaven godlike
Looking out of a wreath of fern and cloud puffs.
Once, when trying with chin against a well-curb,
I discerned, as I thought, beyond the picture,
Through the picture, a something white, uncertain,
Something more of the depths – and then I lost it.
Water came to rebuke the too clear water.
One drop fell from a fern, and lo, a ripple
Shook whatever it was lay there at bottom,
Blurred it, blotted it out. What was that whiteness?
Truth? A pebble of quartz? For once, then, something.

I wish I could say exactly why I feel this poem was faked. I'm certain that "Stopping by Woods" sprang from an actual particular experience of stopping by woods. I'm certain that Frost, like everyone who lives in the country, looked down a well, probably many times. But did anyone ever "taunt" him about it? "For Once" was entirely a studio performance with only a contrived connection to any *particular* experience. Of course if I could explain my feeling about this I would have penetrated to the heart of the problem of art and reality, which is somewhat more than I expect to do in this essay. Nevertheless my feeling is distinct. Perhaps in part it comes from the exact hendecasyllables, a classical meter uncharacteristic of Frost. Perhaps also the metaphor of the well is too pat, too sentimental. But the poem itself reveals more. Its strongest part is the opening, even if it is false; the syntax is strong and interesting. I suspect those "others" actually did taunt the poet, not for his inspection of wells but for his solipsism in general. That was the real occasion for the poem, their taunt and his consequent annoyance; that was the real impetus. But it petered out, and after the first sentence the poem goes downhill rapidly. It becomes tendentious, almost whining with its italicized "once," its repetitious insistence ("something white," "something more," "blurred...., blotted....," etc.), its distractive *rebuking* waterdrop, and its inappropriate "lo" in the midst of otherwise colloquial diction. Then in the last line everything goes to pieces. The poet, in despair, *names* what his poem is about, "truth," thus committing the poet's cardinal sin; and at once the poem is destroyed, the labored metaphor of the well collapses. What lies at the bottom of the well is – is – is ... but of course it *cannot* be named, that's the whole point, any more than the meaning of the snowy woods can be named. Yet Frost did it. He pushed and pressed and tried to coerce his poem. And he did it over and over in other poems, many of them more substantial than this one.

"Two Tramps in Mud Time," another famous poem, is a case in point. It opens with the poet as wood-splitter in the thawing time of late winter, suffering the interruption of two unemployed loggers; this is good localized description, the kind Frost was master of. But then he appears not to know what to do with his opening. The poem wanders into further unnecessary description: the April day, the bluebird, the snow and water; and then it ends in four straight stanzas of editorial matter. The two tramps and the mud time are left stranded. When one thinks of how Frost would have used these figures at the time when he was writing his earlier dramatic and narrative poems, one can see clearly how he had deserted his own imagination and how he tried to make up the deficiency through conscious manipulation and force.

One point remains to be made – an important one – which is that although many of the failures are poems associated with Frost's deliberate optimism, many others are products of his darker intuition, just as his successes too are distributed, though unevenly, on both sides of his spectrum. I don't mean that Jarrell's insight is no longer useful; as a relative judgment it still holds up. But it is not as complete as we once took it to be. What else should we expect? After all, Frost's talent and his vanity both were functions of the whole man; they had to be. And if I think that in his whole career his vanity overcame his talent, and that he produced in consequence far more failures than a poet of his gifts ought to have produced, his successes remain intact – such poems as "Mending Wall," "The Black Cottage," "A Servant to Servants," "The Hill Wife," "The Axe-Helve," "The Vanishing Red," "Acquainted with the Night," and others. These are fine poems. Some have doubtless already taken on the quality of greatness as the term is used by historians. They have been well praised and well celebrated by many writers, including myself. This year they will be celebrated as no work of an American poet has ever been celebrated before (for Whitman and Dickinson, whose poems came to prominence after Frost's first success, have yet to catch up with him). Here in Vermont where I live and where Frost is a tourist attraction second only to skiing, I know many people are counting on the centennial observances to ease them through our new/old economic crisis. So I make no apology for writing a centennial essay on Frost's weaknesses. To be concerned with his weakness is, now, a form of compliment. And to be instructed by him about our own weakness is a greater compliment. I see Frost's error of forced technique repeated again and again in work by other poets, including my own. All of us who labor in vanity have this to learn from him: that only a poet who remains open to experience – and not only open but submissive, and not only to experience but to the actual newness of experience here and now – only such a poet can hope to repeat his successes.

≥⁓ ·

The Sun's Progeny

1976.

IN AUDRE LORDE'S POEMS, technically very advanced though they are, even brilliant, even cool, if by coolness one means not sophistication so much as real controlled passion: in these technically advanced poems I nevertheless find a vision of the primeval more convincing than any other I have seen in American poetry for a long time.

Passion means eternity in her system of magic; eternity means passion.

> *Father the year has fallen*
> *Leaves bedeck my careful flesh like stone*
> *One shard of brilliant summer pierced me*
> *and remains.*
> *By this only*
> *unregenerate bone*
> *I am not dead, but waiting.*
> *When the last warmth is gone*
> *I shall bear in the snow.*

The earth is speaking, the voice of nature, every woman since time began, every feminine thing, and speaking to whom? To what father? He of the "only / unregenerate bone": call him Fate. What echoes compressed in this poem, resonances, mythologies. I can only marvel.

And the language, when one stops to see it, to hear it, is *poetry*. No gimmickry from the Iowa Wrackship. Rhyme and meter in perfect modulations of song, down to that final "snow"; how beautifully, augustly, it closes the poem in a great repose. This is sexual solemnity that only the oldest minds and deepest bodies can know.

Or consider her words of cosmological alienation:

> *I was brought forth in the moonpit of a virgin*
> *condemned to light*
> *to a dry world's endless mornings*

sweeping the moon away
and wherever I fled
seeking a new road home
morning had harrowed the endless rivers
to nest in the dried out bed
of my mother sea.

Time drove the moon down to crescent
and they found me
mortal
beside a moon's crater
mouthing the ocean names of night.

At the center of the universe – far out, far in – is Loneliness, which is a function of Sex and Justice.

Audre Lorde connects it all up, sexual, racial, metaphysical, grief in the webs of nature, injustice the only constant. Her book is called *Coal*, yet it is dedicated to "the People of Sun." Why? Because coal is the sun's progeny, come forth at last to the light, to burn in pain or joy or victory or humiliation or whatever other aspect of mortality it may assume.

I am Black because I come from the earth's inside
now take my word for jewel in the open light.

May I say without overstepping myself that many of us are coal? And that coal is our aspiration, the essence of our randomly pigmented humanity? For us these words indeed are jewels in the open light.

. . . .

Italian Sensibility

1976.

ONE DIFFICULTY in dealing with translations is that we can't be sure if what looks like a shortcoming in the English is really in the original, especially when the original text is not included, which is the case with this translation by William Arrowsmith of Cesare Pavese's *Hard Labor*. Not that I'd be helped much if it were, my Italian being rudimentary.

Put it this way: if we know that a certain intention is clear in the original but not fully realized in the translation, we can still read the English *as if* it carried all the import of the untranslated poem. Don't tell me it isn't possible; we may, if we have the will, read anything whatever in any way we choose and turn *Hamlet* into doggerel, or Samuel Hoffenstein into high art, merely by changing our tone of voice. With translations of poetry this is not only possible but legitimate and necessary. There are poetic qualities, nuances, convictions, which no translator – and Arrowsmith is among the best – can convey. We must intuit them and then inject them sympathetically into the English texts. When the English texts are verbally convincing, as Arrowsmith's are, such intuiting and injecting become no more than the minimal acts of poetic faith required of any serious reader.

Pavese is called a realist, an objectivist, a poet with his eye on the thing itself, who wrote without rhetoric, fancy imagery, or other high-style devices, especially as these were practiced in Italy by the mandarins of Fascist literature. He belonged to the generation of Silone. But he wanted more; he wanted to call out from the thing itself its own greater meanings. "The surest and quickest way for us to arouse the sense of wonder," he wrote, "is to stare, unafraid, at a single object. Suddenly – miraculously – it will look like something we have never seen before." Okay so far. We know what he means and many of our own poets have said the same thing. Roethke said that "any object looked at intently enough becomes symbolic"; Levertov has written often about the innerness of objective identities and how it determines "organic form." Here is part of a poem Pavese wrote in 1936 while exiled in Calabria, far from his home in northern Italy, as a result of his opposition to the official regime:

> *The man alone gets up while the sea's still dark*
> *and the stars still flicker. A warmth like breathing*
> *drifts from the shore where the sea has its bed,*
> *sweetening the air he breathes. This is the hour when nothing*
> *can happen. Even the pipe dangling from his teeth*

is out. The sea at night makes a muffled plash.
By now the man alone has kindled a big fire of brush,
he watches it redden the ground. Before long
the sea will be like the fire, a blaze of heat.

Nothing's more bitter than the dawning of a day
when nothing will happen. Nothing's more bitter
than being useless. A greenish star, surprised
by the dawn, still droops feebly in the sky.
It looks down on the sea, still dark, and the brushwood fire
where the man, simply to do something, is warming himself.

And so on. (I wish I could quote more, but Pavese's characteristic poems are too long.) Here we have a number of Pavese's common themes: the man alone, sexual privation, uselessness, the contrast between cold sea (sterility and death) and warm ground, et cetera. But what about that star? It is "surprised," it "looks down." When I first came to it, it seemed the crassest fallacy – pathetic, romantic sentimentalism. Twenty years ago I'd have dismissed it without a twinge.

Well, Pavese *was* a romantic (he killed himself for love at age forty-two), and in spite of his tough exterior maybe a sentimentalist as well, an inverted sentimentalist; we know the type. I am twenty years older now. What I intuit is that these images ("internal images," Pavese called them) do work in the Italian poems. They are inherent in Italian sensibility. Hence I can make them work in the English too, even effortlessly and even though there are a great many of them. The rewards are worth my effort.

Hard Labor contains stunning poems, especially those about the countryside Pavese came from: the Piedmont's barren hills, vineyards, goats, humid winds, blazing suns, work-torn, love-torn, poverty-stricken people. Pavese himself was sex-haunted, a perennially rejected, and rejecting, lover; a misogynist, in fact; and his poems make a case study in romantic sexism for those who care to read them that way. But he wrote clearly, cleanly, objectively, without self-pity, and the best of his poems, a considerable number, extend beyond personal conflict and into the universally human. Until now we have known him chiefly as a novelist. He himself, however, regarded *Hard Labor* as his most important work, and indeed it does raise many important issues, both intentionally and adventitiously; issues whose urgency, personal, social, and political, is only heightened by the moving poems in which they occur. This is perfectly evident in Arrowsmith's translations.

~ . . . .

Pact of Blood

1976.

POLITICAL poetry may be written in three ways. First, the poet may put together plain statements, declarations of fact and opinion, reinforcing them with all the devices of rhetoric he or she knows how to employ. This sometimes makes good propaganda, a rallying cry, but basically it is sloganeering, not poetry, and it has no enduring value. We have seen a great deal of such writing in the U.S. during the past decade.

Secondly, the poet may transmute political substance – feelings, ideas, events – into symbolic or mythological structures, either personal or public or, often, both. The result is genuine poetry, *imagined* poetry, which nevertheless moves readers to specific political attitudes. Esthetically it is far better than the first kind, and politically it is likely to be more effective in the long run. Mind, I am speaking of political poetry in the narrow sense, poetry written expressly to support a political cause; in the broader sense all poetry, like all human action, is political. Some of our own best poets of recent years have written this second kind of poetry, e.g., Adrienne Rich, Denise Levertov, Robert Lowell, Audre Lorde, Thomas McGrath, and others.

Finally, the poet may achieve so rare a refinement of poetical vision that he can deal directly with political events and politicians and still give them a genuine esthetic quality. The supreme example is probably Dante's *Inferno*, which still moves us in political ways though the politics of Dante's time and place are utterly remote from us. But I know no U.S. poet who has sustained this third mode for more than brief passages (such as here and there in Whitman's "Song of Myself").

Notice I said "U.S. poet" in spite of the awkwardness. Because, as Pablo Neruda reminded us more than once, when we call ourselves American, meaning ourselves exclusively, it may be a grammatical convenience but it is also an insupportable rudeness to the rest of the

Western Hemisphere, and it is exactly in line with the way we have treated Latin America in other respects as well.

Never doubt that Neruda was a revolutionary. His poems in the sequence called *Canción de Gesta* were aimed directly at us, *at* and *against* us, and of course also against our puppet regimes throughout Latin America, our whole imperial mechanism. He named names – Eisenhower, Kennedy, the Central Intelligence Agency – and he named events – massacres, plots, assassinations, sellouts. Yet his poems often rose, it seems to me, into the third category; real poems suffused with poetic vision, bonded to poetic language and imagery, and so thoroughly the works of a poetic sensibility that one can't draw the line between poetic and political effects. Not that all the poems in *Canción de Gesta* are equally good; some fall short. But the majority do not. Neruda was aware of the problem of political poetry, of course. People who are attached to the lyric poems he wrote in other moods (his first book having been published in 1921 and his whole work embracing many moods and modes) accused him of poetic betrayal when he shifted to political themes. He answered them in a poem which ends:

> I have a pact of love with beauty;
> I have a pact of blood with my people.

And it was clear that for him people came before beauty, blood before love – how else could an honest man choose in the world today? Yet in fact he served both, blood and love, and served them equally well.

No other foreign poet has been as often translated in recent years. No wonder. Neruda was a great poet, a Nobel Prize-winner, a poet by turns philosophical, erotic, elegiac, comic, et cetera; and these versatilities and depths, rather than his human radicalism, are what attract most of our scholars and translators. (Significantly, *Canción de Gesta* is not even mentioned in the standard book of translations from his late work.) It would take a specialist just to keep track of all the English versions, however, and I am no specialist. I can say only that every translation I have seen, without exception, strikes me as barely adequate, the present one of *Canción de Gesta*, called *Song of Protest*, being no better than the rest, which is why I quote only two lines from it. Yet Neruda's power penetrates even the most awkward English and makes the translations worth reading.

Canción de Gesta was first published in 1960, then reprinted many times throughout Latin America, occasionally with new poems added or old ones revised. But Neruda was unable to carry it far enough to take in the events in his own country that are so much on our minds now. The cruel overthrow of Allende, designed at least in part by our own Central Intelligence Agency, meant the end of Neruda too, whether directly or indirectly doesn't matter. He died. *Song of Protest* ends, very fittingly, with an account of his funeral, his body lying "in state" in the muddy library of his house. The rightist militia had wrecked it, ransacked it. Then they denied his right to a public funeral. There was a procession through the streets to the burial, the poet's body on a common wagon, the people gathering behind as it went, ordinary people, poor people, who chanted his poems by heart, flouting the militia. What courage. What love. And what poems. We neglect them only at our peril, both poetic and political.

🖎 . . . .

The Question of Poetic Form

1976.

…151. Sometimes when manufacturers go into business for the first time they give their products high model-numbers, as if to suggest that they are old companies with long experience in similar antecedent productions. In somewhat the same spirit, though I hope for reasons less specious, I begin here with paragraph 151. God knows I'm an old company,* and perhaps only He knows the number of my antecedent productions. But more specifically what I want to suggest by my high model-number is the time that has gone into the preparation of this particular product, years of random "scholarship," voluminous notes, fragments, citations, experimental pages, scattered bibliographies, and so on, with which I sit surrounded now – more than enough to fill up 150 introductory paragraphs. Then rejoice with me, they are all jettisoned. No footnotes, no quotations, and as few proper names as I can get by with: that is how I've decided to proceed. Let the thing be ab-

---

* I was 55. Oh, the world-weariness of the young. H.C., 1994.

stract, subjective, principled. Academic critics and philosophers have their reasons, I know, but their reasons are not mine; nor are they the reader's, at least not if my readers are the people I hope to address, fellow poets and lovers of poetry.

152. Yet aside from the fact that I would find it personally too disheartening not even to mention my labors, a further point arises from these missing 150 paragraphs. For a long time I shuffled my papers, trying to make my notes fall into a pattern that would be useful to me, until at last I saw the truth: there is no pattern. And the reason is clear; I knew it all along, but was intimidated from applying it by the manners of the very scholars whose works I was reading. Virtually every important theory of poetry has been invented by a poet. That is the nub of it. And each theory has sprung from the poet's own emotional and esthetic needs in his particular time and place – or hers, for many important statements have come, especially recently, from women – and moreover each theory has been derived from what the poet has observed of his or her own psychology in his or her own workshop. In short, the theories are subjective. Each theorist begins by returning, not to "first principles," since in art they do not exist, but to experience, and this was as true of Sir William Temple and Percy Shelley as it has been more recently of Yvor Winters or Charles Olson. The scholarship is irrelevant. And no wonder the theories are inconsistent and often in conflict; no wonder there is no pattern and the categories break down, so that the scholars end, as one of them has, by calling Pope a neoclassical romanticist or by using every term in their catalogues, ineffectually, for Ezra Pound. Yet the statements of Pope and Pound and other poets remain crucial, the indispensable documents of our poetic understanding. In them I find both urgency of feeling and the irrefragability of knowledge, the real knowledge of what happens when a poem is written. Both qualities are what keep art and the artist alive.

153. I see no pattern then; quite the contrary. And consequently what I am doing here above all is asking for...but I don't know what to call it. It is neither reconciliation nor toleration. Among genuinely conflicting views reconciliation is impossible, while toleration implies indifference or a kind of petrified Quakerish absolutism of restraint. These are not what I mean at all. Yet it is true that I abhor sectarianism in the arts, or dogmatism of any kind. What I am asking for, I think, is

the state of mind that can see and accept and *believe* ideas in conflict, without ambivalence or a sense of self-divisiveness. Call it eclecticism if you will. I've been accused of it often enough, the word flung at me like a curse. But just as I, a radical, distrust other radicals who are not in part conservatives – i.e., who are ideologues – so I distrust poets who cannot perceive the multiplexity of their art, perceive it and relish it. Poetry is where you find it. I am convinced of this: convinced as a matter of temperament, as a matter of thirty years' intensive critical reading, and as a matter of my perception of human reality – the equivalence of lives and hence of values. So if you find poetry in Blake but not in Pope, or the other way around, that's OK, you are better off than people who find it in neither. But if you find it in both, then you are my kind of reader, my kind of human being.

154. Moreover poetry is a mystery. I don't mean the poem on the page, though that is difficult enough. I mean what went before: poetry as process, poetry as a function of what we call, lumping many things together, imagination. Think how long science has worked, thus far in vain, to explain the origin of life, which appears to be a simple problem, comparatively speaking, involving few and simple factors. Then think of trying to explain the imagination; first the imagination in general, then a particular imagination: the factors are incalculable. I believe it will never be done. Hence what anyone says about poetry, provided it be grounded in knowledge, is as true as what anyone else may say, though the two sayings utterly conflict. Yet they can be held in the mind together, they can be believed together. And still the element of mystery will remain. In my opinion anything less or other than this tends toward absolutism, bad thinking, and obstruction in the poetic comity.

155. What about Aristotle? He was no poet; far from it. It shows unquestionably in his theory of poetry. He wrote about art from the point of view not of the artist but of the spectator, the playgoer. He described the psychology of esthetic experience; pity and woe, the notion of catharsis. This is interesting and useful, and from it certain ideas may be extrapolated about the work itself, the play. But about playwriting, about art as process? No. And Aristotle's attempt to do it – the feeble theory of imitation – as well as the attempts of a great many others after him, have produced confusion and irrelevance for nearly 2500 years. To my mind this is the giveaway. A real theory of art begins with pro-

cess and accepts the inevitability of mystery; it rests content with its own incompleteness. A spurious theory begins somewhere else and tries to explain everything.

156. The word that seems to incorporate most fully the essential idea of imaginative process is the word *form*. But at once the element of mystery makes itself known, for the word has been used in so many different ways, with so much looseness and imprecision, that clearly people do not know what it really means; or perhaps the word itself really means more, implicitly or innately, than the people mean, or can mean, when they use it. Hence the imprecision can never be eliminated; the craftiest philosopher will never produce anything but a partial definition. Yet this is no reason for not trying. A few years ago I was attacked by an eminent poet, publicly and bitterly, because in a short piece on another topic I had said that the staggered tercets used by Williams in his later poems are a "form." Granted, I was using the word imprecisely, which is what one must do with these large, complex, enigmatic terms, especially in short pieces, if one is to avoid a breakdown of communication. I am sure my readers knew what I meant. But the eminence was not satisfied; apparently he was infuriated. No, he said, the staggered tercets are merely a style; the form is something deeper, the whole incalculable ensemble of feelings, tones, connotations, images, and so on that bodies forth the poem; and I purposely, if quaintly, say "bodies forth" rather than "embodies" because I think this exactly conveys my attacker's meaning and the distinction is worth attending to. Of course he is right. I agree with him; I agreed with him then and before then. But at the same time he was only partly right, and he was being dogmatic in just the sense I have referred to, that is, by insisting arbitrarily that part of the truth is the whole of the truth, and by pinning everything upon an understanding of terms. This is what dogma is. Yet often enough in the past the meanings of our terms have been reversed. *Form* has meant the poem's outer, observable, imitable, and more or less static materiality; *style* has meant its inner quality, essentially hidden and unanalyzable, the properties that bind and move and individuate. Indeed this was the common use of the two words in literary theory from Lessing and Goethe to T.S. Eliot. And all that is proven by this is that poets are always talking about the same things, but with different names, different tones, different emphases, and different perceptual orientations. How could they

otherwise, when each returns to his or her own experience for the knowledge from which to write?

157. So we see the danger, namely, that experience which leads to knowledge will lead further to dogmatism. It happens all the time, by no means more frequently among poets than among others. Yet it isn't necessary. Neither in human nor in categorical terms is this progression – experience → knowledge → dogma – inevitable, it can be interrupted anywhere by reasonableness and humility. What do we mean by the word *form* in ordinary speech? What for instance is the form of an apple? Certainly it is not only the external appearance, its roundness, redness, firmness, and so on. Nor is it only the inner molecular structure. Nor is it the mysterious genetic force that creates appleness in the apple. It is all these things and more, the whole apple. The form *is* the apple. We cannot separate them. In philosophical terms it is the entire essence of the apple plus its existence, the fact of its being. I think that when we use the word *form* in reference to a poem we should use it in just this way. It means the whole poem, nothing less. We may speak of outer and inner form, and in fact I think we must, provided we remember that these are relative terms, relative to each other and to the objectives of any particular inquiry. An image, for example, may be an element of outer form at one time or of inner form at another: it depends on how you look at it. But the form *is* the poem.

158. As for style, to my mind it is not something different from form but something contained within form, a component of form. True, it is unlike other components. But they themselves are more or less unlike one another, so why should this cause difficulty? The best definition I can make is this: style is the property of a poem that expresses the poet's personality, either his real personality or his invented personality, or most likely a combination of the two. It is manifested in the concrete elements of form: syntax, diction, rhythm, characteristic patterns of sound and imagery, and so on; and if one has sufficient patience these elements can be identified, classified, tabulated, they can be put through the whole sequence of analytic techniques; yet style will remain in the end, like the personality behind it (though not on the same scale), practically indemonstrable. Style consists of factors so minutely constituted and so obscurely combined that they simply are not separable and not measurable, except in the grossest ways. Yet we know a style when we see it or hear it; we recognize it and are attracted or re-

pelled by it. One reason for this is the fact that style is a continuing aspect (or congeries of aspects) in a poet's work. It remains consistently itself from one poem to another, even though the poems in other respects are dissimilar. We speak of the "growth" and "maturity" of a poet's style in the same way that we speak of the growth and maturity of a person. This is an interesting fact; it may even sometimes be a crucial fact, as when we are attempting to explain the incidence of poetic genius. But it can also be a dangerous fact, for it leads to the state of mind in which style seems to be abstract from the poem, abstract from form itself. This is a delusion, and moreover a delusion that brings us near the heart of the question of poetic form.

159. Some people will say that my allegation regarding outer and inner form is sloppy. I don't see why. I am comfortable in my radical relativism (which I call equivalentism), and am frankly unable to explain why others shouldn't be comfortable in it too. Yet I know what they have in mind. Some kinds of outer form, they will say, are repeatable. Sonnets, villanelles, that sort of thing; and of course it is quite true that the structures of meter and rhyme in some such poems may be indicated roughly but schematically by stress marks and letterings, and then may be imitated in new substances of words, images, feelings, experiences, and so on. My critics will say that this repeatability of certain elements of form makes them absolutely distinct from other elements that cannot be repeated. Again I don't see why. To me the poem in its wholeness is what is important, and I do not care for classification. Besides, absolute classifications are a myth. Simply because we can say that two poems written a hundred years apart are both Petrarchan sonnets, does that make them the same? Obviously not. Moreover the statement itself seems to me to have only the most superficial classificative meaning; it is virtually useless. Oh, I know what immense complexes of cultural value may adhere to the Petrarchan sonnet or to other conventional classes of poetic structure, and how in certain contexts, outside the discussion of form, these values may be most decidedly *not* useless. OK. But here I *am* discussing form, and the point I want to make is that in reality no element of form is perfectly repeatable and no element is perfectly unique. Outer and inner form may approach these polar absolutes at either end, but they cannot reach them. They cannot reach them because the absolutes lie outside the poem. A rhyme scheme is not a poem; it is a complete abstraction, a *scheme,*

which has only the absoluteness – if that is the right term – of a Euclidean triangle existing nowhere in nature. Similarly the combination of vital energies and individual referents at the heart of a poem, its inner form, may be almost unique, almost unanalyzable or indiscerptible, but it cannot be absolutely so, for then the poem would cease to be a product of human invention and would assume a status equivalent to that of the creaturely inventor himself or herself, a part of *natura naturata*; and that, I believe – I fervently hope – is impossible. (Though I know many poets who claim just this for their own inventions and their own inventive powers.) In short, it is not a question of repeatability but of imitation. And it is not a question of facsimile but of approximation. All we can say about the abstractability of form, including style, is that some elements of form, chiefly the outer, are more or less amenable to imitation, and that other elements, chiefly the inner, are resistant to it. Yet this is saying a good deal. The form *is* the poem, and all its elements lie *within* the poem. Repeatability is a delusion. Finally even style, though I have noted its continuance from poem to poem, does not continue by means of repetition but by means of self-imitation, that is to say, imperfectly, hence changeably and developmentally; an unchanging style would be a dead style, or no style at all; it certainly could not be a part of poetry.

160. I don't know if what I have written in this last paragraph is clear. Let me reduce it to an analogy. By examining a number of apples one can draw up a generalized schematic definition of an apple, and by using modern methods of investigation one can make this definition account not only for an apple's external appearance but for its invisible internal structure and its animate energy, the forces that determine both its specificity and its individuality. Conceivably this definition might be useful, since by referring to it one could recognize an apple whenever one saw it. Beyond that, if one were inclined to make classifications the definition would help in distinguishing the apple from other classes of fruit. But no one, not even the most ardent lovers of definition, would say that the definition *is* the apple. Obviously the definition is only a definition. And yet some people say that the definition is the *form* of the apple. Can this be? I don't see how. Can a form exist apart from the thing it forms, or rather apart from the thing that makes it a form, that informs it? Can we have such a thing as an unformed form? No, a definition is only a definition, a generalization, an

abstraction; and a form, by virtue of being a form, is concrete. Perforce the apple's form cannot exist outside the apple.

161. When I put the matter this way the source of difficulty becomes clear immediately: Plato and his concept of the ideal. Plato made a shrewd observation of human psychology when he conceived his ideals, or as he called them Ideas; unquestionably our imaginations do contain an abstracting faculty with which we derive and separate ideas from things, and often these ideas become ideals in both the Platonic and modern senses. They are universals, though that is not saying as much as people often mean when they use this word. They are what enable us to be perfectionists, knowing the ideal is unattainable yet striving toward it; which is what accounts for poetry and most other human excellences. Every poet has in his or her head the "idea" of the perfect poem, though it has never been written and never will be. But to infer from this useful but passive quality that ideals – definitions, "forms" – are active or instrumental in the realm of practice, in poetry or in nature, seems to me mere fancy.

162. I should think poets ought to see this more easily than most people. A form is an effect, not a cause. Of course I don't say that in a chain of cultural actions and reactions a form, or rather the abstract definition of a form, may not play a causal role; without doubt it may, and obviously the element of convention in literature is large and important. But considered in conceptual purity, a form is not a cause. Do we work from the form toward the poem? That is the mode of the set piece, the classroom exercise – and we know what kind of "poems" come from that. No, we work from the thing always, from the perception or experience of the thing, and we move thence into feelings and ideas and other cultural associations, and finally into language, where by trial and error we seek what will be expressive of the thing. If we are lucky we find it, and only then do we arrive, almost by accident or as an afterthought, at form. In one sense form is a byproduct of poetry, though this is not to deny its essentiality. Naturally I do not mean either that the actual complicated processes of poetic imagination can be reduced to any such simple progression as the one I have suggested. The whole transaction may occur in a flash, literally simultaneously. Formal intuitions may appear at the very beginning. I am convinced that no method of analysis will ever be contrived which is refined enough to isolate all the energies and materials combined in the poetic

act. Yet at the same time I do suggest that form in itself is never the cause, and certainly never the instrument (the efficient cause), of real poetry, and I believe this is something all real poets can verify from their own experience.

163. Until now my strategy has been to avoid using the two words that in fact have been the crucial terms in all my speculations about poetic form for several years, the words *organic* and *fixed*. Yet they are my reason for these paragraphs. The notions I have set down here have been set down thousands of times before, I'm sure, frequently by writers more skillful and gifted than I. Hence what impels me is my awareness that each age attacks the perennial topics from the standpoint of its particular need, with its peculiar angle of vision and edge of feeling. And our age, speaking in terms of poetry, seems to revolve predominantly around these two terms. Organic form versus fixed form: that indicates how we look at the question of poetic form, and it pretty well suggests the quality of our feeling about it. Certainly we are earnest and combative, we are very acutely caught up. Have poets in earlier times worried themselves quite as much as we do about form in poetry? Even the word itself – *form* – has about it now a flavor of ultimacy, almost a numen, that I don't think it possessed in ages past. Of course there are good reasons for this, at least in terms of literary evolution. Anyone who has lived through the past thirty or forty years of poetry in America knows exactly how the conflict between fixed form and organic form came about, and why. But I am not interested here in the history or sociology of poetry; I am interested in the thing itself, and I hope what I have written so far shows that I think both terms, *organic* and *fixed*, as they appear in common usage among poets today, are misapplied. Clearly this is the case with fixed form. If form cannot be abstracted it cannot be fixed; at best it can only be turned into a definition, a scheme. The case with organic form seems less clear, because in some sense the concept of organic form is close to what I have been saying about form as the effect or outcome of poetry. But frequently the advocates of organic form go further; they say that the forms of their poems are taken, if not from the ideal forms of the Platonic heavens, then from forms in nature, in experience, in the phenomenal world. But forms in the phenomenal world are no more abstractions than any other forms, and transference is impossible. At best poetic form is an analogy to nonesthetic form, but a very, very remote

analogy; so remote indeed that I think it serves no purpose, and the citing of it only beclouds the issue. If what I have argued here is true, that is, that form is the poem, then form is autonomous – it can be nothing else; which is only what poets have said in other ways for centuries. (Though this does not mean, I would insist, that the poem in its totality of feeling, meaning, and value is separable from morality or ordinary human relevance.) Well, if form is autonomous then let us treat it as such.

164. But if form is autonomous it is also indigenous. A particular poetic form is solely *in* a particular poem; it *is* the poem. Hence it inheres solely in the materials of that poem (which by extension or implication may include the poem's origins). From this I conceive that if an analogy exists between a poetic form and a form in nature, this analogy is solely and necessarily a coincidence; and it is meaningless. After all, what functional analogy can exist between the forms of generally differing materials? To say that a poetic form is analogous to a form in nature is the same as saying that a horse is like a pool table, or a dragonfly like a seraph.

165. Going back to *outer* and *inner*, these are the terms I prefer, applied with strict relativism. They are more exact than *fixed* and *organic*. Moreover I like them better because they insinuate no conflict, no war, but rather a consonance. To my mind warring poets, because they are dealing with the very substance of truth – our vision of reality – are almost as dangerous and a good deal sillier than warring generals.

166. Of course I don't mean to deny what is as plain as the nose on anyone's face: for example, that Alexander Pope wrote nearly all his poems in closed pentameter couplets. But I would say three things. First, the misnamed "heroic couplet," which seems to us the height of artifice, was just the opposite in the minds of those who used it. Dryden chose the couplet because he thought it the plainest mode available, the verse "nearest prose," and he chose it in conscious reaction against the artificial stanzaic modes that had dominated English poetry during most of the sixteenth and seventeenth centuries. In short he and his many followers thought they were liberating poetry, just as Coleridge and Wordsworth liberated it a hundred years later, or Pound and Williams a hundred years after that. The history of poetry is a continual fixing and freeing of conventions. It follows that these poets, Dryden and Pope, really were engaged in a liberation; and it fol-

lows too that we ought always to pay at least some attention to history and fashion, the worldly determinants, in our consideration of any poetry. Secondly, I do not think the couplet was a fixed form. I do not think it for the same reason that I do not think any form can be fixed. Granted, it was a pattern that was imitated by many versewriters. But among the best poets it was a form like any other poetic form: the natural, spontaneous (which does not mean instantaneous) effect of the causal topics, feelings, and attitudes from which their poems derived. It is evident in the best of Pope. He himself said: "I have followed... the significance of the numbers, and the adapting them to the sense, much more even than Dryden, and much oftener than anyone minds it.... The great rule of verse is to be musical." Today we do not like "numbers" and "rules"; but I get from this the distinct feeling that when Pope spoke of "adapting," he was thinking about poetic form in a way close to my own. And I know for certain that what he meant by "musical" had little to do with rhyming and everything to do with the total harmony of language and substance. Think of the material of Pope's poems. Could it have engendered any other poetic form? I believe the closed pentameter couplet was natural to Pope, "organic" if you like, and if his poems are not as well unified *poetically* as any others of a similar kind and scope, if the best of them are not *poems* in exactly the same sense we mean today, then I don't know how to read poetry. (But I do.) Thirdly, in another sense of the word, different from the sense I have been using, every poetic form is fixed. It cannot be otherwise. Unless a poem is destroyed as soon as it is written, its form exists as a thing in the world, to be observed by anyone who wishes to observe it, particularly by the poet who created it. Thus every poetic form exists in its permanent concreteness – relatively speaking, of course – and thus it gives rise to influence. It produces a convention, and this convention may reenter the poet's sensibility and become part of the apparatus of imagination. It happens with all poets. After all Whitman continued to follow the conventions of his poems quite as narrowly as Pope followed the conventions of his; and in this sense the "organic" poets of today are writing in forms as fixed as any, as fixed, say, as the heroic couplet. I grant it would be difficult in practice to discriminate between what I am here calling a convention and what I earlier called a style; yet in theory it must be possible, because a style is what is expressive of a poet's personality, whereas a convention is a generalized "feeling" about language and structure, often with broadly cultural associations, which can enter anyone's sensibility, not just its creator's. It would be silly to deny a connection among James Wright, Galway Kinnell, and W. S. Merwin, for instance, or among Denise Levertov, Robert Creeley, and Robert Duncan. And I suspect that in part these connections consist of the poets' common and mostly unconscious awareness of conventions that have arisen from the multiplexity and multiplicity of their own created, "fixed" poetic forms.

167. Poetry is where you find it. Its form is always its own. The elements of outer form, such as language, texture, or tone, may move sometimes from and sometimes toward the elements of inner form, such as structures of imagery and feeling, symbols, or scarcely revealed nodes of imaginative energy. But if the poem is a real poem its whole form will be integrated. No element of outer form, considered apart from the rest, can signify whether or not a poem, an old poem or a new poem, is real; nor can any element of inner form, so considered. Hence the classification of poems, old or new, is a hurtful, false endeavor. Let the warring cease.

🖉 ·

The Act of Love: Poetry and Personality
1976.

A FEW YEARS AGO I wrote an essay about the self-creating function of the poet.* Actually the essay was about the poetry of Robert Lowell, but I had a broader concern. I was using Lowell's poems, especially his autobiographical ones, to show how poets in our time had resolved the moral impasse of the autonomous poem, that fixture of the New Criticism and of much Western literature in the period between the two wars. The autonomous poem, explicable in terms of itself, had for its consequence a dangerous separation of art from reality, which was explicit in some writers and implicit in a great many more. Poets found themselves conceptually stranded on an esthetic plane of being,

---

* "A Meaning of Robert Lowell," p. 70.

divorced from practical or moral responsibility, accountable only to abstract style or to some other aspect of imagined form. In principle they were little more than fantasists.

Of course I am compressing damnably. Readers who are interested must look at the Lowell essay. But the point here is that I showed, or tried to show, how poets of roughly my generation had rebelled against this conundrum of their elders by striking through it, as through a Gordian knot, and declaring their responsibility not to art but to life, which in artistic terms meant to the creation of life, and hence specifically to the creation of their own lives. The poet, I said, was engaged in the conversion of crude experience into personality through metaphor and the other disciplines of the instrumental imagination, and I used the term personality in very nearly the sense given to it by Nikolai Berdyaev, though without his Christian applications – that is, to mean the whole individual subjectivity, the spirit-body-soul. This act of creation I conceived to be a deeply moral, practical endeavor. Certainly the point was not original with me; or perhaps I should say it was original with a great many people during the 1950s and 1960s when the thrust of existentialist ethics was penetrating swiftly into contemporary awareness. One saw it emerging in many forms throughout literature, psychoanalysis, and other sectors of artistic and intellectual life. By now it has filtered down to a younger generation that has no idea of its origins.

In fact one sees it everywhere. But it has suffered an abridgment, a shortcutting. Instead of responsibility to life, instead of responsibility to his or her own personality as the archetype of life, the poet now is responsible to the private personality and nothing more. The danger of the existentialist ethic has always been its tendency to turn into solipsism, and this has happened. All the old terms – authenticity, dignity of the individual, the freedom to be, and so on – have become merely a license to indulge the self, the ego; anything goes. In recent years we have observed a considerable increase in surrealist or semi-surrealist or parasurrealist poetry, in which the poets unabashedly derive their important words and images from private referents that no one else can be expected to understand. The poets may be creating themselves, but they are doing so in privacy. The result is poetry that has achieved another kind of autonomy, the autonomy of isolation; call it singularity in the strictest sense. Yet these poets publish their poems;

they even read them aloud in front of audiences; they do it with eager-
ness and aplomb. One can only surmise that the old notion of poetry
as a social mechanism is dying from self-suffocation.

We need to find a way to link the self-creating poet, at work in the
utterness of his subjectivity, with the community; and we need to do it
without resorting to former externalized or objectified intellectual con-
trivances, such as the idea of the masterpiece or the idea of the didactic
or communicative function of art. In my Lowell essay I suggested that
since people are pretty much alike the poet who is converting his or
her own experience into his or her own personality can presume a re-
sponse from readers with analogous configurations of experience and
personality. This is true, I think, and in a rough way it accounts for the
practical efficacy of a poem. But it is undeniably rough, not to say lame,
not to say feeble. We need something both stronger and more acute, a
concept fully integrated into existentialist feeling and at the same time
close to our practical knowledge of writing and reading. I shall attempt
it. I do so with diffidence, of course – and only partly because the at-
tempt is difficult. The worst is that I have, and in such an undertaking
can only have, my own practical knowledge to go on.

For here, as in the poem and in life, subjectivity is all. To objectify is to
destroy. Yet I must write abstractly, I have no choice. It is a question
then of abstracting oneself. I began writing this essay, abruptly, when I
was reading Berdyaev's *Slavery and Freedom*, a book which seemed to
me an echo not only of much that I had read earlier, from Kierkegaard
to Buber, but also of my own thought and feeling over a long duration;
an echo moreover that was a little off pitch in both cases, enough to
throw my own song, so to speak, into truer harmony. I began to write at
once, laying down the book when I had read only as far as page 59. But
that is far enough for me to see that though I cannot accept all elements
of Berdyaev's personalist philosophy, the basic element seems indis-
pensable, to me and to all poets, and for that matter to all really human
beings – namely, his assertion that personality is an existential phe-
nomenon. It is apart from essence. What this means is that though per-
sonality may be created from components of the objective world, since
there are no other components, it nevertheless passes into pure subjec-
tivity, free and alone, as it comes into being through the agency of

imagination. It is no longer an object; it transcends objects. When it is objectified, as in a discussion among social scientists or psychologists or polititians, it is destroyed; it disappears. Yet in another sense it never disappears; it is universal and relative; it exists in every consciousness. True, it may never be fully realized; its actualization in any consciousness may always be partial and potential, or even impeded and subverted. But at the same time its degree of realization at any moment *is* its fullness, which cannot at that moment be more. And this fullness is the whole subjectivity. Hence, returning to my statement at the head of this paragraph, I can know personality only through my own.

In other words personality is a phenomenon of pure existence. It occurs in what have been called our existential moments, our moments outside time, moments when the person is removed entirely from society, from history, from biology, and from all determinants, even from esthetic criteria and methodologies; for determinants are the depersonalizing, the personality-destroying, forces of the world. Among materialists and positivists an escape from determination is thought impossible, but their view seems shallow now and quaint in the light of contemporary experience. At all events poets know better – they *feel* that they know better. Their existential moments are what they call their "periods of creativity"; they speak of "working freely," "having a hot spell," and so on. They know that when they are intensely engaged in a poem, spontaneously engendering imagery and verbal compounds from the imagined structures of remembered experience, they are wholly beyond determination – they are personalities. Then they have pierced time and entered eternity. They exist. They are free.

It is a spiritual happening – at least I do not know what else to call it even though all my life I've been uncomfortable with irrationalism – and of course it is not confined to poets; quite the contrary. My own existence-in-personality has had its purest moments in jazz improvisation, which I do badly. (But that is a depersonalizing worldly judgment.) A musician engrossed in the swift unwinding of his or her own invention effects an intensity of existence rarely accessible to the poet, because words are more complex and ambiguous, hence more recalcitrant, than a line of musical tones in a clear chord succession. But this is a cavil, an uncertain one at that; poets too have their moments of intensity, what the ancients called fury and we translate as exaltation.

These moments are a spiritual happening. As for other people, I am neither mechanic nor farmer, but at times I have worked at both trades in a half-professional capacity, and I know that personality can flourish, existence can flourish, in the engagement with machines and the land, though this is no longer permitted as an ordinary thing in our civilization. Every consciousness is a personality *in posse*. And we know now, as our ancient forerunners knew also and our more recent forerunners forgot, that we must not exclude the animals – that is, the other animals.

Notice that I say spiritual happening, not mystical happening. The distinction is important. I feel it is more than a matter of degree. I am not a religious person, at least not as this is usually understood; but once or twice I have seen visions and more often I have experienced other hallucinations, chiefly auditory. I do not know how to explain them, though I have made guesses. I do know that the occasions have been painful, not happy. I think true mystical experience must be an ecstasy, which means literally a transportation out of one's place (*ekstasis*): a loss of identity. Spiritual experience is the opposite: an intensification of identity. The poet at work is in firmer command of what he knows, all of what he knows, than at any other time. Indeed *work* is the key word here. The spirit of human beings may be capable of development or mutational stages beyond my comprehension – I certainly do not comprehend visions or the antics of parapsychology – but the stage I do comprehend, which I therefore call spiritual and not mystical, is the stage that is reached through work.

For my part, moreover, I cannot project this concept of spirit and personality onto any traditional religion that I know, though analogues and affinities occur in many of them. Berdyaev's Catholicism seems forced and almost irrelevant to me; not insincere, nothing as gross as that, but still not genuinely necessary. I respect his faith, but I feel he could get rid of it without jeopardizing his moral, psychological, and existential standing.* Yet I do use the word spiritual. I believe that personality is a dynamic process, a process of transcendence, extending always beyond itself, and that if this transcension permanently ceases personality will fall back into objectification and death, or at least into

---

* See Thomas Merton's very important essays on the work of Albert Camus for a remarkably clear, sympathetic statement of the basic positions.

a kind of suspended animation. But I am unclear about the *end* of tran-
scendence, the *toward-which*. I have been for years and I think I always
will be. I am not sure there *is* an end, beyond the realization of person-
ality in itself and for itself. I have no eschatological expectations what-
ever. But I use the word *spiritual* to mean the substance of feeling
when personality passes out of time's determinants and into pure ex-
istence, which I have called (perhaps with the license of fancy) eter-
nity; and in poems I have spoken of meetings there with the holy spirit
or the creative spirit, though my meaning has not been the same as that
which Christians use when they refer to the third attribute of the Trin-
ity. If I have had any externalization in mind it has been something
more pagan, I suppose, something nearer the Muse. At any rate I think
I know what he meant when Paul Goodman in his poems called upon
the holy creative spirit or Saint Harmony. But for me all externali-
zations are weak and vague, a poorer, less helpful mystery than that
which lies within. Chiefly I think of the transcendence accomplished
by personality as a process of innerness; and of the holy spirit as my
own. Inward lies the real spiritual power, if power it be, toward which
transcendence reaches. Transcendence is a pushing through the petals
of memory and feeling toward the deeper center of the flower. No
doubt some will say I am speaking metaphorically, groping after per-
sonal intuition; for them outer and inner are the same, eternity is a
circle, infinity a double loop. Perhaps. I can't say much about that. To
my mind the idea of the spiritual and the idea of the adept are anti-
pathetic. If I am using metaphor it is because I know no other way to
convey my meaning; yet the meaning is there.

How does this bring me toward a linkage of poetry and commu-
nity? We seem to have come to a point where the poet is utterly lost in
himself. But I think a linkage is possible.

First a distinction must be drawn between individuality and indepen-
dence. Of course on one level this is a matter of personal psychology,
personal intuition; but it has general ramifications too. The latter term,
independence, was another catchword popular during the existential
discussions of a few years back, along with dignity, authenticity, and
the like. It was meant as a means to focus down on the primacy and au-
tonomy of the single personality in the great existential transvaluation
of values; down with corporation in all its ugliness, up with men and

women – consciousness is all! "Existence before essence" was another catch phrase, almost a slogan, and *"vive la différence"* turned up in poem after poem during the 1950s. In fact there *was* a shift of values, a shift noticeable especially but by no means entirely among young people, augmenting the shift that had been going on for a hundred years and is still going on. But meanwhile the corporate world has done what we all know it has done, and the outlook at the present moment is not – well, not encouraging to say the least.*

All this throws light on the meaning of independence. But I think the meaning can best be seen through a contrast with individuality, and this requires a look at ego-philosophy and particularly at Max Stirner. Who knows how many millions of people in the world are living by Stirner's philosophy who have never heard of him and who would be shocked to know that their feelings were at least shared if not in part originated by a man who holds an honored place in anarchist lineage. It is true nevertheless. Stirner's *The Ego and His Own*† is in many respects a characteristic work of the nineteenth century, full of ebullience and optimism and hearty rhetoric. It takes off from Rousseauistic political philosophy (its first line is a quotation from Goethe: *"Ich hab' Mein' Sach' auf Nichts gestellt"* – literally, "I have founded my interest on nothing"), with its roots in the Cartesian *cogito*, combined with Malthusian speculations and in vehement reaction against the dominant Hegelianism of the time, all stirred and fermented by the revolutionary feelings of pre-1848. In striking ways Stirner was the double, the inverted double, of Kierkegaard. His book was radical enough, no doubt of that. He called – loudly – for the desanctification of everything: God, church, state, institutionalism of every kind, nationhood, fellowship, marriage, nature, love, custom, law, and so on; nothing stood before the all-compelling supremacy of Stirner's one knowable reality, the individual ego. So far so good. The trouble was that he never developed his idea of ego beyond a rudimentary stage; perhaps in his time and place he could not do so. For him the human species comprised only a miscellaneous assortment of egos, single

---

* And now? After Reagan, Bush, Clinton? The "present moment" in 1976 looks almost rosy. H.C., 1994.

† *Der Einzige und sein Eigenthum* (1845). It was not translated into French until 1900 or into English until 1907, but it was well-known before then among European intellectuals. "Max Stirner" was a pseudonym for J. Kaspar Schmidt.

nodes of consciousness endowed, each one, with demoniac self-regard. At least this is the general impression one takes from his book, in spite of his perfunctory gestures toward mutualism, associationism, and other Proudhonian concepts. Ego was all. Hence *The Ego and His Own*, in which Stirner clearly wished to project a philosophical foundation for radicalism, produced the contrary effect, at least in large measure: it contributed to conservative anarchism and became a support, though seldom openly acknowledged, of laissez-faire. In effect it is the keystone in the arch linking anarchic and conservative thought. Nietzsche, for instance, had read Stirner closely, and one sees more than a trace of ego-philosophy in Zarathustra.

Berdyaev quotes a telling aphorism, which he credits to Péguy, to the effect that the individual is each man's own bourgeois, whom he must confront and conquer. It is true. Yet simply to call individualism the enemy is not enough; it is too much a part of us, too much a necessary part of us. If the war comes between individualists and corporatists I will no doubt enroll myself with the former, feeling the soldier's uneasy sense that his own cause is far from pristine. Yet the distinction between individuality and independence is crucial, especially for the poet. An individual can never become a personality, for two reasons: first because the ego can never remove itself from objectivity; second because the ego can never lose itself in pure existence. Something must be said about each of these considerations.

The ego can never remove itself from objectivity because ego is itself an object, and knows itself to be an object, in the world of objects. It is continually threatened by the objective world – abused, coerced, displaced. In other words its responses are determined; it is an unfree thing. It is caught, as surely as the other egos that seek to catch it. Individuality is the twin of corporatism, and the two dance together always. Only independent consciousness can find real subjectivity and become a personality, because independence is free from ego, free from self-regard, and hence free from the threatening, determining forces of objectivity.

Similarly ego can never lose itself in pure existence, can never experience personality as a process of transcendence, because it cannot let go of itself. Throughout this essay I have avoided the word *self* wherever possible, though it is not always avoidable. Certainly it is an ambiguous word; in its narrowest sense it means ego, in its broadest the whole amalgam of personality, as when a mystic speaks of the confrontation between God and self; and of course it can mean any phase of completeness or incompleteness in between. Consequently there is a seeming contradiction here; I have spoken of personality's transcendence as a process of inwardness and of the poet as a person lost in himself or herself, and I have spoken also of ego as that which cannot lose itself. But clearly in the former case I was using self in its broadest sense, and in the latter in its narrowest. Clearly also the farthermost reaches of self are inaccessible to ego, which means that individuality cannot enter into transcendence or become a personality, while independence can. It is another question whether or not ego is necessary to draw us back from transcendence into the common world or what would become of the unimaginable person who is egoless.

A poet is a personality. He or she is independent, at least to the extent that he or she is a real poet; someone who has conquered his or her bourgeois. When at work the poet is in a process of transcendence – and now I will change the term to self-transcendence – which is a spiritual state of pure existence. He or she is resolutely subjective, completely subjective. And what else?

I hope by now the tendency of these discursions is clear. Transcendence is subjective, but it is directed. Or perhaps it directs itself. Toward what? That is for each consciousness in its own personality to answer, and the answer will be in its own terms. I avoid *other-directed* as jargon from the world of objectivity. Perhaps it is best to say simply: directed away. Berdyaev speaks of the yearning and anguish of personality in its process of transcendence, and certainly one may denote yearning without a referent. It is a state of being. Subjectivity seeks subjectivity, perhaps its "self," perhaps its "other," or perhaps only the universal subjectivity which, though relative, cannot then be apprehended in its differentiations but only collectively – the human presence, or just the presence. The seeking is what is important. It means that pure existence is achieved through an act of love.

Poets know this. I can speak only for myself, I suppose; yet I have never heard another poet deny what I am saying, and I have heard many confirm it, though in very different terms and contexts. I am not speaking of substance, the poem's *materia*. I am not speaking of the poet who is writing an erotic poem addressed to a particular person, for instance, nor of the poet who writes from motives of hatred. These motives are substantial; they are what the poem is about. What I have in mind is what has been called in other places the "esthetic emotion," the feeling that overlies substance and converts substance, whether beautiful or ugly, into something else. Sometimes this "something else" has been called beauty, but the word is likely to be misunderstood. I prefer to call it spiritual love, the state of being a pure existence, and the esthetic emotion is the experience of that state. I believe it is impossible to write a poem, a real poem, that is not an expression of subjectivity moving through and beyond itself.

If this is true it would be impossible to write a poem that contains a contrived private reference, for this would be ego-haunted, pulling the whole process backward into objectivity. But please do not mistake me. A personality is created from phenomenally objective experience imaginatively ordered, and a poem similarly takes its authenticity and independence from the same source – the perception of reality. A poem is a commemoration of personality in process. It is indubitably personal. But a poet in the act of love, existing purely and in subjectivity, in yearning and anguish, will transmute his private reference into generally accessible knowledge, his private feeling into universal subjective feeling, and he will do it *without thought*.

Most of the poems I read – and in my work I must read tens of thousands every year – are ego-haunted. They are riddled with objectivity (though the poems of the so-called Objectivists are often not – but this is a confusion of terms). They fail as poems because they express no spiritual consciousness and are written without knowledge of existential purity. They are the products of objectivity. I repeat: *most* of the poems, the very great majority, are not poems at all. I believe our "creative writing" schools and workshops are conducted in such a way that they prevent the writing of poems. If a poem is a product of subjectivity, then it has no function, no dynamic place, in objectivity, which means that it cannot be manufactured. Writing cannot be taught. The writer is an *amateur*, always.

Of course a poem, once written, takes a place among objects. It endures, it is phenomenal, a quiescent continuance – in an anthology, say, on a library shelf. It has the attributes of other objects, form, texture, and so on. But I am not discussing technique. Only when the poem is taken from the shelf and read does it reassume its subjectivity, and if the reader is an authentic personality then he or she, like the poet who created the poem, passes into the purity of spiritual existence. The reader's work too is an act of love.

It follows that poetry is social, though not in any sense of the term used by sociologists. It follows that poetry is political, leaving the political scientists far behind. Maybe it even follows that if the substance of a poem, or part of it, is expressly though broadly social or political, this fact will reinforce the subjective communalism of the poet's intention in the transcendent act; but that is a question – the interrelationship of substance and the vision of form, or of moral and esthetic feeling – to which twenty-five years of attention have given me no answer. Yet many, a great many, of our finest poems, especially as we read backward toward the evolutionary roots of poetry, seem to suggest some such hypothesis, and in any event we know that political substance is not, and in itself cannot be, inimical to poetry. Finally it follows that the politics of the poet, in his or her spirituality, will be a politics of love. For me this signifies nonviolent anarchism, at least as a means; I know no end. For others it means something else. But we will share, at least in our spirituality, far more than we will dispute.

And perhaps one further consequence should be remarked. All people – but especially poets, if I may for once speak chauvinistically, since they more than any others, workers, artists, or persons of faith, are experienced in the whole spectrum of consciousness; yet still let me say all people – should seek to remember in objectivity what has happened to them in subjectivity. Objectivity is where the worldly effects of the act of love are found, above all the effect known as independence, which alone can afford to be kind.

🖝 ·

The Man in the Box at Walden
1976.

A FEW YEARS AGO I wrote a poem in which I referred to Henry David Thoreau as "that idiot." The response was about what I had expected. Officially, puzzlement; one reviewer even suggested that my term could be understood only if taken in a special inverted sense, as when

Walpole called Oliver Goldsmith an "inspired idiot." But that wasn't what I meant at all, and many readers told me, but unofficially and in private, that they understood me perfectly and for years had shared my feelings.

Of course I didn't mean it literally. Thoreau was intelligent, I suppose; he had a good enough mind. When I called him "that idiot," I was applying the term just as I might apply it, in casual exacerbation, to the local school superintendent or the Secretary of State. It was a putdown, an expression of annoyance. But it was taken, officially, as heresy, and a peculiar heresy at that. I had spat on the sacred cow, and no one even wanted to admit I had done it.

Certainly that is what Thoreau has become. He is as firmly fixed in the American pantheon as anyone, and not just as the candidate of the establishment either. *Walden* is read not only in schools but in communes, not only in the bourgeois suburbs but in the radical ghettos – or at least in the radical countryside. Its author is claimed as a forerunner by everyone from staid conservationists to revolutionary anarchists, and is cited as the authentic exemplar – more than Emerson, more than Whitman, certainly more than poor John Woolman or tragic Black Elk – of native American mystical consciousness.

Well, it seems to me extraordinary that a people should adopt for their favorite Great Work a book written in disdain for the people themselves. That's what *Walden* is: a work conceived in rancor and composed in scorn. It is an élitist manifesto, a cranky, crabby diatribe. Its victims are its readers, and none escapes. Its author was sanctimonious, self-righteous, and ungenerous to the point of cruelty. If I had lived in Concord during Thoreau's time I might have gone out to Walden to see him once – I hope I would have – but I don't think I'd have gone back for a second visit. That Americans should give their devotion to such a disagreeable author is not only extraordinary; it is revealing.

This is not a question of what Thoreau actually had to say. When I boil down his rhetoric to basic ideas, I find myself in agreement with most of them. It isn't hard; the ideas are simple and universal. I too am a New Englander and an individualist (though I prefer the term independentist). I too live in the woods by choice, though not as a hermit, and live, at least partly by choice, in poverty. I too have a strong element of native Yankee anarchism in my thought and feeling. And if

I cannot accept all Thoreau's religious sentiments in the form he gave them, since my branch of the Yankee tree is the pragmatic rather than the transcendental, I can at least, as a fellow poet, see that they are legitimate expressions of spiritual and esthetic sensibility for a man living in his time and place. Moreover I can take real pleasure, with many others, from his nature writing. Not because he was a naturalist, which he wasn't; a comparison of any page from *Walden* with any page by Henri Fabre or John Muir will prove that. No, I think my pleasure and other people's pleasure come precisely from Thoreau's amateurism. The observations he made in his neck of the woods are similar to those we make in ours. His affection for particular trees and rocks, meadows and groves, is what we know in our own lives too. And similarly with his critical views of industrial society, politics, the academic world, Bostonian Brahminism, etc., and with his insistence on the need for meditation and repose in the lives of human beings. We share these feelings. In fact I believe we would feel them no less strongly if Thoreau had never written.

The preachifying is what is intolerable. And the preachifying makes up a very large part of the total product. The first chapter of *Walden* – a long one, fifty pages or more in most editions – is given to the topic of "Economy," i.e., how much Thoreau spent for his project in the woods and how he earned the money to defray his costs. The nub of it is contained in a couple of tables of statistics, occupying less than two pages. The rest of the fifty are given to a protracted scourging of the evils of mankind, under a dozen rubrics: housing, art, education, communalism, religion, fashion, and so on. No one escapes. Over and over Thoreau asserts that there is nothing a man can *do* that is not less worthy than what he, Thoreau, has done. Why? Because he built his own cabin in the woods (on borrowed land) and lived there for a couple of years of leisure, eschewing every obligation except to himself. *Doing* is precisely what Thoreau likes least. At one point he tells how, when he was walking along the railway, he saw a large wooden toolbox, and "it suggested to me that every man who was hard pushed might get such a one for a dollar, and, having bored a few auger holes in it, to admit the air at least, get into it when it rained and at night, and hook down the lid, and so have freedom in his love, and in his soul be free." His very words: "freedom in his love" – in a box! So Thoreau solves the problem of sex by masturbation, and the problems of all humanity by isolation. Again and again, not only in the first chapter but in many other parts of the book, he excoriates his neighbors in Concord, the farmers and artisans, and does so in the most condescending terms. Why? Because they work; which is to say, because they have wives and children. The farmer cultivating his fields is a fool; this is explicit (see Chapter IX, for instance, the account of Flints' Pond). Thoreau playing with himself in his cabin is a wise man; this is scarcely less than explicit. Arrogance, it is nothing but arrogance, and of an extreme order that I can explain only by believing it defensive at bottom and motivated by guilt.

One of the things I have noticed, in my private, unofficial conversations, is that all the people who are enthusiastic about *Walden* are men, while I have yet to meet a woman who cares much for it. The fact is that Thoreau acted out, for a short time and in a limited, easy way, a primary and perennial fantasy of the American male. To escape, to be on one's own, without the anxiety of sex or the clutter of human responsibility: it is the dream of the failed man. Thoreau showed that one man could do it. In the same way he showed failed artists and failed intellectuals how they might escape. Do away with art, do away with history, abolish every civilization more complex than that of the anthill beneath your feet. It is the American dream. And then, because we fail even in this, because we return compulsively to our endeavors, our studies, our poems and paintings, we must permit ourselves to be scorned and reviled and castigated. This is deeply, congenitally American. It is the twist of the Puritan knife, guilt returning upon desire and weakness. Thoreau was eager to do the job for us, and today we have plenty of lesser Thoreaus, equally eager. The magazines and lecture halls, though not the woods, are full of them.

I don't mean that Thoreau had no vision. Obviously he did. As I have said, when you boil down *Walden* to its basic substance you come out with a scheme of values and an envisioned way of life that are consistent, positive, and good. But they are simplistic. Thoreau never took the trouble to argue his case in practical and moral terms, or even in metaphysical or esthetic terms; he never assimilated his vision to the actualities of existence. He simply asserted his feelings. He was, in fact, very much a product of his time, the nineteenth century. He was a utopian, just as much so as his neighbors at Brook Farm, though his was a utopia of one, not a community. And what is characteristic of utopian thought is exactly what we find in Thoreau: a belief that the end justi-

fies the means. For Thoreau his perfected vision, his objective, justi-
fied not only shoddy reasoning or the lack of any reasoning at all – a
typical Thoreauvian paragraph is made of unconnected assertions, not
to say non sequiturs – but also whatever bad manners and violence of
feeling occurred to him in the course of his disquisition. The matter of
his book, in other words, generated a manner which negated the entire
enterprise.

This is more than a temperamental defect, a monstrous lack of sym-
pathy. Other men – Kierkegaard, for instance – have lived and worked
in isolation, yet have penetrated far deeper into the quality of human
existence. When we compare the work of the two men, we see how
shallow Thoreau's vision was. At least partly this was because Tho-
reau was caught unconsciously in the whole romantic, Hegelian, uto-
pian current of his time, while Kierkegaard, who was far more aware of
contemporary intellectual history and its meanings, turned against it.
True, Thoreau from his American vantage point turned partly against
it too, but only partly. He saw a danger in Hegelian concepts of mass
consciousness and historical determinism. But in his own individual-
ism Thoreau (like Max Stirner in Europe) failed to see that there were
equal dangers. Thoreau's individual is only the mass compacted into
one, an autonomous sovereign ego. Individualism and corporatism are
two sides of the same coin. In short, Thoreau made no distinction be-
tween individualism and true existential independence, and conse-
quently ended with no more than an isolated sensibility – living in a
box!

We know today what to think of that nineteenth-century current,
the utopian spirit. We know how it spread and joined with other no-
tions of determinism and ultimacy, until in our own century it issued
into many totalitarianisms, not political merely but in every phase of
life. We know in America where it has brought us, politically, economi-
cally, socially, and all in the name of freedom. Naturally we don't blame
Thoreau for that. But "freedom" was a favorite word of his, and the
meaning he gave to it certainly was close to the meaning it came to have
in American life down to our own time. It is a twisted meaning,
wrenched away from the "liberty" with which we began. For my part I
believe Thoreau, living in his box in the woods, was a captive man, far
less free than, say, Thomas Jefferson wrangling in the Continental Con-
gress or building Monticello. Freedom that merely turns its back is no

freedom at all. Who is more free, in Thoreau's sense, than the demented murderer or rapist, and who more captive?

In other writings, the essay on civil disobedience and the travel books, Thoreau presents a far more modest, reasonable, attractive appearance. My friend Wendell Berry points out that *Walden* was Thoreau's first book and not any of us likes to be judged by our juvenilia. But *Walden* is the book he is known by. It is one of the books that all Americans are known by, and by which we know ourselves. Crabs and cranks and wayward mystics, with violent minds. How many Hollywood heroes have been cast precisely in that mold! They are roaming our streets right now. I suppose nothing is more futile than wishing history could be changed; yet I can't help thinking what a difference it might have made if Thoreau had read Jefferson as closely as he read the Hindu scriptures, or even if he had understood what his neighbor, Ralph Waldo Emerson, was really saying. He didn't. He wrote his book, and it has become our national meditation, our *Bhagavad-gita* and *Tao Tê Ching* rolled into one. I hope it isn't altogether futile to wish that today there may come to be a more general understanding of its flaws, or at least that people will quit knuckling under to the man who sat in his box in the woods and called them, one and all, drudges, nitwits, and slaves.

🖎 ·

Our Man in Twit'nam

1975.

CHRISTOPHER CAUDWELL, the Marxist critic who was killed in 1937 while fighting with the International Brigade, once put his finger on the embarrassment felt by many over their affection for the poetry of Alexander Pope. At least I feel it over mine. He wrote: "Pope perfectly expresses the ideals of the bourgeois class in alliance with a bourgeoisified aristocracy...."* What could be plainer? Pope's concern was for restraint, balance, order, in short, for "reason," as I think is well known and unquestioned, but in our own intellectual world we have

---

* *Illusion and Reality*, 1937, p. 86.

scarcely a single reputable standpoint along the whole spectrum of opinion, radical or conservative, from which we can view such a concern with much sympathy.

> Pope's poetry... is a reflection of that stage of the bourgeois illusion where freedom for the bourgeoisie can only be "limited" – man must be prudent in his demands, and yet there is no reason for despair, all goes well. Life is on the upgrade, but it is impossible to hurry. The imposition of outward forms on the heart is necessary and accepted. Hence the contrast between the elegant corset of the eighteenth-century heroic couplet and the natural luxuriance of Elizabethan blank verse....

So Caudwell pins Pope wriggling, in a time categorically different from ours, on the exact ethos of the rising Protestant middle class, which we have been taught to despise.

Peter Quennell, who is probably the best of Pope's biographers, makes the same point, at least with respect to style, in his discussion of Pope's *Elegy to the Memory of an Unfortunate Lady.** He quotes three lines from Webster's *The Duchess of Malfi:*

> *Now the echo hath caught you...*
> *I told you 'twas a pretty one: you may make it*
> *A huntsman or a falconer, a musician, or a thing of sorrow.*

And next to them he places four lines from a similar "eerie moment" in Pope's poem:

> *What beck'ning ghost, along the moonlight shade*
> *Invites my step, and points to yonder glade?*
> *'Tis she! – but why that bleeding bosom gor'd,*
> *Why dimly gleams the visionary sword?*

Again what could be plainer? The comparison makes Pope seem ridiculous. Often enough he is. And it is a ridiculousness that easily entraps his readers, who move from the brilliance of his best writing,

* In *Alexander Pope: The Education of Genius, 1688–1728,* 1968, p. 145.

lulled by his beat and his music, into passages that are far from his best without noticing the difference, until suddenly they come to and realize that the brilliance has been supplanted by utter rococo nonsense. This too is just what we have been taught to despise, taught by the whole weight of modern literary feeling from the earliest pronouncements of Pound and Williams down to the present day.

Yet Pope at his best still appeals to our sensibilities. The pleasure we get from reading him is unmistakable. Moreover there is nothing antiquarian about this pleasure because the best of the poems – the *Dunciad*, the moral essays and epistles, *The Rape of the Lock*, and some of the minor poems – are living poetry still, which we read in the same way that we read any poetry, old or new. In consequence we more and more are seeking ways to overcome our embarrassment, that is, to retrieve Alexander Pope from the stereotyped figure he has been since the time of Hazlitt if not before, and to make him into a *poet*, one among the company of poets with whom we live on familiar terms. I think this can be accomplished easily enough. We need only pay attention to the quality of his *writing*. Pope was a superb writer, and the wonder is that the job hasn't been done long since, yet it hasn't, at least not adequately and not as far as I know; even Saintsbury's thorough and often agreeable account of Pope's prosody is defective in its post-Romantic dogma of irregularity. Another time I may have a shot at it myself. Now I am more interested in the cultural elements of the stereotype.

Was Pope actually an apologist for the rising bourgeoisie of post-Revolutionary England, as Caudwell suggests? Was he in the midst of the movement, a product of it and spokesman for it? Or was he not rather an outsider? He may have wanted to participate in that upsurgence of new social and economic power; in some sense he obviously did, he even longed for it. But he simply couldn't manage it. He was a Roman Catholic, for one thing, automatically suspect in a society still afraid of Jacobinism; and for another he was a hunchback and almost a dwarf, suspect, again automatically, for his inability to play a "normal" sexual role: no woman would have him. And he was a radical. Of course I don't mean a revolutionary; Pope believed in social order, even in hierarchical social order. But he had a radical's innate distrust of power, whatever form it takes. This was part of what made him a poet, and it grew only stronger as he grew older. Beyond that he was a Lockean through and through, philosophically speaking. How could someone raised on Catholic theology take so wholly to the philosophy of the English revolution? I don't know. Yet Pope did; probably he wasn't a very good Catholic, like Catholics today who practice contraception. And when I recently reread Locke's *Second Treatise of Government* I was pleased to see that with only the ordinary allowances for historical anachronism it contains almost nothing incompatible with the philosophies of Proudhon or Bakunin, which came a good deal later (to say nothing of native American anarchists like Warren and Andrews or even Thoreau). In short, far from being an apologist for his society Pope was a radical critic of it. Has there ever been a more bitter denunciation of the power of money in capitalist society than his *Epistle to Bathurst?* True, Pope's radicalism was very different, as different as can be, in *tone* and *emphasis* from ours. He believed in order, while for us order has become so monumentally oppressive that we lash out against it altogether. Yet where would we be finally without that concept at the bottom of our radical thought and feeling? As for Pope, he insisted always that what he meant by order was *natural* order, and I believe we have good reason to infer that his idea of it was not far after all from what later theorists called the "classless" society. In other words Caudwell has overstated the case. We must read his assertion with an addition and a change of emphasis: "Pope perfectly expresses the *ideals* of the [historical] bourgeois class..., etc."; not the practice but the ideals, which were Locke's ideals – liberty and natural order – and Jefferson's too, and maybe not so far from Tolstoy's or Kropotkin's – or humanity's.

Over the years, in reading Pope and in reading as much as I could about him, I've been struck by the similarity between him and Dante. Both were outsiders, exiles in their own countries; both were poets who conspicuously sublimated their sexual energies in their writing; both were political poets motivated by visions of moral virtue, who dealt with actual political mechanisms in their poems – they named names. I don't mean to exaggerate the resemblances, of either kind or degree. Dante's situation was more propitious than Pope's in almost every respect: culturally, linguistically, philosophically, etc. Hence Pope was a satirist primarily, made so both by the necessities of literary evolution and by the self-consciously settled, uninventive attitude toward values in his time. Yet a distinction exists between Pope and other satirists. Swift – and I do not forget the fourth part of *Gulliver* in what I'm saying here, though I know devoted Swifteans will dispute the point – Swift was fully aware of his situation in the "age of reason" and took every advantage of it in his writing; Pope did the same of course, but in his best work, such as Book IV of the *Dunciad*, he transcended his situation. He transcended satire, as Dante had transcended the *dolce stil nuovo*, and produced work which, though nothing like the *Commedia*, nevertheless stands classically apart from genre and reaches outward to the universal heart of human existence.

At any rate if Dante is the paradigm of the modern poet, Pope fits the model, in his work and his life, as well as anyone and better than most. Thus he ought to be, and I believe he is, accessible to us; more, he is amenable to us. Two recent books, by Patricia Meyer Spacks and Frederick M. Keener, help to show us how.* Unfortunately both books are written by and for scholars. I know there's no use in flogging a dead horse, but damn it, does the experience of humane learning have relevance any more or not? We have reached a point at which the only serious considerations of the poetry of Allen Ginsberg are produced solely for academic ends. Such specialization seems to me pitiable, pitiable – all the more when the people who engage in it have something useful to say. Why can't they write plainly? Professor Spacks has investigated the imagery in Pope's major poems to show how the poet used metaphor, simile, and concrete images of many kinds to convey not only feelings and attitudes but quite precise ideas. The fact is that Pope's poetry contains far less direct statement than you would expect to find when you consider the topics of most of his poems. Another critic, Martin Price, has made the point too, namely, that Pope's poetry gives "more the effect of Metaphysical wit than versified argument; it is dialectical rather than didactic."† *Didactic:* the term stuck onto the poems for two hundred years; no wonder people detested them, or thought Pope no more than a somewhat superior Wigglesworth. I repeat: Pope was a poet, a poet in *our* sense, the sense of a person profoundly engaged in imaginative reconstruction. Naturally he used poetic means. He used wit, by which he meant, as far as I can make

---

* *An Argument of Images: The Poetry of Alexander Pope*, by Patricia Meyer Spacks; *An Essay on Pope*, by Frederick M. Keener.

† *To the Palace of Wisdom* (1964), pp. 140–41.

out, exactly the same thing that Coleridge meant by imagination. He
was "dialectical," in the sense adapted from Kant by modern critics
and applied commonly to such poems as the *Cantos* and *The Waste
Land*. Spacks has demonstrated the case admirably, I think, with close
readings from many texts, extended comparisons backward to Dryden
and Donne and forward to Eliot, and with many citations from her fel-
low scholars. If she nowhere gives us a statement of the meaning of her
work as pointed as the one I have given here, if she fails to see the value
of *Eloisa to Abelard* among Pope's secondary works, and if she writes a
prose that is – well, I've said my say about that – nevertheless and in
spite of all, her book is useful. I think nonacademic people who like to
read Pope (if any are left besides me) could benefit from looking at it.

Professor Keener's book is more critical and less scholarly, a work of
literary intent, and as such is written with at least some ambition to-
ward good style. Unhappily Keener is finical. His writing builds clause
on clause, modification on modification, and so does his argument,
three steps forward and two back, until in some passages the reader is
totally confused. But Keener's objective is clear. It is to study the voice
of the narrator in Pope's poems, the evolving persona from first to last,
and then to relate it to what is known of the poet's life and character.
The result is not biography and not intended to be. It is more a species
of mythography. It is an attempt to describe the poet, the figure of the
poet that Pope progressively invented for our benefit, and to discover
the meanings and values attached thereto. In some respects it is similar
to Maynard Mack's fine book about the relationship between Pope's
poetry and his landscape gardening, country life, and Palladianism in
general.* What Keener discovers of course is that Pope the poet, the
creator revealed inside his poems, is more than a persona, he is a per-
sonality; and he becomes a clearer and clearer personality as the po-
etry matures. When Keener says that "Pope came to incorporate more
personal experience in his poems than had any English poet preceding
him," we can only agree, at least if the "incorporating" is understood to
have been explicit rather than implicit. What's more, the personality
emerging from this personal experience becomes more and more at-
tractive – to my mind right up to the end. Keener (perhaps inevitably,

---

* *The Garden and the City: Retirement and Politics in the Later Poetry of Pope, 1731–1743*,
1969.

considering his focus of interest) prefers the livelier figure of the narrator in the epistles and moral essays, but for my part I would never reject the dark, bitter narrator of the *Dunciad*, whose intelligence and love, half-hidden though they may be, are instinct in every line, especially in Book IV. But mainly what Keener shows us is a *poet using himself*, creating himself, and doing so in terms more realistic and complex than any other poet until Hardy. It is an observation of the utmost importance to our historical understanding because it so plainly develops the affinity between Pope and us.

And perhaps this is the point to emphasize for general readers here. The two books I have reviewed, as well as other recent books I have mentioned and a good number I have not, are aimed toward divesting Pope of the historical inertness that has encumbered him for two centuries or longer. We need a Pope to whom we may not only respond but relate, in the peculiar literary symbiosis that keeps literature – past or present, there is no difference – alive. Between Milton and Blake no poet plays this role for us. Pope is the logical choice, not only for his preeminence but for his own qualities as man and artist, and we need him; we need him there, in that time, speaking to us from that large region of sensibility. Pope can do it. And whether or not I am right in thinking that in spite of his Tory trappings he can speak to us in our radical concern (though to my mind all true poets by definition speak to us in our radical concern), he certainly can speak to us, and does, as a poet who shares our attitudes toward the human predicament. Here is one more quotation, this from G. Wilson Knight:

> His [Pope's] focal centre is man; not man dramatically interlocked with a great mesh of natural and cosmic energies, as in Shakespeare; nor man and his universe torn by the "mighty opposites" of conscience and culture, as in Milton; nor man viewed variously according to the subject, political, religious, or literary, as in Dryden; but Man who in himself must achieve the synthesis or harmonization which religious and political schemes are always claiming to achieve for him, and with no great warlike or other actions to assist his self-escape."*

---

* *Laureate of Peace: On the Genius of Alexander Pope* (1955), p. 9.

In short, existential man. And to my mind existential man is not only Pope's "focal centre," and not only the inferential product of his arguments, but his own mythologized creative self. If such a man cannot speak to us, then I don't know who can.

 ✍ ·

Three Notes on the Versewriting of Alexander Pope
1976.

1.

COMMONLY Pope's use of apostrophes – the mark of punctuation, not the rhetorical device – has been explained by two notions having almost the sanction of proverb. One is that he wished to get rid of extrametrical syllables, the other that he wished to avoid, by means of elision, the awkward little pause that comes when you have two vowels juxtaposed. Both ideas can be found in Saintsbury's *History of English Prosody*, for instance, and in many other places as well. Pope himself gave support to the theory about eliding contiguous vowels, which was certainly current long before him. But did Pope really pay much attention to these ideas when he sprinkled his poems with apostrophes? I doubt it. The poems don't support it. Take the second notion first, the one about elision. In fact there is considerable antecedent evidence that English poets apostrophized to avoid placing two vowels together. Chaucer wrote "thapostel" for "the apostle" (Prologue, *Wife of Bath's Tale*, 64), "thestaat" for "the estate" (*Parson's Tale*, 685), and even "nof" for "nor of" (Prologue, *Wife of Bath*, 660), though this last seems so peculiar that one suspects an error of transcription. But how did he pronounce them? Does anyone know? I am not, though often I wish I were, a philologist; yet in this case it may not matter, because all we have are the written texts and any conclusion is inferential. My inference is that Chaucer was making a typographical imitation of the French, hoping to produce a fashionable effect – since French was still the first language among the aristocratic classes of England in his time – but that in speech he never pronounced "thestaat" with anything like the degree of elision we give to *l'état*. This would be foreign to our whole way of speaking today, and equally foreign, I suspect, to the genius of the English language from the beginning.

   With Pope the case is clear. He uses apostrophes wherever he likes, sometimes to note tempo, sometimes as a mark of conventional typography, sometimes for no reason at all.

> *Twice-marry'd Dames are Mistresses o' th' Trade.*
>
> (*January and May*, 110)

Here there can be no question of elision; "the trade" is unelidible. Hence the apostrophes are notations for speed, and very nicely placed too; aside from irony or any other consideration of substance, they give Pope a strong five-stress line to ride over the basic pentameter, even though the line has eleven syllables altogether and four unaccented syllables in a row. This is just the kind of thing Pope does again and again in a hundred different ways to achieve variety within his pentameters.

> *And All th' Aerial Audience clap their Wings.*
>
> (*Pastorals*, "Spring," 16)

I defy anyone to elide "th'Aërial" (which was certainly pronounced with the dieresis, though the eighteenth-century text does not include the diacritical mark). And if elision of contiguous vowels was desirable, why did Pope regularly write "thy eyes" (*Rape of the Lock*, 118) and "thy urn" (*Epistle to Dr. Arbuthnot*, 260) when grammatical custom and prosodic theory alike would have suggested "thine"? In short, contiguous vowels were no bogey, and the little awkward pause was a help, not a hindrance, in versification. That minute hiatus gave a suggestion of syncopation that was, and is, extremely important in maintaining the liveliness of English verse. Hence the apostrophe for Pope was a notation of speed, a sign that the reader should say "ðə" and not "ði" for the article. But the article was definitely to be pronounced, not elided, a distinct separate syncopated sound, often used with successive unaccented syllables in order to throw extra stress onto accented syllables that fell in normally unaccented positions.

   This itself undercuts Saintsbury's argument that Pope used apostrophization to get rid of extrametrical syllables. Of course Saintsbury needed to prove that Pope was monstrously regular so that he could compare him unfavorably with freer poets a century earlier or a century later. But it won't do. Pope could be as careless as any poet, for one thing. How else can you explain his writing "ere," "e're," and "e'er," all interchangeably – once "howe're" for "however" (*On the Statue of Cleopatra*, 16)! But more important, he did everything he could, within the strict couplet, to relieve the jig-jog of standard pentameter, and one means was to keep extra syllables, not throw them away.

> *Then gazing up, a glorious Pile beheld,*
> *Whose tow'ring Summit ambient Clouds conceal'd.*
>> (*The Temple of Fame*, 25–26)

If extra syllables were forbidden, why not write "glor'ous" and "amb'ent" as well as "Tow'ring"? But no, Pope wanted those unaccented disyllabic beats, and I, at least, am convinced he pronounced "tow'ring" with three syllables, however rapidly. The apostrophe was conventional. It was never used to replace any vowel but *e*.

> *The grave unites[,] where ev'n the Great find Rest,*
> *And blended lie th'Oppressor and th'Opprest!*
>> (*Windsor Forest*, 317–18)

If regularity were wanted it would have been perfectly good eighteenth-century practice to write:

> *And blended lie Oppressor and Opprest!*

– which is probably what Rochester or Prior would have done – and perfectly acceptable in terms of substance too. But Pope wanted those extra unaccented syllables to give the line more speed and take the curse off the weak "and" in a normally accented position.

The case of "'em" is more difficult. Pope used the shortening often, but not as often as "them," and it isn't always possible to tell why he chose one or the other. In jocular or belittling passages "'em" is appropriate, but in one perfectly serious, not to say heroic, passage he uses both forms in the same line:

Tell 'em, I charg'd them with my latest breath…
(The Episode of Sarpedon, 306)

And what about the last line of *Eloisa to Abelard*, which everyone deplores?

He best can paint 'em, who shall feel 'em most.

It would have been quite an acceptable line if Pope had spelled out the pronouns. Instead he spoiled it. Maybe he was self-conscious – it is one of the most revealing lines he ever wrote – or maybe he did it in self-belittlement. Or maybe he fell carelessly into a stereotype, the way he always wrote "tho" for "though." In any case I cannot believe Pope spoke the line – the climactic line in the poem, clearly referring to himself – with much less than a full pronunciation of every word in it, and we shouldn't be misled either by the mere typography.

What it amounts to is that Pope used apostrophes for various reasons and inconsistently, sometimes for metrical effects, sometimes for rhetorical effects, sometimes – I think often – for mere orthographic or stylistic convenience, as we write "and/or," "sonovabitch," etc. But I have been unable to find a single clear case of his using them to make an elision or to eliminate an unwanted syllable.

2.

Pope believed, as he told Spence, that in a pentameter line the caesura falls naturally after the fourth, fifth, or sixth syllable, and since part of his aim was naturalness he varied his caesura among these positions much of the time. Yet in his search for variety he could shift his caesura further along when he wanted to, even to the eighth or ninth syllable; one can find, especially in the later verse, plenty of enjambed lines within couplets and even a few enjambed couplets. This is well-known and I suppose shows no extraordinary skill in the poet. Pope was faced with a greater problem than this, however, which at the same time he turned to his advantage, namely, how to justify (using the term in the typesetter's sense) a line in which a weak syllable falls in a normally accented position. It happens in English pentameters all the time, going back to Chaucer and Wyatt. Milton had been the most adventurous in dealing with it, and Pope learned more from Milton's blank verse than most commentators have recognized. Still, writing in closed and balanced couplets, Pope had to rely chiefly on his own invention to find means for overcoming the difficulty. Frequently in his early poems he failed.

> *A Bosome Serpent, A Domestick Evil,*
> *A Night-Invasion, and a Mid-day Devil.*
>
> > (*January and May*, 47–48)

Here both lines of the couplet have the middle beat on a weak syllable, and the second line, with balanced phrases connected by "and," represents the most common construction in Pope's early and middle verse. There is no way to read these except as four-beat lines in which the heavy caesura takes the place of the fifth beat, which may be all right once in a while, but it leads to monotony and unnatural emphasis if repeated too often – just the effects Pope wanted to avoid. (In other contexts I have sometimes called these weak syllables in accented positions "negative stresses," which we *understand* as a fulfilling of prosodic value, e.g., in "Tomorrow and tomorrow and tomorrow.") As he continued writing, Pope learned how to justify these lines metrically by playing with both the accented and unaccented syllables.

> *Tho'* each *may feel* Increases *and* Decays,
> *And see now* clearer *and now* darker Days.
>
> > (*Essay on Criticism*, 404–5)

Here the weak "and" in the first line is shifted away from the caesura, and the four-beat first line is justified by the six-beat second. Moreover the weak "and" in the middle of the second line is itself justified by two spondees on either side of it ("now clear-," "now dark-"). This use of spondees to overcome a mid-weakness became more and more characteristic.

> *And the pale Ghosts start at the Flash of Day!*
>
> > (*Rape of the Lock*, 5.52)

Almost a nursery-rhyme effect here, anapests in heroic measure; yet the heavy accents hold the line, if barely, to the pentameter and move the emphasis very successfully away from the weak "at," where it would normally fall. By such means Pope learned to vary his rhythms, until in his later verse he could write with extraordinary flexibility.

> *But not this part of the poetic state*
> *Alone, deserves the favour of the Great.*
> >   (*Imitations of Horace*, 2.333–34)

Here in the first line he syntactically forces the accents onto "not this part," followed by three unaccented syllables, so that syntax and meaning combine to give metrical interest to uninteresting words, and the whole is heightened further by the daring runover, which in turn justifies the four-beat second line.

> *Never was dash'd out, at one lucky hit,*
> *A fool, so just a copy of a wit.*
> >   (*Dunciad*, 2.47–48)

And here the first line of the couplet is four-beat dactylic (it could fit without alteration into *The Ingoldsby Legends*), drawn back to the underriding pentameter by the density of the second line, which must be accented on the second, third, fourth, sixth, and tenth syllables.

But single lines and couplets do not show Pope's real versifying ability. Actually his means of metrical justification were extended patterns, whole paragraphs of shifting accents, in which successive lines work forward and backward against one another.

> *What wóful stúff this Mádrigal wou'd bé,*
> *In sóme stárv'd Háckny Sónnetéer, or mé?*
> *But lét a Lórd once ówn the háppy Línes,*
> *Hów the Wít bríghtens! Hów the St'yle refínes!*
> >   (*Essay on Criticism*, 418–21)

These are only four lines, of four, six, five, and six accents respectively, in which the third alone approaches normal pentameter; in the others no pattern of accents is close to its neighbor's. Yet the four work together beautifully. And Pope could do the same thing, and frequently did, in passages of six, eight, ten couplets, or more, continually playing

strong against weak, quick against slow, with syncopated extra syl-
lables in many places, dancing away from the norm and back to it, so
that he achieved great variety while at the same time he justified all the
lines and drew them into the general metrical scheme.

3.

Beyond metric lies the language itself, diction and syntax, the discov-
ering what a particular mode means, what it really *is*. Scholars dispute
the descent of the closed couplet to Pope; one, Reuben Brower, tells us
it was through Waller and Dryden,* while another, William Piper, by-
passes Dryden and says the important influences were Granville and
Walsh.† No doubt there are good reasons for either view. But the im-
portant point is that from Jonson, who complained of "cross-rhymes"
as distractive, to Dryden, who wrote of his own medium as "this
unpolish'd, rugged Verse I chose, / As fittest for Discourse, and near-
est Prose," the couplet was regarded as a plain, ordinary kind of verse,
in contrast to the stanzaic forms used so commonly for long narratives
and to blank verse, which was best suited for tragedy and epic. The
couplet was "nearest prose"; which is to say, our own view of it as
artificial and highfalutin is exactly contrary to the view held by those
who practiced it and who were trying to do the same thing, roughly
speaking, for poetry in their time that Wordsworth and Coleridge did a
hundred years later and Pound and Williams a hundred years after
that. Granted, the idea got lost sometimes, as when Pope used couplets
for his *Iliad* and Addison for his *Cato*. (Just as E.P.'s idea has been lost
often enough in our century too.) But I like to think Pope saw, or at
least half-saw, that his Homeric translations were a mistake, not only
because they ate up ten years of what should have been the most cre-
ative period of his life, but even more because they subverted his own
style and idiom from their natural bent.

Saintsbury, in his mania for irregularity, criticizes Pope and prefers
Dryden because the latter interspersed his pentameter couplets with a
good many triplets and alexandrines, while the former came to eschew
them. As a matter of fact Pope did use triplets and alexandrines in his
early verse. In *The Episode of Sarpedon*, for instance, he inserted an

---

* *Alexander Pope: The Poetry of Allusion* (1959), pp. 12–13.

† *The Heroic Couplet* (1969), p. 121.

alexandrine at one point (l. 96) where he wanted an especially re-
sounding effect, and in *An Essay on Criticism* he used a fair number of
triplets. But he had the good sense to recognize that neither device
worked, not simply because regularity is after all the stylistic essence of
a discourse in couplets, but even more because both devices are dis-
tractive; they were remnants of cross-rhyming and stanzaic verse. He
abandoned them. He wanted verse that did not call attention to its own
external form; he wanted regularity, less for the sake of neoclassical
theory than for the emphasis it placed – where emphasis ought to be
placed – on the poem's inner qualities of style and substance. At the
same time he sought and found, slowly but steadily, the other true
qualities of the couplet.

What are they? Many, no doubt. Poise, sharpness, a certain ele-
gance, humor, etc. – the things so often noted by critics and historians.
But to my mind the most important of them is naturalness, and the
most important element of naturalness in the couplet – that verse
"nearest prose" – is freedom from padding, since in prose there is no
need to pad. It was a hard lesson to learn. The stylish verse of Pope's
early years was loaded with epithets and other automatic adjectives;
this was what the literary age demanded. Pope's early work is full of
such writing, and the habit persisted a long time. Even as late as the
Epistle to Burlington he could be led by it into such a self-evident ab-
surdity as "milky heifer" (l. 186); and here is part of Ariel's speech to
the sylphs in *The Rape of the Lock:*

> *Ye know the Spheres and various Tasks assign'd,*
> *By Laws Eternal, to th' Aerial Kind.*
> *Some in the Fields of purest Æther play,*
> *And bask and whiten in the Blaze of Day.*
> *Some guide the Course of wandering Orbs on high,*
> *Or roll the Planets thro' the boundless Sky.*
> *Some less refin'd, beneath the Moon's pale Light*
> *Pursue the Stars that shoot athwart the Night,*
> *Or suck the Mists in grosser Air below,*
> *Or dip their Pinions in the painted Bow,*
> *Or brew fierce Tempests on the wintry Main,*
> *Or o'er the Glebe distill the kindly Rain.*
> *Others on Earth o'er human Race preside,*

> *Watch all their Ways, and all their Actions guide:*
> *Of these the Chief the Care of Nations own,*
> *And guard with Arms Divine the* British Throne.
> > *Our humbler Province is to tend the Fair,*
> *Not a less pleasing, tho' less glorious Care.*

(2.75–92)

Notice how easily these pentameters can be turned into tetrameters with very little loss of substance, though the change of tone is considerable:

> *Ye know the Spheres and Tasks assign'd*
> *By Laws Eternal to your Kind.*
> *Some in the Fields of Æther play,*
> *And whiten in the Blaze of Day.*
> *Some guide the Course of Orbs on high,*
> *Or roll the Planets thro' the Sky.*
> *Some less refin'd, in pale Moonlight,*
> *Pursue the shooting Stars at Night,*
> *Or suck the Mists in Air below,*
> *Or dip their Wings i' th' painted Bow,*
> *Or brew fierce Tempests on the Main,*
> *Or o'er the Glebe distill the Rain.*
> *Others o'er human Race preside,*
> *Watch all their Ways, their Actions guide:*
> . . . .
> > *Our Province is to tend the Fair,*
> *A pleasing, tho' less glorious Care.*

I don't say Pope or any other poet would be satisfied with this translation; but it does show up, I think, the weakness of the original. The only genuine pentameter couplet in this passage, i.e. the only one that cannot be reduced without serious abridgment of substance, is the one I have left untranslated, the next-to-last. It is not a great couplet by any means; in fact the first line is notably awkward. But it points the direction toward the closed pentameter's true quality of naturalness or prosiness, which lies in language that fills out its own syntax without forcing and with no adjectives unnecessary to the meaning. And I have

faith that Pope was intelligent and sensitive enough to see this direc-
tion and follow it.

At all events when one turns to the later poems, the moral essays,
the epistles, the *Imitations of Horace*, the final *Dunciad*, one has no
trouble finding passages that show the difference. I open the book to-
ward the end and literally take the first paragraph my eyes light on:

> *Well, on the whole,* plain *Prose must be my fate:*
> *Wisdom (curse on it) will come soon or late.*
> *There is a time when Poets will grow dull:*
> *I'll e'en leave Verses to the Boys at school:*
> *To Rules of Poetry no more confin'd,*
> *I learn to smooth and harmonize my Mind,*
> *Teach ev'ry Thought within its bounds to roll,*
> *And keep the equal Measure of the Soul.*
>
> (*Imitations of Horace,* 2.2.198–205)

The point does not need laboring. This passage, like the one from *The
Rape of the Lock*, is not the best of the poem in which it occurs; but
both passages are representative and the difference is unmistakable.
The later verse is natural, and with naturalness came fluency, variety,
and geniality – even if the last was inverted, so to speak, in the
Dunciad.

Then why was so little of this kind of verse written after Pope?
Maybe he wrote it so well that he effectively shut it off to following
practitioners. Maybe the enormous influence of Johnson's more pon-
derous temper was irresistible to writers of the 1750s, 1760s, and 1770s.
Or maybe, in the perversity of literary fashion, Pope's own contempo-
raries and successors misunderstood his achievement, and preferred
and imitated the wrong poems from his collected works. Neoclassical
criticism lagged far behind Pope's accomplishment, and that includes
Samuel Johnson's. At the same time Pope himself had remarkably little
to say about either the style or the form of his later poetry. (One cannot
imagine a modern poet working so intently with a particular literary
mode who would not at the same time expatiate *ad nauseam* on its
meanings and values.) But a minority saw what Pope had done. Gay
unquestionably saw, though he died young, and Goldsmith probably;
Byron saw; Ruskin's few words on Pope are worth all Saintsbury's

thousands. The trouble is that the minority is still a minority. The "common reader" today, or for that matter the common poet, has no idea of the real function of the couplet in literary evolution. It is still ordinarily called the "heroic couplet," after all, which is just what, in Pope's hands, it wasn't and isn't. And until we perceive this and accept it we shall be committing ourselves to historical misunderstanding and depriving ourselves of an attractive ally in the eighteenth century, where we have few enough as it is.

P.S.: Of course one could argue that to choose a passage from *The Rape of the Lock* as a demonstration of padding is unfair because Pope was writing a mock-epic and purposely making fun of the heroic style. But in his other more serious poems of about the same time he used the same overloaded diction. I think the main point of my experimental "translation" still holds up.

P.P.S. [in 1994]: Do I jeopardize my meager reputation among the cognoscenti by reprinting my Pope pieces now, as I did when I first wrote them? I'm aware that I do. Judging by the students and other young people I run into, Pope is even less popular now than he was twenty years ago. Everyone avoids him. For a long time everyone has. Eliot once remarked that if he'd had his choice he'd have chosen to write like Pope but that the cultural conjunctions of his time prevented it; then he wrote essays about dozens of other poets in the English tradition without ever mentioning Pope. Allen Tate wrote a good poem about Pope, but now Tate is as out-of-fashion as Pope himself. A few other poets, Louise Bogan, Carolyn Kizer, Wendell Berry, have shown passing signs of respect. But that is as far as it goes. For myself, I still believe that we drop a whole century from our recent history only at our own peril. I believe that Pope, the inventor of some of the primary attitudinal foci of Romanticism forty or fifty years before the Romantic movement got under way, was a great genius who speaks to us in our own terms if not in our own language. As for insanity, the topic par excellence of the twentieth century, why so much attention to little Kit Smart and poor John Clare when Pope's insanity is ten times more interesting and almost infinitely more significant?

🖎 . . . .

Chants, Oracles, Body-Rhythms

1978.

ALLEN GINSBERG'S poems of the 1970s are a marvel, his new book, *Mind Breaths*, presenting half a dozen poems, probably more, that are first-rate Ginsberg. The fact that they are as good as anything he has ever written delights me (and, I hope, many others), because I feel that his poems of the 1960s in *The Fall of America* were generally not so good, too full of random, unassimilated political rage; neither were his experiments with consciously composed blues a few years ago, as I remarked at the time.

You know how Ginsberg writes. Long circular movements, syntax irregular and interfused, catalogues of parallel thoughts and images extending sometimes for pages: chants, oracles, body-rhythms. Hopeless to try quoting them in a review. To excerpt a few lines would serve no purpose; in fact it would be a positive disservice to the poem.

But let me describe one poem from the new book, called "Ego Confession." A wonderful poem; I've read it five times. It is a mockery throughout: a mockery first of the convention of confessional poetry in recent decades, and then a mockery of the poet himself; it lays bare all his fantastic desires, to be the great poet, the great saint, to stop war, to eradicate viciousness, to gather in from the universal spirit the singing tenderness which will unite us all, etc., etc.; and it is, finally, a mockery of us, the readers and bystanders, silly, fantasizing, unavoidably messianic creatures that we are.

Yet the mockery transcends itself, not at the end of the poem but all the way through, each statement moving in a process of self-transcension toward the higher compassionate understanding that makes our silliness sane, our pathos holy, our "ego confessions" authentic signs of human spiritual desire. The poem is infused with passionate gentleness.

I once referred to Ginsberg's books, as they are published by City Lights in their little square formats, as "mousetraps of love," which is exactly what they are.

Ginsberg is no simple poet, though some people would like him to be – in fact, the technical means by which he achieves his effects are difficult, even obscure. Consider structure. Categorically speaking, there are three kinds of poetry: first, conventional structure imposed from without; second, archetypal structure risen from within; and third, random structure derived, again, from without. In reality these categories are far from explicit, and they shift and meld together; yet I do believe that all great poems, no matter how rigid or free in their styles and appearances, fall within the second category, and this includes the best of Ginsberg's earliest work (though whether or not those poems are truly "great" is something we won't know in our lifetimes).

In his poems of the 1960s Ginsberg strayed into the third category. Structure was derived from random external events, newspaper stories or things seen from the window of an airplane. The result too often was declaration, not poetry. The structure, if it was structure at all, was disintegrative, literally incoherent.

But now he has returned to poems of the imagination, poems arising from within, complexes of feeling that come to consciousness with their own structure already in them. This doesn't mean that they are of necessity mythological, in the Jungian sense. No, the political feeling of the sixties – and of the present – can be as much a part of these inherent complexes as anything else. But the structures are integrated, assimilated; they are products of Ginsberg's unified, multiplex personality. As a result he can now utter explicit political curses, as he does, against the whole nark segment of modern life in such a way that they not only become genuine political statements but also function esthetically and commensurably as elements of his entire poetic vision. They are part of the prophesying. And this has been at least one of the chief poetic objectives through all ages, from Homer and Isaiah down to our own time.

Enough theorizing. The poems are there – on the page, in the book. They are called "mind breaths." No need to speak of kinds, qualities, degrees, the intellect's inevitable meanderings. The poems *exist*. Think of all the millions of things that might have gone otherwise, so that the poems might not exist. Our times are bleak enough, heaven knows, but at least we have this.

The Spirit of Lo Lenga d'òc

1978.

IN THE PREFACE to his *Six Troubadour Songs*, W. D. Snodgrass writes: "In the last two decades, our vision of the Provençal Troubadour and his songs has almost completely changed. Gone is the wistful figure singing sweetly in the twilight of his spiritual devotion to a far-off, idealized lady. Under the impact of certain crucial musicologists and performers – especially Thomas Binkley's Studio for Early Music in Munich – we have accepted a heavy Arabic influence in this music; nowadays, our performances sound more and more like belly-dance music or, more accurately, the Andalusian music of North Africa. Our sense of the texts has altered comparably. By now, we are almost ready to say that Troubadour songs have only two subjects: one, let's go Crusading and kill lots of Moors; two, let's go get in the boss's wife."

Now this is ridiculous on several counts. Naturally in recent studies of medieval Occitanian literature and music we have experienced a movement toward deromanticization similar to what we know in other sectors of scholarship; but no serious student would go as far as Snodgrass suggests. In the first place, what's wrong with Arabic music? Simply because it has been used in North America primarily as an adjunct to drooling tent-shows does not mean that in its own time and place it did not and does not serve far different and more various purposes. Listen to flamenco. I know nothing of Thomas Binkley, but if he has discovered an explicit Moorish element in Mediterranean art, thought, and life, he has discovered what has been known to everyone concerned for hundreds of years.* Today if we look at the trobadors more in an existentialist than Edwardian spirit, this does not mean that anyone with sense ever considered them "wistful figures singing sweetly in the twilight"; nor does it mean that we may discard sound

---

* "Nous retrouvons enfin à travers les échos des croisades de nombreuses évocations de l'Orient et leurs relations incessantes avec le monde arabe sont largement connues." Leon Còrdas, *Trobadors al Segle XX*, Arles, 1975, p. 11. Besides, Andalusian and Catalan music was all there was in the eleventh and twelfth centuries in southern Europe, except for liturgical chants. Moorish music was the rock music of that time.

historical evidence. What is one to do with *trobar clus*, the courts of love or the great Consistori del Gai Saber (established in Toulouse in 1323 to study and sustain not only *las leis d'amor*, i.e., the laws of love, but the linguistic and esthetic qualities of its poetry), the *croix languedocienne* with its hearts which we still see in churches all over the Midi, the concepts of *paratge* (honor), *jòi, pretz* (merit), *valor*, and *mesura* (wisdom) which we find at the center of so much of the literature? No, it was a unified nation and unified culture; religion, at least partly Catharist, was its source and energy (what else would we expect in the medieval world?), and its literature was *not* frivolous. Can anyone imagine the work of Guinicelli, Cavalcante, and Dante springing from the conventions of the music hall?

The first translation in Snodgrass's booklet is of the famous "L'Aventura del Gat," by Guilhèm Peitieu, which is uncharacteristic of the poetry as a whole. It is out-and-out bawdry. (Translated many times and once even published in *Playboy*, as Snodgrass points out, it is the fantasy of a poet who pretends to be mute, and by thus securing them from scandal heroically enjoys two noblemen's wives.) But bawdry it may be, sophisticated vulgarity it is not – and the difference is essential. Guilhèm, the earliest trobador whose name is known to us, was a nobleman (duc d'Aquitaine, comte de Poitiers), intelligent and educated, a poet who certainly was aware of his antecedents from Catullus to the Goliards. His writing, like his attitudes, was firm, straightforward, verbally and prosodically vigorous, obviously the product of a superior poetic imagination. I suppose the closest well-known analogue in English is the Chaucer of the "Miller's Tale." Here is the third stanza of Guilhèm's poem.

> *En Avèrnha vèrs Lemosin*
> *encontrèri sus mon camin*
> *las gentas molhèrs d'En Garin*
> *   e d'En Bernart.*
> *Me saludèron simplament*
> *   per Sant Launart.*

What could be plainer, in spite of the somewhat intricate rhyme and meter? Here is Snodgrass's translation.

> *Down in Auvergne, past Limousin,*
> *Out wandering on the sly I ran*
> *Into the wives of Sir Guarin*
>   *And Sir Bernard;*
> *They spoke a proper welcome then*
>   *By St. Leonard.*

Where does Snodgrass get those extra words – "down," "out wandering on the sly," "spoke a proper welcome then"? It is much too over-written. And the meaning of "per Sant Launart" ("in the name of") is not transmitted, while the syntax and prosody (the enjambment) are too complex. But mainly the *tone* is wrong. I don't think it is simply the similarity of stanza forms that makes me think of Robert Burns; not the Burns of the lovely folk restorations, but the Burns of the comic narratives, epistles, and satires. Yet it's a lang, lang way from twelfth-century France to eighteenth-century Scotland. And the translation shows further overlays as well: Byronesque irony, the jiggery of *The Ingoldsby Legends*, something of Carroll and Lear, a good deal of the archness of W. S. Gilbert and Noel Coward, in short the culture of "high pop" for the past two hundred years. So it goes throughout Snodgrass's versions.

Toward the end of the poem Guilhèm says, "Tant las fotèri, m'ausiretz, / cent e quatre-vint uèit fes." Snodgrass writes: "I screwed them, fairly to relate, / A full one hundred eighty-eight." Forget "fairly to relate" and "a full"; forget the jingly meter; "fotèri" means "fucked," a good old Indo-European word (see Partridge, *Origins*). Why does Snodgrass write "screwed"? He doesn't need it for the rhyme or meter. I presume he does it because it has just the quality of cute sophisticated vulgarity which he likes but which has nothing to do with Guilhèm's straightforwardness or with the practice of trobadors in general.

As for the musical part of Snodgrass's work, since far fewer tunes than poems survive from the culture of Languedoc, he has shifted melodies which originally went with other poems to the poems he has translated and then to his own translations as well. The first part of this seems more or less reasonable; the old texts are singable in the tunes he has given them. But the second part? Why translate the texts but not the music? In fact Snodgrass's lyrics would go much better to something by Cole Porter than they do to the old Catalan airs.

The most important point I wish to make, however, has little to do with Snodgrass, although his preface has brought it to my mind. He refers there to "the Provençal troubadours," but it is a mistake; a mistake, granted, with long historical precedence, going back to the ancient name for southern Gaul (*Provincia romana*) and much reinforced by the work of Frédéric Mistral and the Félibrige a century ago, which was a great but sometimes misguided work of revival; yet it is a mistake nevertheless. Whereas Mistral and most of his nineteenth-century coworkers actually did live in Provence, the trobadors came from all over the Midi, and the center of cultural activity was definitely west of the Rhône. The poets used a language that did not exactly correspond to any of the dialects of Occitan, a *koinê*, a literary language. It was not Provençal any more than it was Limousin, Gascon, Auvergnat, Catalan, or any of the others. No one knows how it came into being, but that it existed before the earliest trobar lyrics is proven by surviving administrative and juridical texts.

Apparently Dante invented the term *langue d'oc* (*De Vulgari Eloquentia*, I, 7, where he opposes it to *langue d'oïl* and *langue du si*, only of course in Medieval Latin, *lingua d'oco*, etc.), but the people of southern Gaul soon took it to themselves as the name of their own country.* So it appears on maps for centuries: Languedoc. But this did not include the whole area in which Occitan was and is spoken, so today Occitan is the preferred word for the language, and Occitania is the whole region south of Lyons, from the Atlantic to the Alps. A real revival, I feel almost an explosion, of Occitanian culture is happening today.

Why is this important? Because the Albigensian Crusade – which is called more accurately by its victims, past and present, "la guerre de conquête"; even Innocent III, who ordered it, admitted that as many Catholics as "heretics" were killed – is still going on. We think of France as a monolithic state, in spite of its democratic trappings, and indeed it is, a nation ruled by one city. Simon de Montfort's brutal invasion was turned back finally by the courageous people of Toulouse, but the damage had been done; and politically, economically, socially,

---

* Simone Weil: "Ils avaient même un nom pour désigner la patrie; ils l'appelaient le langage."

and linguistically the conquest he began has never ended. Today it is proceeding more thoroughly than ever. The bankers, industrialists, developers – well, theirs is an enormous, dismaying devastation, too big to discuss here. We must stay with the linguistic aspect. Paris controls the radio, the television, and the schools, and French is the only language permitted. Yet there are *seven other living languages* in France: Breton, Flemish, Basque, Sardinian (i.e., in Corsica), Alsatian, Catalan, and – the largest in respect of number of speakers – Occitan. In 1972 the Association Internationale pour la Défense des Langues et Cultures Menacées passed a resolution of condemnation against France for "cultural genocide." If the effort was feeble, the term was exact.

I have heard Occitan spoken in the countryside of the Ardèche. (Some scholars say the purest speech remaining is in the village of Largentière.) It *is* a language. One must insist on that because Parisian academic and other snobs call it "le patois," and so, in their ignorance, do many of the *paysans* who speak it. But it is the clear descendant of langue d'oc, a Romance language with as much historical autonomy as French, Italian, Spanish, or any other. In the cities, Nîmes, Montpellier, Toulouse, thousands who have lost its use, chiefly young people, are relearning it, studying in schools they have organized themselves. Hundreds of publications are appearing in it, both literary and journalistic. And all this activity is allied to vigorous action in the political and economic spheres. The commonest graffiti in the Midi are "Décolonisez l'Occitanie!" "Mort aux toutes Franchistes!" etc. Almost every car in the south of France has a decal saying "Oc" in the window; the word is painted and sprayed everywhere, I think literally on millions of walls, road signs, bridges – every available surface. There is no question of separation, of course. France is not Canada. Québec may secede eventually, but for Occitania it is impossible, constitutionally or any other way. The people don't ask for that, and I think very few would even wish for it. What they do ask for is recognition and perhaps some measure of reparations. The force of centrality is massive, we know, in France as elsewhere, but the force of regional feeling is not negligible. Against administrative might it offers moral, cultural, and linguistic right. It has worked elsewhere; possibly it may work in France.

The least we can do is acknowledge it. We can call the people by their right name, Occitanians, their language by its right name, Occitan, and their great poets by their right name, Trobadors.*

🖝 . . . .

Notes on Meter

1981.

A COUPLE OF MONTHS AGO Allen Ginsberg and I were talking about quantitative meter, by no means a dull topic. Allen has become interested in the idea of quantity as a metrical aid, both for writing and for reading; he read me poems by Campion, Watts, and others who have professed to imitate classical quantitative measure in English, and he showed me how the Sapphic measure, which he especially admires, had helped him to straighten out a troublesome passage in his new "Plutonian" poem. Finally he read the famous lines from Canto 81:

> *The ant's a centaur in his dragon world.*
> *Pull down thy vanity, it is not man*
> *Made courage, or made order, or made grace,*
> > *Pull down thy vanity, I say pull down....*

giving them their natural accents, heavily stressed to show how they fall into an irregular order, possibly into quantitative measure. "At least," he said, "that's one way to understand it."

Allen's enthusiasm was unmistakable. I wish I could quote more of what he said. My memory isn't good enough. But I think I am not misrepresenting him if I say that his enthusiasm was impelled by a strongly felt need for a firmer concept of measure than he had had when he wrote, "by instinct," his earlier poems, "Howl," "Kaddish," and the rest. And I know I am not misrepresenting the many other poets of Allen's age and mine, or some younger ones as well, when I say that

---

* To those who wish a brief, recent account of Occitan I recommend highly *La Langue Occitane*, by Pierre Bec, no. 1059 in the "Que sais-je?" series (Paris: Presses Universitaires de France, 1973). There are many larger studies, of course. One of the most respected is *Histoire de la littérature occitane*, by Charles Comproux (Paris: Payot, 1970). Another is *Trobar*, by Robert Lafont (Centre d'Etudes Occitanes de Montpellier, 1973).

they have expressed to me during the past two or three years this same need for some renewed concept of measure in their own writing.

As far as I could hear, in his reading of the various "quantitative" poems in English, Allen used nothing but an ordinary American stress accent. In the lines by Pound, for instance, Allen's quantitative reading did not alter my hearing of the variable iambic pentameter that I believe Pound was using in intentional allusion to English seventeenth-century poetry. Myself, I don't believe quantity can work, or ever has worked, in English. How can it when we pronounce *father*, *gather*, and *bather* with exactly the same stress/unstress in spite of the considerable changes in the "length" of the accented vowel? The same with *booter*, *butter*, *boater*, *baiter*, *beater*, *bitter*, etc. The Sapphic measure is a mixture of trochees and dactyls in a four-line stanza, of which the first three lines are metrically the same and the fourth is abbreviated. It is an Aeolic measure, one of the "lyric" forms, and it worked marvelously in Greek because the language kept a genuine distinction of quantity between long and short vowels and an accent based partly on pitch (as more conspicuously in Chinese and Sanskrit). But in the modern European languages we have neither pitch (though we don't speak in monotone, as some have asserted, and anyone who has lived in France has observed the extraordinary changes of pitch with which a Frenchwoman can say *Oo la la* without breaking from a spoken to a singing voice) nor length; we have stress. We have almost infinite degrees of stress. Contemporary phoneticians, using computers, can show that no two syllables in any English sentence are accented alike. They can show that no two readers of a given line of poetry accent it alike. This is the reason, or one of the reasons, why the imposition of "classical" scansion, with its iambs, trochees, anapests, etc., on English poetry can never work except very inexactly, as prosodists have been saying for generations.* Nevertheless our stress accents do create rhythm; and rhythm by its own nature falls into repetitive patterns, or what we call measure.

Even Latin poets writing in imitation of Greek meters, as did all literary Romans for hundreds of years (though not the folk poets), found their own language unamenable, the accent of stress working against

---

* But see, for example, the beautifully managed Sapphics of Marilyn Hacker in recent years. NOTE IN 1994.

(and eventually supplanting) the accent of length or pitch, so that Horace's Sapphics, for instance, can be read either quantitatively or accentually, with very different but equally "legitimate" effects in either case. (See W. Beare, *Latin Verse and European Song*, 1957, p. 171 *et passim.*)

In the early 1950s I reviewed two or three volumes of *Paterson* as they appeared; the reviews were in the *Nation*. In one of them I asked what principle of metric made the poetry so readable. I couldn't extrapolate any measure from the poetry that would hold up consistently as a poetic construct. (Williams, incidentally, wrote me a long, cordial letter, in which it became clear that he couldn't extrapolate one either.) Twenty years later, in 1973, when I was preparing a selection of my prose for the press, I added a note to this review, but the note was later scratched in order to save space. I have always regretted the loss of that note, however, so I quote it, somewhat shortened, here:

"These questions about line values in Williams's verse (which I put so long ago) were taken up in succeeding years by many people, chiefly by Williams himself and by Charles Olson. The idea of the 'variable foot,' which Williams came to while writing his late poems, was no doubt a clarification of his own metrical instinct, helpful to him in the composition of those superb poems; yet I believe the idea remained for him a sensed thing, nearer to instinct than to precept. A very personal idea, at any rate. And in 'Asphodel' and the other poems of his last period, although my ear does detect a firmer line than in some of the earlier work, I still find passages in which the line structure breaks down, passages I cannot read aloud without either losing the line structure or breaking into elocutionary awkwardness in order to preserve it. (Williams himself had the same problem when he recorded his reading of 'Asphodel.') As for Olson's hypothesis that the line is a unit of breath, this is helpful because it brings prosody back to its sensory base and because we can all confirm it in what we know of our physiology and psychology. Yet in the end I think it has more to do with tone, mood, speed, or style in a poem – with *texture* – than with measure as such.

"Measure is the word to hang onto, and in all its senses. It means not only the way we recognize cadence in a poem, but the way we make relative judgments of space and time; it implies regularity. Inches and feet, minutes and hours. (In Langue d'òc *mesura* means wisdom and justice.) Without them there is no measure. In poetry there is no measure if the reader or auditor cannot anticipate, by inference from the pattern of beats that has already struck his or her senses, the striking of *the next beat*. This does not mean iambic pentameter. It does mean, however, that free verse is a literal contradiction, an impossibility; poetry, if it is really poetry, cannot be entirely irregular. This is as true of Walt Whitman's poems as it is of Alexander Pope's.

"Nothing requires that measure be *verbal*, or that the beat be tied to syllables. Iambic pentameter is not only regular, it is inflexible; the beat is tied to the iambs, that is, to a particular order of syllables. But we need flexibility in our verse as much as we need regularity; we need to be able to anticipate the next beat and to recognize the line structure by which measure is sustained, but we need also to have naturalness of phrasing and freedom of syntax.

"I always revert to Pound, and to his early suggestion that poets 'compose in the sequence of the musical phrase.' How simple. How brilliant. Which perhaps explains why no one has successfully elaborated it, as far as I know. It's a pity because it means that Pound's statement (more exactly his restatement of ancient principle) has turned into a catch-phrase – people speak it and repeat it without bothering to ask what it means. To most it conveys merely a license to compose any way they want – feelingly, *liltingly*, that's the commonest meaning. But Pound was a fair musician; he could read music, he played the bassoon, he composed an oratorio and a number of other pieces; he knew what he was talking about when he spoke of 'the sequence of the musical phrase.' A measure in music, a bar, is a fixed quantity. If the time signature is 4/4, you have four beats to the measure – 'and no cheatin',' as Bill Basie used to say. But within the fixed measure you may have any melodic or phrasal combination you wish, any distribution of accents, any number and variety of notes; you may emphasize the beat or you may syncopate it; you may play around; you may even substitute rests. Indeed, Basie and thousands of other fine musicians have made jazz improvisations that contain rhythmic variations so subtle and intricate that they can be notated only with an oscillograph, yet they always add up to four beats in the measure. Hence there is no question of tying the beat to an inflexible pattern of accentual or phrasal units, such as an endless succession of eighth notes. Yet the measure is preserved. Even in complex music, if one has a trained ear one can hear it.

"When English prosodists tied the beat to an inflexible syllabic pattern, they created a poetry as confining and awkward as music would be if it were limited entirely to eighth notes. Fortunately the tonal and textural resources of language, in both sound and meaning and in the two interacting, are far greater than the resources of unarticulated sound, i.e., music; and this accounts for our rich poetry in traditional meters. (And Bach was no slouch with eighth notes, for that matter!) The poets could stick to the syllabic ding-dong and still get extraordinary variety of stresses into their sentences. (See Pope's late epistles for an extreme example.) But without doubt much of the best poetry of our century, especially in America, has been composed according to notions of free metric. Pound was the master. He kept the measure – often in the Cantos a four-stress line – he kept alive our anticipation of the beat, he was always aware of line values, very keenly aware; yet by using every device of phrasing, including rests and stops, he also kept alive our sense of the spontaneity and natural harmony of poetic language, never forced, never imprecise. His influence is pervasive. It seems to me that the three closest followers of Charles Olson – Denise Levertov, Robert Creeley, and Robert Duncan – come nearer to Pound in the metrical practices I have just described than they do to Olson or to Williams himself.

"There are other quantities, of course, besides the beat, hearable quantities that can be used to establish measure and arouse our anticipation of line length: the accent and alliteration of Anglo-Saxon verse; the syntactical parallelism of Hebrew poetry, especially as it entered English through the Psalter and set off a secondary strain of metrical feeling – Milton, Blake, Whitman, etc. Pound himself was not unaffected by these influences, as we can tell from the surprisingly liturgical chant he used in reciting his own poems. Perhaps it is impossible to track down and methodize all the sources of a poet's metrical practice; perhaps it is unimportant to do so. The point is to write, not to theorize. Yet we were given minds and our minds do nag us, just as Williams was nagged by his until at last he came to the idea of the variable foot; which, whatever good it may be to the rest of us, was an immense good to him."

To this I would add only points of emphasis:

1. The beat is important, in both poetry and music, not because the sounded phrasing is tied to it but because it isn't.

2. No rhythm that does not set up an anticipation of the beat to come is properly rhythmic at all.

3. Any concept of measure, whether vocal or syntactical, even typographical, even pseudo-quantitative or purely syllabic, any concept at all that helps a particular poet to get on with his writing is a good one. What works, works.

4. Different ways of reading, based on different concepts of measure, may be applied to the same poetry with no loss of rhythmic effect or understanding; often the different systems of accentuation will coincide.

5. Not long ago when I was reading Whitman with some graduate students, we all agreed that we were too inhibited vocally to chant the poems as Whitman himself doubtless did. Our grandparents and great-grandparents were taught to read poetry *as* poetry. No doubt many excesses were committed – gestures, declamatory extravagance, etc. – but why did we throw out the baby with the bath water? Now we are afraid to read even our own finicky poems for the vocal acuities they might possibly contain. Our voices are atrophied, no tension in them, no resonance or timbre.

6. Today in this country our best poets, whom I would probably number between fifty and a hundred, are being swept away and drowned in the flood of soft, imitative, academic writing of thousands upon thousands of mediocre poets. (By "academic" I mean belonging to any of our "schools" of ideopoetry. Where is an independent poet now? I haven't heard of any.) One reason for the mediocrity, one among others, is the loss of a sense of measure. This is not enough to create a poetic revolution. Many historical, cultural, and probably political and social elements must coalesce, as they did in 1790 or 1910. Of course I do not know when that will happen again. No one knows.

Here is one of my favorites, by an unknown poet a generation or two before Chaucer:

> *Lollai, lollai, litil child*
> *Whi wepistou so sore?*
> *Nedis mostou wepe*
> *Hit was iyarkid the yore*
>
> *Ever to lib in sorrow,*

And sich and mourne evere,
As thin eldren did er this,
Whil hi alives were.

Lollai, lollai, litil child,
Child, lollai, lullow!
Into uncuth world
Icommen so ertow.

Is this remarkable prosodic sophistication an anomaly? No. Read the praise songs of Numidia, the insult chants of the Eskimos. The important elements of human sensibility haven't changed much, nor are they likely to – if we can hang onto our five wits at all. Is this metrical spirit old or new? As spirit – or intention, affectivity, whatever you will – it is neither. The poem's rhythmic feeling is as permanent as its thematic feeling; it is contemporary with Sappho and Williams. This power of poetic language to move in almost infinitely complex variations over the predictable beat – even when the language prolongs or cuts short the beat – is what permits us to recognize poetry and respond to it, anywhere and at any time.

Notes on Metaphor

1982.

THE SHORT TIME since I began teaching has nevertheless been long enough to show me that most graduate students, to say nothing of undergraduates in their blest innocence or of other poets in their thousands whose manuscripts come to me all the time, do not distinguish between the words *image* and *metaphor*. Or if they do it is fuzzily, glibly. But I am a niggler when it comes to language, and content to be so, though I know the final impossibility of precision.

After Imagism, with its reaching back to Symbolism and to the extreme indirectness of Oriental art, one can see and understand how, in the evolution of sensibility for the next seventy years, an image in a poem became a signal, a Pavlovian stimulus, for the poet's merely in-

ventive faculty to come into play. The result now is poetry clogged
with metaphors; usually they are disparate and, as complements to the
poem's purpose, meaningless. I have said that Robert Lowell's poetry
is a fair example of this, and I say it again, with the understanding that I
could equally well name many more, who are both like and unlike
Lowell in every other aspect of poetic practice.

Years ago the Objectivists announced that metaphor and its inevi-
table outgrowth, the consciously manipulated symbol, are illegitimate
because they arrogate to the poet's personal uses certain properties of
the object, suppressing others and thus wrenching the object away
from its own wholeness and identity. I liked that. It seemed to dovetail
with other aspects of European existentialist thought in the years of
midcentury. If, as Auden said and as I and many others have said in
different terms, human intelligence is "supernumerary" in the uni-
verse, what right can it have to involve itself in the processes of material
existence? None. The biblical idea that the world exists for the conve-
nience of human beings is turned upside down, a colossal inversion af-
ter four or five millennia of belief. It – the inversion – is not accepted
yet by more than a sprinkling of the populace. Then what are we to say
about the exploitation of the world for human ends? Is it human na-
ture? I'd prefer to say human, i.e., perverted animal, instinct, because I
am quite sure that nothing properly called "human nature" exists. And
of course the exploitation is evident, appallingly so. Even today, with
some hedging, scientists continue to act on the proposition that the
power to reason is what differentiates human beings from other animal
species. So do I, but I believe the "power to reason" means the "will to
dominate." Intelligence is the perversion of instinct. We cannot not use
it, but we must somehow, by force of self-denial or power of self-
transcendence, bring it into consonance with the superiority of non-
intelligence.

I am straying. For my purpose here I should narrow the question
and ask: what are we to say, in the face of our need for some modicum
of philosophical consistency, about the thousands and thousands of
metaphors in poetry of the past that thrill us each time we encounter
them? More particularly, what are we to say about Baudelaire,
Rimbaud, and Mallarmé, who together invented modern poetry? Can
we call "L'Après-Midi d'un Faune" an illegitimate poem, even though
it works better than any other poem of its kind in Western literature?

Shall we throw away Hofmannsthal, Rilke, Char, Stevens, Levertov – almost everybody?

Perhaps metaphor is inevitably built not only into our instinct but into our language. Even the most doctrinaire Objectivist would not shy from "the birdsong at twilight." Yet we know that birds do not *sing*, not in any sense that has a true connection with our use of the word. Can we disclaim *birdsong*, therefore, on grounds of anthropomorphism? What about *wave?* – a word I have chosen completely at random except that I wanted an Anglo-Saxon monosyllable. Which came first, the motion of the hand or the motion of the sea? Partridge in *Word Origins* traces it to "ON -*vafa*, itself akin to OE *wafian*, to wave esp with the hands, ME *waven*, E 'to *wave*,' whence the n *wave*, a billow." But this is too easy, it doesn't help, it leaves me unsatisfied. When I look under cognates I find Latin *uibrare*, to vibrate, which is "perh akin to L *uipera*, ML *vipera*, a viper." Well, this is more like it. A snake undulates. But Partridge does not affirm the cognancy, and he goes no further back than Latin, not even to Greek, not to the conjectural Indo-European root he loves so much. And suppose he had done it. Would we even then know if the hand were snakelike, the snake sealike, the sea handlike? No. Metaphor is as deeply and obscurely implanted in our cognitive procedures as any other equal, but no more than equal, viciousness: sexism, rationalism, the urge to quantify.

When Zukofsky's *A-24* was published, with its four disparate lines of text and one line of music going in concurrence from page to page, I wrote to him and said, among other things, that my experience of reading the five lines simultaneously was like lying on the deck of a sailing ship and watching a point of Saint Elmo's fire on the mast-tip swing back and forth across the constellations. Louis, who was the most adamant of the Objectivists, replied (and I quote from memory because his letters are elsewhere): "If I must accede to a simile, then let it be an exact one, like yours." Flattering. But the simile was a total fabrication. I have never been on a sailing ship in my life, I have never seen St. Elmo's fire at sea (though I have in the woods). Upon further investigation I find that St. Elmo's fire is most likely to be seen during a storm when the constellations would be hidden. Obviously Zukofsky had never been on a sailing ship either. It shows what frightening risks, philosophically speaking, human imagination is liable to, this perverse faculty. Zukofsky and I were both making fools of ourselves. But at least we had the sense to do it in private and with a mutual understanding of what we could permit ourselves and with what provisos. Which cannot be said for the great preponderance of poets working today, including most of my good friends.

Reality is a false hope. Metaphor is the falseness abstracted and ideationally embodied. The fact that absurdity exists as much within oneself as without does not relieve the poet – or anyone else – from the need to stand against it, defiant for the sake of supernumerary humanity. We must constrain and subjugate our imaginations and ourselves.

Here are three lines from a poem called "In the Hawk's Eye," by R.T. Smith:

> *Some of us live down here*
> *at the center of his circling.*
> *We watch him caper in the wind.*

Smith is a poet whose work I like. His perceptions are keen and personal, his feeling is strong but never strident, his mind is acute (as in that "some of us"), his writing is tonally, texturally, rhythmically good. Moreover he is a countryman whose vision of nature is similar to mine in its mixture of menace and pathos, and he can write of these complexities in simple words, something I often cannot do and hence admire considerably. But I do not like that "caper." Why? Most of my students and friends would approve that verb expressly. They would applaud its originality and therefore the apparent authenticity of the experience or perception behind it. Nor can I find fault on that account, for although most large hawks glide or soar in their circling flight, I have seen them (accipiters and falcons more than buteos, I think) fluttering, feathering, maneuvering quickly for the precise angle of stoop; in effect, "capering." Is it the anthropomorphism bothering me? Maybe. But if *birdsong* is OK, why not *caper?* For that matter is there anything in the meaning of *caper* that limits its application to human beings? Well, for me, though the dictionary does not say so, I think I do feel that the word primarily describes a human action, and only at a great remove and with a certain inaccuracy can it be applied to hawks. This remoteness and inaccuracy – or perhaps better, unfitness – overcomes in my mind whatever Smith may have gained by originality.

Think of the recurrent passages in which Pound described the little lighted candles floating out on a slow tide in their paper boats at nightfall, the rite for Tammuz. They are precisely descriptions or picturings, the simple scene without metaphor either explicit or implicit. The language is Pound's, hence an almost transfiguring clarity, yet nothing is twisted, nothing parted. At the same time the imagery is laden with unstated meaning. Can clarity alone be "transfiguring"? The Cantos are a treasury of such images set down in purity, without the forcing of metaphor. And exactly the same can be said of Frost's imagery, e.g., woods filling up with snow.

Yes, clarity does transfigure. "Intensely seen, image becomes symbol," said Roethke, and his poems contain many examples too.

Like everything in the mess of human intrusion upon natural order, metaphor is a vexing question. I see no course to take but to avoid a doctrinal answer. Since metaphor is fixed ineradicably in language and probably in consciousness, and since the great poets have given us great metaphors beyond counting, we can only bow, as to the inevitable. But this doesn't mean we must give up our good sense. For myself, I believe that metaphor generally does not work as well as direct statement, and further that the tediousness and friability of most current American poetry is owing to the overuse of metaphor more than to anything else. I wish Smith had written "soar" or "tilt" instead of "caper." *Caper* is a word that carries human, emotional, and hence valuative connotations and it cannot be properly objective. Pound would have used a more original word that was still true to the hawk's identity rather than to the poet's or reader's; or he would have used the plainest words he could find, giving them fullness of original meaning through his remarkable spontaneous strategies of syntax, tonality, and measure.

Four summary admonishments:

1. Use metaphor sparingly and only when it accords well with all the poem's other components and is fully integrated with them. The metaphor must arise naturally from the things of the poem. Never invent a metaphor for its own sake.

2. Give up the long-standing notion that metaphor is somehow innately "poetic," "the soul of poetry," that which produces "awareness," "the shock of recognition," etc. Granted, the poetic faculty is a synthesizing imagination, but what it brings together are relevant and com-

patible feelings, thoughts, and words, not extraneous and far-out irrelations. And the bringing together is a natural thing, not an artifice. Comparison, simile, metaphor, these are the rhetor's tricks of methodized imagination, taught in the schools of rhetoric (creative writing workshops).

3. Intensity is what counts, as Roethke said and many others too, Levertov, Hopkins, Blake, Longinus, etc. Intensity of perception, intensity of experience. To see, to hear, to feel. It is not easy, but without it no true poetry can occur. Nor may it be counterfeited, or its lack made up by verbal invention. Stephen Dedalus believed in "the eternal affirmation of the spirit of man in literature," with appropriate Joycean and/or Irish irony. I believe in it without any irony at all (although I would not say "eternal").

4. Today especially, in the extremity of the human existential predicament (for one cannot conceive a further extremity that will not simply remove human existence once and for all), we can no longer practice the will to dominate through more and more human impositions upon things as they are, things in themselves, impositions of whatever kind and in whatever sphere, intellectual, artistic, or material. We must acknowledge the equivalence of all identities, our own included. We must execrate the capitalist bastards who urge otherwise. This is not philosophical idea-spinning. It is practical in the most immediate sense: we cannot survive without it, a total inversion of attitudes and values. Who knows if it can be done? But my own wish, at least, is to be counted among those who tried.

🖎 . . . .

With Respect to the Infuriating Pervasiveness of Optimism

1983.

WHEN EZRA POUND was a young man, he assumed his intellectual character in a phase of Anglo-American culture created by one man, Matthew Arnold. When Pound went to London in 1910, he landed in an Arnoldian *milieu*. These are, I imagine, sufficiently extravagant generalizations, which is what I intend them to be. I am not speaking of Pound the poet, the student of comparative literature, the technical innovator, and so on. I am speaking rather of Pound the exemplary figure, the young intellectual among other intellectuals, who took on unavoidably and unconsciously the optimism of the nineteenth century's greatest English arbiter of cultural understanding.

But Arnold was no featherbrain. He was a poet. He was also a critic, an educator, a public administrator, and a hardheaded practical man. He had functioned imaginatively in precise reaction against the Byronesque romanticism that had lingered in English sensibility beyond the middle of the century. Nor was Arnold a utopian in any sense, being distinct in this from many of his great contemporaries, Ruskin, Morris, Marx, Spencer, Darwin, and others. Arnold was, if you like, the Grand Reformer, the exponent of Liberalism Writ Large; and his attraction for later generations, perhaps especially in the USA (Eliot included him among the luminaries of Cousin Harriet's parlor library), was his essential pragmatism, even his cultural relativism, and his disdain for ideological thought in general, whether Positivist or Tractarian.

Yet Matthew Arnold was the one who said that art is "a criticism of life," and what could be more optimistic than that? In his work the idea of criticism became almost ideological; it acquired an expansiveness and aggressiveness it had never had before, making it truly functional and directive, not in a Johnsonian or didactic manner, but expressly in and through the imagination. Art became criticism, and criticism became art, in both senses of "becoming." Thus artists were not only recorders of change in human affairs, they were moderators and mediators. They could be and should be assessors, instigators, and moral henchmen.

Arnold was the Aristotle of the modern world, at least in the parts of it that speak English.

When Pound became an old man, he fell into a deep depression. I ignore for the present whatever biographical, read pathological, factors may have induced it. "I can't make it cohere," he said. And since he was decidedly a human being he took his failure personally. Yet what in the *Cantos* themselves requires such a failure? When I think about that huge poem, though I find parts of it odious, I see nothing that could not have been structured systematically by an imagination as inventive as Pound's. No. The incoherence lay not in the poem but in the world.

Pound was born in 1885, three years before my father. Both men lived from the world of Arnold into the world of the hydrogen bomb. What Pound had begun in cultural optimism could not be sustained, certainly not beyond the horrors of World War II and Hiroshima. Optimism gave way, the idea of coherence gave way, the poem gave way. My father, though he wrote no big poems, wrote little ones, and he too, like who knows how many others of that generation, ended in the silence of despair, so bitter that his not speaking was a kind of incandescence.

Someone will no doubt suggest that Pound was saturated with the tragic view and that this cannot be equated with optimism. But I believe – I've come to believe after decades of studying and leaning heavily on the tragic view – just the contrary. The tragic view of life and art, which pits human intelligence against the incoherence of fate and celebrates, however negatively, the authenticity, solidity, and *value* of human experience, is, I believe, from Sophocles to Shakespeare to Schopenhauer to Sartre, at bottom not only a mode of optimism but essentially more optimistic, not less, than the progressivism of Hegel and Whitman and Henry Ford, to say nothing of Plato. Yet a work begun in the optimism of tragedy is self-contradictory. It must admit failure in the face of incoherence in order to make its point. It becomes a comedy, what we call a black comedy. And I am by no means the first to point out that the *Cantos*, like *King Lear*, are comedic.

Is optimism then an inevitable component of any constructive human effort, meaning effort aimed at change? Is it a part of human "nature"? Perhaps it is. (And let's avoid the riddle of what, if anything, human nature means.) My own historical imagination suggests to me, however, that another mode is possible, a mode in which optimism is not present at all, either positively or negatively, a mode in short based upon the ante-modern belief that time is linear and eternity is circular. If I look at the mind of Dante and compare it with the mind of Descartes, I see that at some point between them linearity became progress and circularity became utopianism – striking variances. And to my mind it is by no means incidental that the *Divina Commedia* is a good deal more coherent than the *Discours de la méthode*.

As for myself, I have come to the age of sixty-two, and in considering the failure of my own work, I am struck, not for the first time but now very forcibly, by the extent to which my life has been lived in a Poundian mold. I mean unintentionally as well as intentionally. (But I do *not* mean ideologically, in case anyone should think otherwise.) In my writing, but even more in my work as editor, reviewer, and general entrepreneur, I have been imbued, though I am temperamentally, read pathologically, as solemn and forlorn a creature as anyone would care to meet, with Arnoldian optimism. I am my father's son, as well as Pound's. I and my friends believed we were still part of a beleaguered avant-garde, and we had good reason for that belief in 1945. Such poets as Pound, Williams, and Cummings were still unable to find publishers, still unknown to educators. We thought that if we could shift the focus of American culture, especially in the schools, away from the line of taste established in Cambridge, Mass., in 1870, then we could effect a real and significant change in our civilization. Indeed this was what we must do, as Allen Tate remarked to me in 1947; and though Tate had many disagreements with other avant-garde writers of the time, from Yvor Winters on the West Coast to Archibald MacLeish and F.O. Matthieson in New England, *everyone* agreed on this. Well, we succeeded. In the ensuing years we effected that real and significant change. We succeeded to such an extent that we are now almost rueful, seeing that children no longer read *Evangeline* or "I Must Go Down to the Sea Again" and that Ph.D. dissertations are now being written on the poetry of Howard Nemerov, for God's sake! And has American civilization changed? Yes, but only in the direction that was evident forty years ago. It has gotten worse.

At any rate this is how the problem presents itself to me now. The efficacy of art, if there is to be any, must depend on some truly fundamental change in consciousness. On this matter it is hard not to think backwards. Gary Snyder would say, I believe, "Let's regress to the purity of the animals." Clayton Eshleman, "Let's get back to the Aurignacians." Wendell Berry, "The essential values and practical techniques are to be found in a peasant culture." And so on. To my mind any such nostalgia is flawed by the historical delusion of Unprogress, which is just as bad as Progress. It is a type of sentimentality; reduced to doctrine, it is the motive of the reactionary State. For what has been done cannot be undone, and we can look only forward, whether we like it or not; that is, toward tomorrow and the day after tomorrow, but never

beyond our own lives, since that would be the sentimentality of uto-
pian progress and the motive of the progressive State. (Is not our un-
sentimental tomorrow the basis of the tragic view?) We must enter –
soon! – a phase of consciousness beyond – well, I do not know what
word to use here, and I must resort to jargony wordmaking in the style
of the politicians – hence, beyond implementalism. Writers must be
authors, not agents. Authorship, not agency, is our service. Note the
difference well.

What are the alternatives? Several, I suppose. Certainly one is the
horrid game of literary politics, so empty and fatuous, which we pri-
marily associate with New York City, though it is played everywhere.
The game is ruled by greed, of course; but its impetus and energy
come from an attempt to escape the failure of optimism, which is to say,
an attempt to prolong the Arnoldian tragic view, coherence embattled
within incoherence, in spite of the Poundian *débâcle*.

Some of my friends will be snickeringly surprised by what they per-
ceive as a turn toward religion in these remarks. Others will think just
the contrary and will say, "Aha! See how he leans toward the Decon-
structionists." But myself, I am not surprised. For one thing, both ele-
ments have been present in my mind and work for many years, al-
though the tasks I undertook prevented them from being developed or
emphasized; for another, I am confident neither will emerge in a doc-
trinal orientation.

Now another alternative occurs to me, in addition to game-playing.
It is the kind of criticism that exhibits itself as a system, sometimes
even a program. Critics like Hugh Kenner and Richard Ellmann, who
believe they can produce a work that is, however circumscribed, not
only coherent but comprehensive, are perhaps the greatest, most de-
luded optimists of all. Their counterparts among poets are those who,
like Francis Ponge, insist that one can achieve an exact, complete de-
scription of one's big toe, or at any rate that it is worth dying in the at-
tempt to do so. As for me my excuse, if I need one, for packing such
huge and crudely drawn concepts into this brief essay is that I think no
other way is possible. I take my leave of the whole shebang. I decline
optimism in all its forms at last.

But is it optimistic to believe I have the choice?

ع٠ ·

Paul Goodman and the Grand Community

1982.

AS AN ARTISTIC PERSONALITY Paul Goodman was so cohesive in his concerns and beliefs, so altogether yoked and bonded within himself, that one can make no analytical statement about him without falling into paradox, by which I mean opposites held in tension, and this is one reason why his writing has been little tested by the critics. For my part I have always preferred to call myself a reviewer, not a critic, and the distinction is important to serve as a disclaimer, for myself, of any systematic view of literature, especially as derived from sociology, linguistics, esthetics, or any standpoint outside literature as such. I don't mean to be falsely modest. It's no news that we live in a low and narrow literary age. My kind of spadework is what we need now, both to sort out our jumbled tastes and to make possible a future criticism that will be serious and responsive. More than eight years ago I began to attempt these sentences, and even now I do not know where they will lead. Nevertheless there is a point in my following my broadest impressions of Goodman's sensibility, since precisely these may lead into the self-enclosure of his remarkable fluency, which was not a matter merely of words, but of thought, feeling, perception, cultural reference; in short, the pattern-making awareness of experience that he himself called "the continuum of the libido." It was in fact his natural facility of imagination, driven always by his pervasive, many-tempered lust, and it never deserted him.

The first thing to be said about Goodman, therefore, is that his integrated sensibility was in some manner achieved; not imposed, not revealed, not fortuitously agglomerated.

And the second thing – still staying within one's broadest impression – is that Goodman's integrated sensibility nevertheless had two foci. Culturally speaking, Goodman lived in two places at once. More than any other important American writer of the twentieth century, he was European. Hemingway, Faulkner and the others of the "Southern renaissance," Williams, Stevens (in spite of his mannered elegance), even Eliot and Pound (in spite of their European allegiances), as well as such members of Goodman's own generation as Schwartz, Jarrell, Shapiro, Lowell, Bishop, etc. – all were American, whether determinedly or unselfconsciously. It is not a question of style. (If it were, Stevens would be from Paris, circa 1880.) It is a question of vision, angle of approach, the way experience is seized and organized esthetically. Goodman was precisely *moderniste* in the European tradition, a companion of Kafka, Gide, Rilke, Brecht, Aragon, and Cocteau; especially Cocteau. He disclaimed the impersonal and conventional; he celebrated the personal and mythological. His procedure was that of dreaming awake, its wit as well as its profundity. He was absurd, practical, deeply moral, shocking, and polemical. He was a superb technician and had a philosopher's sensitivity to the humanity of language (somewhat akin to Heidegger, though I don't know if he had read him); at the same time he had little use for linguistics as such, or for structuralism or concretism or any other conceptualist theory of art. He was devoted to *meaning*. In all these qualities he was a European man, and not simply European but Continental. He was a romanticist in the post-post-post-romanticism that this implies. I am reminded of the absolutely necessary apothegm somewhere in the writings of Albert Camus: "Classicism is nothing but romanticism with the excess removed."

Further, a point can be made about the deliberately "American" writers of the first half of the century, namely, that many of them, often including Williams (whose work I admire enormously), fell into a kind of rhetoric of America, exaggerated, in effect chauvinistic. The American Experience, etc. Goodman was far too sophisticated, too analytical, too well trained philosophically to fall into that. He knew how important the city of Paris was to the modernist movement. There really is a sense of place in the works of Cocteau, Gide, etc., to say nothing of Proust, whereas with American writers place tends to become exclusively subject, to move from the background to the foreground. With Goodman, as with the Europeans, it is in both places. As for Whitman, I think at some deep level – below style, topic, and mode of thought – Goodman shared with him the bedrock humanism or artistic altruism, close to but never the same as messianism, that saved the older poet, if barely, from chauvinism. In some poems, though not many, I detect phrasings by Goodman that could have been taken word for word and rhythm for rhythm from Whitman, though almost certainly they weren't.

Having said this about Goodman's Europeanism, however, I think at once of the ways in which he was so thoroughly American that my remarks seem crazy. No other American writer of his time dared to be patriotic in Goodman's fundamentalist sense. In the midst of his sophistication he was plain and straightforward, not to say homely; in the midst of castigating contemporary American civilization he would stop to proclaim, in tones of injury, his faith in the Jeffersonian archetype. It was almost a tic, but no less serious on that account. He truly believed that the Lockean presence in the American Constitution made it not only one of the world's most beautiful political documents but still the best hope of mankind. He took off his hat when the flag went by. And his love of the American scene, urban or rural, was clear in everything he wrote. He called himself a "Jeffersonian anarchist." What's more, he made it stick, he turned the seeming contradiction into a unity. He was American even to the extent of accepting necessity in politics, moderating his revolutionary zeal and despair to a reformist optimism, at least from time to time – and what could be more American than that? Sometimes he seemed in danger of turning into an ordinary Anglo-American liberal, a fault his critics on the left were always glad to point out. At all events he made us see that *radical* and *conservative*, if they remain useful terms at all, are only so in combination. We cannot say one without meaning the other. He was practical and pragmatic, like all Americans; but always haunted, like all Americans, by the ideal.

But I see that already I must correct myself, the difficulty of dealing with such a complex personality is so great. It was not that Goodman "moderated his revolutionary zeal"; he advocated short-term changes which in themselves were nothing basic but which he saw as necessary little elements of the social revolution (after Kropotkin) that would, if it were accomplished, make the later political revolution more secure. Something like that, at any rate. He felt that it would be a mistake to leap over these little changes because they were not revolutionary in themselves. He also felt – and this may be the heart of the matter – that it was important to avoid despair, depression, etc., since political activity, especially revolutionary, requires energy and hope.

Yet how many times, again in paradox, he castigated Hope as the enemy of reasonable endeavor!

Perhaps, refining the point further, it is possible to say that in effect Goodman believed in an underlying *nature*, in which human beings participate, though at the same time he recognized the danger of such a belief, its outworn transcendental simplicity. Cautiously but clearly, he believed that at all moments of political or social vitality (in history) one will see glimpses of this underlying nature, and one will be able to say why the particular political form sustains it, frees it, nurtures it, etc. This thought, and his preference for simplicity, entered actively into the aspects of his mind that can be called conservative. In an analogous recognition of its danger, he tempered his romanticism, his native libidinous exuberance, with a classical and historical mode of reasoning. And all this was deeply characteristic of Western intellectual life during the years of Goodman's active maturity, 1940 to 1970, though it obviously appeared in many shapes and colors.

In the back of my copy of *The Empire City* I jotted some of the names which occurred to me in my rereading: Rabelais, Cocteau, Aristophanes, the Old Testament (but more *Genesis* than *Isaiah*), Swift and Hogarth, Proust, Joyce (but with a question mark), Twain, Voltaire, Handel, Poulenc, Thurber, "even in parts Francis Ponge," "the orchestrations of *The Critique of Pure Reason*," and Buster Keaton. A random list; obviously many others were tributary to Goodman's confluence: Aristotle, Villon, Wordsworth, Freud, Louis Sullivan – the names keep surfacing – perhaps Kafka most of all. Two temperaments so unlike, Kafka and Goodman, their positions worlds apart, their concerns scarcely touching; yet Goodman found in Kafka something necessary to himself. I think it was the figure of the alien first of all. If Kafka was an artist too, so much the better. But the isolated man, the cut-off imagination, these were the paradigms Goodman needed for himself. If he loved America, he did not love Americans, any more than he loved Libyans, Finns, or Trobrianders. Before each act of thought he had to touch, as if it were his talisman, his own freedom in all its chordal changes – independence, solitude, alienation, horrible messianic loneliness. Otherwise he could not think deeply at all.

(And was he, parenthetically, touched and reinforced by his own style of language and thought as it had appeared in prior American civilization, in works by Thoreau, Alcott, the other tax-dodgers, or by

Dickinson and Hawthorne? The styles were close to his in many ways, yet the distances were great as well. He seldom spoke of them. I feel that Goodman's cultural temperament made him think of his American forerunners as unwanted rivals, and of their Transcendentalism, especially in its withdrawal from social process, as too puny a human endeavor to warrant his attention. Yet Brook Farm was important to him.)

Now in the course of a couple of pages, following my sentences where they go, I have been led through a considerable number of opposing coordinates on the circle of Goodman. The European American, the socialized alien, the practical utopian, the conservative radical, the pragmatic idealist, the self-explaining mystery and self-disclosing secret; for like all writers, but more manifestly than most, he was an Indian giver. If he disclaimed, as he characteristically often did but sometimes did not, the conventional post-romantic role of prophet, *homme d'esprit*, and vatic spirit, nevertheless he promised what he could not deliver. This was not, as one might be tempted to say at first, the "unutterable" word; Goodman was too thoroughly Aristotelian and psychoanalytic in his bias to accept ultimately the idea of a secret, mystical, supraverbal *logos*. It was simpler than that. What he sought was the word, the combination of words, that could contain all his own contradictions. This was humanly impossible, itself a factor that would have to be incorporated in the "word," with emphasis on "humanly." So he wrote around it and around it, forty books on almost as many topics, explaining himself again and again, laying everything bare except the one real object of his and our desire, that which has no name though a thousand synonyms. Goodman is the perpetually fading echo that reverberates between the cliffs of consciousness. Call them being and nothingness. That inexactness will do as well as any other.

A system of opposites lined up like the intersectional points of diameters along the circumference of a circle. As with all metaphor, this from geometry is inaccurate in its application, yet it is useful. In its typicality it represents one observable and so to speak certifiable aspect of the continual negotiation between reality and human mental capacity or incapacity; it is inevitable, it is there in our heads, beyond the control of "reason" or "will," and its success in any particular operation will be relative. This Kantian view (though Kantian only to the extent that much else proposed by Kant himself is disregarded) would have been agreeable to Goodman. He was an anarchist, meaning by definition a mind limited and undoctrinal; a pragmatist, a relativist, a humanist, a moralist, a personalist. I don't know if he read Nikolai Berdyaev, but he would have gone part way with that philosopher's peculiar Catholic anarchism, as he would have gone part way or further with Tolstoy and Buber and many other religious radicals; and the points of separation from them would have come over disagreement about terms – the definition of the social context, the exact specifications of spiritual awareness – more than from conflict of ideas. Part way was Goodman's perennial journey.

So he chose more and more to live in the countryside of northern New England where some half-articulate philosopher might be milking cows on the next farm down the road. He was a city Jew drawn like a moth to the light of backwoods Yankee nonconformity. His place (near Stratford, New Hampshire) was as far from Cambridge as he could get without leaving New England. He shunned as well the objectivism of William Carlos Williams, Louis Zukofsky, and George Oppen, with their insistence on the purity and autonomy of the thing-in-itself. Yes, he might have said to them, metaphor has its dangers, including the risk of phenomenological distortion; but lo! (for he was our only modern writer who knew how to get away with the marvelous archaisms) see that metaphor pure and shining in this poem by Wordsworth, and another here in Villon! They work, they function, they are useful. How can one deny so natural an expedience of human invention? He demanded to be taken as a "practical" man, the esthetician of the possible. And just as he shunned the objectivists, he shunned everyone else.

Goodman could make friends with no one who was not either a disciple or dead – and the longer dead the better.

One cannot avoid the inference that Goodman's oppositionism was as much a matter of temperament as of principle. Yes, he complained of loneliness and he welcomed new friends eagerly; but he could stick with no group for long. He preached communalism, yet was the last who could have accepted it. Notice how quickly, after he had attained success and had won a following among the young advocates of counterculture in the 1960s, he turned against them, or partly against them, and began writing books and essays to distinguish his positions from theirs. These distinctions were and are important, he was perfectly right to insist on them; but he could have written his books and essays as a leader, rather than as a critic. The chance of leadership was handed to him, the gift of history that most ambitious people pray for and that he himself had prayed for (e.g., in *Five Years*). But Goodman threw it away, abruptly, almost at times disdainfully. He knew what he was doing. Then was he unambitious? Not a bit; his need for recognition was enormous, a principal theme of his poems. But so was his need for independence. He was in conflict with himself – the point is worth repeating – and what is interesting, indeed crucial, is the way he kept his conflicts under control, brought them into the circle of tension that was his whole sensibility, and thus held himself and his work together.

But I have no wish to anticipate Goodman's biography. That job is being done superbly by Taylor Stoehr, whose work, when it is finished, will be an indispensable history of Goodman's era. (I knew Goodman only briefly in the time before his public success.) One point of biography is well known already, however, Goodman himself being always eager to publish it, and is important and worth emphasizing here. He belonged to the generation of New York intellectuals, mostly Jewish, who dominated much of American political and literary thought in the late thirties, forties, and into the fifties; such writers as Philip Rahv, Lionel Trilling, Hannah Arendt, Delmore Schwartz, Dwight McDonald, Mary McCarthy, Saul Bellow, and many others. A cardinal point with these brilliant men and women was precisely their alienation from the main currents of American life and thought; yet Goodman was alienated even among them.

It was an earlier instance of what happened in his relationship to the young people of the 1960s. But his estrangement from his own contemporaries was more fundamental, perhaps more painful, more damaging. He bitched about it endlessly. I think even he, however, knew how much he needed that damage, that extreme intellectual and even personal isolation. He continually took positions, consciously or unconsciously, that would reinforce it. No line could be laid down by the group, whether political, artistic, or philosophical, that Goodman would not bristlingly object to. He was an alien among aliens, ignored, scorned, refused access to the alien magazines and publishing houses. You might think he would have been published regularly in *Partisan Review*, the *New Leader*, the *Nation*, and the other radical noncommu-

nist magazines of that time based in New York, but he wasn't. Irregu-
larly, yes; but he never had ready entrée to any means of publication
before 1960. He complained about this, bitterly and with justice. It was
easier for T. S. Eliot, royalist, reactionary, and a snob, to get into *Parti-
san Review* than it was for Paul Goodman. Yet his predicament was his
own doing as much as anyone else's, more than anyone else's, and his
complaints were in fact triumphs of self-celebratory exuberance.

Goodman was the self-justifying, self-congratulating pariah; not
quite a martyr, he knew he was too intelligent to play that role convinc-
ingly; but he was wily enough to know too that he could be comfort-
ably downtrodden and make a public virtue of his perpetual auto-
nomic dissidence. Not that the "virtue" was "public" at the time. The
factions within intellectual life in New York during the late thirties, for-
ties, and early fifties were many and minute; but they themselves pro-
duced hardly any public impact. How could the one who dissented
from the dissidents expect recognition for it, all the more since the dis-
sidents, when he attacked them, failed to counterattack? They just ig-
nored him. Yet Goodman knew himself well enough to recognize that
he could function best as philosopher and artist in an attitude of per-
sistent opposition, and he hoped – he always hoped! – that ultimately
this private necessity would become a public virtue. This is exactly
what happened in the sixties when all his works, earlier and later,
came, however briefly, into public prominence.

Even anarchists, whose base in thought denies them the comfort of
ideology, need something to rest on, i.e., that base itself, which thereby
becomes a kind of ideal or absolute. It is, of course, the notion of free-
dom. Freedom complete and unconstrained by anything except con-
siderations of "public safety." What ensues from this has been debated
for a century and a half, with tactical and philosophical consequences
to my mind both fascinating and illuminating; but I have no need here
to try even the sketchiest recapitulation. Goodman's use of the idea is
my concern. His freedom was less that of the utopian theorists of Eu-
rope than of the nostalgic theorists of America. He called himself a
"Jeffersonian anarchist." But the term did not satisfy him, and else-
where he equated "anarchism" with "libertarianism" and "rebel hu-
manism" in the attempt to pin down in a word his own undogmatic
and ideologically unideological desire for freedom, practicality, and
love. His view of the early history of the United States was sentimental,

perhaps wrong; but it was crucial. "During the first thirty years of the Republic only five to ten percent were enfranchised and as few as two percent bothered to vote. But the conclusion to be drawn from this is not necessarily that the society was undemocratic. On the contrary, apart from the big merchants, planters, clerics, and lawyers, people were likely quite content, freed from the British, to carry on their social affairs in a quasi-anarchy, with unofficial, decentralized, and improvised political forms. It was in this atmosphere that important elements of our American character were developed." And those elements were kept alive today, Goodman insisted, primarily in his own writing.

Yet he never forgot "our moronic system of morals and property," nor that this system emerged constitutionally from the political forms of the Republic, nor that the only recourse of honest people in American has almost always been political illegitimacy.

Goodman was a radical who dreamed backward more than forward, and whose view of the present was more often vague than precise, more often anxious than expedient, in spite of his commitment to "practicality." "Perhaps it is because I am so crazy with hope that I live in constant terror," he wrote. But also: "I fail to experience myself in groups that I cannot immediately try to alter by personal decision and effort." Again: "To dance into the present with the force of the endurance of the world." And elsewhere still: "With much of the business of our society, my intuition is to forget it." Finally: "On the advice of Longinus, I write...for Homer, for Demosthenes, and other pleasant company who somehow are more alive to me than my contemporaries, though unfortunately not available for comment." But if Homer had been alive in New York in 1940, Goodman would have dismissed him as inhumane and doctrinaire.

Goodman was not divided, he was torn. All his writing, seen from this standpoint, was an effort to patch himself together. It worked, and that is what is so remarkable.

The temptation at this point becomes obvious, namely, to reduce these various dualisms to the basic one that Goodman called his bisexuality. In one way or another sex is his tonic from first to last. Aside from the explicitly erotic poems and stories, sexual energy is present in all his writing; at least so I would argue – I don't know how to prove it. But when Goodman speaks of "the force of the endurance of the world," a statement that can be found in different formulations throughout his works, I believe he is thinking of a nature that by no means excludes Newtonian, Darwinian, Freudian, Einsteinian, or any other modes of "objective contemplation," but that nevertheless is basically and simply generative – he is thinking, however metaphorically or unconsciously, of sex. His dualisms are sexually informed. His manner of argument is the same. The sensuality of his style, by which I mean its "poetry" or "music," its syntactical sinuosity and almost tactility, is clear to me in even his most abstruse discussions. This uninhibited fluency, so remarkable in a writer given to making distinctions, is the one element that pervades all his writings: the fiction and poetry, of course, but also the declamations, the private jottings, the philosophical and critical exegeses – everything. And he kept this sexual energy flowing all his life, through to the final poems of sexual melancholy written when he sensed death not far away.

Yet I find none of these considerations convincing when it comes to assigning reasons for the dichotomies of intellect and feeling in Goodman's work. First, although he usually called himself bisexual, in at least one prominent passage of his writing he called himself homosexual. Secondly, one cannot avoid seeing that among his poems, the expressly erotic ones are to, for, or about men, while those addressed to his wife (and to his children as engenderings of his marriage) are distinctly different in tone; the latter being warmly and deeply affectionate and companionable, so that often they move the reader more genuinely than do the former poems of lust. And thirdly, I dislike and distrust any of these quasi-clinical, reductionist analyses in literature, and I would not resort to them even if I were competent to do so. For Goodman himself, psychoanalysis was without question the single self-enclosed theoretical structure that most clearly determined his view of reality, yet he was prudent, as he would say, in his application of Freudian concepts, even in the derived Gestalt-analysis he favored, to artists or their works.

To my mind Goodman's propensity for dualistic modes of experience was forced on him, as on most of us, by his own temperament or by human temperament in general, and perhaps also by his early philosophical training, his graduate studies at the University of Chicago when Richard McKeon and Neo-Aristotelianism were the vogue there.

Aristotle's Pity and Woe, Pathos and Purgation, were important cat-
egories to the young intellectual of 1938 because, not only esthetically
but socially and psychologically, they substantiated his instinctive
awareness of art as a functioning thing, if not dialectical at least media-
tive. No doubt he found further support for his pragmatic view in the
Kantian notion of a priori limits, popular with John Crowe Ransom
and other New Critics. (Part of the avant-garde rejection of Hegel and
Marx in general during the late thirties was expressed in a reversion to
Kantian concepts, but bypassing the Romantic excess, along with new
interest in such writers as Kierkegaard, Dostoyevsky, and Kafka, all of
whom were important to Goodman.) But mainly Goodman had no in-
terest in faddish philosophy. Conflict for him was a practical or proce-
dural necessity, but he was always engaged in more or less holistic
analysis, or at least the hope of it. He resorted, or was forced to resort,
to dualistic modes in some books, e.g. *Compulsory Mis-Education* and
New Reformation, but more often he regarded himself as a person in
the main line of honest souls, from Aristotle, Longinus, Descartes,
Spinoza (whom he reverenced), Kant, James, Nietzsche (though he
discounted the *übermensch* as a form of neurotic yearning), Dewey,
etc., down to his own knocked-together but generally unitary "system."
He shows little liking for Cartesian or, in his own time, Sartrean dialec-
tics. And if it is true that the more he insisted on the ideal oneness of
society and the individual person, the more he found himself pushed
toward equations, dichotomies, and oppositions, nevertheless he held
the ideal – a functional unity – before his mind as the only reliable goal
for anarchistic and loving ways of thought. If this meant, psychiatri-
cally speaking, some scarcely appraisable but pervasive form of sexual-
ity, so much the better.

Goodman's sexuality, however, does remain a question needing fur-
ther explanation. He did not explain it himself, which is significant. He
explained everything else about his poetry, repeatedly and lengthily,
but he ignored this. He is rightly credited for his courage as a forerun-
ner in the movement toward gay liberation; that is, for his open avowal
of homosexuality in his poetry. But his silence elsewhere seems to indi-
cate some deeper embarrassment. Goodman knew that his concept of
love was unitary and that it was fundamental to his notion of the good
community. Only love can hold people together (as Locke had said),
and this love must be whole and wholly free. Yet community necessar-

ily entails the ideas of fertility and generation, which were traditionally associated with the loving heterosexuality of the human animal. And Goodman himself was a traditionalist. He does not say, however, what his communalism means in this context, beyond his insistence that love, like everything else, must be free.

It is as if the division of love into *eros* and *agape* dear to the Catholic theologians and invidious to at least some of the rest of us (so that we have denied it and said that the two are really one) does in fact exist in Goodman's life and work, and expresses itself in his attitudes toward his family on one hand and toward his sexual adventures with males on the other. Thus we come round to bisexualism again, but at a deeper level of meaning, and I think this is valid. Goodman tried to make a unity of *eros* and *agape,* and at times succeeded (or thought he did), but ultimately he really is stuck with some kind of separation. His inability to *rest* in any group and his obsessive need to keep talking, both of which he confessed readily, as well as his preference for being the critic in opposition, since he was always more adversary than advocate except in cases where he found himself in such primary opposition that he could "afford" to lean toward conciliation (e.g., his almost innate divergence from established religion and his final attempt to come to terms with it in *Little Prayers and Finite Experience),* all these elements of his own "nature" indicate to me a practical alienation from the social values of love. This would explain both his yearning for community and his inability to come to rest in a community. It was a deep duality, perhaps the deepest of all, far below his bisexuality. Nevertheless this is what I am talking about, this source, when I say that all his thought and writing are informed by his sexual energy.

Goodman was not famous, God knows, for laconism. By his own account he wrote "forty books," a nice round number such as authors are frequently heard to let fall. Yet in his case it seems that this may be an underestimation; his bibliography is huge, and since his death in 1972 newly uncovered works have continued to appear with regularity. He was a man of many words, for "to me it is panic to be speechless." At the same time he knew the values of brevity. (So complete was his proficiency that I find myself wanting to say, against reason, that he knew *all* the values of *all* literary strategies.) As he grew older and his imagination progressively consolidated and simplified his vision, he turned often to the Japanese hokku, for example, and wrote a few so poignantly right that they wring your heart.

> *If they were to say*
> *that this hokku was the last*
> *poem that he wrote*

Yes, he knew *all* the values: how the strict armature of traditional artifice glows and comes alive in the broken language of unutterable, or nearly unutterable, feeling; the sentence left unfinished eternally. Yet he had a sharp, epigrammatic wit at times.

> *I must be thirsty,*
> *man, to make love to such a*
> *long drink of water.*

In the prose too, which gives the impression of almost uncontrolled discursiveness, organization by caprice, one finds nevertheless embedded apothegms, these less the consequence of conscious effort perhaps than of the unmitigated force of invention. Imagine him at work, hunched over the battered old Underwood, his pipe fuming and clenched between what remained of his teeth. The sentence, the *sentence* – it was for him an act of imaginative compression, though he knew how to hook them together and keep the cadence rolling. It was the ideal expression of a thought, a single movement of the mind. The sentence was for Goodman what the image had been for Ezra Pound. Here are a few that have struck me particularly over the years.

The givenness of Creation is surprise.

•

This world is purgatory. I have plenty of proof that I am not damned – I understand that it is heretical to say so – but I am being tried, I have no notion why. Maybe that's what I'm supposed to learn.

•

Yet men have a right to be crazy, or stupid, or arrogant. It is our speciality. Our mistake is to arm anybody with collective power.

•

"Stand up for the stupid and crazy," Whitman said. Is there a connection? I can say only that either way I wouldn't be surprised.

•

When Isaac was saved on Mt. Moriah, Abraham must have gone into a towering anger. The Bible, written as God's history, tells us nothing about this. All that heartache for nothing.

•

There are too many missionaries among my friends.

•

Spite is the vitality of the powerless.

•

It is astounding how natural and few the fine arts are.

•

A style of speech is an hypothesis about how the world is.

•

Despite its bloodlessness, the tradition of literature is a grand community and, much as I envy the happy and the young, I doubt that they have as good a one.

•

The color of the Burning Bush is thought-passing-over-a-face color (but it must be a *thought*, not one of the vagaries of the likes of you).

•

Any workman putting away his tools is among the lovely dancers of this world.

•

For whatever is a human passion may be expressed in music, and whatever is music is in the human throat to imitate it.

•

... the bondage of peace ....

•

The thing is to have a National Liberation Front that does not end up in a Nation State, but abolishes the boundaries.

•

Literature is not a "linear" unrolling of printed sentences and it is not a crude code; it is artful speech. And speech is not merely a means of communication and expression, as the anthropologists say, but is a chief action in our human way of being in the world.

•

The case is that our society is in a chronic low-grade emergency.

•

In the breakdown of repression, the artists do their part by first dreaming the forbidden thoughts, assuming the forbidden stances, and struggling to make sense. They cannot do otherwise, for they bring the social conflicts in their souls to public expression.

•

Certainly we are in a political crisis, for, though the forms of democracy are intact, the content is vanishing.

•

Yet it is a melancholy but common thing in the world (and makes for a melancholy world) that while the one fighter is for some reason single-mindedly bent on destroying a man, that man does not want this fight; he does not believe in it, he does not think that it is worth the hurt and damage involved. He has been forced into it, and it happens that he cannot quit the field.

•

Goodman could never quit the field. He would stalk off, muttering his disgust, but the next day – the same afternoon! – he would be back, his pipe fuming.

What made Goodman so blithe a philosopher was his understanding that philosophy is of the heart. He loved Kant almost because the Koenigsburgher was so often wrong; or rather not wrong but incomplete – stopped by the limits of mentality. And this is the pathos that makes the Beautiful, surpassing every secondary esthetic principle of inclusiveness, dynamism, control, or whatever. *The Critique of Pure Reason,* read in this way, is Western man's greatest oratorio of ideas, a triumph of art; so huge, so majestically orchestrated, touching so many of the unnotable, unsoundable limits.

In this Goodman was closer, on second thought, to his American forerunners than to his European. He was a little Emersonian, but of the jumbled Notebooks (though I don't know if he read them) more than of the finished Essays. An important distinction. In spite or because, whichever, of his haste and vitality, Goodman was always feeling his way, touching one after another of the objects, often books, presented to him by chaos, repulsing most, taking a few to himself. It was intuition at work, his rule of thumb, which left him sometimes in contradictions he cared nothing about. But we, his readers, may care. Inconsistency is no hobgoblin, but it makes strangers where there should be friends.

"...my trouble is that I have to be that kind of poet who is in the clear because he has done his public duty. All writers have hang-ups, and mine is To Have Done My Duty. It is an arduous taskmaster, but at least it saves me from the nonsense of Sartre's poet *engagé*, politically committed. How the devil could a poet, who does the best he can just to get it down as it is whispered to him, decide whether or not to be morally or politically responsible? What if the Muse won't, perverse that she is? What if the Truth won't, unknown that it is?"

"The ability of literature to combine memory and learning with present observation and spontaneous impulse remarkably serves the nature of man as the animal who makes himself...."

Strange. The terms are Sartre's yet the drift seems blindly anti-Sartrean. How is it that the "animal who makes himself" has a "nature"? Impossible, the Frenchman would say, unless mere self-consciousness is a "nature," which it is not. Can a person be both created and self-creating? Yes, Goodman would exclaim, why not! And then he would go on to say, perhaps, that the fact that a man "makes himself" does not contradict the idea of a prior givenness, or nature, but instead refers to the aspects of evolution that proceed from human culture. Science and technology, applied to agriculture, improve the diet, and after a few generations the average man is 5'10", and has bad teeth instead of good ones. But obviously this takes more intellectual, more spiritual, forms as well.

Sometimes it seems as if Goodman ought to have found in Sartre, as he did in so many other European writers, a companion-at-arms. Very little necessary conflict existed between them. Sometimes Goodman's rejection of Sartre seems merely vanity, parochialism, defensiveness, the feelings that made him flare out at anyone who seemed, however distantly, to be treading on his own ground. But if there were no necessary differences between them, certainly there were practical differences, stylistic differences. Sartre was an ideologue, after all. In politics he supported the invasion of Hungary. To this Goodman could have uttered only a gigantic NO! Freedom and love come before ideas. And to Sartre's word-spinning, the house of cards built for Jean Genêt, the strange tenuosity of "existential psychoanalysis," Goodman could have responded only with another negative.

For it is after all more than a question of vanity, parochialism, and defensiveness. And Goodman is closer to Emerson than to Sartre and the other European secular existentialists (though I wish he had written something about Camus). The poet "who does the best he can just to get it down as it is whispered to him," – what is he but the Kantian, the Emersonian, the Romantic?

I do not doubt for a moment Goodman's sincerity in avouching what was "whispered" to him. He is a poet of intuition. And yet – was he not as well a poet of "responsibility," of "authenticity"? Emerson had thought he was a Kantian, but was at best only loosely so. Goodman brought to American "romanticism" the inner moral voice, the imperative, of Kant, the poet's due to the Greater Spirit, his *intuition*. Goodman repaired the ruin of Transcendentalism with an esthetic accountability that could have come, but didn't, straight out of Sartre's theory of literature. For of course and without the slightest question, large parts of Goodman's poetry and fiction are political. He was being only petulant, denying the obvious, to say otherwise. The notion that somehow his polemical writing, his participation in rallies and demonstrations, left him free to be a "pure" poet was deeply at variance with many statements of his belief in the unity of literature and life and of his sensibility. Even on the same page with the last quotation above he wrote: "The habits, genres, and tropes that have been developed in the long worldwide literary tradition constitute a method of coping with reality different from science, religion, political power, or common sense, but involved with them all. In my opinion, literature, although it is a method *sui generis,* is not a specialized department of learning but a good way of being in any department. It is a part of philosophy, which as a whole has no department."

Incidentally, watch out for Goodman when he says "in my opinion." It means a whopper – right or wrong – is on the way.

Yet, with nearly the whole span of twentieth-century American poetry before us – so many politically inspired poets who failed to transform their politics successfully into their poetry compared with the few who did – we can see how the trap that Goodman fell into was tempting enough; I myself have not avoided it. I used to think, indeed I said publicly, that Goodman's broadly political books which brought him to the attention of a wider audience than usually reads good poetry and fiction – and I had in mind such books as *Growing Up Absurd, Compulsory Mis-Education,* and *People or Personnel* – were in some sense a misfortune, though no one could honestly say they should not have been written; a misfortune because they distracted attention from his "creative" writing; and I expressed the hope, I think even the belief, that in the long run these polemical works would be forgotten and his poems and fictions would remain alive in the American consciousness. I no longer make this distinction. His best poems and fictions *will* remain alive in the American consciousness (if the American consciousness survives, which it well may not), but so will many of his other books. They go together. Goodman's topics were many, but his theme was always himself; and he could no more refrain from inserting into his polemical works remarks about his own beliefs as an artist than he could refrain from breathing. He was an organic whole. No other writer in America of this century – not Pound, not Williams, not Olson, though these are more nearly identified with the concept – represents so well the organicity of thought and feeling, of sensibility, implied in the title he gave himself, a Man-of-Letters.

Which is not to say that everyone must read every book in Goodman's "forty." Some are more important than others. For my part, I feel that the minimum for every reader's bookshelf is the following:

Art and Social Nature, The Copernican Revolution (edition of 1947), *Kafka's Prayer* (extremely important), *Communitas* (written with his brother Percival), *The Structure of Literature, The Empire City, Growing Up Absurd, The Lordly Hudson, Utopian Essays and Practical Proposals, Compulsory Mis-Education, Five Years, Hawkweed, Like a Conquered Province, Adam and His Works* (collected stories), *North Percy, Homespun of Oatmeal Gray, New Reformation, Speaking and Language, Little Prayers & Finite Experience.*

All these were published during Goodman's lifetime. Since his death more systematic collections of his short works (stories and essays) have been edited by Taylor Stoehr and others, including a few pieces not previously contained in books, and also one whole novel found hidden away among other papers, *Don Juan,* written around 1940. Goodman always had a difficulty – a heartbreaking struggle; see his negative paean to despair and survival in *Five Years* – in seeking publishers for his work, and heaven knows (or maybe Mr. Stoehr) what further unknown works may still appear.

Finally, the *Collected Poems* of 1973. Goodman was working on this, assembling, cutting, revising, when he was struck down; the further work of completing the manuscript and seeing it through the press fell to Stoehr, who did his best to ascertain and follow Goodman's last wishes. He could do neither less nor more. But I have considerable doubt of the wisdom of Goodman's own revisions, as I shall explain hereafter. Probably the *Collected Poems* must be added to the list because it contains poems not included in any earlier books while some of the earlier books themselves are hard to find. But the original books of poems are to be preferred, at least for the present.

A month or six weeks ago I found myself needing a copy of *The Lordly Hudson,* published in 1962. Mine was in Vermont, but I was in Syracuse – Syracuse, New York, which is not exactly Alexandria but is still a big enough, rich enough American city, with some pretentions to civic intelligence. Well, the neglect of Goodman's work during much of his life and still continuing has been a long source of pain to me, and of astonishment. I could not find the book in any library, public, academic, or private, in this city. And is it any different in Lexington, Kentucky; or Hot Springs, Arkansas; or Salem, Oregon? (You other Americans, you pious four-flushers and grandstanders, what the hell is one to say to you?)

I don't know how to account for the neglect of Goodman's work. Time after time I have met people who should be attracted by his poems and fictions, young and old, rich and poor, male and female. They have heard of him, those who are old enough have read *Growing Up Absurd* or attended a symposium on alternative schools in which he took part, but beyond that he means no more than the statue of President Harrison in the park. They do not know, have not even heard of, his poems or *The Empire City* or his short stories.

One explanation has occurred to me, wild as it seems, which is that Goodman's writing is too clear and that whatever exegesis it needs has been given by Goodman himself. The critics have nothing to do, and of course readers will not bother with anything that hasn't been hashed over a dozen times in the fashionable quarterly maggot-scenes.

"As a man of letters, I am finally most like Coleridge," he wrote. Then in parentheses: "With a dash of Matthew Arnold when the vulgarity of liberalism gets me by the throat." It was true. There is, if I am not mistaken, a universal turning point between Enlightenment and Romanticism, in the histories of individual men and women as in the histories of civilizations. It is a dangerous point because, for the vulgar liberals, who are the vast majority of mankind, it devolves into sentimentalism. But for the few, including Coleridge when young, it is a point of extraordinary freedom, the well-trained mind releasing itself into spirit. That point was where Goodman lived.

"Poets contrive to make interjections an organic part of their language by inverting the word order, distorting the syntax, and adding rhythm and resonance. Ordinary folk in a passion give up on the language." To which one need add only Goodman's own innermost thought, that poets ultimately are ordinary folk, that poems ultimately also must give up, e.g. the hokku with no conclusion.

Kafka was Goodman's closest literary friend, the young Jew of Prague, the writer whose greatness was like a dreamt castle with its towers vanishing upward in the mist.

Why am I so polemical about recent language theory...? Why don't I let those scholars do their thing, while I, as a man of letters, do mine? Frankly, I am made polemically uneasy by it, by the thrust of cultural anthropology, Basic languages, scientific linguistics, communications engineering, and the Theory of Communications. They usually treat human communication as far more mechanical than it is; they are technological in an anti-humanistic sense. They suit State and corporate policy too well and have crashingly pre-empted too many research grants and university appointments. My own bias, to be equally frank, is to play up the animal, spontaneous, artistic, and populist forces in speech. These forces are both agitational and deeply conservative – as I think good politics is. And as a writer, I want to defend literature and poetry as the indispensable renovators of desiccated and corrupt language.

Agitational and deeply conservative: mind soaring into spirit. (Reason, order, objectivity submitting to love.)

A poem is one inseparable irregular conglomeration, chanted. The word order is likely to be twisted. The names are particularistic and anomalous. New metaphors are invented. There is use of echoic meaning and expressive natural signs. There is strong use of tone and rhythm, sometimes even meter. The syntax is manipulated more than is common, sometimes "incorrectly," to give it more meaning. The exposition of the sentence follows the speaker's exploration of the subject rather than a uniform rule. All of this is for the purpose of saying a feelingful concrete situation, rather than making discursive remarks about it.

•

A generalist is a man who knows something about many special sciences, in order to coordinate their conclusions in a system that has little relation to reality. A man of letters knows only a little about some major human concerns, but insists on relating what he does know to his concrete experience. So he explores reality. A generalist is inter-disciplinary. A man of letters finds that the nature of things is not easily divided into disciplines.

•

When I do what is called "thinking," muttering to myself, I never use words like God or Faith, and they are in no way premises for my behavior. When I talk to other people, I sometimes use them, but not authentically; I might use such language, as I have said, to facilitate earnest conversation with a believer, though I am not a believer; or I might use them to cut short a boring conversation with an unbeliever, when I am too tired to explain myself better. When I write, however, I readily use this vocabulary and apparently seriously. How is this?

•

In *Defense of Poetry,* I suggest a possible reason: "Maybe it is that when I think or talk to myself, I am embarrassed; but when I write, I am not embarrassed" – since writing is my free act. But there could be a simpler reason, more *prima facie,* more what it feels like; I use this language because it is a poetic convention, a traditional jargon, like wearing old clothes because they are comfortable. It means what is the genius of the language of billions of human speakers – not my business. As a writer my business is only to be as clear as possible and say a work that has a beginning, middle, and end.

So we see Goodman clinging to his web of contrarieties.

Poetry is an empty act that is unfinishable but that has a beginning, middle, and end. But it is an *act.* Thinking is not an act. When the catcher signals to the pitcher, this is a thought; when the pitcher nods his head and goes into his windup, this is an act. Mind and imagination are connected, but the connection is tenuous, sometimes unlucky. The pitcher may shake off the sign, in which case the thought is useless. Or he may throw a bad pitch, in which case the act is a failure. But in all cases the pitcher's act is free, empty, isolated, internal, and its consequences, whatever they are, do not change it; no, not even if he beans the batter, who then suffers irreparable brain damage. Failure is failure, Goodman would say; it is a condition of human (self-conscious) existence, and so are punishment and misery and guilt. We can and must act with good faith and clarity, though these will never save us.

Thought is an argument with an imaginary companion. Making poetry is an act whose thought and content come from elsewhere, performed deliberately and in a conventional manner; its concreteness comes from its singularity – no act completely duplicates another, and a machine does not act but only moves in a meaningless transference of energy – and from the style imparted to it by the particular combination of attributes in the poet. (A machine is closer to thought than to a poem. A machine cannot have style.)

One may think at times that Goodman has painted himself into the same corner as the linguists and post-structuralists, as when he insists on the conventionality of language and artistic form. Yet the whole force of his argument, to say nothing of his poems, is to distinguish himself from those who would dismiss meaning from poetry. He too insists that the poem is "concrete," but he goes further. One must always remember that the poet does not believe in meaning as thought. Meaning is morality; morality is right feeling; and right feeling in concrete language is beauty. Sometimes I think Goodman yearned for "pure" poetry as much as Mallarmé before him. But I also think that such was not his case with poetry, no matter how he yearned. His poems are political. Impossible to think of them as anything but political, moral, practical acts, "empty" and "free" only in their disconnection from objective determinants. Poetry is given. But so is life.

Another distinction, which Goodman did not make (as far as I recall) but which I want to make for him is this: on one hand, style with a small s, being the techniques of syntax, grammar, and prosody contained in the grand and good and almost immemorial poetic convention; on the other hand, Style with a capital S, being the self-consciously fabricated verbal idiosyncrasy of poetic caprice or, worse, poetic fraud. Goodman's style was the former, and in fact he does not think about style explicitly and rarely uses the word. Moreover, as he knew, as we all know, convention in Goodman's sense is not always reliable. John Berryman could compose his *Dream Songs* in a Style that gave them a consistent superficial tension and density, while Goodman's poems in a plain style, as fine as the best of them are, especially in comparison with Berryman's, are more uneven. The fact that Berryman has been the darling of the critics while Goodman has been neglected shows the insensitivity of critics, who are always suckers for artifice.

But if in his poems Goodman conventionally used the conventional signs of a conventional religious language, and if as an unbeliever he conventionally knew that they were conventionally worthless, this is by no means the whole story. He was a practical man, i.e. a poet, i.e. a man

of faith. Often he adverts to the idea of the earth beneath him support-
ing his footsteps as he walks idly along, thinking of something else.
This is his faith. He was able, I don't know how, to shrug off the truly
immense apparatus of his learning, experience, and thought, and to
put himself again into the attitude of a child; or, more rigorously, cer-
tain constellations of traits and actions in the mature man reveal a
childlike quality, the panicky, needful child who is very much afraid,
but at the same time reliant on an unselfconscious prudential wisdom
and joy. A child does not touch a porcupine even though he has never
seen one before. "Nothingness" is a useful concept, and it may well be,
as many have said, that if one pursues it far enough it turns into the
same thing as "somethingness." But Goodman was a practical man. He
worked with his experience of "this only world," and for him "some-
thingness" was truly somethingness: the given reality upon which we
unselfconsciously, faithfully rely. He worked with his experience,
which was this simple faith, through years and decades, writing poems
in which the conventional signs took on more and more a personal, in-
dependent significance. Astonishing how simply and clearly he could
say his complicated relationship to reality.

> *O God, there must be some way*
> *that he and I (and many another)*
> *can be a little happier.*
> *Whisper it to me in my ear.*

He was like a child. A wise, suffering, hopelessly hopeful child. Neither
a literal nor a mystical way exists to define what the word "God" says
in this quatrain. Yet I know what it says, and I am confident that my
readers know what it says too. I don't have to try to explain it.

Goodman was *like* a child. But this is not to say that he was a child. On
the contrary it is to say how he was in his yearning, which was how he
was in the world. And the words of children were often – but others
just as often – expressive of how he was. "Whisper it to me in my ear,"
he says.

    And then many times this poignancy eluded him, and he spoke out
like the tough existential man he was, the Jewish Yankee.

For the beautiful arts
are made of cheap stuff,
of mud and speech
and guts and gestures

of animal gaits
and humming and drumming
daylight and rock
available to anybody.

This also is saying how he was in the world. And the names in these eight lines are not as random as they may seem at first, but were chosen in wisdom and placed with care. How else could he ever say how it *really* was for him in this world?

As for how it would be out of this world, Goodman did not write of death as much as one might have expected, knowing his metaphysical consternations. When he did write about it, he took it for what his experience – e.g. as a motorist (he loved the road) – told him it would be, and put it down on the paper more and more simply (though simplicity was one of his virtues from the beginning), and so in some sense dismissed it.

Chuangtze is dead as I shall die
unnoticed by the wayside,
his spirit does not haunt the world
and his death-grip is relaxed.

So. Finished and decomposing, no haunting spirit. Chuang-tzu, more than two thousand years ago, the great interpreter of Taoism to the world.

Returning again to the matter of style (with a small s), I wonder what poets were Goodman's models. He does not say much about this. Poets generally don't. Villon was obviously important to him, Wordsworth more than important – crucial. I know he read Milton's essays. I suspect he may have looked once at Donne's sermons and several times at Aubrey's *Brief Lives* and Pepys's *Diary*. And I am convinced, myself, that he must have read Bradford's *History of the Plymouth*

Plantation, that great distressed American epic, though I have only intuition to support me. But one can multiply the inferred influences indefinitely: Anacreon, Swift, Woolman, Catullus, Burns, the "Shepherd's Calendar," Rimbaud, and so on. Is there no contemporary instance? I can scarcely think of one (still adverting to style alone), though a wild guess might be that his deep interest in Kafka came through the translations of the Muirs, and that this might have led him to seek out Edwin Muir's own poems earlier than other Americans did; more than a trace of dictional and prosodic similarity exists between the two. And then Robert Frost – what about him? In an astounding number of ways Frost and Goodman echo each other, in many more ways than the devotees of either poet are likely to let on. But see, for instance, Frost's "The White-Tailed Hornet," especially its conclusion, which is Goodmanian in substance, tone, texture, and style.

But the point needing emphasis more than any other is that Goodman's instinct for the tradition took him not to individual models as much as in the direction of a persistent sub-part of the tradition, somewhat difficult to define but roughly identifiable in his own thought and feeling. It was the pathos and sweetness and power of plain song that held his loyalty. The mandarins, the official poets – from Virgil to Eliot they were not for him though he could pick out a genuine strain from any poetry wherever he found it. Thus his poem in praise of his brother Percival is in the "manner of Pindar"; and some of his poems in couplets have traces of Pope's last epistles and satires, though not of the earlier poems or of anything by Dryden but his songs. But not to individuals did he attach himself; rather it was to the company of poetic craftsmen who fashioned the long sigh of humanity; before them he knelt in genuine humility. In his polemical writing he could be as egomaniacal and offensive as anyone, and even worse in his private behavior if we are to believe those who knew and loved him best; but to the real achievements of human genius he paid nothing but respect. And shall we blame him if his respect was surer and more readily accorded the farther back he looked? Time in its passage clears away our doubts, and Galileo seems a firmer friend than, for instance, Darwin (as Darwin in turn seems a firmer friend than the authors of *The Double Helix*).

Yet the paradox persists. Goodman's esteem for the tradition is a conspicuous part of his poetic attitude, both in explicit statements and in the intimations of his style; at the same time he was distinctly an experimental writer – perhaps more in his prose fiction than in his poetry – and probably the last of the important modernists in American literature of the present century. He stood at the end of the long tradition, but he cut out his immediate predecessors; he insisted on standing alone. The generation of Pound and Eliot did not much appeal to him, the generation of Auden and Spender even less. Whereas with all of his own prominent contemporaries – Jarrell, Schwartz, Shapiro, Lowell, Bishop, Rukeyser, Roethke, and so on – I can perceive immediate derivations from their forerunners, with Goodman I cannot. In a few other cases I see experiment and individuality – William Everson, James Laughlin, Kenneth Patchen, Charles Olson – but even with these I can trace immediate influences more easily than I can with Goodman, and besides, they do not – for whatever reason, narrowness of view, smallness of output, confusion of cultural locus, quirkiness of temperament – stand in Goodman's rank.

Down, my dears, my students – I said it and I mean it. Paul Goodman was a better artist and arguer than Charles Olson, far better, and hence, if you knew it, is more valuable to you in your present plight, you with your workshop verses! (Yet Olson at his best had the sweeter, more generous temper, and for this reason has exerted the greater influence.)

The thing is that Goodman reached backward to go forward. He was a heretic, outcast in his era, like all his heroes of old. Better than anyone else he understood the poet's need to exist consciously in the continuum. Granted, Eliot and Pound in their own ways had said the same thing and to a certain extent had shared similar tastes; but their views of contemporary literary society were élitist and their politics disreputable. (Not that Goodman was free from élitism, the élitism of one, which he called – and so do I – independence.) Nor was Goodman a mannerist, not in the slightest degree, which is what one cannot say of Pound or Eliot or many other poets in the earlier part of the century. Goodman's archaism of diction and syntax came naturally, came from the whole sound of the great writing of the whole past, from folk tales and legend, from hymns, from everywhere; and it was combined inextricably with the jargon and street talk of his own time. Goodman in fact levied upon every linguistic force at his command, shamelessly raiding both the elegances of gentility and the argot of hipsters. He made it all his own.

> *This lust that blooms like red the rose*
> *is none of mine but as a song*
> *is given to its author knows*
> *not the next verse yet sings along.*

This is genius, not typographical confusion. Stein, Proust, Joyce, and Faulkner made languages out of cultivated complexity, hard to unravel. Goodman is as clear as glass (or the peals of English bells, and indeed his songs remind me of the little changes rung by children there). But you will not find any grammarian after 1700 – and before that who cared for grammar? – to parse Goodman's sentence logically. To my mind, to my ear – I having read this stanza many, many times – these four lines are magical, balancing forward and backward on the fulcrum of "author," that many-meaning, many-feeling word. (And only two polysyllables, that and the final "along," in the whole quatrain.) This strange syntax is not, I insist, a mannerism. It is the spontaneous speech of a man as much immersed in *The Anatomy of Melancholy* as in *The Neurotic Personality of Our Time,* a man to whom Cardan, Emerson, and Whitehead were all contemporaries.

How much would I have to quote to convince the reluctant reader that this is *typical,* that Goodman does it again and again (though naturally he became more skillful as he went on)? Too much. I refer the reluctant reader to Goodman's books. But I will quote once more, this time an entire poem.

> *I lustily bestrode my love*
> *until I saw the dark and poured my seed*
> *and then I lay in sweetness like one dead*
> *whom angels sing around him and above.*
>
> *I lay with all my strength embraced*
> *then swiftly to a quiet grave withdrew*
> *like a grotto with the sea in view*
> *surging and pounding, till the spell was past.*

> *Since then, my hours are empty of*
> *everything; beauty touches me*
> *but is like pain to hear or see;*
> *absent among the tribes of men I move.*

I cannot imagine, after this, that I need say more about diction and syntax. The fourth line is a wonder. A few additional points may be helpful, however. First, I take this poem from the same place in the book where I found several other quotations used already, where the book fell open randomly on my table. Secondly, how rarely do poets have the courage to take up what seem utterly worn out metaphors – orgasm as death – and try to give them something new. Thirdly, the stanza suggests, but only suggests, the English lyric of the seventeenth century, something by Herrick (for Goodman too is a son of Ben, among other things); or perhaps it suggests Tennyson's wonderful "In Memoriam"; yet notice how the meter meanders between tetrameter and pentamenter and how the accents fall not quite in order. Many have tried it and some have succeeded – Louise Bogan, Theodore Roethke, J.V. Cunningham, Stanley Kunitz, Richard Wilbur, and others – but none quite as well as Goodman. He is, if only by a shade, the most himself within the tradition. Finally, notice the perfection of cohesiveness among the poetic elements, how archaism ("bestrode") and inversion ("swiftly to a quiet grave withdrew") and backward-harkening syntax ("whom angels sing around him and above") all combine without the least sense of rhetoric, overwriting, or strain. It is the most natural poem in the world. And I think the reason for this is precisely Goodman's humility, which so many doubt; his capacity to write simply with little words, yet always in deference – to time, to poets, to the poem, and to the reader – never in condescension. At least never in his best work.

It is an astonishing poem. It has no "right" to succeed. Bestrode, my love, seed, angels, grotto, spell, beauty, tribes of men – no, this is a wierd, romantic/biblical vocabulary, of attitudes as well as words. The truly remarkable thing is that this vocabulary really is Goodman's, is not just literary. Yet one reads the poem, at first, with little tics of embarrassment along the way, embarrassment for the poet and his naive words; and then, such is the force of the poem that when one re-reads it, as one inevitably does, the tics are gone. Something powerful

is at work here, some strange alienation in the poem from the very be-
ginning, deeply underlying the words, so that the sexuality of it dis-
perses quickly and one is drawn down into the deeper matrix – of
what, one hardly knows. The whole poem is about utter aloneness, but
aloneness drained of its suffering. (Compare the *basic* mood with
Frost's "Stopping by Woods.") Esthetically what happens in Good-
man's poem is so complex that even in this apparently boundless essay
I cannot try to analyze it. Why does the poem work? What is behind
the poet's humility? Goodman not only respected experience, the
what-happens of life, he was often enough overwhelmed by it, like a
child exposed to too many things, too much to handle. He wanted to
freeze it, hold it *out there,* control it; but he couldn't – he was too hun-
gry for it. His earnest defenses continually broke down, and the world
crashed through. Such pathos! On the other hand Goodman would
have defined an academic as one whose defenses are, alas, entirely suc-
cessful. The question for him – and not only for him – was: how much
experience can I stand?

But I pause, I haul myself down. As always when writing about poetry
I become diffident and doubt myself. Do other people hear what I
hear? And if not how can I explain? The first line of the third stanza in
the above poem, for instance – does Goodman get away with that con-
trived enjambment for the sake of the rhyme? Can one read it with any
accent on "of" and still read in justified, justifiable English? I know I
could never do it aloud; my voice will not hesitate on that syllable with
the precisely needed degree of indeterminacy, though people tell me I
am a good reader. In my head I can do it. But I am not willing for this
reason to admit that the weak final accent is a flaw. It is a contrivance,
and not *all* contrivances are artificial. If Donne can get away with:

> *Love's not so pure, and abstract, as they use*
> *To say, which have no mistress but their muse....*

(and he does), then Goodman can bring off his irregular line as well.
And if my ear is more attuned to convention, and my mind more ready
to accept it, than is the case with many other readers nowadays, then I
can only agree, though ruefully and wishing otherwise, that this is so.
Contrivance works when it is conventional; and convention works

when it is (1) not presently so widespread that it is meaningless, (2) not followed slavishly but with daring and independence, and (3) not of the voice alone but of the mind and spirit. In short, the relationship between the artist and his convention must be inventive and must subsist in a nice proportion of humility and self-assurance. Contrary to popular belief, convention in itself is neither alive nor dead, these being objective and verifiable conditions. It is an attitude, a feeling, almost a fantasy. Only its effects are demonstrable, never the thing itself.

Goodman had, like most full-time, long-time poets, many voices and modes, and he was not shy in using them. I have already spoken of his hokku. Then there are his sonnets, the ballades and ballads, the blank verse, free-form poems, songs, especially the quatrains composed of two loosely rhymed couplets with the second indented below the first, to which he turned more and more for his prayers and elegies as he grew older. What were his attitudes toward these different forms? It is enough to say here that he did feel differently about them and turned now to one and now another, half instinctually, as his moods changed and different topics occupied his mind. And it is notable that in organizing his collected poems he lumped certain ones together by genre, the sonnets, ballades, etc., showing that he had a literary feeling for them, even though the stronger linkages throughout the whole collection fall clearly within thematic, not generic, configurations. The further question is, did he have a single voice observable throughout? And the answer is yes, definitely, although only the most painstaking statistical analysis could discover the particular verbal usages that embody it. They are there, I am certain of it. But beyond the few that I think I recognize in my casual reading and that I therefore do not want to put on display, I can only point again to his remarkable control of syntax as the one talent that permitted him to move readily among and within the various forms; for all but a few of his poems were occasional and extemporaneous. (Which does *not* mean that he did not work hard and with the utmost seriousness.) Syntax, meaning the art of the putting together of sentences, as opposed to grammar, meaning the science of taking them apart: this is the quintessence. And perhaps his sonnets show it as well as anything.

For those who cannot perceive in the poems themselves Goodman's affection and respect for the sonnet as a special, long-standing convention that he could take to himself, among many other conventions, in his state of being as a poetic master – and I am not speaking invidiously, because I know many people today who through no fault of their own have tin ears when it comes to the great traditions – for such readers Goodman's analysis of Milton's sonnet on his blindness, done in the most caring manner of *explication du texte* and contained in *The Structure of Literature,* will be helpful, as, for that matter, will all the rest of that book.

Goodman did not have a tin ear – anything but. Of the sixty sonnets included in the *Collected Poems,* only two or three seem to me unreadable. I have checked five as sufficient to stand in the first rank, meaning that for me they are alongside the sonnet by Milton and the one by Shakespeare that begins "Let me not to the marriage of true minds" and the one made by Wordsworth when he was standing on the bridge in Westminster. Another way to say it: Goodman wrote the best American sonnets after Longfellow, although I like very well a few others by Lizette Woodworth Reese, E. E. Cummings, Edna Millay, Yvor Winters, and Allen Tate. This is astonishing, almost miraculous (maybe it was). Goodman wrote in a time when even the most determined traditionalists did not care much for fixed forms; the sonnet, in spite of its provenance at the very center of Renaissance poetry, was still thirty-odd years ago too closely associated with *fin-de-siècle* hearts and flowers. Pound wrote many but published none. Even Yeats, who one might have thought would have taken to the sonnet eagerly, did not, but preferred instead the stanzaic forms of his own invention. And taking Goodman's poetic generation as a whole (1935–1970), its most popular model by far was precisely in Yeats's later work. To all this Goodman paid no mind, going his own way in his "only world."

The first sonnet by Goodman that I ever read was "In Lydia," which I believe was submitted in a group of poems to *Poetry* when I was a member of the staff there, circa 1947–50.

> *I am touring high on the Meander River*
> *the scenery never varying. The land*
> *is Lydia, the wheat rich, the climate bland,*
> *and very sweet the modus of the zither.*
> *Our queen is Omphale, for never never*
> *cut was the curving cord in which we end*

– when shall we arrive? I round a bend,
the view is changed, and forward is another.

That's not a woman in the palace yard
spinning! unwillingly – breathing hard –

Hercules! here, for pity's sake
the thread is long enough, it leaves the wheel
and tangles, and the world is areel.
My hands have hold upon it; shall I break?

I don't know whether the wording here, taken from the *Collected Poems,* follows the original version (I suspect the thirteenth line may have been weakened in Goodman's final revision), but I do know definitely (because it struck me forcibly when I first read it and influenced the invention of a form I myself have used often, which I call the paragraph) that I have printed the poem in its original shape, that is, with the couplet displaced from the end and set apart by space-breaks in the middle. I had never seen this before. For reasons I cannot fathom, Goodman chose to run the couplet into the last four lines when he revised his poems for the collected edition, thus de-emphasizing his rearrangement of the usual form and giving the sonnet a conventional-looking sestet. It is a fine sonnet in any case, though I wish Goodman (in violation of his usual practice) had written "and the world's areel," thus making the thirteenth line a clear metrical equivalent to the short eleventh line, the whole final quatrain easier and stronger.

God damn and blast and to a fist of dust
reduce me the contemptible I am
if I again hinder for guilt or shame
the blooming of my tenderness to lust
like a red rose; I have my cock traduced
to which I should be loyal. None to blame
but me myself that I consort with them
who dread to rouse me onward and distrust
what has a future.
                    Let me bawl hot tears
for thee my lonely and dishonored sex

> *in this fool world where now for forty years*
> *thou beg'st and beg'st and again thou beg'st*
> *because this is the only world there is,*
> *my rose in rags among these human wrecks.*

Is it half jocular? Of course, all poems about sex are; this is the human sensibility, "primitive" or "refined." But notice the strong movement of the sentences through the octet, the power yet naturalness of the rhymes, and then in the sestet Goodman's giveaway, "the only world": whenever he says that he is serious, let no one misunderstand him. This is a sonnet so packed with tonal, metrical, dictional, and thematic intricacies that I doubt a thorough explication could be made in less than many pages; I mean this – no exaggeration. Yet any reasonably experienced reader will be able to do it just in the reading. The poem is crystalline.

At the same time it's necessary to point out, not only in prudence but in the humility I more and more feel before my task, that Goodman's sonnets do not appeal to everyone, and that this sonnet in particular has been attacked by an acute critic who was also one of Goodman's most sympathetic readers, my friend George Dennison. The poem – I paraphrase George – is dishonest and spiritually ugly. Only an intellectual, full of ideas as well as hurt and having a long history of attempts to heal the splits between mind and body, passion and thought, etc., could be so arrogantly *loyal* to his cock. "Rouse me onward," ha! – Goodman was compulsive and fetishistic, self-aroused and continually so. How can diction, syntax, etc., be of any force when the poem itself (and the evidence is in the poem) displays such a disgusting mess of illness, attitudinizing, self-protective lying, etc.? I can only answer that to my mind the literary quality of the poem does in fact overcome these ugly revelations, which are revealed in plenty of other poems too. Goodman was a man of letters indeed. He revered prosody. The arrogance and dishonesty patent in the poem, especially in the octet, are retrieved for me by the prosodic power of the whole poem and by the authentic universalization of feeling in the sestet. A great many of us can "bawl hot tears" for our "lonely and dishonored sex." But see how crazy and silly the words sound when quoted outside the poem? They are. Yet the whole verbal and structural and imagistic complex of the sonnet holds its substance together and elevates

it, I feel, to the plane upon which personal dishonesty and braggado-
cio become realized esthetic paradigms. It was a terribly risky sonnet
to write. But Goodman took the risks. Isn't this what being a poet
means?

> *Grief how into useless age away*
> *ebbed youth and I was unhappy all those years*
> *I also do not feel, for now new fears*
> *possess me and I steel myself today*
> *today's pain to endure, so I can die*
> *without a reckoning and weep no tears*
> *for promises deceived. Maybe my peers*
> *or my disciples will this tribute pay.*
>
> *Oh, when He bound my arms behind my back*
> *and threw me in the sea, I heard Him call*
> *"Swim! swim!" and so I have swum to this hour*
> *breathless in the cold water rough and black*
> *where many have already drowned and all*
> *shall drown in the swells that sink and tower.*

Is it necessary to point out the poetic self-faith expressed in the metri-
cal irregularity of the two opening lines? Yes, they are crabbed, incred-
ibly so, arrogantly and intentionally so. (It would have been child's
play to put those two lines in "right" order.) To me the force of feeling
in them is the force that justifies and demands them, and they are beau-
tifully expressive.

> *One thing, thank God, I learned, the grisly face*
> *of Hope to abhor, her eyes bloodshot with dreams,*
> *her hair unkempt with fury. Lying streams*
> *out of her mouth and men drink it. Alas,*
> *if you look ever in a looking-glass*
> *and see an ugly Hope in hungry flames*
> *devouring you, so the unreal seems*
> *real and the impossible to come to pass*
> *possible, see, when you look again*
> *Disappointment! But this face of pain*

is mine, which I and all my family have,
my mother wears it in her southern grave,
my sister grown old woman has it, and
my brother building buildings rich and grand.

The couplet at the end makes us think of the great tradition, and no one has better extended the sonnet's essentially Shakespearean movement, pushing the runovers and enjambments *just enough further.* Goodman's verbal instinct is here at its best. See "mother/southern" in line twelve: did it fall accidentally that way? or did Goodman think it up? In either case the force of years of poetic thought lies behind it. Note also the movement of imagery in this fluent poem, from horror and Dantean grotesquerie to the more human "face of pain" and ending in the last line – the reference is to his brother Percival, the architect, with whom he wrote *Communitas,* his most important early statement of social criticism and also, incidentally, a hopeful book – with "buildings rich and grand." Who could have expected such a swift, complex modulation of images and feelings?

Students have said to me that they dislike Goodman's inverted syntax and archaism because such writing seems to them awkward. They wonder why Goodman let himself be pushed around by form. But there is no question of being pushed around. Goodman was a *writer,* a *versewriter,* among other things, which entails a skill that young readers seem ill-equipped to recognize, even now when so many of them are turning back to conventional fixed forms. (I've read hundreds and hundreds of sonnets recently, from students, from people who submit to magazines, from entrants in contests, from quite well known poets, but have not seen one with any hint of the tensile lyricism, however many-tempered it has been, that the sonnet has required from good poets since the thirteenth century.) Goodman wrote his sonnet this way because he wanted to, because this was the effect consonant with his own temperament and the poem's feeling. He could just as easily have written:

Thank God I learned one thing, to abhor Hope's
grisly face, her eyes bloodshot with dreams,
her hair unkempt with fury. Lying streams
from her mouth and men drink it. If you perhaps

should look in a mirror and see Hope's hungry shapes
of flame reaching to devour you, your own schemes
raging there..., etc.

This would have accorded well enough with his usual rhyming and metrical practice. Indeed something like this might have been a first draft of the poem. But Goodman *chose* the inversions, the archaic "Alas," the whole inner strategy, and his choice was intentional, if not at the moment of writing, then certainly in the long course of self-training that led up to it. In fact I am struck now by the possibility that some of Goodman's contemporaries may have had more influence on him than I suggested earlier; but a negative influence, not a positive one. Delmore Schwartz and John Berryman, for instance, were both writing sonnets at about the time Goodman was beginning his. He may have seen very early that he needed something different from their styles, plainer than Schwartz's Marlovian grandness, simpler and easier than Berryman's extreme contortedness. This would have been in keeping with his desire to be separate.

This sonnet is called "The Americans Resume Bomb-Testing, April 1962."

My countrymen have now become too base,
I give them up. I cannot speak with men
not my equals, I was an American.
Where now to drag my days out and erase
this awful memory of the United States?
how can I work? I hired out my pen
to make my country practical, but I can
no longer serve these people, they are worthless.

"Resign! resign!" the word rings in my soul
– is it for me? or shall I make a sign
and picket the White House blindly in the rain,
or hold it up on Madison Avenue
a silent vigil, or trudge to and fro
gloomily in front of the public school?

Clearly this is *in extempore*. Goodman's spontaneous anger is too great, forcing him into egomania and dishonesty, permitting him to make the easy identification of "my countrymen" with the State, which elsewhere he would not have done. The rhymes are too easy; only a trifle, but noticeably. And why when force, measure, and colloquial value demand it did he not insert "out" after "gloomily" in the final line, to give it more weight in the pentameter? Nevertheless I include it among my five because it shows so trenchantly how the surplusage, so to speak, of feeling can drive through the poetic form in Goodman's flexible syntax and carry all before it. This it does *as* a sonnet: the movement from octet to sestet exactly what the original lyric impulse (back to Pier delle Vigne in the *trecento* as Arthur Symons said) pre-scribes; *pre-scribes,* the word is worth considering.

Finally –

> *Foster excellence. If I do not*
> *who will do it? The vulgarity*
> *of this country makes my spirit faint, what we*
> *have misdone to our history and what*
> *to the landscape. The tasteless food we eat,*
> *the music, how we waste day after day*
> *child, woman, and man have stunned me to dismay*
> *like an ox bludgeoned, swaying on his feet.*
>
> *John, rescue me by becoming. I have well*
> *deserved of the Republic, though it has*
> *rewarded me with long oblivion.*
> *Make you me proud and famous as the one*
> *who thought that we could be what Florence was*
> *when angry men made rough rocks beautiful.*

Notice how Goodman has no metrical force-of-habit, but starts off this sonnet in a totally different, short and punchy syntax. Also how the hackneyed images follow one another in perfect originality because the language will not let them slump back on their cushions of hebetude. Lastly how Goodman, like the rest of us, was grandiose and greedy in his demands on his personal friend, in this case John. Why should

John do what the "Republic" will not, what the poet cannot? Because, goddamn it, *somebody* must! Who better than a lover to assuage the injury dealt by unjust Time and the State. Catullus, Villon, Swift, Leadbelly, etc.

In part I choose to emphasize Goodman's use of the sonnet because it seems to fall more or less midway between his use of the larger fixed forms, especially the ballades, and his own invented forms, both the deliberate and the impromptu. But no consideration of his writing can be let go without at least a glance at the quatrains he came to appreciate more and more as the poetic shape most amenable to his needs. Here is a bit of a poem, no more than a tag stuck on at the end of a sonnet about a glimpse of a handsome, inaccessible young man.

> *Some happy folk their faith*
> *and some their calling doth*
> *justify, but Lord,*
> *I am justified*
>
> *by the beauty of*
> *the world and my love*
> *of Your animals, though I*
> *may not be happy thereby.*

This is characteristic; the involved, pivoted sentences, the rhymes ranging from near to remote, the archaism both reinforced and contradicted by the irregularity of rhythm, and then the grand affirmation given and at once partly withdrawn. It occurs to me too that many, a great many, of Goodman's poems end in their beginnings, as here with the repetition of "happy." It is the lyric circle around whose perimeter the contraries align themselves.

I choose two more, untitled:

> *I ask the Lord, "Who are You?"*
> *though I know His name is "Spoken to."*
> *Hoping but I am not sure*
> *His name might be "I am who answer."*

With certain faith let me continue
my dialogue with Spoken-To.
  Hope has always been my curse,
  it never yet came to pass.

The crazy man that you meet
talking to himself in the street
  is I, please gently lead him home.
Creator Spirit come.

Again a small poem, probably impromptu or near it. Technically it is very fine, revealing Goodman's faculty for reducing brilliance to what seems offhand, so many fortuities that we know they cannot be fortuitous. I will point only to the second stanza, how there "certain" and "curse" are linked internally, as are "spoken" and "hope," "always" and "pass," so that the stanza is aurally compressed and unified, and then how the rhyme in the first couplet, "continue" and "Spoken-To," an unaccented sound rhymed with an accented one that nevertheless is a very small word, a preposition, how this assembles behind the meaning a huge power of prosodic reinforcement. But perhaps we have had enough discussion of technique. "Spoken-To" is a term used by some orthodox Jews as a euphemism for the divine name, which is taboo, and so Goodman's poem is immediately rooted not only in his own people's religion, a backward reach emphasized by further biblical-sounding language ("come to pass," "lead him home," etc.), but also in the structure of spiritual taboo in all human consciousness, as amplified sophisticatedly in our awareness of cultural anthropology and Jungian psychiatry. It is a poem about fear and craziness and unnamability, pathos as the gross matter of the human condition, profoundly Hebrew and also profoundly Greek; a poem which ends on our one solace as the poet utters his own euphemism, "Creator Spirit." This is no cheap-shot poetic aggrandizement; quite the contrary. The humility of utterance is plain, it is sincere. (Goodman did talk to himself on the street.) Yet the poem is far from any orthodoxy, and it does almost heretically link the human person's esthetic mentality with the sense of religion. It makes no claim for the poet as prophet, but every claim for the poet inhabiting all souls. It reaches back, far back, through the shadows of anonymity which time gathers around the early members of "the grand community," back to the earliest, the greatest Anonymity. I cannot help thinking of the painting that shows God touching Adam's finger. In this poem Adam (one of Goodman's favorite names) touches back. It is a poem as swift as lightning, a spark leaping across an infinite gap, and it is as succinct, lucid, and profound a statement of modern man's religious nature as Goodman or any other poet has written.

Now another in the same stanza, opening with the line that was the earlier poem's close, this one written a couple of months after the death of the poet's son Mathew.

> *Creator Spirit come*
> *by whom*
>   *I'll say what is real*
>   *and so away I'll steal.*
>
> *When my only son*
> *fell down and died on Percy mountain*
>   *I began*
>   *to practice magic like a pagan.*
>
> *Around the open grave we ate*
> *the blueberries that he brought*
>   *from the cloud, and then we*
>   *buried his bag with his body.*
>
> *Around the open grave*
> *I laid the hawkweed that I love*
>   *which withered fast*
>   *where the mowers passed.*
>
> *I brought also a tiny yellow*
> *flower whose name I do not know*
>   *to share my ignorance*
>   *with my son. (But since*
>
> *then I find in the book*

it is a kind of shamrock
    Oxalis corniculata,
    Matty, sorrel of the lady.)

Blue-eyed grass with its gold hexagon
    beautiful as the gold and blue
    double in Albireo
that we used to gaze on

when Matty was alive
I laid on Matty's grave
    where two robins were
    hopping here and there;

and gold and bluer than that blue
or the double in Albireo
    bittersweet nightshade
    the deadly alkaloid
        I brought for no other reason
        than because it was poison.

Mostly, though, I brought some weed
beautiful but disesteemed,
    plantain or milkweed,
    because we die by the wayside.

(And if spring comes again
I will bring a dandelion,
    because he was a common weed
    and also he was splendid.)

But when I laid my own forehead
on the withering sod
    to go the journey deep,
    I could not fall asleep.

I cannot dream, I cannot quit
the one scene in the twilight

that is no longer new yet does
not pass into what was.

Last night the Pastoral Symphony
of Handel in the key of C
*   I played on our piano*
*   out of tune shrill and slow*

because the shepherds were at night
in the field in the starlight
*   when music loud and clear*
*   sang from nowhere.*

Will magic and the weeks placate
the soul that in tumbling fright
*   fled on August eighth?*
*   The first flock is flying south*

and a black-eyed susan
is livid in the autumn rain
*   dripping without haste or strain*
*   on the oblong larger than a man.*

Creator spirit come
by whom
*   I say that which is real*
*   and softly away I'll steal.*

It was not so long after this that Goodman did steal away, joining
Mathew, and he did it softly enough too, like the rest of us.

From this longer poem I have learned how not to care overmuch for
the design I had chosen from artifice to suit my poem; the seventh
stanza is shaped differently to accommodate the change of rhyming, yet
the next-to-last stanza, which has the same rhyme in abba, is shaped
like the rest. In the ninth stanza he thought of an extra couplet – before
or afterward? I don't know. He could just as well have used the third
couplet as the first of a new stanza. He didn't.

Another point. Goodman was his own closest reader. He remembered when he had found a scrap of language that suited him and compressed his meaning. He repeated it, using it as often as he liked, deepening its meaning in the variety of contexts. In this poem "we die by the wayside," just as in the poem about Chuang-tzu.

And for a while I thought, foolishly, that I could leave this poem about the death of Mathew Goodman with no more than my few technical observations. I felt so fine a poem, so clearly embodying the elements of Goodman's practice, needed no further commentary. I was attempting – but not consciously – to disguise or dispel my own and the reader's sense of self-revealment after reading this almost unbearably moving poem. Why are we overcome with shyness just as we find what we go to art to seek, this ultimate human actuality? I don't know, but I believe this phenomenon underlies the predicament of the arts in our civilization today, our willful concentration on mediocrity.

The poem is as fine an elegy as any I know. Do I mean it is as good as the dirge in *Cymbeline* that I have had tacked to my cowshed wall for twenty years? Yes. How do I know it is as good? Knowledge has nothing to do with it; both poems are pinchbeck to the *cognoscenti*. I feel the goodness, and I speak to those who feel it with me, or who may come to feel it. Shall I define the human heart in an essay?

At the beginning and again at the ending, the poem advocates magic, invokes our primal intellection. It is another reaching back; it is paleolithic. Indeed the opening stanza and the closing one are the same, which gives the poem Goodman's characteristic circularity, but in this case gives it even more than that: the almost strict repetition is like the magician's clap at the beginning and end of his trick, for the poem occurs outside of time, outside of experience, as if in the science-fiction writer's favorite time warp. It is a true act of ecstasy (*ex stasis*). So simple the device, known well to children; so complex the psychic action. Then while we are "away," we live only ritualistically, the bringing of flowers again and again, their parts and properties named (with perfect correctness) in the magic of evoking the reality we can say but never understand, the music, the seasons. And the references all appear to us like waves from the same source, the mowers, the lady, the star, the poison, the music "from nowhere": all are the same, the waves falling on our shore of consciousness from "nowhere," from far out, from grief as the mythologos, the word that cannot be said. It is a poem of transcendent negation.

Milton praised Lycidas, Shelley Adonais, Goodman says of his "only son," Mathew, no more than that he was a "weed" and "splendid" and that he "fell down and died," having brought blueberries "from the cloud": no more. Yet to my mind Goodman's elegiac intensity is greater, and on my ear his words fall, without loudness, without formal declamation, still with more sweetness and resonance. I call it "transcendent negation" because I cannot define it except by saying what it is not, and even then only very imperfectly. An elegy without praise? It seems odd, yet now that I stop to think I see that this is the poem of our time, written again and again, by Ransom, Roethke, by many others, because our "hero" is always this young person who is "real." And "the oblong larger than a man" is real. But the reality is more than we can take, except in the time-out-of-time, the poem, the myth. This movement, as of mercury in a balancing tube repelled by negative magnets at either end, myth and reality falling toward and away from each other, is the magic of minds reverting through our kind's ten thousand years or our own ten thousand days of reason, to unending agony and fatigue again.

Goodman wrote:

> *I cannot dream, I cannot quit*
> *the one scene in the twilight*
> *   that is no longer new yet does*
> *   not pass into what was.*

I feel in this the ache of implacability as in few other pieces of literature. I know it is the simplicity of it, the negative refusal to say more, that makes it, technically speaking, so effective. But I cannot hope to understand the means of it much further. So much does not pass into what was. Stonehenge. Ozymandias.

"The soul that in tumbling fright / fled on August eighth" – was it Matty's? Yes. Was it Paul's too? Yes. Was it the Creator Spirit, was it Death? Yes. Will it be placated? No. Do affirmation and negation mean the same thing? No. Yes.

Now approaching, if it hasn't long been passed, the permissible limit of an essay, I still have written almost nothing about Goodman's prose fiction. Obviously, anything near an adequate discussion must wait for another occasion, and probably I won't do it, but will leave it to others better fitted than I am. My own feeling – and I hope it does not come merely from my own greater interest in poetry – is that Goodman's mind and temperament were not as well suited to prose narrative as they were to poetry. Here I must make a clear distinction between Goodman's fictional prose and his philosophical, critical, and polemical prose. The latter is mostly superb. And the modes of poetry, though most people do not recognize this, are closer to argument than are the modes of prose narrative. To say it another way, his poems are more like his essays than either are like his novels and stories. This is hair-splitting, I admit. A dozen of his short stories are among the best by any American writer of this century. And his big novel, *The Empire City,* though it probably fails some of the ultimate tests, the standards of structure and tightness demanded by the creative writing workshop, is so spirited and intelligent that I would rather be amused and stimulated by it than sedated by any number of our pretentious current metafictions. Sometimes it is such joy to throw the "ultimate tests" out the window!

Goodman had great hopes once for *The Empire City.* The first section, entitled "The Grand Piano," enjoyed a fair success when it was published separately in 1942. According to Taylor Stoehr (see his introduction to *Don Juan),* one of Goodman's literary friends wrote to him: "Paul, I congratulate you on your immortality." Statements like this were not made lightly in New York in 1942, when literature was still a serious and dangerous business. But Goodman's reputation fell off sharply after that. The second section, "State of Nature," was ignored. When the third section of the novel was completed, Goodman could find no publisher for it, though he tried and tried, as always, even in his darkest despondency. At last he published "Dead of Spring" himself, and sold the copies to friends through the mail, as I recall for $2 each; and strange books they were, printed on cheap stiff paper held in spiral plastic bindings, apparently produced in some job-shop that normally specialized in calendars and appointment books. Now they are collector's items. It seemed at the time a pitiable effort. How many copies could he have sold? A couple of hundred if he was lucky. But now, looking back, we see the courage of his persistence, a courage he needed all his life, for although the novel was eventually published in one volume – including the previously unpublished fourth section,

"The Holy Terror" – by a commercial publisher and then later in a paperback edition, and although I salute Bobbs-Merrill and Random House for their editorial perspicacity, *The Empire City* still did not receive the attention it deserves from reviewers or readers, and has not till this day.

Is it a novel? I don't know and don't much care; call it whatever you like, the internal monologue of the man in the moon. In historical terms it can with perfect justice be called an allegory, a picaresque tale, a philosophical novel, a comedy of humors, a panoramic adventure, and possibly a tractatus. For myself, certain no one will ever define its essences in a simple statement, I am content to say that *The Empire City* is a phantasmagoria of ideas whose hero is Horatio Alger, whose secondary personages are a very mixed group of imagined and real people, whose structure is random, and whose purpose is to investigate through episodes of comic pathos the *truth* of human life at the middle of the twentieth century in the greatest city on earth. Its antecedents are legion, but mostly from para-literature: *commedia dell'arte*, Rabelais, *The Canterbury Tales*, Hogarth, Artemus Ward and Mark Twain, Krazy Kat, Chaplin and Cocteau – the list could go on and on, and why do I call it "para-literature"? That is an academic way of putting it. What I mean to say is that almost anything you can take from outside the "main current of literary evolution," anything from Petronius to Ring Lardner, will find its echo in *The Empire City*.

As for the short stories, they are various yet mostly also of adventuresome intents and methods. They are not well wrought in the Mansfieldean manner, nor in the Hemingwayan either, but rather they effloresce from Goodman's exuberance with only his own cogent imagination to supply their limits. I cannot describe them, nor attempt to say in a paragraph how they were made. I think all of them are a delight to the mind, some a delight to the heart, and a few are, after the poems, extremely important. I do not think any reader can go into a bookstore and take up a copy of *Adam and His Works,* if he is lucky enough to find it, or one of the three new volumes of collected stories edited by Taylor Stoehr, if he is lucky enough to find them – I do not think he can pick it up and read one story, any story – say, "The Complaint of Richard Savage," but none will take more than a few minutes to read – and then walk out without buying – or stealing – the book. Like almost all true writing, the stories are immediately gratifying.

But Goodman was no perfectionist, never that. Rather he wrote at a dizzy pace, I think, his sentences of prose (more than his sentences of poetry) scarcely able to keep up with his flying thoughts, and he cared little about revision, so that sometimes he wrote stories which had no real purpose, no sufficient prior envisioning, such as the posthumously published novel *Don Juan,* which bears some connection to the early parts of *The Empire City* but becomes tedious after the first fifty or sixty pages because the theme is too tendentious for the narrative, being lyrical rather than active, to sustain.

Failure, especially youthful failure, is predicated if not by the limits of the human mind then by the nature of post-romantic ego and of post-impressionist language, both of them riddled with the sense of their own inadequacy. Yet the grand company continues in spite of all.

A number of times in recent years I have complained about the mess of Goodman's *Collected Poems* and asked for a selected edition that would contain the best versions of the poems, not simply the last versions. I made an extended case for this in the present essay as it was originally published in 1982. Now, I'm glad to say, we have good news. Geoffrey Gardner, a writer, critic, and editor, a friend of Goodman and his family, a man completely qualified to do the job, has put together such a selected edition, an ample selection which includes all Goodman's well-known poems in their best versions, a number of previously unpublished poems found among the poet's papers after his death, notes, variant readings, etc. It is a fine piece of work and desperately needed. It will be published, if all goes well, in 1991.

I still wish, however, to discuss the case of Goodman's best-known poem, "The Lordly Hudson," because it is so instructive. Here it is, as it was printed in 1962, the title work in Goodman's best-known book of poetry.

> *"Driver, what stream is it?" I asked, well knowing*
> *it was our lordly Hudson hardly flowing,*
> *"It is our lordly Hudson hardly flowing,"*
> *he said, "under the green-grown cliffs."*
>
> *Be still, heart! no one needs your passionate*
> *suffrage to select this glory,*

this is the lordly Hudson hardly flowing
under the green-grown cliffs.

"Driver! has this a peer in Europe or the East?"
"No, no!" he said. Home! home!
be quiet, heart! this is our lordly Hudson
and has no peer in Europe or the East,

this is our lordly Hudson hardly flowing
under the green-grown cliffs
and has no peer in Europe or the East.
Be quiet, heart! home! home!

We all know many ardent wordings for a river, mountain, highway, glen: our only world, the earth *in loco parentis*. After the wrack of sex, this is the singer's most passionate human testimony. But I know no other that surpasses this in simple expressiveness. Such poems bear the authenticity of universal knowledge and feeling. They are beyond the bounds of judgment, beyond relativism, in the realm of equivalence and essential anonymity.

This is the text as it appeared in the *Collected Poems*, revised by Goodman a few weeks before his death:

"Driver, what stream is it?" I asked, well knowing
it was our lordly Hudson hardly flowing,
"It is our lordly Hudson hardly flowing,"
he said, "under the green-grown cliffs."

Be still, man! no one needs your passionate
suffrage to select this glory,
this is our lordly Hudson hardly flowing
under the green-grown cliffs.

"Driver! has this a peer in Europe or the East?"
"No no!" he said. Home! home!
be quiet, heart! this is our lordly Hudson
and has no peer in Europe or the East,

> *this is our lordly Hudson hardly flowing*
> *under the green-grown cliffs*
> *and has no peer in Europe or the East.*
> *Be patient, Paul! home! home!*

By such small stitches may passion be clothed in art or left shivering and naked. Three alterations: the change from "heart" to "man" in the first line of the second stanza; the deletion of the comma between "no" and "no" in the second line of the third stanza; the substitution of "Be patient, Paul" for "Be quiet, heart" in the final stanza.

One can reconstruct Goodman's probable motives in making these changes. "Heart" is a genteel and banal word; how much better to generalize and universalize by saying "man." Or, more likely, "man" was addressed to himself in the street idiom of the sixties and seventies. But in his haste Goodman did not see that "man" points directly and reductively back to "Driver" in the stanza before, and is thus both a spoiling of the poem's universality and a misplaced colloquialism in a poem whose simplicity is still very formal. Moreover the effect of the original poem was exactly *in* its repetitions: "heart," "heart," "lordly," "lordly," etc.

The excision of the comma between the "no's" was in keeping with Goodman's later typographical style, and is not of much moment – one doesn't wish to be finicky. Yet I must add that for me the comma was part of the poem's celebratory, ode-like, formal expressiveness, and I miss it.

The greatest damage is the final change. Yes, Paul wanted to get home; he was on a plane while he read and corrected the manuscript for his *Collected Poems*. He had been teaching in Hawaii. He had had a heart attack not long before. The exotic environment of the Islands suited him far less than the plain hayfields and hawkweed of New Hampshire. But "patient" is not the same as "quiet," again the wonderful repetition is lost, and "Paul" is a long, long way from "heart."

"The Lordly Hudson" is an early poem, probably from before 1940. I am told its occasion was Goodman's homecoming to New York after an unhappy stay in Chicago. He was strong, his poetic instinct was working beautifully, and he was in no haste. More than thirty years later when he revised the poem, he was coming home again. He was weak and in pain; he knew his death was not far off. He made the three

little changes on the spur of the moment, and a great poem was re-
duced to an ordinary one. It was a misfortune. But now we can go back
to the original version in the new *Selected Poems,* and the two versions
do give us a fine example of the place and mystery of craft in poetry, an
example every student should examine carefully.

I don't want to leave the *Collected Poems,* moreover, without saying
my admiration for the memoir by George Dennison that serves as the
book's introduction. A vigorous piece of writing that needs to be pre-
served.

To the two sequences of poems he wrote for Mathew, Goodman gave
the title "Sentences." Here is one of the poems:

> *"Great Tao is a ship adrift" – awakes*
> *at sunrise asking, where am I?*
> *and deviates forward slowly to nowhere.*
> *What does he know? to front afraid the gale*
> *and painfully climb the next oncoming wave.*
> *It is by an inevitable mistake*
> *that the ten thousand cheer and shake their flags*
> *lining the shore in the indifferent port.*

Nevertheless, and Goodman would have said so too, to be one of the
ten thousand is something.

A sentence is an always potential construction of language. Good-
man gave it his devotion for a lifetime. It is also "the opinion pro-
nounced by a person on some particular question" (*OED*). Finally it is
what the judge hands down. Those who fail to recognize behind
Goodman's "Sentences" the weight of all these meanings and the
weight of some of his favorite word-works from the past, *The Testa-
ment* of François Villon or *The Trial* by Franz Kafka, will perhaps miss
nothing essential. But those who do recognize these things will be en-
riched humanly by them, and will thereby become themselves in some
part members of Paul Goodman's Grand Community. For the tradi-
tion is what we as mankind travel on, the Tao, wherever we are going.

🖙 . . . .

Richard Hugo

A review of *Making Certain It Goes On: The Collected Poems of Richard Hugo*. 1984.

RICHARD HUGO IS DEAD. He died not long ago. Now this new book contains, practically speaking, all his poetry, meaning each of his previous books in full, plus twenty-odd pages of poems written after the last book issued during his lifetime. In such circumstances a reviewer is expected to make some sort of summary. Can it be done? Not well; not within the confines of an ordinary review. Nevertheless one tries to be useful.

First summation: *Making Certain It Goes On* is as tedious a book of poems as anyone could be asked to read, in spite of a few, very few, good and moving poems here and there.

Second summation: it puts me in mind of a time many years ago when I bought the complete poems of Robert Herrick, a poet I admire very much, granting the offensiveness of his cavalier affiliations. Before I had read half the book I was fed to the ears with Herrick. To this day I have not read the second half. For lovers of poetry an anthology is a blessing, even an inferior one.

Third summation: with truly great poets this is not the case; e.g., I can read, seriatim and with pleasure, all of Ben Jonson's lyric poems.

Beyond this I have only inferences, and the easiest way into them is a small segment of personal history. Several years ago I set out to write a book about the generation of American poets roughly ten years ahead of my own: Lowell, Bishop, Berryman, Olson, Schwartz, Rukeyser, etc. It was to be called *Poets of Responsibility*. A publisher offered me a contract and an advance, which, with more sense than I've shown sometimes, I turned down. I began with Paul Goodman; eventually I produced an essay that was published separately. Next I went to Theodore Roethke. Because I had, over more than twenty years, reviewed nearly all his books, always favorably and often enthusiastically, I felt sure I would find my task easy and enjoyable. For a year I studied Roethke: the poems, the essays, the published notebooks and letters, the works of biographers and critics. At the end I threw up my hands. More and more I was turned off by the man's overweening esthetic and

spiritual solipsism. Why? Roethke's anguish was genuine, many read-
ers shared it, and playing cat and mouse with God is after all a long-
sanctioned literary schtick. But where other poets had been content to
let God play the cat, for Roethke God was the mouse. And for me, an
atheist, this was intolerable, all the more as reinforced by his fierceness
toward Eliot, Yeats, and every other poet in the life-or-death competi-
tive struggle Roethke took writing to be – clearly, explicitly revealed in
his letters and journals. One effect was an imputed confidential inti-
macy between the cat-poet and cat-reader on spurious grounds.
Roethke was a superbly talented poet, perhaps better equipped than
any other of his age, but all his verbal enticements did not overcome
his hugely egotistical intention, the comfort of his separate soul. In
short he was not a responsible poet at all.

Because I could not write about Roethke with enthusiasm, I gave up
my book altogether, even while I acknowledged to myself the essen-
tially uncritical attitude implicit in my decision.

Hugo was born in Seattle, lived there a considerable time, and was,
I believe, a student in Roethke's writing class at the University of Wash-
ington. His early admiration for Roethke is unmistakable. Many people
– not including Hugo, whom I never met – have told me Roethke was a
good teacher. Indeed the notion of Roethke's success in the classroom
is mythological, used by thousands of teachers of creative writing to
encourage themselves in the wastefulness and boredom of their jobs. I
am not convinced, however. Roethke was a persuasive teacher – who
can doubt it? – but this does not mean he was good; being good re-
quires more receptivity to differences and more responsibility to indi-
vidual talents than most poets can muster. What Hugo got from
Roethke, at any rate, the heavy iambic pentameter of "Four for Sir John
Davies" and the attitude of poetic megalomania, he was ill-equipped to
use: he had neither the verbal talent for the one nor the illusionist meta-
physical imagination for the other. Hence what we see in the first hun-
dred or so pages of his book are poems loaded with awkward pentam-
eters – since for whatever reason, apparently a tin ear, Hugo was unable
to give his lines the variability and balance that Roethke was master of –
and a rapidly deepening decline into pessimism.

But the point is that it was a phony pessimism. Hugo had no god to
play the mouse for him, so he substituted what was left, the world and
all its creatures, including especially its nonpoetic, non-Hugovian

human creatures, with all their thoughts and feelings. A nest of vipers. There was nothing original in this, of course. But inevitably Hugo himself was drawn into the nest; he became a reputable and rewarded de Sade. (Masochism and sexism are conspicuous threads through all his work.) Nowhere is Hugo's pessimism sustained by any thoughtful attitude toward causes, such as Roethke – and de Sade – could offer. All is vague, a kind of inverted Darwinism, evolutionary despair.

In the poems of his middle years, which are probably his best, Hugo loosened his prosody, though you can still find plenty of heavy-footed iambs and buried pentameters. The pessimism becomes only grayer and grayer – his favorite color, as *abandoned* was his favorite word. The poems are cryptic, portentous, and above all confidential; they refer us to places we have never heard of as if we had lived there for years, and they tell of people identified only by pronouns, *he* or *you*, as if they were our next-door neighbors. This is not obscurantism, I've come to feel, as much as befuddlement. He writes:

> *I like bars close to home and home run down,*
> *a signal to the world, I'm weak....*

That's from a poem published in 1975. In fact, many of Hugo's poems occur in barrooms, and the tone is exactly that of the self-pitying drunken stranger who leans on you and erupts his unconnected life and philosophy into your ear. I am reminded of certain popular singers who have cashed in on their ability to sound drunk or stoned.

Fourth summation: Hugo's poetry is not only obviously derivative but degenerative.

Fifth: Hugo's poetry is the dominant influence upon the common American poetic style of recent years, as one may observe in thousands of books and periodicals. Here I know I'm on uncertain ground – if only because at other times I've felt the same thing about other poets. But Hugo's poems are genotypical: the same "free" meter that is nevertheless imbued with a stiffness recognizable as the mark of academicism, the same pronouns without antecedents, the same present tense (what used to be called the historical present but has now become a nonsensical eternal present), the same unearned sentimental misery, the same specious confidentiality. All this has become the poetic convention of the 1980s.

Finally: if one may relinquish the socio-literary mode demanded of reviewers and take the poems separately as phenomena rather than symptomatologia, then one can – I think almost anyone – choose a good small selection of Hugo's poems for an anthology. This is important. The selection will include some of the few poems in which Hugo speaks from outside his solipsism, poems like "Living Alone," but also some that do not, like "The River Now." Such poems will probably always be among the best of their limited kind in American literature and thoroughly representative as well. We must be leery of the kind, aware of its narrowness and its intellectual and artistic shabbiness – by which I mean that James Wright's poetry, for instance, is of another kind in spite of superficial similarities – but we certainly cannot leave it out in our account of American cultural schizophrenia during the Seventies.

David Ignatow

A review of *New and Selected Poems, 1970–1985*, by David Ignatow. 1985.

"THE SOLDIER is convinced that a certain interval of time, capable of being indefinitely prolonged, will be allowed him before the bullet finds him, the thief before he is caught, men in general before they have to die. This is the amulet which preserves people – and sometimes peoples – not from danger but from the fear of danger, which in certain cases allows them to brave it without actually needing to be brave." This wisdom from the world before apocalypse was written by Marcel Proust.

Poetry is "braving it." One among the many ways. If it has peculiar virtue, this must be its music, by which one does not at all mean its mellifluous syllables but rather its mythifying imagery that orchestrates the complications of existence and concentrates them. Existence as such is grotesque. It is noise. It is alien. George Gershwin, that light-hearted, light-minded man in the best sense, said: "I frequently hear music in the very heart of noise." The last poem in David Ignatow's book is called "The Image":

The image in the mirror feels nothing
towards him, though it is his image. He
weeps, and it weeps with him, but is merely
the sign of his weeping, yet he knows
he cannot eat, drink, or make love
without that image. He is in awe of it.

Though it does not need him,
he is its servant as he stands there,
doing what is necessary
to keep it in the mirror – humbled
and grateful for its presence,
that which reveals him to himself.
If there is a god, this is he.

Is god the mirror image then? Camus wrote: "God being dead, there remain only history and power." But the poet, growing old, knows that history is not merely error but caprice, the grotesque of the imagination, while power is useless because there is nothing against which to exert it. The poet, growing old, knows that the certain interval allowed him before his death can be prolonged only in thought, a noisy interfabulation of thought, a whimsical technicality. The old poet is "braving it" more and more bravely.

Music is that-which-is-almost-harmonious-but-not-quite. The music of one's self is always a rondo, obsessions that overlap but do not coincide, the merry-go-round of psychiatric causality. Notice that the image in the mirror is not exact. It has no depth. Its color is light, not pigment. It is an image, not a thing. The music of the looking-glass is unnatural; it was invented; it was invented long ago by poets, who gave the idea to smiths and glaziers; it is wonderful music because it simplifies and generalizes the thing that is imaged. As long as one does not go too far – that is, as long as one remains aware of the danger of Plato's narcissistic Ideas – this music of self-reflectiveness is salutary in its capacity to evoke awe. Not going too far is another term for braving it.

Oh yes, old age does awesomely compact the music! The image seems almost evanescent, the sound of falling snow. In the great grotesque of noise the image becomes a shocking whisper, smaller and smaller, closer and closer, until the poet swallows it and for a fraction of a second is conscious of silence.

Not all Ignatow's hasty readers will respond to the music of the last poem in his book. They will want something more conventionally lyrical than this language that contains only itself. (Yet there is a compelling argument for the poetry of language that contains only itself.) Fortunately for these readers, this is a big book, in effect the whole second half of Ignatow's lifework, the first half having been published in *Poems 1934–1969* – and of course the work is still going on. (Both this earlier collection and the present one are handsome, ample volumes. We owe thanks to Wesleyan for this, and for the smaller books of Ignatow's poems that have been published along the way.) Plenty of incidental modulations of harmony in Ignatow's writing, as in "One Leaf," a truly splendid modern lyric poem:

> *One leaf left on a branch*
> *and not a sound of sadness*
> *or despair. One leaf left*
> *on a branch and no unhappiness.*
> *One leaf all by itself*
> *in the air and it does not speak*
> *of loneliness or death.*
> *One leaf and it spends itself*
> *in swaying mildly in the breeze.*

So many delicate changes leading up to the high, long vowel in "breeze"; so many just-right rhythmic variations in the interplay of four-, three-, and two-beat lines and in the runover phrasings. Poets will notice these, and will think of a song from one of Dryden's plays or a stanza in the *Rubaiyat*.

The thing about god is that he – or she – or it – is neither dead nor alive but *in conceptuo*. The black hole is always inverting itself, the molecule of hydrogen is always at the instant prior to the instant of its transformation.

Here is an untitled poem by Ignatow:

> *Paint a wall*
> *cover the weather stains*
> *and spider webs: who's happy*

You who don't exist
I make you
out of my great need
There is no prose for this
no ordered syntax
no carefully measured tread
I am falling beyond depth
into oblivion
I hear breathing
Something must be said
of nothing

I am as queer as the conception of God
I am the god and the heaven
unless I scatter myself
among the animals and furniture of earth.

The breathing heard in oblivion, the cows at night: that's music. Otherwise the world is a disease of the retina. "The birth of the reader must be at the expense of the death of the author," wrote Roland Barthes, which seems to make the book reviewer both executioner and midwife, as he is. How revolting! But at least everyone is humming bits of music. "Without music life would be a mistake," wrote Nietzsche, who was also, like Ignatow, a great redundancer. Without music a mistake would be life.

Tom McGrath is Harvesting the Snow

1985.

AFTER THE WAR, in 1946 or possibly 1947, I first encountered the poems of Tom McGrath in Shag Donohue's bookstore on 57th Street in south Chicago. I had been born an Easterner, but from the back hills of New England, not the city, and I had a mixed heritage anyway. My grandfather had founded the first newspaper in the Dakotah Territory in 1885; my father had been born in Sioux Falls. My grandfather told me of hearing Bryan and of working with Debs in the years before World War I. In other words I had a pretty good dose of prairie populism in my childhood, and actually it fitted quite well with the eighteenth-century libertarianism of the hillside farmers who were my neighbors. Naturally McGrath's poems appealed to me.

But I was puzzled too. Why wasn't McGrath a fixture in *Partisan Review*, for instance, or the *New Leader?* Why wasn't he right in there with Delmore Schwartz and the rest of the gang? He wasn't, of course. Even though he hewed close to the Communist Party line in his poems of the late thirties and during the war, McGrath was still a fly-weight corn-hoer to the élite. Do you remember Pound's disparaging remark – he who had been born in Idaho – about Harriet Monroe with "the prairie dust swirling in her skirts"? Unless one ascribes rank ingratitude to Pound, which would seem an overreaching, the remark has less to do with Harriet than with some of the poets she published in *Poetry:* Sandburg, Lindsay, Neihardt, who were absent from the *Little Review, Vortex, transition,* etc., as McGrath was absent from *Partisan.* The New York radical élite, oriented toward Europe, had always ignored "native" radicalism. I mean the continuous tradition of the Eastern élite from Johann Most to Alexander Berkman to Philip Rahv. What a pity! I am as strong for upholding literary standards as anybody, but why should *Partisan* have given us so much warmed-over Sartrean engagement when the conditions of the American working class and intelligentsia were so obviously different? What did Sartre know about the House Un-American Activities Committee? And why was *Partisan* so damned eager to publish poems by T.S. Eliot and not Tom McGrath, to say nothing of Dr. Williams?

A significant attempt, perhaps partly unconscious, was made to subvert the tastes and opinions of my generation of American youth, and it largely succeeded.

But not with McGrath. He continued writing, he published his poems wherever he could, he refined his radicalism, moving away from Marxist simplicity toward a functional American anarcho-socialism, and he extended the scope of his poetic vision. For a time he lived on the West Coast and was, at least so I infer, turned on to the pseudo-radical antics of California's senile infants; but his roots were always in the plains. The harsh land had made his sensibility: stone and gravel,

wind and snow, rust and poverty. And in the end his sensibility re-
mained faithful to the land. He moved back to Dakota. I don't know
exactly when that was, but I think perhaps around 1968.

Let me make it clear that I'm not talking about some social-realist
hack. I'm talking about a poet with as great a voice as Whitman's, and
with a devotion to the American language (and its English anteced-
ents) the equal of anyone's. A superb talent, a splendid imagination. A
poet. I give myself credit for recognizing this from the first; and when
I made my anthology (*The Voice That Is Great Within Us*), I tried to
indicate it by giving McGrath as much space as most of his contempo-
raries, Jarrell, Berryman, and the rest. But I've yet to see another an-
thologist who has picked up the cue, and only very infrequently do I
meet young poets who know what McGrath has done.

He has persevered. He has been fantastically consistent, loyal to
himself. Here is a poem, a late one, called "Ordonnance":

> *During a war the poets turn to war*
> *In praise of the merit of the death of the ball-turret gunner.*
> *It is well arranged: each in his best manner*
> *One bleeds, one blots – as they say, it has happened before.*
>
> *After a war, who has news for the poet?*
> *If sunrise is Easter, noon is his winey tree.*
> *Evening arrives like a postcard from his true country*
> *And the seasons shine and sing. Each has its note*
>
> *In the song of the man in his room in his house in his head*
>   *remembering*
> *The ancient airs. It is good. But is it good*
> *That he should rise once to his song on the fumes of blood*
> *As a ghost to his meat? Should rise so, once, in anger*
>
> *And then no more? Now the footsteps ring on the stone –*
> *The Lost Man of the century is coming home from his work.*
> *"They are fighting, fighting" – Oh, yes. But somewhere else. In the*
>   *dark.*
> *The poet reads by firelight as the nations burn.*

Notice how the tenderness for the poet winds into McGrath's desperate anger, almost disillusioned anger. Yet he perseveres. The poem is in hard-sounded prosody, done with perfect verbal tact. This is the poet at work, the poet transmuting his political and social anxieties into *memorable* structures. I emphasize memory. Isn't that what art wants, to make politics a part of culture? Homer could have and would have made as much of Daniel Shays as he did of Odysseus. But the poet today has many voices. Here is a poem called "When We Say Goodbye":

> *It is not because we are going –*
> *Though the sea may begin at the doorstep, though the highway*
> *May already have come to rest in our front rooms . . .*
>
> *It is because, beyond distance, or enterprise*
> *And beyond the lies and surprises of the wide and various worlds,*
> *Beyond the flower and the bird and the little boy with his large*
>   *questions*
>
> *We notice our shadows:*
> *Going . . .*
> *– slowly, but going,*
> *In slightly different directions –*
> *Their speeds increasing –*
> *Growing shorter, shorter*
> *As we enter the intolerable sunlight that never grows old or kind.*

Notice here the remarkable rolling control of the long lines. As I have said, Whitmanian. You cannot find more than a few American poets who can do this, though the ephebe says it is easy. Notice also the sentiment, very congenial to a fellow northman, that says the sunlight is intolerable. Is this not the hardihood that old radicals and young poets, who are the same, must assimilate to their deepest impulses? In spite of everything, the whole goddamn mess, McGrath says:

> *I'll have to walk out in the snow*
> *In any case. Where else is there to turn?*
> *So if you see me coming, a man made out of ice,*

Splintering light like rainbows at every crazed joint of my body,
Better get out of the way: this black blood won't burn
And the fierce acids of winter are smoking in this cold heart.

No, we have nowhere else to turn, McGrath and I, though we have never met and when we die our graves will lie far apart. But they will be among the speaking graves, the orating graves, sounding forth from under the heavy depths of snow. Watch out, all you smushy flatlanders. Fold your dewy palms, and listen to the brilliant voice of midnight.

🖎 ·

The Blues as Poetry

1985.

I AM NOT speaking of the part of traditional blues that qualifies as literature on poetic grounds, but of the use of the tradition, both thematically and formally, by poets.

Poets who love the blues are moved quite naturally to try composition in the traditional form. For one thing, the form is another proof – here in our midst   that complex rhyming and metrical schemes, such as, in the past, the French *villanelle* and *triolet*, the *cansò* of the trobadors, the *cansone* and *sonnetto* of northern Italy, do derive ultimately from the folk, no matter how they may be trivialized and overrefined by poets of the aristocracy and the academy later on. (Examples even more extreme may be found in Sanskrit, in pre-Mohammedan Arabic poetry, in medieval Celtic, and in many other "primitive" literatures.) That the blues are a folk invention, even in some cases today, is self-evident to anyone who listens to them. That the tradition is a difficult one for poets is only somewhat less self-evident, since published examples are still both few and inferior a good sixty years, at least three poetic generations, after the blues were popularized in the 1920s. David Budbill of Vermont has written good blues. June Jordan has poems that remind me of the blues, which obviously was her intention, although as far as I know she has not written an explicit blues. Gwendolyn Brooks has written a few fine blues; Langston Hughes also. Allen Ginsberg has written many blues, unfortunately not fine at all in my opinion; they sound like the very minor, white, watered-down, blue-grass imitation-blues of the Tennessee backcountry, as sung once by Joe Hill and Woody Guthrie. Raymond R. Patterson, in his *Elemental Blues* (Merrick, N.Y., 1983), has written some excellent blues – when I read them I hear lost voices, Ida Cox, Mildred Bailey, Lil Green – and has made a few experiments with variations on the basic form that are illuminating though to my mind they don't go far enough. In some of his poems the diction is too sentimental and old-timey. I myself have written a few blues, but none I care to publish.* Since I have been playing and singing the blues for more than fifty years, perhaps this is as good an indication of the difficulties as any.

What is wanted is a poem in the conventional three-line stanza, at least to begin with, that can be sung but that can also stand by itself in print, without music, as poetry. The lines should rhyme; the second line should duplicate the first, that is, the refrain, so to speak, should come before the main element of each stanza. Each line should assimilate itself both to twelve beats of music in the stanza, the underlying measure, and to some shorter, more comfortable rhythmic and prosodic arrangement of spoken language.

Problems, formidable ones, emerge at once. To avoid triteness and tedium in the repeated lines, to impart phrasal variation and appeal to language not strictly metered (though a remarkable number of blues lines do fall into pentameter), to decline the temptation to try for effects that can be accomplished only in music, and so on. Some degree of literariness – and I use the term without deprecation – is almost certainly necessary. In one of her early blues, for instance, Billie Holiday sang the line:

> *I ain't good-looking, and my hair ain't curled ...*

She held the "I" for something more than six beats, a beautifully effective musical maneuver. But in literature no punctuation, no typography, not even Robert Duncan's innovative spacings and markings (though they function pretty well in his poetry), can force the reader's eye to linger that long on a single syllable. If you printed the "I" alone

---

* I did include one blues, written after this essay, in my *Collected Shorter Poems* (1992), and I have used the word *blues* in the titles of a fair number of other poems.

on one page and continued the rest of the line on the next page, or even after twenty blank pages, the reader would still go as immediately as possible to the continuation, and the phrasing enforced by the beat in music would be lost. It is not a question of what the reader should do, but of what he or she inevitably will do. Responsible writers must take this into account.

Within the boundaries of literature-as-such, however, considerable rhythmic and phrasal variation can be created. Let me set down a few rudimentary observations.

1. Conventional punctuation is of little use. The most critical part of the blues line is the caesura. Very few lines consist of a single syntactical unit. Hence variation from the first line to the second in each stanza can best be accomplished by moving the caesura, indicating a pause that is either metrical or ametrical; singers do this all the time. But a comma will not suffice in a printed blues, nor will any mark, especially as one reads stanza after stanza. A line break is more effective. Thus the stanza from which I quoted above:

> I ain't good-looking
>   and my hair ain't curled
> I ain't good-looking and my
>   hair ain't curled
> but my mother she gave me something it's going to
>   carry me through this world.

This is literary, not musical, that is, not exactly as Holiday sang it. But for me it works better than a mere transcription would. No punctuation therefore. How about the hyphens and apostrophes? I think I'd omit them too:

> I aint good looking
>   and my hair aint curled

This appears cleaner and better to me.

2. The more difficult question arises of whether or not to attempt orthographical reproduction of speech, our literary koine having deviated so far from our pronunciations – or "t'other way abaout," as Pa McCabe used to say. Holiday sang "lookin," not "looking," and in the

third line she sang neither "going to" nor "gonna," but "goin to." It is a matter of taste, subjective and relative, and of what one wants to do; and also, inevitably, of one's capacities. Ezra Pound could not write dialect, though he liked to try. Mark Twain could and did. My own thought is that if verse forms arise in the folk, and if, as I said at the beginning, they evolve necessarily toward literature, then the shift of street language to literary usage is not to be deplored, provided the poem does not become pedantic. The artful poet today will in fact use the whole range of diction from vulgar to technical – as Derek Walcott mixes Jamaicanese with the language of Fleet Street – and he will know when to resort sparingly to orthographical divergence and when not to. Such mixtures would be not at all unsuitable to the blues. (Cf. also ballads by Auden, Thomas, Robert Hayden, and many others.)

3. Variations of form have been introduced by the musicians themselves already. Here is another stanza from Holiday's blues with a four-part first line, each part on roughly two accents:

> *my man wouldnt give me no breakfast*
> > *wouldnt give me no dinner*
> > *squawked about my supper then he*
> > *put me outdoors*
> *had the nerve to lay*
> > *a matchbox on my clothes*
> *I didnt have so many*
> > *but I had a long long ways to go*

Then there is the final stanza, in which the four-part first line is rhymed:

> *some men like me cause Im happy*
> > *some cause Im snappy*
> > *some call me honey*
> > *others think Ive got money*
> *some say Billie*
> > *baby youre built for speed*
> *now if you put that all together*
> > *makes me everything a good man needs*

With these hints and others, such as the fairly common two-line and four-line stanza in the sung tradition ("How Long Blues," the first stanza of "Easy Rider" in its original version or many of the 16-, 18-, and 32-bar blues), poets should be able to think of further variations that will augment the formal latencies of the blues.

4. Bessie Smith's "Young Woman's Blues" was first recorded in 1926, yet any poet who could today attain the same formal complexity, consistency, and momentum in a written blues would be famous immediately.

5. One variation from standard form that at first seems simple – it has occurred to a fair number of musicians and songwriters in the past, e.g., Lee Wiley, Johnny Mercer, etc. – is the use of a stanza with three separate lines and three rhymes:

> *well in new york baby*
> *you cant hardly ever see the sun*
> *and in la and miami*
> *the fuzz is always reaching for his gun*
> *lets go to your town baby*
> *and sit and watch that old green river run*

You see at once how this upsets and weakens the dynamic of structural attitude and expectation in the stanza: repetition of the first line seems necessary, though this may be something that poets, rather than songwriters, can work out. Other traditional variations, such as the separation of the first two lines in each stanza while the third line repeats from one stanza to another, which is again close to the lyric impulse of the jongleur, work quite well and indicate directions in which literary development might go.

6. Why bother? Someone will ask it, inevitably. Because the blues, altogether aside from their music, are often more expressive than conventional poetry, by which I mean virtually all poetry written in the U.S.A. today.

> *blues jumped a rabbit*
> *run him for a solid mile*
> *well the blues jumped a rabbit and they*
> *run him for a solid mile*

> *rabbit turn over and he cry like*
> *a little baby child*

This goes back at least to 1925, probably to a time twenty or thirty years earlier than that. Or consider the final stanza of a much later blues, sung by Holiday twenty years after the one I've quoted above.

> *love is just like a faucet*
> *it turns off and on*
> *love is like a faucet it turns*
> *off and on*
> *sometimes when you think its on baby*
> *it has turned off and gone*

Two similes, many years apart, one from rural life and the other from urban, yet both naturally related, spontaneously and integrally related, to the common culture around them; and they are original and inventive too. Are these tropes less poetic in the blues than they would be in poetry? They are *expressive*. This, it seems to me, is what so much of our poetry has lost. Ginsberg is at least correct in his intention: to get back for our poetry what the blues already and naturally possess. Then notice the purely poetic values in the last stanza quoted, the modulation – not rhyme, not assonance – of verbal sound: love/just/faucet/turns/off/on/gone. Such delicacy! Louis Zukofsky did no better, though he did as well.

7. Raymond Patterson has written, in the introduction to his *Elemental Blues*, "...the subtleties of this American verse form have yet, in America, to receive the attention given to the haiku, the Sapphic, or the ghazal." He is absolutely right. The situation is absurd. Many will remember when, fifteen or so years back, the classical Persian ghazal seized the imaginations of American poets like Adrienne Rich and Jim Harrison and others. Fine work was done, at least in part because some foundation or other offered fellowships for translations from the ghazals of Mirza Ghalib. But how could these poets resort to a kind of poetry so remote and alien, and not give at least equal attention to the only major kind of poetry invented in our own country and our own time? The blues are not only expressive, they are ours. All the more

reason to begin writing them, and I wish some foundation would sponsor the attempt.

8. As I say, I've written no blues I think good enough to publish, and I should add that I've written only a few and only in recent years. I wish I had been writing blues from the beginning, or at least that they had been a persisting formal – rather than associative or textural – element in my poetry. I have written many other kinds of song, why not the blues? And now I see – for the first time utterly clearly! – how I was inhibited by the cultural chauvinism of the literary community. This was not conscious in me; I have played and sung the blues, and have written and talked about them, for many, many years, without the least feeling of condescension. I have been scornful of writers and critics who could not or would not acknowledge the determinative place of African-American music in our contemporary civilization. Yet I did not write blues. The whole apparatus of literary production in this country, publishers big and small, editors, magazines, critics, universities, etc., militated against the idea of writing blues, militated against the idea even occurring to me. Yet I do believe that what Cummings did with the conventional sonnet, to take a conspicuous example, could be done with the blues, if one had a lifetime to give to it. Now of course it is too late for me. But not for others.

🖙 . . . .

Mystery and Expressiveness

1985.

THE TWO KINDS of expressiveness in art, sensual and conceptual, are separable from substance only in theory, in analysis; this is understood. And I no longer believe, as I once did, that theoretical and analytical discussion, whether public or inside one's head, is necessary to understanding. Blest are they who respond fully to poems, paintings, musical compositions, and so on, without thought; for thought is the only product of theory and analysis, which are exercises of the mind for their own sake, or for intellectual pleasure, and though many of us become addicted to them, they serve only a cognitive function and have little, if anything, to do with understanding.

Young people, when they read a poem or look at a painting, do not ask whether and how it is expressive, but only what it says, what it shows, what it means. This is as it should be. Contrary to the notion of certain sophisticated critics, what we ask of a work of art in ordinary, pragmatically verifiable experience is what it signifies. From the point of view of the artist and the spectator – that is, leaving the critic aside – if significance were nugatory, the compositional process would break down, as indeed we have seen with certain third- and fourth-generation abstract expressionists who ended up in one or another order of minimalism, complaining that they had no more "problems," by which they meant invented formal incompatibilities on the surface of the canvas, to solve. Every artist must have something to make art about.

To these ideas a corollary must be added: perhaps the greatest utility of theory and analysis is their indication of their own limits. No matter how far one may press an investigation of expressive means, no matter how near one may edge to "final knowledge," a cognitive ending or point of rest will never be reached. An effective line of poetry, for instance, will never disclose all the subtle elements of its own prosody. Even the most elaborately programmed computer could never find them, which is to say that every line of poetry, in all its prosodic combinations, is unique. Thus mystery lies at the extreme of knowledge – at the end or at the center, depending on how you look at it. Those who pursue knowledge the furthest will see most clearly, not the mystery, for it is precisely hidden, but the inevitability of mystery, though whether this vision is an aid to understanding I do not know. But the acknowledgment of mystery is at least salutary.

Expressiveness in art derives from the work's embodiment, the work's presence and actuality, as opposed to its substance, which was once called content, an unreliable term. Substance is meaning; expressiveness is means. Someone will say that the means are part of the meaning, and I agree, of course. But let's keep the discussion as simple as we can, granting that any analysis of a work, any wrenching apart of the whole, is already complex and abstract. Then what is meant by the two kinds of expressiveness? Conceptual expressiveness derives from abstract technique: in poetry from figures of speech and from imagery, both direct and metaphorical; in painting from composition; in music from tempo, dynamics, keys, modes, and anything that has to do with combining and contrasting tonal and rhythmical patterns; and so on. Sensual expressiveness derives from the medium or from – excuse the expression – concrete technique: in poetry from the sounds, rhythms, and other verbal manifestations; in painting from pigment and its liquifacient and fixative agents; in music from tones, which are frequencies of vibration, what some people call notes or distinctions of pitch; and so on. At any rate these are the best approximate definitions I can come up with at the moment. It will be seen that expressiveness, both kinds, is a function of what has been called either style or form at different times and places, for, contrary to much current belief, these terms have been used not only variably but interchangeably in the evolution of Western criticism and esthetic philosophy; but here the emphasis is on the function, not on the static, achieved artifact in its inertness, which is how critics usually perceive a work of art. Expressiveness is an active quality, not a passive one.

But really I find myself embarrassed to be discussing such simple and rudimentary matters. I do so only because I so often come into contact with artists who do not discuss them or who are not even aware of them. Yet artists, as distinct from spectators, are the ones who need to be concerned. Not so much with conceptual expressiveness perhaps, because this is fairly steadily dealt with in workshops, whereas I have the impression that sensual expressiveness is not. Here, however, I am getting onto shaky ground. I do not know enough about painting, sculpture, filmmaking, architecture, etc., to generalize the degree or kind of self-scrutiny common among their practitioners and teachers. What I do know about are jazz and poetry.

Several times in recent years I have given a talk called something like "Mystery and Expressiveness in Jazz and Poetry," and I have thought about turning it into an essay, but have been stumped by the impossibility of representing some of the materials on paper: my "talk" consists in large part of playing tapes as well as reading poems. I begin my talk with the last recording of Billie Holiday, taken from a live television concert not long before she died. I wasn't lucky enough to see the original program, but I have several times seen a film of part of it. Holiday – her face a little worn but still very beautiful – sits on a high stool among some of her favorite musicians, Ben Webster, Lester Young, Henry Allen, and others, and her voice is much stronger, much less quavery, than it was on the last studio recordings she made. (To infer, as I have heard some people do, that she had been permitted a controlled dose of heroin by the producers of the program is unfair to them and to her, and is reductive with respect to the power of the music.) She sings a blues, nodding her head to the beat, smiling. She sings simply but with her superb sense of timing and phrasing intact. It is a somewhat slow blues but not a drag or a dirge; it is what Holiday used to call "finger-snapping music"; the words are silly in some verses, quite meaningful in others. (This blues and other excerpts from the concert were issued by Columbia on an album entitled *The Sound of Jazz*, CS 8040, 1958.) At the end is a one-bar tag by Webster on tenor, and at the very end, just after the final beat but while the tone is still sounding, somebody moans. It is scarcely audible, but in my talk I play the final bars again with the volume turned up so that the audience can hear it easily. (The voice sounds to me like Vic Dickenson's, but that's a guess.) Then I ask the audience what this moan means.

And I have had dozens of improbable answers, everything from pain because the tenor tag ends on a fourth instead of the dominant, which is ridiculous, to joy, love, sexual frustration, understanding, sympathy, sorrow, etc. When I say to the audience that the moan does not *mean* anything, that it is an involuntary response to a purely sensual experience, that it suggests deep feeling but no specifiable emotion, nothing that a literary label can be attached to, that the feeling expressed is of undifferentiated physical experience, like the sound a person might make upon hitting a tennis ball or waking with a hangover or experiencing orgasm or death, when I suggest these things, the people in the audience begin to feel uncomfortable, and they shift around in their seats and lift their hands to rub their noses or pat their hair. From the platform it looks like a little flutter or spasm passing through them. Have they been taken so far out of their own bodies that they cannot deal with sensuality as such any more?

After the blues by Holiday I play another by Joe Turner, recorded at a concert in 1967 when he was still at his best (*John Hammond's Spirituals to Swing 30th Anniversary Concert*, Columbia, G 30776, 1967). The tempo is slower this time, the words are in some verses more sorrowful, and in some passages Turner sings with a modified sob in his voice. In the middle, when the vocal leaves off and an instrumental ad lib begins, there is a loud, high-pitched yell, "Wahoooo!" – I presume from Turner himself. At the end I ask my audience what this means,

and again I am given the names of emotions, and a few people are likely
to be quite insistent, even testy, about it. But am I wrong? Does a musi-
cal pitch *mean* anything in our minds? Let's say an E-flat coming after
a D and accompanied by a diminished chord: does it *mean?* This is a
question of vibrations-per-second striking against eardrums and other
sensory receptors. Can this mean something in itself? No, meaning is
always in part a product of mind; the precisely appropriate response to
musical pitch is a physical one – horripilation, a writhing sensation in
the spine or a wrenching in the gut, a wince, a scowl – and if in the pro-
cess a groan or yell escapes, the fact that it is a vocalization does not
make it a verbalization. Many people, apparently, don't know this dis-
tinction. Which perhaps is natural.

After the music I play tapes of sounds from nature, peepers in
spring, wind in a spruce forest, wild geese passing overhead at night,
and then tapes of manufactured sounds, a train whistle, the din of mas-
sive machinery; and in none of these cases can the audience make an
authentic specification of meaning, which causes them to be even
more uncomfortable. Yes, I do understand the temptation to say that
the sound of the geese flying overhead in the dark is the voice of God
or one's ancestral spirits passing and calling, or that the train makes a
"lonesome" sound. This is what primitive people have always done.
But I think such people, whose lives were immediately and intimately
connected with nature, knew what they were doing and did it con-
sciously, the fantasizing and symbol-making, the superimposing of cul-
ture upon sensory data, and they kept clearly in mind the reality of
their situation, their place. A goose is a goose is a supper. This double
talk or double thought is just what the human species in a situation of
contrived existence has lost the capacity for, in spite of all the high-
powered attention devoted to poetic ambiguity in our time. Of course
we cannot be primitive (though we can be savage, God knows). Per-
haps it behooves us therefore to be realists, in which case we must be
extremely wise and cautious in the choice of words to apply to the
sound of the geese. (Writers know that adjectives always weaken the
nouns to which they are attached, even when they are necessary.
Modification entails diminution. The folk know it too, which is why
our language in recent decades has shifted so far in the direction of ad-
jectival nouns and compound nouns.) Yet we must talk, we must write
poems; which means that we must put ourselves into relationships

with other people that require explanation and description, something more than finger-pointing. What shall we say, that the sound of the geese is eerie and yet appropriate? – as the sound of ghosts might be? This in fact suggests the ghosts or God, and the geese are geese. Better to describe the effect produced, a nostalgia for the unknown that is, as we say, felt "in our bones" and transmuted immediately to tension in muscles and nerves. Better to talk only to those who have heard the geese themselves, those who respond in the same way you do, at least more or less. And this is what is meant by community.

How much we have lost verbally in our forced civilization, which is the inflation, not to say exploitation, of community.

After the tapes I begin to read poetry, passages or whole poems in which the substance is either so foolish or so obscured that it becomes functionally irrelevant, especially in aural apprehension: things like John Lily's "Cupid and My Campaspe...," a particularly turgid page from *Paradise Lost*, some vacuous Dryden, a spun-out commonplace from *The Prelude*, and so on, down to Swinburne, Pound, Duncan, Gary Snyder; it is not at all difficult to find such pieces even among contemporary poets whom we think of as utterly substance-oriented, lovely, musical, sonorous, swinging, or foamy, and meaningless, passages that will evoke a *frisson* from everyone in the audience who has ears to hear and nerve-endings to feel. This of course does not mean everyone, for some are, it seems, genetically unable to respond to poems, just as some are unable to respond to music, and many others, legions of others, have been turned off to poetic values by our schools and by the vocal dullness of much American poetry of the twentieth century. It takes more than a public lecture to reawaken them. Yet not much more perhaps. People have told me that my talk has helped them.

And at this point in the talk I scarcely need to say anything more: the point has been made by the examples. Expressiveness in art is not a function of substance. Not at all. Originality of thought and feeling, novelty of event, cogency of allusion, and all other elements of substance are, in the best sense of the word, literary; they are what poets *do*. The sensual and conceptual elements are, so to speak, what poets *are:* the conditioned and/or instinctive skill within which they exist. Expressiveness is what draws poets to poetry in the first place, and it is what older poets more and more return to as they consolidate and simplify their poetic visions. And the same holds in all the arts.

Does this mean a work can be done with no substance at all? At one time or another workers in all the arts have tried it, but I am certain it is impossible except in music. I believe that, speaking theoretically and analytically, a musical pitch is pure and has no meaning. I believe – though how can one be sure? – that my own musical "ideas" occur to me, when I am improvising, only as sequences of pitch, texture, and rhythm, with no literary or cultural attachments whatever. I am not a singer, and I care less for vocal music than for instrumental. Yet it is obviously true that much music, probably most music, does occur in what we may call a literary or cultural context. Practically speaking, pure music may be as impossible as pure art in general, pure expressiveness. Nevertheless music *tends toward purity*, and to my mind Schopenhauer was right when he suggested that the other arts aspire to the condition of music, except that I wish he had said "ought to aspire."

A great many artists from all times and places have attested that the inception of a work of art, its origin, its "inspiration," is a combined event, the simultaneous, mutually reinforcing emergence of substance and its expressive means, both sensual and conceptual. This is particularly evident in the improvisatory art of the twentieth century, whether it be a solo by Cannonball Adderley or a circus by Peter Schuman's Bread and Puppet Theater.

The truth of course is that in this time we have many poems and other artworks that are inexpressive; it has become the norm. Composers and performers make music without much concern for its impact on the body of the auditor, and poets conventionally write prose, or at best poems radically tending toward prose. In architecture the concrete block has become a model, and in painting we have super-realism on one hand and blank canvas on the other, equally inexpressive. In jazz the conservatories and workshops have introduced an imitative academicism, finicality, and virtuosity that seem – at any rate to me – extraordinarily boring.

But I see counterindications too, artists who recognize that the attitudinal significance of pop culture, with its rock music and heavily metered greeting-card verse, is worth paying heed to. Young composers, like my friend William Duckworth, are not only acknowledging their roots in the blues, jazz, and rock – which are, and this is no overstatement, whatever the *New York Times* says, the classical music of America – but also showing that they understand their roots. (Not the case with Copland, Gershwin, and other composers of that generation.) And although much of the music composed during the past twenty-five years on synthesizer and tape, *la musique concrète*, seems to me artistically insincere, some is not, and the search for new expressive means with electronic instruments continues to be rather exciting. In jazz some musicians are using the voice primitively, i.e. instrumentally, and are using instruments more, rather than less, bluesily, i.e., outside the diatonic modes. Notice the increasing popularity of string quartets in jazz, and the skill of the performers on unfretted string instruments that can be easily tuned to any scale and played in any mode. The performance of Thelonious Monk's piano pieces by the Kronos Quartet is a case in point; the quartet can *play* what Monk could only intimate on the piano. (But Paul Zukofsky's performances of rags, which are a legitimately pianistic music, are no better than travesty.) In poetry I see many young people scouting the fringes of literature, both the conventional and the unexplored fringes – as suggested, for example, by Jerome Rothenberg's anthology, *Technicians of the Sacred* – in search of ways to make their poems more sensual, more expressive. And painters like Susan Bush are finding quite new and expressive means in their graphic use of commonplace materials for effects of sensual immediacy. In sculpture Judith Brown is a good example.

At all events I think I perceive the closing of the time when one will hear of a literary work the criticism that "it is too well written," of a piece of music that it is "too sonorous" or "too mellifluous," or that any musical or literary or painterly qualities are "distracting." (I have heard all these within the past three days.) The signs are not as clear as one might wish. They never are. But I suggest that works like the recordings of simple songs in the earlier African-American tradition by Horace Parlan and Archie Shepp, in which – at least in the best of them – the musical expressiveness is new, moving, yet firmly integrated with substance, or like the novel *Luisa Domic* by George Dennison, or *Suttree* by Cormac McCarthy, in which the writing is both gratifying in itself, to anyone with an ear for the possibilities of American speech, and thoroughly at one with the novel's remarkable substance and vision – I suggest that such works as these, and a good many others, do manifest a turning away from inexpressive formulaic virtuosity and a desire to meet the real needs of the human mind and spirit, which are perennial. But I do not wish to be misunderstood. Raymond Carver has been called a "minimalist," a "writer of fragments," a "stylistic vacancy," etc., but to my mind he is none of these, and his best stories are expressively and substantially complete, trenchant, compelling, and in their way beautiful. Naturally Carver has accepted the limits of his verbal imagination, or rather he has partially accepted them while he continues to push against them. What else can any artist do? The artist who functions equally well in all conventions does not exist, and all expressive works – even the largest, e.g., *A la recherche du temps perdu* – can *be* expressive only within their own acknowledged frontiers.

Already what we must watch out for is the coming upon us of the *baroque nouveau*. In the main lines of every American art today we see powerful tendencies toward the pedantic, the establishmentarian, and the hyperesthetic. In short, a new decadence. Without denying the appeal exerted on us by a less than responsible art, I believe we must reject it – as serious artists always have. But this isn't easy. In particular cases the artist will very often be hard-pressed even to decide what must be rejected, and how, and when. This tension is the source of expressiveness in our lives, or at least one source. Probably we need it in order to know how to be expressive in our work.

At the far end of expressiveness, or at its center, its point of impulsion, lies the mystery. The mystery is not cryptic, though some artists choose to believe it is and even derive from it, as cryptesthesiatically from "another source," their own artistic vision. If this works for them, then who objects? But for my part a distinction exists between the *cryptic* and the *labyrinthine*. The cryptic is a hiddenness associated with another order of perception, whether finite or infinite. It is totally outside my competence. But the labyrinthine is a hiddenness associated with human perception, our way of seeing; it is an obscurity of finite complications too distant, minute, and tangled for our finite discernment to clarify. No one will ever penetrate to the heart of the labyrinth. If my powers of analytical and theoretical intelligence are too weak, as they are, and if my capacities of imagination are too limited to allow me a complete realization of the procedures of expressiveness, then I rejoice as much as anyone in what surpasses my understanding and in the wonderful fortuities, the instances of what-happens, that occur when I am putting together a work of art. This always had been and, as long as artists exist, always will be the greatest joy we have in our finite, contingent, and terrified lives.

🖎 . . . .

Duncan's Dream

1986.

> *Aimai-je un rêve?*   MALLARMÉ

IN REREADING Robert Duncan's poems of a decade or so ago – rereading them, I should add, for the first time since they appeared, the life of a reviewer being what it is – I am taken by surprise at the power of my own response, even though I expected it. The sense of confirmation, the degree of it, is what seizes me. I am confirmed, confirmed again, almost "over-confirmed," in my subjection to nearly every aspect of his writing. It is a good and willing subjection. It is a case almost of chemical, physiological reagency, although it works in the solid jointure of intellect and sense and would not occur without a mutuality of concern, of ideas by which we both are held. But the ear is fundamental to the jointure, our kinship in musical sensitivity.

Passages 36 bears a bracketed subtitle:

> THESE LINES
>
> COMPOSING THEMSELVES IN MY HEAD AS I AWOKE
>
> EARLY THIS MORNING, IT BEING STILL DARK
>
> *December 16, 1971*

I line it out this way because that's what Duncan did, I'm certain not randomly. Jonson and Wordsworth might have, and in our esthetic environment would have, done the same. Poets write poetry all the time. Most people, nonpoets, would have written "composed," not "composing," and in that, as well as in the lining, a world of difference lies. Duncan lives in the *flow* of language, meaning the flow of time, ideas, emotions, memories, sensory feelings, everything: he lives *in* the flow, not apart from it, as most poets do; and this is one reason why, when he arrests the flow, it is so effective.

The poem begins:

Let it go. Let it go.
Grief's its proper mode.
But O, How deep it's got to reach,
*   How high and wide*
*   it's got to grow,*
Before it come to sufficient grief...

I know but part of it and that   but distantly,
a catastrophe in another place, another time,
    the mind addresses
and would erect within itself   itself
    as Viet Nam,   itself as Bangla Desh,
itself exacting revenge and suffering revenge,
    itself the Court and before the Court
where new judges disloyal to the Spirit of the Law
    are brought. All forces conspire
        to seat them there.

Notice in the second strophe here the distinctions between a comma, a space, and a comma followed by a space. I believe even an untaught reader could sound these differing pauses properly, for Duncan's at-home-ness in language bestows on him a power to enforce his music (as in "that   but distantly, / a catastrophe": perfectly natural and perfectly beautiful, as so much in his poetry is), and to enforce it without violence. Nor is it craft, because "craft" suggests wiliness, of which I discover none in his mature work, but only the kind of spontaneous expressiveness that ensues upon complete absorption of technique. Notice further how the syntax – not simply the parallel clauses, but the phrasings within the clauses – creates a rising tension, how it lunges forward on the beats, over the beats, a wave cresting and falling against a shore. Then notice particularly the first strophe, the italicized poem that came to the poet in darkness while he was half-awake. This is the lyrical instinct in language at its best, impossible to analyze. One can point to the rhythmic patterns, how they recall yet make impromptu deviations from the English convention, and also to the diction, how it combines the contemporary vocabulary, e.g., "got," which in me evokes an impeccable thrill of vulgarity, though like everyone I use it constantly in my speech, with touches of archaism, as in the capitalizations and the subjunctive mood at the end. But these are crude academical observations. They do not explain. And hence I must say again, as I have been saying, no doubt tediously, for thirty years, that responsiveness to art is subjective, that the finest, most profound expressions of it are, no matter how clear-sighted, impassioned and in a good part reverential, and that for this we ought to be thankful.

It strikes me that people like me who love music but have very little technical knowledge of it have an advantage when we are listening to music with friends, for when the question inevitably arises, "How did he do that?", we have no answer but to play the record again; whereas with literature, in which the technique, at least on a rudimentary level, is so much simpler, we have a disadvantage because we are always tempted to try to explain.

What is the "it" in Duncan's poem? Awareness. Knowledge. (Here, of violence and terror.) Knowledge is suspect for the poet, always. It is not a mode of understanding, even though our "civilization" for centuries has been trying and trying to convince us that it is. The poet says: "Let it go." But on the other hand knowing *is* a mode of being human. It is not only inescapable, it presents us with the wish to escape only at the cost of our own unworthiness. To be human we must accept the burden of knowledge, including its damnable usefulness. This is the tension of the poet's mode of understanding, the mode which always undermines itself, and from it all the other tensions, and hence the dynamisms, of poetry arise.

Later the poet says:

> *Eat,*
> *Eat, eat this bread and be thankful*
> *it does not yet run with blood*
>
> > *At the mill the wheel no longer turns;*
> > *the fields are in ruin.*
>
> *Each day the planes go out over the land,*
> > *And revolution works within*
> *to bring to an end in the rage of power*
> > *the works and dreams*
> *of a governing Art. The air is darkened.*

> *Drink, drink, while there is water.*
> *They move to destroy the sources of feeling.*

Notice the simple perfection of Duncan's compelling us to see and hear the primary meaning beneath the common meaning of "source" (from Latin *surgere:* in French it still means a "spring").

The poem is somewhat long, like all the *Passages*, and is full of conflict, the poet's direct attachment to myth against the world's sundering violence, with Poundian suggestions of the Consistori de Vrai Amor and how the poet has been advocate there of *mythopoios*. Then at the end:

> *I do not as the years go by grow tolerant*
> *of what I cannot share and what*
> *refuses me. There's that in me as fiercely beyond*
> *the remorse that eats me   in its drive*
> *as Evolution is   in*
> *working out the courses of what will last.*
> *In Truth 'tis done. At last. I'll not*
>
> *repair.*

It is a resolve to be in Truth, this simple eloquence: *a poet not unaware.* Taken from the moment of half-dream. Of twilight. A tension.

"These Lines" contains much more than is indicated by my excerpts, and of course Duncan's whole work much more than that; considered as an oeuvre, it is extremely complex. (And the poem quoted is a kind of reversal against Duncan's earlier commitment to "nonpolitical" poetry, if there is such a thing.) But the work as a whole is firmly, finely integrated, as good an example as we have in English of the poetic imagination continuously evolving within the overlapping cycles of personal and social, intellectual and emotional experience. One can find loose ends and ragged patches here and there, as in anybody's lifework, and one can find also – or at least I can – places where comprehension breaks down. I am more inclined than I used to be to ascribe these latter to the poet's failing, not mine. But the success of the whole is what I emphasize, the way the poet's life has been lived on the page in remarkable candor and in even more remarkable poetic control and distancing: perhaps the most consistent, most energetic conversion of experience into art. I do not forget W.C. Williams or anyone else. But I believe the older poets had not quite Duncan's finesse of sensitivity to the meaning of mythopoios in poetry of the present and to the complicated intermixture of ambition and humility demanded by its expansive potentiality.

I see such need for this kind of poetry now, this understanding. More than during the atrocities of Vietnam and Bangladesh, if that is possible. Yet I do not see younger poets who recognize this, or who even try and fail in attempting it. Again and again Duncan holds out a torch in the darkness, and no one takes it from his hand.

What Does Organic Mean?

1988.

CHUANG-TZU, the master, is said to have said: "To have an environment and not treat it as an object, is Tao." How beautiful! One smiles and sighs, and one is truly grateful, the happiest of feelings. But then difficulties begin to appear. No doubt the first part of the statement – about having an environment – is the thorniest, but let's not discuss that now; let's agree that an environment is an environment in the ordinary sense and that each of us "has" one all the time. What about the second part? If we do not treat the environment as an object, how shall we treat it? As a subject? This is the implication. But how as a subject? A subject in our consciousness only? Or somehow a subject in itself, a subjectivity? I think the Taoist meant the latter. Our environment is intrinsically a subjectivity, perhaps a congeries of subjectivities, or at any rate we should treat it with that possibility in mind. And what is a possibility? A dream, a wish, a fiercely ardent *desiderium*. In a by no means inauthentic sense, what is desired enough, good or evil, exists. To all this I think Denise Levertov would assent.

One day in autumn we were walking through a young woods in the interior of Maine, where Denise then lived. It is upland country. We saw many old stone fences that had marked the boundaries of pastures and meadows a generation or two earlier, even a small graveyard overgrown and untidy. The fields had come up in popple and birch and willow, hardhack and goldenrod and asters. We walked on an abandoned road. I remember a number of such walks, but no longer which walk I am thinking of, nor when it was, nor who were the others with us. The leaves of the young trees were intensely yellow in the October sunlight; they shimmered in the breeze and threw shadows, faint and dappling, on the leaf-strewn ground. It was as Denise has written in her poem about the "goldengrove."

> *Goldengrove*
> *is unleaving all around me; I live*
> *in goldengrove; all day*
> *yesterday and today the air has been filled*
> *with that hesitant downwardness;*
> *the marigolds, the pumpkin, must be sought out*
> *to be seen, the grass*
> *is covered with that cloth, the roads'*
> *margins illuminated.*

I was walking ahead, conversing with someone. I heard Denise exclaim behind me, and when I turned I saw her kneeling, holding a little brown snake close to her face in order to feel its tongue flickering against her cheek. Her expression showed neither enchantment, nor wonder, nor sensual delight, nor the gratification of worldly knowledge, but some feeling perhaps at a point where all these cross one another.

Snakes appear often in Denise's poems. As she says in one of them:

> *No man is so guileless as*
> *the serpent....*

The environment contains then, not an object, but a thing. Let's call it a stone. Denise would say, I think, that the stone is – not that it has or possesses, but that it is – a subjectivity. Notice that this goes further than the insistence of the Objectivists, such as Williams, Oppen, and Zukofsky, upon the inviolable identity of the stone, which the poet may subvert by symbolic imputations only at the risk of hubris. Notice that it goes further even than the Swedenborgians, who declare all things expressive of the Godhead's loving omniscience. Identity and expressiveness are not as much as subjectivity. How does one treat another subjectivity in a nonobjective way, since in some sense, as Sartre maintained, all subjectivities are the Other? How does one know another subjectivity when knowing must be ultra-verbal, as with the stone? These are supremely difficult questions. Usually they have been answered in the formulas of mysticism, but in the present context (namely, nonascetic) these seem to me wrong. Mysticism entails transcendence, which must then be defined in special terms, quite uncustomary terms, if one is to avoid the idea of the environment as the transcended, the subordinated, the objectified. Instead we should speak of art, of esthetics, the way of the spiritual imagination, for this is a transaction among equals, or at least among equivalents – poet and stone. And for me, as I think for Denise too, this is very important. It comes as close as anything can to dispelling my fear of the human species and its lust for dominion. But is art still a mode of forcing, however slight? Is the simplest, loveliest poem flawed by an unappeasable human will to intervene? I suspect it, but I don't know it – although I know that the snake may not have been consentient in its handling – and I don't even feel able to discuss it. Does anyone now?

It was a little brown snake with a pink belly. One sees them all over northern New England. Their name is always "little brown snake," which is sufficient. What I would leave with the reader is the subjectivity of that particular little brown snake, so crucial to Denise's poems, and Denise herself as she knelt, attentive, in the golden glow of the young woods.

Lear

1990.

ONE LINE from *King Lear* that all poets remember comes at the end of the play when Lear, carrying his dead daughter Cordelia in his arms and struggling to take in the fact that he will never know her alive again, says: "Never, never, never, never, never." Is that a good line prosodically, or isn't it? In an early poem of mine, consciously imitating, I wrote:

"O river, river, river, river, river." The effect pleased me then and it still does. But a friend of mine, a poet and playwright, told me recently that Shakespeare's line is bad both poetically and dramatically. And I know that most younger poets today, my students and others, would consider such passionate and lyrical writing inadmissible.

When I was young we not only studied Shakespeare, we read him for pleasure – as we read all the good poets of his time. He seemed in a sense one of us, a poet in our immediate succession, someone from whom we could learn. To young poets today he is utterly remote, I think, as far removed as Virgil or the author of *Beowulf* – of no use at all to their own work. I have noticed that on their applications for admission to the graduate creative writing program at Syracuse, in answer to the question about which older poets have influenced them, students rarely name any poets born before 1940. They never mention Shakespeare. Perhaps they are, collectively speaking, the first poets in English since the seventeenth century who have not taken the greatest poet in English for one of their models.

Probably this isn't their fault. On any semester's list of graduate offerings, at least at Syracuse University, these days you may not find a single course on Shakespeare.

But going back to the line near the end of *King Lear*, contextuality, as the theorists say, is all. This play is an impassioned poem. Extreme diction, reiterative diction, is common throughout. At the beginning of Act I, Scene ii, Edmund says:

> *Why brand they us*
> *With base? with baseness? bastardy? base, base?*

Later in Act I Lear says, striking his own head:

> *O Lear, Lear, Lear!*
> *Beat at this gate that let thy folly in....*

And again:

> *O let me not be mad, not mad, sweet heaven!*

At the beginning of Act IV Gloucester says:

> *But who comes here?*
> *My father, poorly led? World, world, O world!*

which may be the dead-center of the whole play. In Act IV, Scene vi,
Lear says: "Now, now, now, now!" and a few lines later he says: "Then
kill, kill, kill, kill, kill, kill!" – actually one more reiteration than in the
line which disturbs my friend. Indeed, near the very beginning of the
play, when Lear asks Cordelia what she can say about her love for him
that will justify a share in his bequests, the little dialogue occurs from
which the whole action springs:

> *Cor. Nothing, my lord.*
> *Lear. Nothing?*
> *Cor. Nothing.*
> *Lear. Nothing can come from nothing. Speak again.*

Thus the play is framed between five *nothings* and five *nevers*. What
could be more indicative of Shakespeare's purpose in this gaunt but
complex poem? And what could be more revealing of the lyric impulse
behind it? From first to last it is about people who are suffering ex-
tremely. The language does not seem to me excessive.

Nor is lyricism, of whatever kind, a departure from real speech. At
moments of heightened feeling we all use broken syntax and repeat the
same words over and over. And sometimes we sing. Most contempo-
rary poetry, on the other hand, gives us language that is intentionally
false, a language that could never be spoken by anyone, hence, how-
ever plain, a literary language, an artificial language. Lear in his mad-
ness speaks with a naturalness that young poets today can't hear, ap-
parently because their own verbal sensibilities have been warped away
from naturalness by the academic milieu in which they spend most of
their lives.

For that matter Lear, though very hard-driven in most of the play,
especially in the storm scenes, is not as crazy as many readers think.
He is "out of his mind," but not far out. Like others nowadays I have
served a hitch or two in that second great institution of our time, the
psychiatric hospital, where I've heard and seen people whose speech
and behavior were far more violent and irrational than anything Shake-
speare assigned to Lear. What we get from our newspapers every day is

what is excessive. What we observe on the streets of our cities is excessive. But not the language of *Lear*. And in response to my friend's feeling that the line in question is poor drama, though in some sense I am disqualified from answering since during most of my life I have been prevented from even entering a theater, nevertheless in my mind's voice, with which I sound all poetry, I can arrange those five repeated *nevers* in half-a-dozen ways that are easily enunciated and appropriate. It goes without saying that they should not be shouted. When the line is spoken, Lear himself is dying, and his words should be uttered in moans and whispers.

Some critics and dramaturgists, like A.C. Bradley and Harley Granville-Barker, have contended, against the majority, that *Lear* is feasible in dramatic production. In spite of my ignorance I must disagree. The problem is not the violence of the play, not the probability in Act III that the storm will drown out the dialogue, not the constant reference to fiends and monsters, not even the destruction of Gloucester's eyes in full view of the audience – "Out, vile jelly! Where is thy lustre now?" – but rather the fact that these elements of the play and everything else in it are real. Any attempt to push them in the direction of fantasy, stereotype, or the surreal, which would be the tendency of most producers and directors faced by such horrors today, would weaken the play. Influenced as we are in our century by our own kinds of represented horror, Kafka, Brecht, etc., we can hardly think of *Lear* without turning it into a morality, an allegory, a parable, a symbolization or typification of some kind; that is, without giving it what we call "esthetic distance." But the blinded Gloucester says: "World, world, O world!" He means this actual world, our own, from which we have no distance at all. We cannot schematize the events of *Lear* according to psychoanalytical, sociological, mythological, Marxist, or any other abstract conceptions without destroying the validity of these events in the experience of real persons. Shakespeare himself emphasized this by departing so far from the conventions of even the bleakest Greek or Renaissance drama. *Lear* from inception to catastrophe to dénouement, if these terms apply, is entirely downhill; it is a straight-line disaster with no structure beyond the scene-to-scene interweaving of the two stories of Lear and Gloucester. Cordelia could have been saved at the end without weakening the tragedy of the old king, as indeed she was saved in the bowdlerized version of the play that was put out for general consumption in both print and performance for a century or more, and this would have seemed perfectly correct to most playwrights and playgoers of Shakespeare's time. Or Gloucester, Lear's counterpart in the subsidiary plot, could have been saved, which would not have weakened the tragedy either. But in the world, Cordelia and Gloucester are not saved. No one is saved. Immediately after Lear's death Kent says:

> *Vex not his ghost. O, let him pass! He hates him*
> *That would upon the rack of this tough world*
> *Stretch him out longer…,*

and a few lines later implies his own death in the near future. Albany, the goody boy, and Edgar, the juvenile hero, are the only ones left at the end. It is a "tough world" indeed – and how contemporary that sounds! It is a cruel and absurd world. If at the ends of his comedies Shakespeare, following the convention, made everything right with the world, and if in his other tragedies, again following convention, he made everything wrong with the world, at least in those plays the world itself is left, and the suggestion is made that the larger order will endure in its essential rightness. But in *Lear* the world is condemned outright, existence is rejected, reality itself is scorned, and nothing persists anywhere but disorder and mindlessness, the human condition. Thus the play is not only Shakespeare's most realistic but his most existential, in our own sense of the term.

If we except, as we must, the original predicament of the play, Lear's irrational favoritism among his daughters – which in fact is not as unusual as it seems to be in the play's abrupt, foreshortened opening; vanity and folly are not unknown in our time either – then the rest of the play is altogether realistic, and this is the way it must be played if justice is to be done to it. I cannot imagine it on the stage. I cannot imagine a realistic reproduction of Act III, the storm and the dialogue and action of Lear, the Fool, and Poor Tom, on any stage I've ever heard of. Yet only strict realism can sustain our interest in Acts IV and V after the violence and insanity, the tension, the perfection, of Act III. In film it could be done, I think, if the direction were good enough.

But don't we always say that Shakespeare's stage was anything but realistic? Yes, and I think that's wrong. It was a bare stage. It was the minimum of artifice. It was scarcely a stage at all, meaning that the scenes and actions of the plays were contained, either explicitly or implicitly, in the plays themselves, the texts. Shakespeare's "stage" could represent anything. Moreover realism is not simply a matter of props and sets. It is a way of playing, a way of reading. It is an attitude. Everything in *King Lear* points to Shakespeare's conception of the people in the play as real individual human beings, not primarily kings, earls, dukes, peasants, etc. On a bare stage or in a naturalistic film this is what they can be. Anything less, any artifice, distorts them.

Perhaps this in part accounts for the relatively fewer productions of *Lear* than of *Hamlet, Macbeth,* and *Othello,* and for the fact that many people think of *Lear* as an anomaly among the tragedies. It is without doubt the bleakest of them, meaning the most realistic; the others, as I've said, have about them at least some saving reassurance. *Lear* came from the center of Shakespeare's black period, written probably in 1606, after *Hamlet* and *Othello* and before *Macbeth* and *Antony and Cleopatra.* Lear is not a misanthrope like Timon, not a power-seeker like Coriolanus, not a sexualist like Antony, not a paranoid schizophrenic like Hamlet or Othello; he is an old man crushed by reality, destroyed by things as they are. We identify ourselves with Lear in a way that we never do with Hamlet or Othello. Lear comes closer than anyone else in Shakespeare to the sufferer of gratuitous adversity whom we encounter in so much of our contemporary literature; he is the alienated victim par excellence. Yet we should not make the mistake of classifying *King Lear* along with the novels of Céline or the later poems of Robinson Jeffers. Pessimism is not necessarily mean. *Lear* has an amplitude and scope of sympathy, in spite of its bleakness, that makes it, at least in my view, much closer to Malraux's *Man's Fate* or Paul Bowles's *The Sheltering Sky* than it is to the merely sadomasochistic strain in Western literature from de Sade to, say, John Berryman and Vladimir Nabokov. *Lear* is a work that leaves us devastated but still aware of our own humanity. We are not revulsed by the play. We may prefer to see performances of *Hamlet* or *Othello,* which move us to the leniency of pity, but we return as readers to *Lear* rather regularly for its horror and wisdom.

To say nothing of its language. *King Lear* is a poem more than it is a play, as I've said already. It is a lyric poem of great spontaneity, as evidenced by the large number of irregular lines, hexameters and trimeters, scattered through the basic pentameter. It flows. The wise insanity of Lear and Poor Tom on the heath has been imitated thousands of times by other writers in all kinds of contexts, but has never been given to us with the acuteness of Shakespeare's dialogue. Lear's Fool is the best – wittiest and wisest – Fool in all Renaissance literature. And in spite of the violence of action throughout the play we find many beautiful lyric passages, especially toward the end. When Lear, recovered from his madness but still feeble and confused, is captured with Cordelia and sent away under guard, he says to her:

> *Come, let's away to prison.*
> *We two alone will sing like birds i' th' cage.*
> *When thou dost ask me blessing, I'll kneel down*
> *And ask of thee forgiveness. So we'll live,*
> *And pray, and sing, and tell old tales, and laugh*
> *At gilded butterflies, and hear poor rogues*
> *Talk of court news; and we'll talk with them too –*
> *Who loses and who wins; who's in, who's out –*
> *And take upon 's the mystery of things,*
> *As if we were God's spies….*

What marvelous writing. And notice that Lear does not abjure the court and its worldliness, as other Renaissance heroes in similar circumstances certainly would have. His personality remains consistent; no matter how feeble or mad, he is a politician to the end. In these two qualities, a gift for writing and boldness in verisimilitude, Shakespeare's genius predominates over all his Elizabethan and Tudor contemporaries. In fact it is interesting to note that in these two respects he is closest in that time, not to Sidney, Spenser, or Jonson, but to John Donne, as far apart as they are in most others. But the play is a poem in all its aspects, perhaps especially in its unity and integration. This is not simply a matter of Shakespeare's skill in adding the invented story of Gloucester to the medieval legend of King Lear (Leir) and interweaving them so well together. Rather it is the way the whole work moves with such fluidity from beginning to end, as if the constraints of stagecraft and dramatic structure did not exist. It is a work written in the fullness of poetic imagination. It is propelled by the same concentrated vision and intensity of feeling that characterize the best lyric poetry, in other words by the same force and singleness that impel the best of Shakespeare's sonnets. And perhaps this is part of the difficulty of producing it in the theater.

One goes to the breadth of Shakespeare's accomplishment for many different gratifications. No writer is more various. I can't say I prefer *King Lear* to his other works, and I would be suspicious of anyone who did. But I can say that I value *King Lear* especially because, among all the plays, it has the least artifice, and because it tells the truth.

𝒦⁓ . . . .

Emily Dickinson's Unexpectedness

1991.

AMONG THE HUNDREDS of "critical interpretations" of Emily Dickinson's work that have come along in recent decades, most are devoted to finding the origins of her poems in her experience, that is to say, in every foible from masturbatory fantasy to mystical vision to out-and-out schizophrenia. Who was Emily Dickinson, the scholars and critics ask insistently, not who is she. To my mind this latter question is the only one we may ask with any hope of a reasonable answer or for that matter with any regard for ordinary decency. The Dickinson who is important to us, or should be, is the woman in the poems. The woman in history is for genealogists; the shadowy figure in the upper window of the house on Main Street in Amherst is for tourists.

I am interested, more and more as I grow older, in the application of intelligence to the topics which intelligence itself informs us are the most likely to yield useful knowledge; and gossip, no matter how scholarly, is not one of these. Biography is a tawdry art – if an art at all. We have seen many, many awful examples of this in the past couple of decades.

No doubt Dickinson could sound her own verses in ways that made good sense and good poetry, and no doubt she did. Any writer knows this. But for whatever reasons – one can think of several, or many, but again one is not compelled to mention them – she wrote in an eccentric manner with respect to both punctuation and grammar that does not help anyone else to sound them. People often complain that her use of the dash as her primary mark of punctuation was inconsistent. Yet in fact it was the opposite, quite consistent within the poetry, because she used it to signify anything and everything that any mark of punctuation can signify, with the result that it signifies next to nothing at all to readers who have not heard the poems in her voice, i.e., all of us. Similarly with her compacted, twisted, sometimes Latinate syntax, which may or may not have been influenced by the Protestant hymnal and the religious prose of the seventeenth and eighteenth centuries. (You can find the same grammatical constructions commonly in Bradford's *History of Plimmoth Plantation* and in the poetry of Paul Goodman, for whatever this is worth.) Because of these idiosyncratic usages – and because she apparently wrote without expectation that her work would be published – some critics have referred to her poetic language as a kind of shorthand, notes jotted hastily for herself in the language that came most easily to hand. But the woman who is evident in the poems is anything but a stenographer, and the critics of various occult persuasions who suggest that Dickinson was in fact setting down materials "given" to her by agents outside her consciousness are doing the woman in the poems a grave injustice. Whether and to what extent she revised individual poems, she did work at her writing, she worked hard, and the density of her language, in sound, syntax, and sense, will permit no other inference.

This is true of her rhyming as well. One cannot doubt her ability to make rhymes as correct (in Saintsburyan terms) as those of Christina Rossetti or Alfred Tennyson or any other poet of her time. She chose to let her aural imagination range freely, and one result is that her off-rhymes, which vary from close to distant, together with her reliance on well-known rhyming patterns (hymns, ballads, etc.), force the reader to hear rhymes where none exists. The first three stanzas of the poem numbered 410 (in Thomas H. Johnson's edition of the *Complete Poems*) are a good example, though you can find others even more extreme:

> *The first Day's Night had come –*
> *And grateful that a thing*   .
> *So terrible – had been endured –*
> *I told my Soul to sing –*

She said her Strings were snapt –
Her Bow – to Atoms blown –
And so to mend her – gave me work
Until another Morn –

And then – a Day as huge
As Yesterdays in pairs,
Unrolled its horror in my face –
Until it blocked my eyes –

The progression from "thing/sing" through "blown/Morn" to "pairs/ eyes," from full rhyme to off-rhyme to no rhyme, is remarkable in its manipulation of the auditor's rhyming sense, making one "hear" what isn't there in the third stanza, and except for one student in the graduate writing program at Syracuse University, who came by it independently, I know no one else before or after Dickinson who has attempted just this, and I do not forget Yeats, Ransom, Muir, and the thousands influenced by them.

In short, the reader confronting a poem by Emily Dickinson must make a few decisions on the spot, perhaps to a greater degree than with any other premodernist poet in English, though Donne, Herbert, Hopkins, Hardy, etc., come to mind as possible rivals. Obviously Professor Johnson was right in reproducing the texts of the *Complete Poems* as they were found in Dickinson's holographic manuscripts, not as they were "corrected" by her friends after her death; but just as obviously – though it has rarely been suggested – the reader must change these texts in his or her mind to make sense of them. This is especially true of the poems written in the early 1860s, which often do seem to have come tumbling out of the poet's imagination in a kind of careless verbal exuberance, left unrevised. Yet I feel that these poems are anything but careless. They have great power, and part of their power is their strangeness. Here is number 422.

More Life – went out – when He went
Than Ordinary Breath –
Lit with a finer Phosphor –
Requiring in the Quench –

A power of Renowned Cold,
The Climate of the Grave
A Temperature just adequate
So Anthracite, to live –

For some – an Ampler Zero –
A Frost more needle keen
Is necessary, to reduce
The Ethiop within.

Others – extinguish easier –
A Gnat's minutest Fan
Sufficient to obliterate
A Tract of Citizen –

Whose Peat lift – amply vivid –
Ignores the solemn News
That Popocatapel exists
Or Etna's Scarlets, Choose –

There it is, a genuinely great poem, but left hanging on a dash, like so many others. The dashes do not help at all. To my ear they impede and confuse a good reading. The capitalizations don't help either. Some adjectives are capitalized, like "Ordinary," "Renowned" (which surely she pronounced with three syllables), and "Ampler"; others, like "finer," "keen," and "vivid," are not. Some readers are certain that the capitalized pronoun in the first line refers to Christ; but if this is so, then the poem leads radically, not to say irreligiously, away from this first reference as it proceeds. In any event the capitalized "He" cannot necessarily indicate a divine person, as it would in most other Christian poetry. The rest of the punctuation, three commas and a period, is capricious. And how is one to read: "So Anthracite, to live – "? It is utterly extra-grammatical, so that the dash for once really does indicate broken syntax. But how is one to distinguish this dash from the others? Well, the poem is full of surprises, but it is clear. What the reader must do, I believe, is reduce the poem to something like the following more conventional arrangement, which is perfectly legitimate provided that he or she then returns to reading the poem as Dickinson wrote it. A sufficiently adroit and experienced reader will perform these two operations so nearly at the same time that they are effectually simultaneous.

> *More life went out when he went*
> *Than ordinary breath,*
> *Lit with a finer phosphor,*
> *Requiring in the quench*
>
> *A power of renownëd cold,*
> *The climate of the grave,*
> *A temperature just adequate*
> *So anthracite may live.*
>
> *For some an ampler zero,*
> *A frost more needle keen,*
> *Is necessary to reduce*
> *The Ethiop within.*
>
> *Others extinguish easier,*
> *A gnat's minutest fan*
> *Sufficient to obliterate*
> *A tract of citizen,*
>
> *Whose lift[ed] peat, amply vivid,*
> *Ignores the solemn news*
> *That Popocatapel exists*
> *Or Etna's scarlets Choose!*

I use an exclamation point after the last word because the ending is such an astonishing, commanding leap out of the syntax, point of view, and tone of the rest of the poem. At first it seems to say that we must choose between Etna and Popocatape(t)l, which is not much of a choice (though we can read possible cultural allusions into it if we want to); in effect we are thrown with some violence back into the body of the poem, forced to reread and understand, e.g., that the "some" who require "an Ampler Zero" are to be identified with the intentionally camouflaged "He" of the first line, as differentiated from the

"Others" who may be extinguished by the wind from a gnat's wing. Is the poem saying that some people die out of this world harder than others because they love – or esteem or comprehend – it better, and that we are with the poet in having the capacity, at least theoretically, to choose which kind of person we shall be? Yes, this is part of it. But whose is the power of "Renowned Cold," whose is the "Gnat's minutest Fan" that obliterates – stark verb! – the "Tract of Citizen"? (The poem was written during the Civil War when "tracts" of military graves became common.) Is it God's? Is the woman in the poem capable of throwing dust in our eyes with that capitalized "He" in the first line and then reversing our expectations, leading us to blasphemy, and hiding the whole maneuver beneath her "carelessness"? I believe this is the poet Dickinson's sensibility in a nutshell.

Why did she do it? What reader was she anticipating? Only herself? These are not biographical issues. If we could answer such questions we'd go a long way toward a better understanding not only of her poetry but all poetry. But our answers can be only conjectural.

The reduction of the poem to conventional syntax and punctuation spoils it and leaves us with a relatively insipid piece of work, though one that most of us would be glad to have written. For instance, the change from "He" to "he" in the first line confuses the rhythm, obscuring the abruptly declining accentuation of the last two syllables, which is essential to the sound/sense of the poem. This makes us see that part of Dickinson's power, though a secondary part, really is her quirkiness. And what a fine poem it is. No careless mind came up with "Ampler Zero," "A Tract of Citizen," or the rhymes in the first and fourth stanzas. This is what we mean when we talk about poetic genius, or at least what we ought to mean. Even more extraordinary is the way such simple words as "amply vivid" in the last stanza are lifted into brilliance – in this case brilliant horror – by the strangeness of "Peat lift" just before them, and the way this in turn sets up the extreme irony of another commonplace word, "solemn," in the next line. We know what "Peat lift" means; it cannot mean anything but burial (or, even more horrifying, exhumation); and yet it means much more. The commonness of peat suggests not only the commonness of huge graveyards but perhaps the ancient, anonymous graves of anthropological "digs" in the peat bogs of Europe. Moreover "Peat" picks up and contrasts to

"Anthracite" in the second stanza, since both are fossil fuels, one distinctly inferior to the other. Notice the subtlety of "needle keen," which brings to mind not only the sewing needles of nineteenth-century housewives but the frozen needles, almost equally sharp, of spruce and fir in a New England winter. The force of concentration in this one poem is such that we would not believe it if we didn't see it before our eyes. Nor can we analyze it sufficiently. One could say that fire is what holds this poem together from "Phosphor" to "Etna's Scarlets," though the word itself is never used. Or one could say just as well that blackness holds it together (granting the unintended misfortune of "Ethiop" in our regenerated consciences), though black is never mentioned. What is happening is simply too numerous to be seized in any single reading. And as far as I know this poem has never been much considered by scholars and critics.

Emily Dickinson, whoever she was, is the most significant woman in Western literature after Sappho. I don't mean she is "greater" than Jane Austen or Simone de Beauvoir. Who knows about greater? Nor do I mean to emphasize gender, which usually seems so obvious that it is not worth talking about in literary terms. (Politics is another matter.) But Dickinson is the only poet in our language, as Sappho and Lady Murasaki may be the only ones in other languages, or at least in what we call major languages, who forces us, actually coerces us – though this could not have been her objective – to think and imagine in feminine modes, which she accomplishes through the nearly absolute power of her artistic sensibility. She arouses in us an almost extravagantly heightened consciousness of metaphysical issues and existential emotions, such as we associate with only the supreme intelligences of our species. She convokes our being, so to speak, and she does it as a woman. I am not fool enough to try to define that womanness, but I am confident all willing readers can recognize it.

Who the "He" in the first line of her poem may be is unimportant. She says everything about him that needs to be said for her purpose. In a similar sense the problems of Miss Dickinson of Main Street, whether she was afflicted by chronic agoraphobia, religious hysteria, sexual frustration, or none of these, are unimportant. That is, we are affected by Miss Dickinson in the same way and to the same degree that we are affected by Miss Farquhar, the great beauty of the other side of town, who died painfully at the age of nineteen from scrofula and shingles. The poet Sappho exists only in her poems. Likewise the poet Dickinson.

Here is poem number 443, which I've not seen much commented on either:

I tie my Hat – I crease my Shawl –
Life's little duties do – precisely –
As the very least
Were infinite – to me –

I put new Blossoms in the Glass –
And throw the old – away –
I push a petal from my Gown
That anchored there – I weigh
The time 'twill be till six o'clock
I have so much to do –
And yet – Existence – some way back –
Stopped – struck – my ticking – through –
We cannot put Ourself away
As a completed Man
Or Woman – When the errand's done
We come to Flesh – upon –
There may be – Miles on Miles of Nought –
Of Action – sicker far –
To stimulate – is stinging work –
To cover what we are
From Science – and from Surgery –
Too Telescopic Eyes
To bear on us unshaded –
For their – sake – not for Ours –
'Twould start them –
We – could tremble –
But since we got a Bomb –
And held it in our Bosom –
Nay – Hold it – it is calm –

> *Therefore – we do life's labor –*
> *Though life's Reward – be done –*
> *With scrupulous exactness –*
> *To hold our Senses – on –*

Another quirky poem that leads us a long way from its opening. The rhythm is more jog-trot than in the other poem I've quoted, and the imagery is less exotic. In some ways it is a rather ordinary poem about ordinary actions and feelings, and I'm sure this was intentional. But it comes from the same period of acute poetic endeavor. Like the other poems it moves from the commonplace to the expressly personal and original, the "Telescopic Eyes" and the "Bomb": what could be more compelling? And notice the precision throughout, from the emphatic "do" in the second line to the "stinging work" in the middle and then to the tiny, momentous "on" at the very end. This poet is a woman immersed in womanly concerns, but at the same time left, by the power of life confronting spirituality and death, in a condition of undiluted exigency. This is rare enough in our frightened and evasive species; to find it combined with eloquence, with a verbal resourcefulness beyond our wildest dreams, is unexpected, unexpectable. Facing this, the critical mind is reduced to stammering, which is what I am doing here.

Isn't it a penetrating poem? One is tempted to call it free, because it moves so directly toward its object. But then one notices all the constraints, and one is tempted to call it artifice. The fact is that it shoots between these opposites like an arrow splitting a leaf, and between many other pairs of opposites too.

Finally, a poem written about a decade later, number 1259:

> *A Wind that rose*
> *Though not a Leaf*
> *In any Forest stirred*
> *But with itself did cold engage*
> *Beyond the Realm of Bird –*
> *A Wind that woke a lone Delight*
> *Like Separation's Swell*
> *Restored in Arctic Confidence*
> *To the Invisible –*

The cadence has become calmer, the language more spare but more fluent and spontaneous too, without any syntactical resolution. (Surely she is the first poet in English to use the uncompleted participial phrase as a comprehensive verbal gesture, and to do it repeatedly.) The movement of these lines embodies the movement of existence as simply and purely as words can. Was Camus the one who spoke of the "dark wind" always blowing toward us from out of the future? I believe so. The coinciding of Moment and Eternity, Dickinson's invisible cold wind that does not stir the leaves. Have the spinster from Amherst and the workman from Algiers anything in common? Almost everything, I'd say. The loneliness of a village room and the loneliness of the African desert are not much different. The artist knows that this isolation is madness (see poem 410), and that madness is the same as ultimate insight, which inevitably is of the limits of insight. Hence the Greeks' anthropomorphizing condescension to their gods. And Tertullian's to his? This is the absurdum. It is a glory in the mind, a gentle glory pervaded by sorrow, but beyond hope and despair, far beyond ego; it is the person become impersonality, the nobody to whom the finest genius assimilates itself. How different from the procedures of ordinary fine poets! What the mind makes, even in ecstasy, in fury, is always implicated in nonbeing, the void of God, call it what you will; and thus when Dickinson writes in dialect – poem 426, for instance, in which her writerly ear for speech-sounds is working beautifully – she does so partly to humanize her mythos, but more largely to humor, to placate, her ignorance, which is my ignorance too. And that is as far as I can go in responding to her poems.

It is far enough. It is never far enough.

彡 ·

Essays for Wendell

1992. I was invited to contribute an essay to a festschrift for my friend Wendell Berry, but what came out when I sat down to write was verse.

> I write to you, brother, to tell you
> that the young sycamore,
> princely as a yearling elk,

is dying. The bedrock of this place
is too near the surface, I think;
the tree hasn't enough root-space.
Which is an observation, at best a reason.
But this is June, my soul is sore
to study such gracefulness, so well started,
sturdy and well limbed, thirty feet high,
which now in the spring season
shows bare twigs and withered leaves.
How can I not feel downhearted
to watch the young tree die?

*   *   *

Brother, our family is pretty large,
you might say enormous,
and we don't speak to most of them,
and they don't speak to us.

*   *   *

Two-thirds of my barn
fell down long ago,
long before it was mine,
collapsed, the rusty
roof-metal now flattened
on the ground. The loose loft door
in the remaining third
sobs in the wind.
The barn looks perfectly
natural among the cedars
in the tall grass where
flowers grow – dame's rocket,
stitchwort, and buttercups.

*   *   *

And yesterday my wife found

at the edge of our woods the flower
of the May apple, suddenly there
on the ground.

Two big leaves, intricately cut;
beneath them the six-petaled
delicate white blossom shut
from the sun.

We could not recall
having seen it before, either of us.
It seems the May apple
often does not achieve flower hereabouts.
Or had we been too dull?

In flowers and all its natural
parts the world has kept
delight. Last night when we went
to our rest, we clasped one another
against insomnia, and slept.

I woke once, near dawn,
and her arm still held me.

This morning I saw – and marked well
on the windowsill –
a jumping spider. Such
a pretty thing.
Its two front eyes touch
and are as blue
as my wife's lapis ring.

*   *   *

One cannot act well or beneficently in a
place until one has understood its nature,
precedent to human intrusion. Thus, in a
country originally forested, the farmer must

study the forest, because, to be healthy, the
field must be an analogue of the forest; in
analogy its nature is remembered.

On its steep hillside your farm once, eons ago,
in nature's fierce competition came to stasis.
Trees, immense trees for your region, held
the slope against the water's continual surge
that would carry away the brown dirt to the sea.
The river down below ran clear. For even
early woodland hepaticas can hold
a grain or two of soil in the freshening season.
You've contemplated this a many a time
in your walking and working – I know because
elsewhere I have too – and have found in it
propriety and the importance of propriety
in farming and in poetry. Then of course
you found decadence when the woods were cut -
those bleeding trees – and corn and tobacco
were planted on the hill. Your mythic river
runs muddy still, muddy and bitter. No
propriety in that. Yet your fields now
after extraordinary labor – brother,
I do not know how you can have done so
much – and after extraordinary thought
and study are secure, right with the world,
proper, and full of meaning, which is love
in action, as your poems are. And what
a blessing this has become for us all.

*   *   *

My place is on a hillside too, and looks
over the Stockbridge Valley to the opposing
hill ten miles distant, a remarkably
green and fertile American intervale.
In winter when my trees are bare I see
twelve working farms, their multi-tinted

meadows and pastures, woodlots and gravel-pits,
through the picture window next to my
computer. Leave out the army, leave out
all such aberrations, this is by my count
my seventeenth place in my life; I live here
with my fourth wife, who yesterday gave me
a watch that tells the time in seconds, the day
of the week, the date and month, and I can time
a horse race with it too – yet I've been called
a "farmer poet." I'm not. Alienation
has been my life, even though I've spent
most of it living and working on the land.
Now I'm too old. I write blank verse (sometimes)
not from principle but because I like it –
the privilege of a crank. I trim my fruit trees
and vines, I tend my flowers, mow my lawn,
my hayfield is sown to Panama grass,
timothy, and alfalfa, my woods are
grown-over pasture with too many thorntrees
but some friendly ash and maple on the upper
side, basswood, cherry, hornbeam, locust.
Now the orioles in the dooryard have fledged
two offspring, and vetch and daisies and hawkweed
are in the meadow. Summer is here. I can't
do much to help it, but, brother, I talk with it,
and what we mostly talk about is you.

*   *   *   **

You wrote: "The god I have always expected
to appear at the woods' edge, beckoning,
I have always expected to be
a great relisher of this world, its good
grown immortal in his mind." That
was in Farming: A Handbook, *1970. And how*
wonderfully the idea works, your expectation,
like your analogy, permitting many
possibilities. I have expected that god too,

and I'm still expecting him, the joy
of the world like Pan or Sasquatch
risen among the flowers or in the pristine
winter morning with new snow on the mountain.
To you, as I know from more recent poems,
he has appeared. What a striking, original
event in any world but especially ours.
I am astonied, as they used to say, I am glad.
For you, he is. And I think for you he is also
a source of authority, what you wanted
all along, to make the system go. For me
the system goes by itself – not very well.
Last year a big asteroid missed us by only
a few million miles. Yet in marriage
the orioles possess, at least for this season,
what I would call "perfect authority," such
as one can know it objectively, with their two
fledglings, carnelian in the appletree.
Now the melilot has bloomed near the barn,
a fountain of feathery yellow, and its authority
has brought it all the way here from Transylvania.
As Edmund Husserl said, values are
the "objectivities of practice," properly classed
under the formal heading of "something in general."
Something. An existent. An objectivity of practice.
And an authority too, even from broken marriages.
From the orioles and the melilot one moves
among formal headings, searching, searching.
I am expecting the god any minute, somewhere
near the barn. I like your faith, brother, and your
authority, so beautiful and important in this world.

*   *   *

One comes to a new place
with marriage in mind,
a new light on the belovèd face,
which one had expected to find.

* * *

"What is left is what is" –
a few more years maybe
(one wants to finish at least
some of what one began),
a few moments of the fizz
of dawn in the east
before I go to bed,
a few more nights to see
my way in the dark. A man
like me likes to describe
things, who knows why? –
how the sunset's soft red
lights the orange lilies by
the dooryard, their coarse brocade
as if under a pink film
of pure imagination laid
upon them – a consequence
none could have foreseen
though it can overwhelm
anyone. And once a tribe
of ancients did see it. How
they responded I don't
know, except in their sense
they knew it, as I do now.
Flowers in the light mean
beautiful changes. How still
are the leaves in the trees.
How quiet are valley and hill.
It is getting dark. The ways
of the night are memory.
We are very remote here.
But in your Kentucky days
and in spirit you are near.

* * *

Maybe the sycamore
will make it after all.
Its crown is thickening;
I think more dark than light
might show in a photograph.
And if it dies, come fall
it will make a modest store
of heat for this heteroclite –
about a cord and a half.

🖛 . . . .

James Laughlin

The Introduction to *The Collected Poems of James Laughlin*, 1994.

JAMES LAUGHLIN invented his way of writing poems when he was still an undergraduate at Harvard. But it didn't come out of the blue. We know that William Carlos Williams, who was Laughlin's friend and whose poems were among the first publications of Laughlin's New Directions publishing company, established in Cambridge in 1936, often composed his poems on a typewriter, and we have reason to think that in part Williams' metric was determined by the look of the typewritten poem on the page. He didn't like his line-endings jagged. So when he came to the place where his line more or less matched up with the lines above it he hit the carriage return and went on to the next one. Sometimes he even hyphenated an end word and ran the second half over to the beginning of the next line. Well, prosodists have talked for years about enjambment in WCW's poems, as if he had been imitating Gerard Manley Hopkins or somebody like that, and I don't mean to say that the arrangement of lines and syntax in a poem by Williams has no poetic value, which would be ridiculous. But Williams was delighted by visuality too, by paintings, by the appearances of this world, and I suspect he wanted his poems to look right, to show movement, balance, sturdiness, etc., in their printed representations and moreover to be unmistakably distinct from the sprawling effusions of the vers-librists – Amy Lowell and that crowd – who were so conspicuous in American writing of the teens and twenties.

Williams never systematized his feelings about prosody, though from time to time he tried to defend them, usually not very well. For Laughlin, however, system was necessary. He decided he would compose on the typewriter and that each line of a poem would deviate in length no more than two typewritten spaces either way from the length of the first line. In effect the shape and line-structure of each poem would depend on the length of the beginning line, written more or less at random. At first this seems the height of artificiality. For one thing, before the advent of electronic typewriters, all typewritten characters had the same width, unlike the variable width of characters in printing type. Consequently a poem which lined up perfectly on the typewritten page according to Laughlin's metric would lose its shape when set in type by a printer, and the reader would never recognize Laughlin's prosodic accomplishment. For another, has any formal device anywhere in literature ever been so inflexible, so difficult? These are objections that have been raised by many. But I want to argue strenuously against them, against the idea that the technical and structural elements of poetry are artificial or somehow external to poetic purpose. On the contrary they are *intrinsic* to the poem. Even a metric as arbitrary as Laughlin's when considered schematically, i.e. abstractly, like the lettered rhyming pattern of a sonnet, becomes necessary and inevitable when embodied in the concrete poem; without it the poem could not exist. All poets in all times, writing in all languages and traditions, even poets of our time who write in free forms (since their freedom rapidly becomes conventional), have used such components of form, not as impediments – why in the world would they want to do that? – not even as compositional aids, but as the very source from which expressive language, via the imagination, derives.

Laughlin would deny the charge of artificiality categorically. In the poem "Technical Notes" he begins:

> *Catullus is my master and I mix*
> *a little acid and a bit of honey*
> *   in his bowl love*
>
> *is my subject…*

and he continues:

I prefer

to build with plain brown bricks
of common talk American talk then
set 1 Roman stone

among them for a key I know Ca-
tullus knew a poem is like a blow
an impact strik-

ing where you least expect this I
believe and yet with me a poem
is finally just
a natural thing.

Which was the title of his first book, *Some Natural Things* (1945). Yet this poem, though containing an uncharacteristic short line in each stanza, is written in Laughlin's typewriter metric and is a remarkably succinct explanation – and illustration – of what he has aimed for. It isn't easy. Most natural things aren't.

At any rate Laughlin, who was trained in the classics and was at the same time steadfastly attached to *avant-garde* writing, has held to his own way of writing for many years, at least fifty-five altogether. A lifetime. And what a marvel this new collected edition is! As he progressed Laughlin began to allow a three-space deviation from the first line in some of his poems, occasionally more than that. And he did poems in other styles too, long-line poems and prose poems. His typewriter prosody was never a *must*. Yet he has stuck with it for by far the larger part of his work, and has enlivened and varied it in many ways: by using decidedly colloquial diction interlaced with occasional elegant phrasings, by running many different syntactical and rhetorical arrangements across his strict line structures, by adopting into his own style words and idioms, especially those taken from classical models, that would be called poeticisms by most other contemporary writers, by infusing his poems with very original observations and with strong comic, ironic, and erotic feeling as well as with intimations of political, social, and cultural criticism. Which brings us to the substance of his poems.

If Williams was the primary influence on Laughlin's metric, Ezra Pound was his most congenial tutor in matters of cultural affinity. Laughlin has told how Dudley Fitts at Choate loaned him books and gave him guidance, with the result that Laughlin became a lifelong reader of the classics. "Catullus started with Fitts," he has said. At the same time Fitts put Laughlin onto important contemporary poets, including E. E. Cummings, whose poems were full of typewritten effects that possibly influenced the young student and whose erotic mode without doubt did influence the attitudinal feasibilities of Laughlin's mature work. At Harvard Laughlin continued his studies, then took a year off to enter the "Ezuversity," that is, he lived in Rapallo and saw Pound often, talked with him (or mostly listened), took Pound's advice about what to read and how to read it. He became acquainted with modern European languages. What an extraordinary educational boost for a young man! Politics was another matter, however. Laughlin has at times professed an interest in Social Credit, as have many others who understand monetary issue – for my part socialized credit, if cooperatively administered, seems a fine remedy for our crisis in banking today and the general economic iniquity – but Laughlin never caught Pound's ranting style of argument. Even in 1936, Laughlin has said, he detected signs of Pound's disabling paranoia and obsessive behavior.

What Laughlin got from Pound, I think, was something of the grand spirit of the older poet's vision of a multicultural, polylingual, fundamentally agrarian, craftsmanly, and austerely mercantile civilization, held together by history, by the secular order of justice, and by the spiritual order of the natural world. Beyond this he got a sense of the pleasure, the constructive gratification, to be found in playing with language. No other American poet I know has come as close as Laughlin to using language as Pound did in the *Cantos*. Yet the styles of the two poets are completely different, almost at odds with one another. Pound went at language in grim seriousness, he learned smatterings of Chinese, Egyptian, and other faraway languages; he relied tenaciously on tags from Greek and Latin as mementos of consolidated meaning, what he called glyphs; he interspersed his poems with passages in modern European languages, including not just French, Italian, and German, but Portuguese, Slavic bits, and of course La langue d'oc, or more properly Lo lenga d'òc, as linguists refer to it today. (In Pound's time and earlier the language was called, inaccurately, Provençal.)

Laughlin's practice, in contrast to Pound's, has been lighter, more comic and ironic, and in fact, though the forcefulness of Pound's language-joining cannot be denied, Laughlin has integrated different languages more closely than Pound did. Here is part of one of my favorites, "In Another Country":

Giacomino!

*she called vieni qua splashing her
arms in the clear green water vieni
subito and so I followed her swim-
ming around a point of rock to the*

*next cove vieni qua non hai paura
and she slipped like an eel beneath
the surface down through the sunken
entrance to a hidden grotto where*

*the light was soft and green on fine-
grained sand é bello no? here we can
be together by ourselves nobody else
has ever been here with me it's my se-*

*cret place here kiss me here I found
it when I was a little girl now touch
me here é strano questa luce com' un
altro mondo so strange this light am*

*I all green? it's like another world
does that feel good? don't be afraid
siamo incantati we're enchanted in
another world O Giacomino Giacomino*

*sai tu amore come lui è bello? com' è
carino sai quanto tu mi dai piacere?
sai come lei ti vuol' bene? lie still
non andare via just lie still lie still.*

How poignantly, excitingly this evokes the sense of a love affair in a for-
eign country! And part of the effect comes from the interfusion of lan-
guages, which is no impediment to most readers. I've never studied
Italian, but I can take in the Italian passages in this poem easily, even
the ones not translated in the poem itself, and if I am unable to pro-
nounce them correctly I can still say them in a way that is pleasing to
me. Has any poet other than Laughlin done this as well? The closest is
Hemingway in some of his stories, or Joyce in parts of his monumental
fictions, but I think Laughlin does it better, more completely, and less
laboriously – that is, more naturally.

Then there are the comic poems in ski-German, a language half-
Austrian and half-American, all mixed together, which Laughlin
picked up during his many skiing expeditions in the Alps. (He was a
fine skier and wrote articles for ski magazines.) Funny, ironic, touching
poems. No one has a better understanding of the American in Europe,
the sense of mingled inferiority, arrogance, confusion, relish, and time-
sorrow that all of us feel over there.

But his French poems are the most varied and numerous of Laugh-
lin's experiments with other languages, and are among my favorites of
all his work. Some are in correct French, touching or ironic love
poems, others are in Americanized French, some play with French
argot and double entendre. Myself, I hear most of them as decidedly
Americanized, perhaps because I've heard Laughlin speak French and
that's the way he speaks it; I can understand him easily though I have
trouble with native Francophones. People who don't know French at
all will no doubt find these poems difficult and I suspect some who
know French well may find them ill-advised or even offensive. But
Laughlin wasn't writing for either group; rather his aim originally was
for the thousands of us who know enough French to understand, say,
two-thirds of *Paris Soir*. Now for this collected edition he has made for
the first time American translations – trots really – in the hope that
these will assist readers whose French is less than mediocre or doesn't
exist at all.

But the important, the imperative thing to understand about these
poems is that he wrote them to say what can't be said otherwise. I
don't mean ideas or images; these may be conveyed in any adequate
language. I mean feelings, the unparaphrasable minutiae of feelings. In
poetic theory recently, languages have been held to be codes intrinsi-

cally identifiable with particular classes and cultures. Then how is a poet to get outside the codes, beyond arbitrariness, free from the social and political stereotypes? One way is by working on the edges of the codes, at the point where codes intersect. This is what Laughlin has done. In his French poems he gives us nuances of feeling and attitude, chiefly comic and ironic and almost always erotic, that aren't accessible in any other language. The result is poetry lighter and generally more ingratiating than Pound's, for instance, poetry I like very much indeed.

In effect Laughlin has created his own code. It is French of a kind, but upon it he has imposed his own rhythm, syntax, and intonation. Readers in France might say it is flatter than real French. But Laughlin, knowing his own precise cultural location, would answer, okay, but it's also more *natural*. Of course it has references outward to thousands of cultural antecedents, all languages do, but it remains self-bonded and infrangible. And incidentally what it registers are not simply nuances of feeling but touches of intonational and prosodic finesse unavailable anywhere else. Many of these poems seem to me remarkably beautiful. Try this one.

LA LANGUE ENFANTINE

Quand elle dort et s'éveille
pour un instant (comme si elle

était troublée par un rêve) elle
parle dans un langue enfantine

une langue très douce et presque
imperceptible qui est difficile

à comprendre parfois c'est un
discours amoureux racontant des

choses qu'elle hésite à dire en
plein jour j'attends avec im-

patience cette langue enfantine
et ses petites histoires tendre.

Easy enough to read if you have any French at all, but here is Laughlin's translation.

THE INFANTILE LANGUAGE

When she's asleep and wakes for a moment
as if she were troubled by a dream
she speaks in an infantile language
a language that's soft
and almost inaudible, difficult to understand
sometimes it's an amorous story
telling things she'd be reluctant to say by day
I wait with impatience for this infantile speech
with its tender little tales.

It's clear right off that Laughlin is unable to translate his poem any better than anyone else would. *Douce* means much more than *soft,* if only because it's the word one uses to a French child who's being too loud-mouthed: "Douce, douce, chéri." And of course he has had to abandon the couplets and the metrical scheme. But would a gifted French translator be able to put it into French either? I'm not a linguist, but for me the straightforward Americanized syntax takes it out of French almost entirely. And this cultural doubleness is what gives the original poem its edge. For isn't it clear in Laughlin's French that the poem is, however light, a poem of amorous jealousy, that these "petites histoires tendres" are much more than "tender little tales"? The sexuality of the poem is what Laughlin's Americanized French conveys but the translation does not. And I suspect that a translation into full literary French would have to be, not necessarily more explicit, but more heavily couched in innuendo to capture this same quality.

Here is another I particularly like.

LA LUCIOLE

Je te vois voltigeante dans la
nuit et je te poursuis pour t'at-

traper tu es presqu'insaississable
mais à la fin je te tiens mais

quand j'ouvre la main tu n'es
pas là tu m'as échappé de nou-

veau qu'est-ce que tu chasses
c'est clair que ce n'est pas

moi je plains la vélocité de
tes alternances affectives

mais je ne sais pas si je veux
te faire changer car si tu é-

tais toujours prévisible serais
tu rasante comme les autres?

And the translation:

THE FIREFLY

I see you flashing in the night and try to catch you
But it's almost impossible to seize you
When I open my hand you're not there, you've escaped me again
What are you hunting for?
It's clear that it's not me
I begrudge the speed of your changes of affection
But I don't think I'd want to change you
If you were always predictable
Might you not become as boring as the others?

Here the big difference between the original poem and the translation hinges on *rasante* in the last line. The translation lays all onus of disaffection on the "firefly," but *rasante* means something like "sating" or "surfeiting," not just "boring," which when you think about it lays equal onus on the one who is, or might be, sated, the one who is doing the chasing. Still, this is a difference between pure French and pure English. The spirit or dharma of the poem comes from the intersection of codes, the language neither French nor English. Would any French poem begin with the two straight declarative statements of Laughlin's poem? Immediately the tone of gentle but edgy sexual jealousy makes itself heard. When I first saw this poem in manuscript three or four years ago, I read it with perfect understanding – all except the title. After I had read the text I had to go to my Larousse to find out what *luciole* means. I had guessed it must be something like "firefly," but the topic of the poem is so plainly a young foxy French woman teasing the speaker, who is unmistakably American, that the simile becomes extraneous. And notice the elegance of "tu es presqu'insaississable / mais à la fin je te tiens...." This is very good lyric writing indeed.

Is it that Laughlin's Americanized French sounds a little archaic too? These poems remind me more of something from Auvergne in the old language, descended perhaps through the "Roman de la Rose," parts of Villon, and Du Bellay, than of anything in contemporary French. I think Laughlin would not be displeased by this.

And of course Laughlin's poems are unpunctuated because medieval manuscripts were unpunctuated too.

Most of Laughlin's French poems are love poems, and so are most of his others. The point has been made that we are deficient in love poems. It's true. You can go through hundreds of books and magazines of serious writing from the past ten or fifteen years and you'll find very few. Why? I don't know, though I'm sure the answer would comprise many complicated factors. But after teaching graduate workshops for ten years I do believe the young people's failure to write poems to their boyfriends and girlfriends is part of the general demoralization caused by the inanity of our popular culture today and the outrage of our political and economic culture. Because young people don't write about much of anything else either, and that's a fact. They have no overriding passion, beyond perhaps an anger too diffuse to be expressed. I'm not surprised that the best love poetry by young people I've read lately has been by Black, Latino, Native American, Asian, and lesbian and gay poets. Well, Laughlin is of the old school. His love poems are not angry, not beset by any problems that weren't problems for Catullus, Propertius, and Arnaut as well. The freshness of Laughlin's poems, the part that is not old school, comes, first, from their settings in our own time, the hotels of London and Paris, the restaurants of New York and San Francisco, etc., the undifferentiated inevitable contemporaneity of our own minds; second, from their diction, which is our own natural spoken language minus the jargon; and third, from their authenticity. Without going into Laughlin's personal life, one can say that his love poems are authentic. They were written to or about particular women. Were these women loved in the way of eros or in the way of agape? It is a question people ask. But to my mind, though the terms are classical the distinction between them is decidedly post-classical, not to say churchly and finical. Laughlin's poems, in which you find sexiness but not much sex, are written in the lovely integrated paganism that Christianity comes round to at last in pursuing its own loving ends, and are conceived with this whole evolution in mind.

TO LOVE IS TO HOLD DEAR

to hold the hand if it is
given   or to hold only a

finger if the hand is clo-
sed   to hold all that is

dear be it near or far be
it seen or heard   and if

it be in the unseen that
too is ever close & dear.

Such stunning lyricism within the rigorous metric of counted em picas. One could do a prosodic analysis of this poem that would go on and on and would be rewarding down to the last trembling of the oscillograph.

I SAW HER FIRST

on the red-on-black amphora
in the museum at Delphi and

knew at once she was Helio-
dora the girl in Meleager's

poem with her hair in a fil-
let and her tiny feet & her

breasts like white roses then
thirty years later we were to-

gether in a faded room in that
small hotel in the rue de la

Harpe she spoke French of
course and at first she was

shy but then she was tenderly
passionate yes it was Helio-

dora will she ever come back
to me might she even come to

stay I make my prayer to the
Gods that Heliodora return.

Many of Laughlin's love poems use classical names and references –
never in pedantry but rather for the resonances, the almost tactile
warmheartedness, of human eroticism from the beginning. And I can't
resist quoting another, which is more than a love poem; it is a com-
pressed philosophy of morals and esthetics.

CARITAS PERFECTA

absolute love was defined by
the Scholastics and Pascal was

not bad on the subject either
but for me it's a personal &

concrete matter that has to
do with you & the way you are

with me which is all of it &
as absolute as anything can be.

You must turn, however, to the poems themselves as they fold against one another in the leaves of this book. Many of them, the love poems and others, may seem rather alike at first, yet each is written with a subtly different focus, a perceivably special gleam of feeling. They support one another, making together a context stronger than the mere linearity of a series. One must gather them into one's reverie collectively, like the tiles of a mosaic.

James Laughlin was born in 1914 in Pittsburgh into the family which had a founding interest in the Jones & Laughlin Steel Corporation. But he left Pittsburgh at an early age – in effect when he went to Choate School in Connecticut at the age of fourteen – and later divested himself of whatever holdings he had in the steel business and, one gathers, of much – but not all; he has always held the family name in good esteem – of the familial and class loyalties he had as a boy. Many of his poems about his childhood are so ironic that they almost, though never quite, break through into asserted bitterness. In "Easter in Pittsburgh," for instance, he refers to "the strike," when he and his brother were sent "out to the farm with mother" for a week for their own protection, and though I'm not sure which strike this was – from the time of the great Homestead strike against Carnegie in 1892 until well into the 1930s strikes by steelworkers in Pittsburgh were common – the attitude of the poet toward his family's involvement in the oppression of the workers is unmistakable. And many other poems, a great many, reflect a similar cast of mind. Laughlin was not a child of the 1960s, however. His rebellion consisted of becoming a businessman on his own, as in the development of the ski resort at Alta, Utah, which has been a huge success. His rebellion consisted of becoming a writer, a friend of writers – Gertrude Stein, for instance, for whom he worked as chauffeur and general aide in the summer of 1934 – and the publisher of many writers whose works his family and their associates would have found shocking, enigmatic, and probably despicable. It consisted of an invariable and mostly serene independence, which led him, for instance, into competitive skiing at an early age and a bad crash and back injury on the Sherburne Trail on lower Mount Washington (yet he continued skiing enthusiastically and many, many years later taught me the rudiments of cross-country skiing in the Litchfield Hills of Connecticut); into a desire to travel in India and Burma in the early 1950s and to study the literary and spiritual traditions of those countries, an interest which shows up in many poems; and into a desire for romantic, practically chivalrous, adventures in practically every corner of the world. An exotic then? A playboy? A prodigy? Yes, something of all these; but a hard-working, ordinary guy as well. At New Directions he has done everything: published, edited, designed and produced, written ad copy and blurbage, peddled books to the stores, and answered his own phone. Until recently he calculated the royalties himself, and he still sends out handwritten royalty checks against his personal bank account. At his home in Connecticut, where he lives in virtual retirement, he receives and reads copies of outgoing mail from the New York office, and his decisions on new undertakings are final.

I wonder how many people would be surprised to learn that New Directions, which has published Stein, Pound, Williams, Henry Miller, Rexroth, Patchen, Oppen, the surrealists and lettrists and language poets, has also published Conrad Aiken, Yvor Winters, Mark Van Doren, John Crowe Ransom, and Robert Penn Warren. In connection with his proprietorship of New Directions, Laughlin once wrote: "... for better or worse, there has been no editorial pattern beyond the publisher's inclinations, his personal response to the manuscripts which came his way." Thus an additional confirmation of independence.

Incidentally, some years back when I wrote that Laughlin had hurt himself when skiing down Mount Washington as fast as he could, he corrected me. "It was the Sherburne Trail near the bottom of the mountain," he said. In other words Laughlin is a literalist, factualist, and precisionist – you see it if you look at the details in his poems – and it's worth remembering that when he was younger he was a close literary and personal friend of Marianne Moore. Was she an influence too? Her insistence on unsentimental accuracy can be found in his writing, and maybe her complex syllabic verse reinforced Laughlin's typewriter metric as well.

Beyond his friendships with the great originators of modernism, Laughlin has been close to many writers of his own generation, people like Delmore Schwartz, Thomas Merton, Kenneth Rexroth, Edward

Dahlberg, Kenneth Patchen, Tennessee Williams, Dylan Thomas, Lawrence Ferlinghetti, Denise Levertov, and dozens of others. Yet in his own work he has never, I mean never, shown the least tendency to imitate any of these writers, and this is impressive. What is also impressive is that with a few important exceptions – Schwartz, Ferlinghetti, Levertov – none of these writers has shown much regard for Laughlin's own poetry nor any notion of helping to promote it. Perhaps they thought he must be powerful enough to promote it himself. Or perhaps – just perhaps – writers are such monsters of ego that they can't take an interest in any writing unlike their own, especially a publisher's. Fact: a publisher's or editor's role is to be on the receiving end of a constant one-way stream of authorial self-aggrandizement. It gets pretty tiresome.

But Laughlin did not promote himself. His first four or five books were small, were published obscurely and distributed primarily to friends. Much of his writing was filed away in typescript. Though he won awards and distinctions as a publisher, both in this country and abroad, few people knew his poetry and he remained in the literary background. (The only prize he has won for his poems, a good one but a foreign one, is the Prix Malrieu, which was given in 1987 to a book of translations from his poetry by Alain Bosquet.) Then his *Selected Poems,* a book much smaller than the present *Collected Poems* but still comparatively sizable, was published in 1986 by City Lights in San Francisco, and more readers, including a few critics and reviewers, became acquainted with his work. At the same time, or a little earlier, Laughlin had begun publishing essays about his experiences with Stein, Pound, H.D., Djuna Barnes, Williams, and other early modernists, and about his understanding of their lives and works, from which it was clear that he was extremely knowledgeable and critically sensitive. His years of editing had given him more insight into and sympathy for different kinds of creative aptitude and disposition than he – or probably anyone – could have gotten in school. As a consequence he was invited to various universities to lecture. He was an adjunct professor for two years at Brown University, for instance, where he did courses on Pound and Williams; he traveled to other universities for conferences and seminars. He became, in other words, a more conspicuous figure on the general literary scene than he had been before as a publisher and editor. And now this hefty new collection of his own poems in all their variety and brilliance will certainly bring much more attention to his work and verify his place among the best American poets of his time.

In a letter to me Laughlin once wrote: "What my poems are about is the juxtaposition of contemporary life with ancient culture." He was trying to do what writers always try to do: boil it all down to the nub. This is how writers save their lives and consciences, by doing their damnedest to be *objective* about the long, long, devilishly hard work into which they have put their hearts and souls and minds. And no doubt Laughlin's letter does in a way offer an approach to his intentions. The destruction of cultures, the loss of values and meanings, is for him simply awful. The continuity of human imaginative goodness, from Lao Tzu and Li Po and the masters of the Hindu classics to Homer, Catullus, Dante, Villon, and so on down to the few splendid writers of our own time, is for him indispensable and is what all of us, in our extreme predicament, can truly rely on. In his small poems, which are not so small, this idea is what he has fortified and nurtured; his poems are a work of salvage. On the other hand the statement in his letter is reductive, obviously. His poems are also about language, about sex, love, injustice, the poignancy of existence, about a thousand other things, as every reader of this book will discover.

Even this does not go far enough, however. For no poet can say what his or her poems are about, because no poet can *see* what his or her poems are about. Isn't it so? James Laughlin's poems are about James Laughlin. No felicity of attitude nor fervor of intention nor incisiveness of topic or belief can add one atom to the enduring resources of human culture. Without Laughlin's unique joining of knowledge and feeling in his own mind – and I say *unique* advisedly – without his independent sensibility, his poems would be no more than the products of any good workshop in the schools. But how far they are from anything of the kind! It is plain as the nose on anyone's face that these poems are exceptional. Nothing else like them exists. I have not mentioned, in the interest of decent brevity, his translations, his poems in what he calls "dog-Latin," his picture poems (done with scissors, rubber cement, and a Canon copier), his long-line elegies and other discourses, his parodies, or the really wonderful poems by his friend Hiram Hand-spring, an obstreperous comic doppelgänger who can say things that wouldn't fit into poems written in propria persona. And then, finally, those poems about the death of his son Robert, few in number but among the most compelling of their kind I've ever read – see if it isn't so. All these add variety and liveliness to this collection; all add to the representation of Laughlin's sensibility. And this – what we sometimes call "voice" or "personality" or "spiritual propensity" or even "genius," but which is rather the whole individual human indescribability – is what makes James Laughlin's poems a distinct and fascinating part of the literature of this century and, in the manner of classical impersonality – for who was Catullus but a name? – of all the centuries before.

🖊 . . . .

The Nature of Art

Written for a symposium in *The Ohio Review*, 1993.

THE ASSIGNED TOPIC IS: "The ways the relationship between Nature and Art may have changed and may be changing." An embarrassing topic for me. From the beginning, from my earliest memories, I have known that no relationship pertains between nature and art at all (and I prefer not to use the capitals). Relationships can exist only among things in nature, and art is one of them. Nature is everything, OK? It is all material reality, and material reality includes absolutely everything, all there is, not merely stones and oceans, butterflies and flowers, but ideas, poems, dreams, spiritual intimations. I neither know nor need a supernatural, an other-than-natural. The supernatural is by definition inconceivable, and the inconceivable is of no use to poetry – or to anything. That frisson of mystical hyperawareness which so many people, including my friends, say they have felt – and which I myself have felt – is for me a movement of neurons, proteins, electrical pulses, who knows what, within the human (natural, material) body, primarily the brain.

And what is nature if not change, the Heraclitean flux? Certain observable regularities and periodicities occur, from which we invent, for our convenience in keeping appointments and giving meaning to death, the idea of time, but this idea will not endure. Suppose you awoke tomorrow morning and learned from your TV that scientists had discovered a slight but measurable cooling of the sun and a decline of two centimeters in the orbit of Venus. The sun's mass is increasing; a black hole is beginning; into it before long the whole world, including the *Divine Comedy*, the Yokohama Express, and the Prophet of Islam, will be plummeted and compacted to the size of your shoe. Talk about frissons! Yet if people continue on this planet for the sufficient length of time, this, or something like this, is what they will hear on their TVs. And elsewhere – anywhere out there in the vastness – people – that is to say, living, sentient, intelligent beings – have doubtless heard it already. Think of that.

Ethnographers have been known to declare that the greatest change brought by human civilization has been our withdrawal from, or our subduing of, the wilderness, and that this can be demonstrated by changes in the art and literature of the ages, beginning with the drawings on the cave walls of the Dordogne and other such very old compositions. Maybe so. But what a small notion of wilderness this supposes. The wilderness is not the woods beginning behind my house and extending in patches to the Catskill Mountains, inhabited still by a few other-than-human predators, though not many. No, the wilderness begins at the edge of my body, at the edge of my consciousness, and extends to the edge of the universe, and it is filled with menace – that is, with change, violent change, *extremely* violent change. This is what I have always known, as if it were implanted in my genes. It is the suboctave of every song I've written. My personal death is the most insignificant possible paradigm, though still real and expressive, of cosmic débâcle; the only destiny is extinction.

The nineteenth century in its optimism and progressivism interpreted Darwin to mean something rather cheerful, at least for the human species. The survival of the fittest meant a better and better community of being for the earth. But today our experience has taught us to see more clearly. The survival of the fittest means the devastation of the rest – what else can it mean? – until finally, whether sooner or later, the fittest will have destroyed their own base, their own "support system." Repeat: extinction is destiny.

To be aware of this is what Albert Camus called lucidity. To choose to be aware of it is what Jean-Paul Sartre called authenticity. Lucidity and authenticity remain the two ideal virtues toward which self-conscious humanity, personally and collectively, must strain, coming even before honesty and ordinary decency, immensely important though these are. This is what I believe first and foremost.

The other course, straining in innumerable ways to perceive and represent an imputed value in Mystery, in what we cannot or do not yet know, is easier. It has in every age including our own been accounted the intrinsically "poetic" thing to do. It is universally acknowledged to have all the poetic advantages. But here I must offend most of my colleagues, including many who have produced work for which I have the deepest respect and warmest affection, by saying that this course – mysticism, ultra-naturalism – is not only easy but cowardly. It is a cop-out. Note, I'm talking about people who are some of my closest personal friends, with whom I have been in conversation for years and years. I understand what they will say. "Nonsense. We know. And you cannot logically or epistemologically dispute what we know in our own minds, hearts, and spirits." Agreed. But is knowledge so important at this point in our history, any kind of knowledge? Hasn't the whole drift of recent intellectual and spiritual advancement shown us that knowledge is no more consequential than other transient human acquirements and that frequently we don't know what to do with it? Knowledge doesn't amount to so much, after all – not as much, I'd say, as minute-to-minute uncodifiable experience. Knowledge taken altogether is a natural datum, comprised of natural data. Which means that what was bravery during most of human history, the attempt to push "knowledge" beyond the frontiers of nature, has become cowardice, the accepted and acceptable thing to do, in our time. It behooves us as poets to acknowledge this and accept it. All great poems – and this is demonstrable   have been works of confrontation and valor in their own time, and if we seek greatness now, as we should and must, we can only strive for the same qualities in our own productions.

But what does all this have to do with the assigned topic? Surely the editors did not want a metaphysical discussion. Nevertheless they did ask me, among others, to say what I think. Well then, I recapitulate. A poem is an existent; it has the same status as a pebble or a galaxy. It has no relationship to nature, but only to other existents within nature. And what I think is that any work of art not informed by a bold and determined regard for this equivalency and its effects is deficient intellectually, emotionally, and spiritually, and cannot speak to the discerning contemporary sensibility. Let the fundamentalists rage. Poets are quiet seekers unwilling to be deluded.

But the editors are still unhappy. They want an essay directed toward the particular artist's relationship to his or her particular natural environment. And as in my larger remarks I have been a realist, here I must choose realism as well. Most poets nowadays can't tell a blue jay from a bobolink, a hepatica from a harebell. For that matter I know a "nature writer," as they are called – and this a very eminent nature writer, believe me – who can't tell a salamander from a skink, which would have been elementary to most rural Americans a couple of generations ago. Rural Americans are a diminishing stock. Granted, a good many middle-class and literate people live not in cities but in suburbs, in parkland developments, in university towns, where the air is supposed to be cleaner and the view more gratifying. But what is their distinguishable natural environment? A strip of lawn with some clipped evergreens. Yew? Hemlock? Juniper? They have no idea. Why should they? Their true natural environment, which is altogether natural and cannot be anything else, consists of brick and concrete, utility poles, air-conditioned rooms, etc. And it also consists of the depleted ozone layer, the DNA complex, the volcanoes of the Pacific, the geological faults beneath California, and all the other esoterica they read about in the Tuesday edition of the *New York Times*. For them, indeed, the most conspicuous elements of nature are its immediate calamities, auto wrecks, cancer, and AIDS. For them nature is depressing.

Since we are talking now about this lesser relationship, i.e., of the particular artist to the particular natural environment, we must say that of course it too is changing. It is changing fast. Very few true country dwellers, like John Haines, Don Lee, David Budbill, Wendell Berry, and R.T. Smith, are poets. Most farmers and woodsmen care nothing for poetry and never did. And what do poets care for? More and more they want to be academics. They want to live in the environment of the classroom and the faculty club. If they can't tell the difference between a blue jay and a bobolink they don't care; in their poems they are satisfied to say simply *bird*. This sorrows me personally because I have lived most of my life in deep woods and far fields and I know about them and have written about them, but at the same time it does not greatly upset me. Good poets will always find their way into their environments whether these be rural or urban, wild or tame. Paul Goodman said that poetry is the poet's way of "being in the world," and I have never found a better or more accurate and expressive formulation of what we do. The world is changing, it is changing rapidly; the poet's response to it must change as well. This is natural, a part of nature. And as a matter of fact most poets are sensible people and will contribute to the Wilderness Society and the Sierra Club and stand with other concerned citizens on the right side of ecological issues.

Wallace Stevens said that "death is the mother of beauty." A banality. But if Stevens, who shied from the banal like a horse from a yellow jacket, could utter it, so can we. In fact we live in banality, our poems are full of banality, the age of cleverness for its own sake – natural as it was – is over. The only ways to go out now are either drugged and furtive or lucid and authentic. And of course, of course, beauty is in the eye of the beholder. It's a function of self-conscious intelligence and perfectly natural. The corollary to Stevens's two cents' worth is this: "fear is the mother of art." We write our poems out of terror. It isn't that we don't understand reality, we understand it only too well. Reality is not a mystery. Beauty and ugliness are what we invent, but fear is what invents us. And now our fear is great and becoming greater. It may be greater than at any other time since Abraham cowered on the starlit desert and invented monotheism. (Whereupon Thoreau crouched in his pitiful ego and reaffirmed it.) Knowledge has not freed us – how could it? We know. We know more than enough (although this does not assuage our natural curiosity). We see a natural calamity, one of the untold and untellable zillions throughout eternity and infinity, befalling us in our littleness and remoteness and insignificance, our cosmic paltriness. Probably sooner than later. We receive news on our TVs every day which is the equal in our lives of an exploding nebula in the universe, news that would have driven our ancestors out of their minds. We have always understood that life is fragile. Now we understand that its foundation in reality is not only fragile but evanescent.

Hence we write poetry, we who are any good at it, I won't say of greater seriousness than poetry of the past (though I think this may be the case), but certainly of very great seriousness and very great intensity – love poems, poems of political outrage, elegies, paeans, whatever. They are in a thousand different ways propelled by and embedded in our fear. So be it. Regret is useless. For my part, I'm getting up in years, as Ida Cox used to say, and won't be much of an accomplice in American poetry to come. But I'm concerned. I say to young people: embrace your fear, study your lucidity and authenticity, know reality, and write like the devil. Because all this dogpaddling around in the wreckships ain't getting nobody nowheres fast – and that's the McCoy.

🙠 . . . .

A Further Note on LEAR

1994.

YES, as the Theorists say, contextuality is all, by which they mean generally the social, cultural, and political context in which particular works of art occur – and I use the word Theorist with a capital to mean all the various branches of contemporary criticism that have reacted and rebelled against modernism and the New Criticism in the earlier years of our century, i.e., in my youth. I admire the Theorists enormously for what they have done to make us aware of the biases inherent to our literature and all literature, the presuppositions and slants, especially in matters of gender and matters of social and economic classification. But certain works, both great and small, resist such judgments. And *King Lear* is one of them.

What is the context of *Lear?* The facts of its conception in London in 1606, and its materialization in the English language seem to me altogether inconsequential. The heath in Act III, where the storm rages and Lear goes mad, is nowhere – and everywhere. Its context is nothing – and everything. It is the continuum of human misery and has no history, no anticipation – no time. It is almost a void, the void of reality, which contains so much that it cancels itself out and becomes the undifferentiated plane of experience. It is the eternal present, for which so many poets today strive vainly and unimaginatively in the mere technique of the present tense. It is all languages, all places and times, all cultures. And these considerations apply to the rest of the play as well. The particulars are folly, violence, love, and woe – I'm tempted to say in that order – and these are surely universal. They are everywhere, everywhere.

Certain works – not many – share this divorce from context. Where are the town and mountain in *The Castle* by Kafka? When does the land surveyor come there? We can say, because we know, that the novel was written in the aftermath of World War I and that certain factors of mode, mood, and value may be ascribed to this. But it could just as well have been written in the aftermath of the Peloponnesian wars or the conquest of Langue d'oc by the Franks or the bloody rise of the Aztecs against the Mayans and Toltecs, it could have been written after any cataclysmic human craziness, and the factors of mode, mood, and value would have been the same. Notice that this quality of placelessness and timelessness, of purely imaginary provenance, does not imply literary superiority. *Pilgrim's Progress* occurs in a specific context of western Christianity and is almost ludicrously deconstructible in Theoretical terms. The same may be said even of the *Divine Comedy*, in spite of its many analogues in other cultures. But *Lear* and *The Castle* and other works like them escape contextuality, or at least reduce it to something conceptually so flimsy that it loses its serviceability in literary investigations. The existence of such works suggests, at least to me, that many avenues lead toward literary and artistic understanding, though of course none ever reaches it.

When I began my brief life as a professor in 1980, the English department in which I worked was split by many personal and intellectual differences, which often produced lively discussions, yet a high degree of integration prevailed and few of the discussions led to in enduring animosities. More particularly the creative writing program was fully and comfortably incorporated within the department. Students from the program were required to take the same kinds and numbers of courses as other candidates for the Master's degree – which is why I chose to work there – and they were almost always welcomed by teachers of history and theory because they were, in fact, often among the best, most interested students in the department. Similarly we on the writing staff were invited to teach courses in history and theory if we wished to. We were on altogether friendly terms with the rest of the faculty, the historians and theorists. (I'm using theory with a small letter here to show that it then meant the study of everything from Aristotle to Northrup Frye.) Eleven years later, when I resigned from the university, affairs in the department had become decidedly less amiable, more disrupted, and to my mind a good deal duller.

Students in the creative writing program were no longer welcome in courses taught by Theorists, and were in some cases treated so badly that they had no choice but to abstain or abscond. A faculty which had fought tooth and nail against discrimination in earlier years became discriminative. A degree of frigidity I could not have imagined set in, both professionally and socially, between many of the scholars and the teachers of writing. It was awful. When I told my students in poetry that they should take courses in Theory, that all writers should be aware of the critical and philosophical currents of their own time, they looked at me as if they thought the old guy had gone over the edge for good. All this was the extreme of human blundering, not to say mania, and I was delighted to get out of there.

As an old-line anarchist – which is to say, someone devoted *first of all* to the notion of universal freedom – I am in solidarity with those who discover and publicize the prejudices, power plays, and other oppressive elements in any sector in any culture. But when these people themselves become oppressors, what could be, to say the least, more unproductive? Nor do I blame the Theorists entirely for what happened in my English department, and I believe in many others, because the further, egregious overspecialization and overacademicization of writing in our universities is to my mind equally unproductive, equally stupid, equally devastating to the good minds and wills in our civilization that would change it rationally and make it freer.

Sometimes I wish I could go back and teach a course in *Lear* that would attempt to identify these issues, not in order to make a synthesis – that awful word – but to use our resources in concert rather than in discord. No text could be better for the purpose.

✍ ·

God Sniffed and Said

"AT ALL EVENTS, Adam, the time has come for you to start naming, whether you like it or not." And He looked somewhat frowningly around Him.

"I don't like it," Adam said.

"Evidently not. But why?"

"It wasn't part of the bargain."

"Bargain? What bargain? There wasn't any bargain."

"Implicitly in the act of creation You – "

"Nonsense," God interrupted. "What is this *implicitly?*"

"It means – "

God interrupted again. "What is this *means?*"

"I'm trying to tell You if You'd only let me."

"Tell Me? What can you tell Me that I don't already know. Knowing is my business."

Adam took a deep breath. "Then why don't You know that when You create somebody You become responsible for him and You're supposed to do the dirty work?"

"Responsible? I absolutely disacknowledge any such principle in My Absoluteness. Besides, I thought naming would be fun."

"Maybe," Adam said. "It does have a kind of exciting promise. Yet at the same time it fills me with strange foreboding. Something tells me that – "

"Foreboding? That's not supposed to come until later. After all, I only created you a few minutes ago."

"Oh? Funny, I feel as if I'd been here a long time already."

"Only in My mind," God said.

"Yes, that's just it – in Your mind. And if I'm supposed to do the naming, then the naming must exist in Your mind too. Why don't You go ahead and do it?"

"You don't understand."

"That's a fact," Adam said. Then: "Who the hell am I anyway? Do You know?"

"I know everything."

"Then what's this all about? And why won't You tell me?"

God sniffed again. "This is getting too complicated. Let's start over."

"OK," Adam said. "What do I do?"

"Take a look around."

"At what? You mean all these ... these *things?*"

"There. You see? You've already started."

"You mean *things?*"

"Obviously. A fine name. Fundamental, in fact."

"You mean these ... these *objects?*"

"Aha! Already beginning to perceive abstractly."

"These ... *subjects?*"

"Wow! A real leap. You're doing splendidly."

All at once Adam began rattling off names. "*Spinach. Crustacean. Helicopter. Bargain basement. Dinosaur. Asia Minor. Mincemeat. Thorn. The Sleeping Beauty. Heliotrope. Pork chop. Bread-and-butter pickles. Muskrat Ramble. Polar bear. Cadillac. Grandson. Vibration. Macaroni. The Monroe Doctrine. Dodecaphonalism. Rattlesnake. Clan. Cypress. Missing link....*"

"Wonderful!" God said. "You got the range now."

"*Ox. Yoke. Wagon. Wagon wheel. Squeak. Grease. Petroleum. Rockefeller. Exxon. Imperialism. Starvation.* I could go on forever."

"Marvelous! Superb!" God beamed.

"Yeah, maybe," Adam said. "But I don't – quite like it."

"Why not?"

"Because every time I say a name, something comes busting out at me, shining all over with ... with *reality*. Hey, how's that for a name?"

"Fine. Fine. But let's not get carried away."

"That's just what I mean. I am getting carried away. That's what gives me the foreboding. Don't You see? I thought this was Your job."

"Well, I did My job, didn't I? I'm the One who created all these ... these ..."

"*Things?*" Adam said.

"I guess so."

"But *things* is my invention. Do You mean You created all this mess without any reality? That's ridiculous."

"Now then. Don't be presumptuous."

"Presumptuous! If Somebody around here is presuming, I guess we know Who."

God sniffed. "Maybe. Maybe not."

"Holy cow," Adam said. "Don't pull that Godliness on me."

"Cow? What holy cow?"

"Why, that one over there. That cow."

"I don't see anything holy about that. It doesn't even look like *cow* to Me."

"Of course it's *cow*."

"Why?"

"Because I said so. Why else? Look, You're the one that got me started on this."

"OK. Calm yourself. But why is that a cow?"

"Because ... because ... Damn it, she's a cow, that's all. She's – "

"*She? She* doesn't exist yet. That's the next thing on the program."

"Don't be silly. I've known *she* as far back as I can remember, which is getting to be more or less like a million years."

"Hmmm."

"How can you have *things* without *she?*" Adam paused. "Still, if she isn't created yet, maybe that's what gives me this sense of foreboding."

"Why?"

"Well, I have this feeling somebody is going to screw her up."

"Who?"

"Don't ask."

"This is getting us nowhere," God said. "Let's go back to the cow."

"A damn fine cow, if you ask me."

"I'm not sure I did. But what's so special about it? Looks like an ordinary cow to me."

"It? Ordinary? She's a *she.* And if she's a cow, she has to be a fine one."

"How come?"

"Because ... well, because she's Hathor, she's Devi, she's – "

"Names. Names."

"You bet. She's Ishtar, she's Aphrodite, she's covered all over with a golden aura." Adam squinted dreamily. "Why, a hell of a long, long way down the line I can even dimly see a poem called 'The Cows at Night.'"

"*Poem?* What's that?"

"You wouldn't know."

"Another one of your names, I suppose."

"So what? I did my job, didn't I? I did what You told me. I named everything."

"I reckon you did at that."

"All except one," Adam said.

"Which one?"

"Me! Me! *Adam!* You're the Namer who invented that name. Now I've been telling you what everything means, why don't you tell me what that means? Damn it, I've got a right to know."

"So you say."

"And what about the name *God?* Who invented that?"

God gave His Final Sniff. The discussion ended.

HAYDEN CARRUTH was born in 1921, and for many years lived in northern Vermont. He lives now in upstate New York where until recently he taught in the Graduate Creative Writing Program at Syracuse University. He has published twenty-nine books, chiefly of poetry but including also a novel, four books of criticism, and two anthologies. His most recent books are *Suicides and Jazzers* (1992), *The Collected Shorter Poems, 1946–1991* (1992), *The Collected Longer Poems* (1994), and *Scrambled Eggs and Whiskey: Poems 1991–1995*. He has been editor of *Poetry*, poetry editor of *Harper's*, and for twenty years an advisory editor of *The Hudson Review*. He has received fellowships from the Bollingen Foundation, the Guggenheim Foundation (twice), the National Endowment for the Arts (four times), and the New York Arts Foundation. He has been presented with the Lenore Marshall Award, the Vermont Governor's Medal, the Sarah Josepha Hale Award, the Brandeis University Award, the Carl Sandburg Award, the Whiting Award, the Paterson Poetry Prize, the Ruth Lily Prize, nominations for the National Book Award and the Pulitzer Prize, and the National Book Critics' Circle award for poetry, among many other awards. In 1988 he was appointed a Senior Fellow by the National Endowment for the Arts.

BOOK DESIGN and composition by John D. Berry, using Adobe PageMaker 6.0 and a Power Computing Power 120. The typeface is Monotype's digital version of Bulmer, which was originally cut by William Martin for the printer William Bulmer in 1790. Martin's type was first used for an ambitious "national" edition of Shakespeare, printed by William Bulmer's Shakspeare Printing Office in London; this and later books from the same press are credited with materially raising the standards of printing in England. Bulmer is a transitional typeface, taller and narrower than Baskerville, with some of the characteristics of later, "modern" faces such as Bodoni. *Printed by Edwards Brothers.*